The Many-Headed Hydra

The
MANY-HEADED
HYDRA

Sailors, Slaves, Commoners, and the
Hidden History of the Revolutionary Atlantic

Peter Linebaugh and Marcus Rediker

BEACON PRESS

BOSTON

Beacon Press
25 Beacon Street
Boston, Massachusetts 02108-2892
www.beacon.org

Beacon Press books
are published under the auspices of
the Unitarian Universalist Association of Congregations.

05 04 03 02 01 00   8 7 6 5 4 3 2 1

This book is printed on acid-free paper that meets the uncoated paper
ANSI/NISO specifications for permanence as revised in 1992.

Text design by Dean Bornstein
Composition by Wilsted & Taylor Publishing Services

Library of Congress Cataloging-in-Publication Data
Linebaugh, Peter.
The many-headed hydra : sailors, slaves, commoners, and the hidden history
of the revolutionary Atlantic / Peter Linebaugh and Marcus Rediker.
p.   cm.
Includes bibliographical references (p.) and index.
ISBN 0-8070-5006-7 (alk. paper)
1. Capitalism—Social aspects—Great Britain—History.   2. Capitalism—
Social aspects—West Indies, British—History.   3. Slave trade—Great Britain—
History.   4. Slave trade—West Indies, British—History.   5. Great Britain—
History—Puritan Revolution, 1642–1660.   6. Mutiny—Great Britain—History.
7. Radicalism—West Indies, British—History.   8. Radicalism—United States—
History.   9. United States—Social conditions—To 1865.   10. Great Britain—
Colonies—Social conditions.   I. Rediker, Marcus.   II. Title.
HC254.5 L715   2000
909'.0971'24106—dc21
00-008881

To Christopher & Bridget Hill

Contents

Introduction · 1

1. The Wreck of the *Sea-Venture* · 8

2. Hewers of Wood and Drawers of Water · 36

3. "A Blackymore Maide Named Francis" · 71

4. The Divarication of the Putney Debates · 104

5. Hydrarchy: Sailors, Pirates, and the Maritime State · 143

6. "The Outcasts of the Nations of the Earth" · 174

7. A Motley Crew in the American Revolution · 211

8. The Conspiracy of Edward and Catherine Despard · 248

9. Robert Wedderburn and Atlantic Jubilee · 287

Conclusion: Tyger! Tyger! · 327

A Map of the Atlantic 1699 · 354

Notes · 355

Acknowledgments · 413

Index · 417

Introduction

WITH RACHEL CARSON, let us first look from above: "The permanent currents of the ocean are, in a way, the most majestic of her phenomena. Reflecting upon them, our minds are at once taken out from the earth so that we can regard, as from another planet, the spinning of the globe, the winds that deeply trouble its surface or gently encompass it, and the influence of the sun and moon. For all these cosmic forces are closely linked with the great currents of the ocean, earning for them the adjective I like best of all those applied to them—the planetary currents." The planetary currents of the North Atlantic are circular. Europeans pass by Africa to the Caribbean and then to North America. The Gulf Stream then at three knots moves north to the Labrador and Arctic currents, which move eastward, as the North Atlantic Drift, to temper the climates of northwestern Europe.

At Land's End, the westward foot of England, break waves whose origins lie off the stormy coast of Newfoundland. Some of these breakers may even be traced to the coast of Florida and the West Indies. For centuries fishermen on the lonely shores of Ireland have been able to interpret these long Atlantic swells. The power of an ocean wave is directly related to the speed and duration of the wind that sets it in motion, and to the "length of its fetch," or the distance from its point of origin. The longer the fetch, the greater the wave. Nothing can stop these long waves. They become visible only at the end, when they rise and break; for most of their fetch the surface of the ocean is undisturbed. In 1769, Postmaster General Benjamin Franklin noted that packets from Falmouth took about two weeks longer to reach New York than merchant ships took to sail from Rhode Island to London. In talking to Nantucket whalers, he learned about the Gulf Stream: the fishermen and the whales kept out of it, while the English captains stemmed the current, "too wise to be counselled by simple American fishermen." He drew up some "Maritime Observations" in 1786, and with these the chart of the Gulf Stream was published in America.

I

✳

The circular transmission of human experience from Europe to Africa to the Americas and back again corresponded to the same cosmic forces that set the Atlantic currents in motion, and in the seventeenth and eighteenth centuries, the merchants, manufacturers, planters, and royal officials of northwestern Europe followed these currents, building trade routes, colonies, and a new transatlantic economy. They organized workers from Europe, Africa, and the Americas to produce and transport bullion, furs, fish, tobacco, sugar, and manufactures. It was a labor of Herculean proportions, as they themselves repeatedly explained.

The classically educated architects of the Atlantic economy found in Hercules—the mythical hero of the ancients who achieved immortality by performing twelve labors—a symbol of power and order. For inspiration they looked to the Greeks, for whom Hercules was a unifier of the centralized territorial state, and to the Romans, for whom he signified vast imperial ambition. The labors of Hercules symbolized economic development: the clearing of land, the draining of swamps, and the development of agriculture, as well as the domestication of livestock, the establishment of commerce, and the introduction of technology. Rulers placed the image of Hercules on money and seals, in pictures, sculptures, and palaces, and on arches of triumph. Among English royalty, William III, George I, and George II's brother, the "Butcher of Culloden," all fancied themselves Hercules.[1] John Adams, for his part, proposed in 1776 that "The Judgment of Hercules" be the seal for the new United States of America.[2] The hero represented progress: Giambattista Vico, the philosopher of Naples, used Hercules to develop the stadial theory of history, while Francis Bacon, philosopher and politician, cited him to advance modern science and to suggest that capitalism was very nearly divine.

These same rulers found in the many-headed hydra an antithetical symbol of disorder and resistance, a powerful threat to the building of state, empire, and capitalism. The second labor of Hercules was the destruction of the venomous hydra of Lerna. The creature, born of Typhon (a tempest or hurricane) and Echidna (half woman, half snake), was one in a brood of monsters that included Cerberus, the three-headed dog, Chimera, the lion-headed goat with a snake's tail, Geryon, the triple-bodied giant, and Sphinx, the woman with a lion's body. When Hercules

*Hercules and Iolaus slaying the Lernean Hydra, Eritrian amphora,
c. 525 B.C. Collection of the J. Paul Getty Museum, Malibu, California.*

lopped off one of the hydra's heads, two new ones grew in its place. With
the help of his nephew Iolaus, he eventually killed the monster by cutting
off a central head and cauterizing the stump with a flaming branch. He
then dipped his arrows in the gall of the slain beast, which gave his pro-
jectiles fatal power and allowed him to complete his labors.

From the beginning of English colonial expansion in the early seventeenth century through the metropolitan industrialization of the early
nineteenth, rulers referred to the Hercules-hydra myth to describe the
difficulty of imposing order on increasingly global systems of labor. They

variously designated dispossessed commoners, transported felons, indentured servants, religious radicals, pirates, urban laborers, soldiers, sailors, and African slaves as the numerous, ever-changing heads of the monster. But the heads, though originally brought into productive combination by their Herculean rulers, soon developed among themselves new forms of cooperation against those rulers, from mutinies and strikes to riots and insurrections and revolution. Like the commodities they produced, their experience circulated with the planetary currents around the Atlantic, often eastward, from American plantations, Irish commons, and deep-sea vessels back to the metropoles of Europe.

In 1751 J. J. Mauricius, an ex-governor of Suriname, returned to Holland, where he would write poetic memoirs recollecting his defeat at the hands of the Saramaka, a group of former slaves who had escaped the plantations and built maroon communities deep in the interior jungle, and who now defended their freedom against endless military expeditions designed to return them to slavery:

> *There you must fight blindly an invisible enemy*
> *Who shoots you down like ducks in the swamps.*
> *Even if an army of ten thousand men were gathered, with*
> *The courage and strategy of Caesar and Eugene,*
> *They'd find their work cut out for them, destroying a Hydra's growth*
> *Which even Alcides [Hercules] would try to avoid.*

Writing to and for other Europeans assumed to be sympathetic with the project of conquest, Mauricius cast himself and other colonizers as Hercules, and the fugitive bondspeople who challenged slavery as the hydra.[3]

Andrew Ure, the Oxford philosopher of manufactures, found the myth to be useful as he surveyed the struggles of industrial England in 1835. After a strike among spinners in Stayleybridge, Lancashire, he employed Hercules and his rescue of Prometheus, with his delivery of fire and technology to mankind, to argue for the implementation of the self-acting mule, a new machine "with the thought, feeling, and tact of the experienced workman." This new "Herculean prodigy" had "strangled the Hydra of misrule"; it was a "creation destined to restore order among the industrious classes, and to confirm to Great Britain the empire of art." Here again, Ure saw himself and other manufacturers as Hercules, and the industrial workers who challenged their authority as the hydra.[4]

Dutch soldiers and guide in a Suriname swamp, c. 1775, by William Blake.
John Gabriel Stedman, Narrative of a Five Years Expedition
against the Revolted Negroes of Surinam *(1796).*

When the Puritan prelate Cotton Mather published his history of Christianity in America in 1702, he entitled his second chapter, on the antinomian controversy of 1638, "Hydra Decapita." "The church of God had not long been in this wilderness, before the dragon cast forth several floods to devour it," he wrote. The theological struggle of "works" against "grace" subverted "all peaceable order." The controversy raised suspicions against religious and political officials, prevented an expedition against the Pequot Indians, confused the drawing of town lots, and made particular appeals to women. For Mather, the Puritan elders were Hercules, while the hydra consisted of the antinomians who questioned the authority of minister and magistrate, the expansion of empire, the definition of private property, and the subordination of women.[5]

It would be a mistake to see the myth of Hercules and the hydra as merely an ornament of state, a classical trope in speeches, a decoration of ceremonial dress, or a mark of classical learning. Francis Bacon, for example, used it to lay the intellectual basis for the biological doctrine of monstrosity and for the justifications of murder, which themselves have a semantics of Latin euphemism—debellation, extirpation, trucidation, extermination, liquidation, annihilation, extinction. To cite the myth was not simply to employ a figure of speech or even a concept of analytic understanding; it was to impose a curse and a death sentence, as we will show.

If the hydra myth expressed the fear and justified the violence of the ruling classes, helping them to build a new order of conquest and expropriation, of gallows and executioners, of plantations, ships, and factories, it suggested something quite different to us as historians—namely, a hypothesis. The hydra became a means of exploring multiplicity, movement, and connection, the long waves and planetary currents of humanity. The multiplicity was indicated, as it were, in silhouette in the multitudes who gathered at the market, in the fields, on the piers and the ships, on the plantations, upon the battlefields. The power of numbers was expanded by movement, as the hydra journeyed and voyaged or was banished or dispersed in diaspora, carried by the winds and the waves beyond the boundaries of the nation-state. Sailors, pilots, felons, lovers, translators, musicians, mobile workers of all kinds made new and unexpected connections, which variously appeared to be accidental, contingent, transient, even miraculous.

Our book looks from below. We have attempted to recover some of the lost history of the multiethnic class that was essential to the rise of capitalism and the modern, global economy. The historic invisibility of many of the book's subjects owes much to the repression originally visited upon them: the violence of the stake, the chopping block, the gallows, and the shackles of a ship's dark hold. It also owes much to the violence of abstraction in the writing of history, the severity of history that has long been the captive of the nation-state, which remains in most studies the largely unquestioned framework of analysis. This is a book about connections that have, over the centuries, usually been denied, ignored, or simply not seen, but that nonetheless profoundly shaped the history of the world in which we all of us live and die.

CHAPTER ONE

The Wreck of the *Sea-Venture*

ON JULY 25, 1609, the sailors of the *Sea-Venture* scanned the horizon and spotted danger. Separated from their convoy of eight other vessels sailing from Plymouth westward to Virginia, England's first New World colony, they spied a tempest—or what the Carib Indians called a hurricane—scudding swiftly toward them. With "the clouds gathering thick upon us and the winds singing and whistling most unusually," wrote passenger William Strachey,

> a dreadful storm and hideous began to blow from the northeast, which, swelling and roaring as it were by fits, some hours with more violence than others, at length did beat all light from Heaven; which like an hell of darkness, turned black upon us, so much the fuller of horror and fear use to overrun the troubled and overmastered senses of all, which taken up with amazement, the ears lay so sensible to the terrible cries and murmurs of the winds and distraction of our company as who was most armed and best prepared was not a little shaken.

The approaching fury "startled and turned the blood and took down the braves of the most hardy mariner of them all." The less hardy passengers aboard the ninety-eight-foot, three-hundred-ton vessel cried out in fear, but their words were "drowned in the winds and the winds in the thunder." The shaken seamen recovered and went to work as the ship's timbers began to groan. Six to eight men together struggled to steer the vessel. Others cut down the rigging and sails to lessen resistance to the wind; they threw luggage and ordnance overboard to lighten the load and reduce the risk of capsizing. They crept, candles in hand, along the ribs of the ship, searching and listening for weeping leaks, stoppering as many as they could, using beef when they ran out of oakum. Water nonetheless gushed into the ship, rising several feet, above two tiers of hogsheads, in the hold. The crew and passengers pumped continuously during "an Egyptian night of three daies perpetuall horror," with the common sort "stripped naked as men in Galleys." Even gentlemen who had never worked took turns pumping, while those who could not pump bailed with kettles and buckets. They had no food and no rest as they pumped an estimated two thousand tons of water out of the leaky vessel.[1]

It was not enough. The waterline did not recede, and the people at the pumps had reached the limits of their strength, endurance, and hope. Now that the exhausted sailors had done all that was humanly possible to resist the apocalyptic force of the hurricane, they took comfort in a ritual of the sea, turning the maritime world upside down as they faced certain death. Defying the strictures of private property and the authority of Captain Christopher Newport, as well as the Virginia Company gentlemen such as Sir George Somers and Sir Thomas Gates, they broke open the ship's liquors and in one last expression of solidarity "drunk one to the other, taking their last leave one of the other until their more joyful and happy meeting in a more blessed world."[2]

The *Sea-Venture* was wrecked—miraculously, without loss of life—between two great rocks in the islands of Bermuda on July 28. The 150 wet and terrified crew and passengers, men and women originally intended by the Virginia Company of London as reinforcements for the company's new plantation, straggled onto a strange shore, a place long considered by sailors to be an enchanted "Isle of Devils" infested with demons and monsters, and a ghoulish graveyard for European ships. Charted in 1511 but shunned by seafarers for a century afterward, Bermuda was known mostly through the accounts of a few mariners, renegades, and castaways, such as Job Hortop, who had escaped galley slavery in the Spanish West Indies, passed by the island, and made it to London to tell his tale. Silvester Jourdain, a passenger on the *Sea-Venture,* would later write that Bermuda afforded "nothing but gusts, storms, and foul weather, which made every navigator and mariner to avoid them as Scylla and Charybdis, or as they would shun the Devil himself." The eeriness of the place owed much to the harsh, hollow howling of nocturnal birds called cahows, whose shrieks haunted the crews of passing ships.[3]

The reality of Bermuda, as the shipwrecked soon discovered, was en-

tirely different from its reputation. The island, in their view, turned out
to be an Edenic land of perpetual spring and abundant food, "the richest,
healthfullest and pleasantest [place] they ever saw." The would-be colonists feasted on black hogs that had swum ashore and multiplied after a
Spanish shipwreck years earlier, on fish (grouper, parrot fish, red snap-
per) that could be caught by hand or with a stick with a bent nail, on fowl
that would land on a man's or woman's arms or shoulders, on massive tor-
toises that would feed fifty, and on an array of delicious fruit. Much to
the chagrin of the officers of the Virginia Company, Bermuda "caused
many of them vtterly to forget or desire euer to returne from thence, they
liued in such plenty, peace and ease." Once the common people found
the land of plenty, they began "to settle a foundation of ever inhabiting
there." Theirs was "a more joyful and happy meeting in a more blessed
world" after all.[4]

It is not surprising that the shipwrecked commoners responded as they
did, for they had been told to expect paradise at the end of their journey.
In his "Ode to the Virginian Voyage" (1606), Michael Drayton had insisted that Virginia was

> *Earth's only Paradise*
> *Where nature hath in store*
> *Fowle, venison, and Fish;*
> *And the fruitfull'st Soyle,*
> *Without your toyle,*
> *Three harvests more,*
> *All greater than you wish.*[5]

In 1610 Robert Rich would conveniently confuse the Bermuda and Virginia experiences in his poetic propaganda for the Virginia Company:

> *There is no feare of hunger here,*
> *for Corne much store here growes,*
> *Much fish the Gallant Rivers yeild [sic]*
> *'tis truth, without suppose.*

He concluded that in Virginia, "there is indeed no want at all." Another
Virginia Company advocate knew that such reports were false, that some
in England had dismissed them as utopian, but he nevertheless main-

The New World as paradise, by Theodore de Bry, 1588. Thomas Hariot,
A briefe and true report of the new found land of Virginia *(1590).*

tained the lie, promising prospective laborers a six-hour workday in
which the "sappe of their bodies" would not "be spent for other mens
profite."[6] Many colonists had headed toward Virginia, on the *Sea-
Venture* and other vessels, with the "heate and zeale" of a "romain year of
Iubile." The biblical jubilee (Leviticus) authorized the call for an end to

bondage and for the return of the commons to the dispossessed. Bermuda seemed the perfect place to enact this biblical prophecy.[7]

Strachey, a shareholder in and secretary of the Virginia Company, noted that among the shipwrecked there quickly arose "dangerous and secret discontents" that began among the sailors and spread to others. A "disunion of hearts and hands" soon followed: those who wanted to go on with the money-making adventure in Virginia were at odds with those whose hands were supposed to get them there. The chief complaint of the seamen and the other "hands" was that "in Virginia nothing but wretchedness and labor must be expected, with many wants and a churlish entreaty [i.e., poor provision], there being neither that fish, flesh, nor fowl which here . . . at ease and pleasure might be enjoyed." They somehow knew whereof they spoke, for colonists in Virginia were at that moment eating leather boots and serpents, looking "lyke Anotamies [skeletons] Cryinge owtt we are starved We are starved." One man killed his wife, chopped her up, and salted her for food; others dug up corpses from graves and ate them. The Bermuda castaways wanted, meanwhile, "to repose and seat where they should have the least outward wants the while." The comparative demographic facts support their claim. The other eight ships and 350 people originally in convoy with the *Sea-Venture* arrived in Virginia only to encounter a catastrophic mortality rate that over two years reduced 535 settlers to about sixty. The Bermuda settlers, by contrast, experienced over ten months a net loss of three people out of 150: five died—only one of these apparently of natural causes; two others were murdered and two more executed—while two were born. Strachey wondered, "What hath a more adamantine power to draw unto it the consent and attraction of the idle, untoward, and wretched number of the many than liberty and fullness of sensuality?"[8]

To defend their liberty, some of shipwrecked "promised each unto the other not to set their hands to any travail or endeavor" that would take them off the island, and with this vow they withdrew into the woods to form their own settlement. They later planned to settle another island by themselves. A strike and marronage thus stood at the beginning of English colonization. Among the leaders of these actions were sailors and religious radicals, probably antinomians who believed that God's grace had placed them above the law. The effort to establish an autonomous community failed, but the struggle between heart and hand continued. Stephan Hopkins was a learned Puritan and follower of Robert Browne, who advocated the creation of separate, congregational churches in which governance was based on mutual consent rather than on deference to elder, king, or nation. Hopkins extended the logic of the sailors' ritual in the storm as he argued that the magistrate's authority had ended the moment the *Sea-Venture* was wrecked. He affirmed the importance of "abundance by God's providence of all manner of good food" on the island, and he resisted proceeding to Virginia, where the common people would only slave for the adventurers. Hopkins's mutiny, too, was defeated, but he himself was not, as he survived to make another mutinous speech aboard the *Mayflower* as it approached America in 1620.[9] Other conspirators on Bermuda were likewise unvanquished, for no sooner had the manacles been slapped on Hopkins's wrists than a third plot was afoot, as another band of mutineers plotted to seize the supplies saved from the shipwreck and to attack the governor, Thomas Gates. Although their plan was disclosed to the authorities, resistance continued. Another rebel was soon executed for verbal mutiny against the governor and his authority, in response to which several others took again to the woods as maroons, where they lived, grumbled Gates, like savages.

Eventually the authorities prevailed. They built two vessels, pinnaces named the *Deliverance* and the *Patience,* to continue the voyage to Virginia, and launched them on May 10, 1610. Yet during their forty-two weeks on the island, sailors and others among the "idle, untoward, and wretched" had organized five different conspiracies against the Virginia Company and their leaders, who had responded with two of the earliest capital punishments in English America, hanging one man and executing another by firing squad to quell the resistance and carry on with the task of colonization. As the others sailed off to Virginia, two men, one a seaman, decided to stay and "end their daies" in Bermuda. Joined by another man, they "began to erect their little common wealth . . . with brotherly regency."[10] One sure sign of the wisdom of those who stayed behind came less than a month after the ships' arrival in Virginia, when Sir George Somers was dispatched by Sir Thomas Gates to Bermuda to get food, a six-month provision of meat and fish, for the struggling mainland colony. Sir George himself, however, never made it back to Virginia:

having rediscovered the joys of Bermuda, he expired from "a surfeit in eating a pig." Although we do not know what individual fates befell the sailors and passengers who sailed from Bermuda to Virginia, it is likely that many of them shared in the frightful mortality of the mainland settlement and died soon after they arrived. Collectively, however, they made up what Virginia's swashbuckling leader, John Smith, called the third supply, an infusion of humanity that helped the young plantation to survive.[11]

The wreck of the *Sea-Venture* and the dramas of rebellion that played out among the shipwrecked suggest the major themes of early Atlantic history. These events do not make for a story of English maritime greatness and glory, nor for a tale of the heroic struggle for religious freedom, though sailors and religious radicals both had essential roles. This is, rather, a story about the origins of capitalism and colonization, about world trade and the building of empires. It is also, necessarily, a story about the uprooting and movement of peoples, the making and the transatlantic deployment of "hands." It is a story about exploitation and resistance to exploitation, about how the "sappe of bodies" would be spent. It is a story about cooperation among different kinds of people for contrasting purposes of profit and survival. And it is a story about alternative ways of living, and about the official use of violence and terror to deter or destroy them, to overcome popular attachments to "liberty and the fullness of sensuality."

We are by no means the first to find historic significance in the story of the *Sea-Venture*. One of the first—and certainly the most influential—was William Shakespeare, who drew upon firsthand accounts of the wreck in 1610–11 as he wrote his play *The Tempest*. Shakespeare had long studied the accounts of explorers, traders, and colonizers who were aggressively linking the continents of Europe, Africa, and the Americas through world trade. Moreover, he knew such men personally, and even depended on them for his livelihood. Like many of his patrons and benefactors, such as the Earl of Southampton, Shakespeare himself invested in the Virginia Company, the spearhead of English colonization.[12] His play both described and promoted the rising interest of England's ruling class in the settlement and exploitation of the New World. In the pages that follow we will use the wreck of the *Sea-Venture* to set out four major themes in the origins and development of English Atlantic capitalism in the early seventeenth century: expropriation, the struggle for alternative ways of life, patterns of cooperation and resistance, and the imposition of class discipline. Within the story of the *Sea-Venture* and its people lies a larger story about the rise of capitalism and the beginning of a new epoch in human history.[13]

EXPROPRIATION

The wreck of the *Sea-Venture* occurred at a crucial moment of imperial rivalry and capitalist development. Indeed, the formation of the Virginia Company reflected—and accelerated—a fundamental shift of power taking place in the early seventeenth century, as the Atlantic maritime states of northwest Europe (France, the Netherlands, and England) challenged and overtook the Mediterranean kingdoms and city-states of Spain, Portugal, Algiers, Naples, and Venice as the dominant forces in Europe and, increasingly, the world. The faster, better-fortified, less-labor-intensive northern European ship, the most sophisticated engineering feat of the time, eclipsed the Mediterranean galley. The ruling class of England was especially eager to challenge the Iberian countries' grip on the New World and to enrich itself while doing so. A group of English investors thus in 1606 formed the Virginia Company, which according to its leading chronicler, Wesley Frank Craven, was "primarily a business organization with large sums of capital invested by adventurers whose chief interest lay in the returns expected from their investment." Here, in the pooling of capital for a new world-trade organization, lay the origins of the voyage of the *Sea-Venture*.[14]

The advocates of the Virginia Company engaged in a broad public campaign throughout England to rally support for colonization, explaining again and again why their private capitalist initiative was good for the nation. They advanced multiple arguments: All good Protestants in England had an obligation to help convert the savages in America to Christianity and to battle their Catholic enemies abroad; all had a duty to extend English dominion and to embrace beckoning national glory. But the most insistent, and most resonant, argument they made presented colonization as a solution to domestic social problems in England.

The company, its propagandists never tired of repeating, would provide a necessary public service by removing the "swarmes of idle persons" in England and setting them to work in Virginia, as Richard Hakluyt, the main propagandist for English colonization, had been suggesting for twenty years. The New World was the place for "irregular youths of no religion," for persons dispossessed by "ract rents," for anyone suffering "extream poverty"—in short, for all those "who cannot live at home." Although we do not know the names or the individual backgrounds of most of the people aboard the *Sea-Venture,* we know that a number of dispossessed were among them. In 1609 the Virginia Company applied to the mayor, aldermen, and companies of London "to ease the city and suburbs of a swarme of unnecessary inmates, as a contynual cause of death and famine, and the very originall cause of all the plagues that happen in this kingdome." Robert Rich, a gentleman shipwrecked on Bermuda, would write of "those men that *Vagrants* liv'd with us," while an anonymous author close to Sir Thomas Gates (perhaps even Gates himself) would complain of "those wicked Impes that put themselves a shipboard, not knowing otherwise how to live in England."[15]

The Virginia Company, like capitalism more broadly, originated in a series of interrelated social and economic changes in late-sixteenth- and early-seventeenth-century England, changes that propelled the *Sea-Venture* toward Virginia in 1609 and informed the writing of *The Tempest* soon after. We can list these changes as the shift in agriculture from arable subsistence to commercial pasturage; the increase of wage labor; the growth of urban populations; the expansion of the domestic system of handicraft or putting-out; the growth of world trade; the institutionalization of markets; and the establishment of a colonial system. These developments were made possible by a profound and far-reaching cause: the enclosure of land and the removal of thousands of people from the commons, who were then redeployed to the country, town, and sea. Expropriation was the source of the original accumulation of capital, and the force that transformed land and labor into commodities. This is how some of the workers aboard the *Sea-Venture* had become "hands."

Shakespeare recognized the truth of expropriation in *The Tempest* when he had the "savage and deformed slave" Caliban assert his own claim to the land against his aristocratic master, Prospero:

> *This island's mine by Sycorax my mother,*
> *Which thou tak'st from me.*

This was the crux of the epoch. As landlords dispossessed European workers and as European merchants dispossessed native peoples in the Americas, the Dutch jurist Hugo Grotius asked, "Can any nation . . . discover what belonged to someone else?" Whose was Bermuda? Whose was America? Whose was Africa? Whose island was England? Since the peoples of the world have, throughout history, clung stubbornly to the economic independence that comes from possessing their own means of subsistence, whether land or other property, European capitalists had to forcibly expropriate masses of them from their ancestral homelands so that their labor-power could be redeployed in new economic projects in new geographic settings. The dispossession and relocation of peoples have been a worldwide process spanning five hundred years. The Virginia Company in general and the *Sea-Venture* in particular helped to organize the middle passage between Old World expropriation and New World exploitation.

How did expropriation happen in England? It was a long, slow, violent operation. Beginning in the Middle Ages, lords privately abolished their armies and dissolved their feudal retinues, while in the early sixteenth century the rulers of England publicly closed the monasteries, rooted out the itinerant friars, pardoners, and beggars, and destroyed the medieval system of charity. Perhaps most important of all were the actions taken by big landowners in the late sixteenth and early seventeenth centuries as they responded to new national and international market opportunities. They radically changed agricultural practices by enclosing arable lands, evicting smallholders, and displacing rural tenants, thus throwing thousands of men and women off the land and denying them access to commons. By the end of the sixteenth century there were twelve times as many propertyless people as there had been a hundred years earlier. In the seventeenth century almost a quarter of the land in England was enclosed. Aerial photography and excavations have located more than a thousand deserted villages and hamlets, confirming the colossal dimensions of the expropriation of the peasantry. Thomas More had satirized the process in *Utopia* (1516), but he himself had enclosed land and had to be restrained. Shakespeare, too, participated in enclosure. He owned a half share in a lease of tithes at Welcombe, whose open fields William Combe proposed to enclose in 1614. Shakespeare did not object since his income would be undiminished, but the would-be dispossessed objected, filling in the ditches newly dug for enclosing hedges. Combe, mounted on horseback, opposed the diggers, calling them "puritan knaves & underlings in their colour," but Thomas Green, the leader of the diggers, returned the next day with women and children to continue the resistance. Green petitioned the lord chief justice and the Privy Council and eventually obtained a warrant to remove the enclosure.[16]

Most agricultural laborers were less fortunate. Unable to find profitable employment, without land, credit, or occupation, these new proletarians were thrust upon the roads and ways, where they were subject to the merciless cruelty of a labor and criminal code as severe and terrifying as any that had yet appeared in modern history. The major statutes against robbery, burglary, and stealing were written during the sixteenth and early seventeenth centuries, as crime became a permanent part of urban life. Laws against vagabondage meanwhile promised physical violence against the dispossessed. Under Henry VIII (1509–1547), vagabonds were whipped, had their ears cut off, or were hanged (one chronicler of the age put their number at seventy-five thousand).[17] Under Edward VI (1547–1553) they had their chests branded with the letter V and were enslaved for two years; under Elizabeth I (1558–1603) they were whipped and banished to galley service or the house of correction. The criminal code elaborated under Edward VI was scarcely less vicious toward the propertyless. The Statute of Artificers and the Poor Law likewise sought to legislate taking hire, or wage labor.[18]

Masterless men and women were the defining feature of late Tudor and early Stuart England, producing the characteristic turmoil of the era. Vagabonds were, A. L. Beier has written, "a hydra-headed monster poised to destroy the state and social order." This description echoes the argument of philosopher and Solicitor General Francis Bacon, who from personal experience considered such people the "seed of peril and tumult in a state." The combination of expropriation, industrial exploitation (through mining and the putting-out system), and unprecedented military mobilization resulted in the huge Tudor regional rebellions—the

Cornish Rising (1497), the Lavenham Rising (1525), and the Lincolnshire Rebellion (1536)—as well as the Pilgrimage of Grace (1536), the Prayer Book Rebellion (1549), and Kett's Rebellion (1549), all of which took place in the countryside. Urban insurrections for their part intensified toward the end of the sixteenth century with the Ludgate Prison Riot (1581), the Beggars' Christmas Riot (1582), the Whitsuntide Riots (1584), the Plaisterers' Insurrection (1586), the Felt-Makers' Riot (1591), the Southwark Candle-Makers' Riot (1592), and the Southwark Butter Riot (1595), whose very names evoke the struggle of handicraft workers to preserve their freedoms and customs. When Oxford commoners sought alliance with London 'prentices in the Enslow Hill Rebellion (1596), Bacon and Attorney General Edward Coke tortured one of the movement's leaders and argued that any attack on enclosure was tantamount to high treason. The largest rebellion of the age was the Midlands Revolt of 1607, which transpired partly in Shakespeare's home county and influenced his writing of *Coriolanus*. Those who took direct action to remove enclosures were now for the first time called Levellers. The exuberant resistance to expropriation slowed the pace of enclosure, delayed the undercutting of wages, and laid the basis for the concession and compromise that we misleadingly term "Tudor paternalism," as if they had been a pure gift of parental goodness.[19]

When it came time to sort out and analyze the dispossessed, Sir John Popham, chief justice of the King's Bench from 1592 to 1607 and a leading organizer of the Virginia Company, listed thirty different types of rogues and beggars and classed them into five main groups. First there were the chapmen, the tinkers and peddlers, the men and women whose little transactions constituted the commerce of the proletarian microeconomy. Second were the discharged or wounded, or the pretended discharged and wounded, soldiers and sailors, whose labors provided the basis of the expansionist macroeconomy. Third were the remnants of the surviving substructure of feudal benevolence: the procurers, the proctors, the pardoners. The entertainers of the day—the jugglers, fencers, minstrels, keepers of dancing bears, athletes, and players of interludes— made up the fourth group. Next, in mentioning those feigning knowledge of a "crafty Scyence" such as palmistry or physiognomy, as well as fortune-tellers and "persons calling themselves Schollers," Popham designated a fifth group that supplied the intellectual and philosophical wants of the people. Finally, his preamble named "all wandring persons and common Labourers being persons able in bodye using loytering and refusing to worke for such reasonable wages as is taxed or comonly given in such Parts where such persons do or shall happen to dwell or abide, not having lyving otherwyse to maynteyne themselves." Thus falling within the statutory meaning of "sturdy rogue and beggar" were all those outside of organized wage labor, as well as those whose activities comprised the culture, tradition, and autonomous self-understanding of this volatile, questioning, and unsteady proletariat. Marx and Engels called the expropriated a motley crowd.[20]

Expropriation and resistance fueled the process of colonization, peopling the *Sea-Venture* and many other transatlantic vessels during the first half of the seventeenth century. While some went willingly, as the loss of lands made them desperate for a new beginning, many more went *un*willingly, for reasons explained by Bacon in the aftermath of Midlands Revolt: "For the surest way to prevent *Seditions*" was "to take away the *Matter* of them. For if there be Fuell prepared, it is hard to tell, whence the Spark shall come, that shall set it on Fire." Arguments in favor of colonizing Ireland in 1594 or Virginia in 1612 held that the "rank multitude" might thus be exported and the "matter of sedition . . . removed out of the City." An entire policy originated from the Beggars Act of 1597 (39 Eliz. c. 4), whereby vagrants and rogues convicted of crimes (mostly against property) in England would be transported to the colonies and sentenced to work on plantations, within what Hakluyt saw as a "prison without walls." Here was the place for the inmates of London and indeed the whole realm. The first known English felon transported to the Americas was a dyer's apprentice who took his master's goods and absconded from a workhouse before being sent to Virginia in 1607. Thousands more would follow.[21]

ALTERNATIVES

The partisans of the Virginia Company knew that expropriation created "swarmes of idle persons" who had once been sustained by the commons. The merchant, investor, and publicist Robert Gray recalled a time when the

commons of our Country lay free and open for the poore Common[er]s to injoy, for there was roome enough in the land for every
man, so that no man needed to encroach [on] or inclose from another, whereby it is manifest, that in those dayes we had no great
need to follow strange reports, or to seeke wild adventures, for
seeing we had not onely sufficiencie, but an overflowing measure
proportioned to everie man.

His tendentious view that encroachment and enclosure had been caused
solely by population growth and overcrowding notwithstanding, Gray
understood that many people in England had once lived differently—
more freely, sufficiently, even abundantly. When the commoners of the
Sea-Venture decided that they wished to settle in Bermuda rather than go
on to Virginia, they explained to the Virginia Company officials that
they wanted the ease, pleasure, and freedom of the commons rather than
the wretchedness, labor, and slavery awaiting them in Virginia.[22]

Inspired by the actions of the shipwrecked commoners, Shakespeare
made alternative ways of life a major theme in *The Tempest*. Gonzalo, a
wise old counselor in the play who is cast away with the king and other
aristocrats on Bermuda, muses about the ideal "commonwealth" he
would establish "had I plantation of this isle":

> *I' th' commonwealth I would by contraries*
> *Execute all things; for no kind of traffic*
> *Would I admit; no name of magistrate;*
> *Letters should not be known; riches, poverty,*
> *And use of service, none; contract, succession,*
> *Bourn, bound of land, tilth, vineyard, none;*
> *No use of metal, corn, or wine, or oil;*
> *No occupation: all men idle, all;*
> *And women too, but innocent and pure:*
> *No sovereignty—*

He continues,

> *All things in common Nature should produce*
> *Without sweat or endeavour: treason, felony,*
> *Sword, pike, knife, gun, or need of any engine,*

Would I not have; but Nature should bring forth,
Of it own kind, all foison, all abundance,
To feed my innocent people.

His commonwealth, he concludes, would "excel the Golden Age."[23]

The people of the *Sea-Venture* shared with Shakespeare numerous sources of knowledge about alternative ways of life, including the classical Golden Age, the Christian Garden of Eden (Gonzalo's "innocent people"), and a broad array of popular traditions: antinomian (no law, or felony, or magistracy); anarchist (no sovereignty or treason); pacifist (no sword, pike, knife, or gun); egalitarian (no riches or poverty); and hunting and gathering (no mining or agriculture). A society without succession was one without aristocracy of birth, while a society without use of service was one without wage labor. These traditions were enacted in pageants of the "world turned upside down," featuring motley-clad jesters such as Shakespeare's Trinculo amid the banners, horses, artwork, and extravagance of courtly carnival, incorporating pagan rites, peasant traditions, and otherworldly utopian settings (*alterae terrae*, like Bermuda) into new, inclusive, spectacular entertainments. George Ferrers, lord of misrule at Edward VI's celebrations of 1552, entered the festivity "vppon one straunge beast," as "the serpente with sevin heddes cauled hidra is the chief beast of myne armes." Comic fables such as the "Land of Cockaigne" deriving from medieval satire kept a type of utopia alive, painting a picture of indolent pleasure and absolute satiation.[24]

The most immediate alternative, of course, was the experience of the commons, with its absence of the private property suggested by words such as *tilth* and *bourn*. *Tilth* was an ancient Frisian word referring to a plowing or a harrowing—that is, to specific labors, and by implication to the condition of cultivation that stood in contrast to pasture, forest, and waste. It evoked, by association, a return to woodland conditions, which still existed in England and especially in Ireland, where English conquerors had already begun to defoliate the woods to defeat a kin-based society that shared its principal resources. *Bourn* was a more recent term signifying the boundary between fields, much used in the sixteenth century in the south of England and hence associated with enclosure. Those who had been expropriated had not only a grievance but a living memory and lore of open-field agriculture and commoning. Thus for many people the

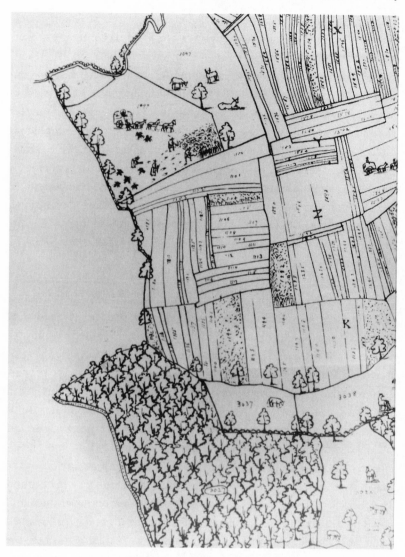

Open-field farming in Laxton, England, 1632.
Booke of Survaye of the Manor of Laxton *(1635).*

absence of "bourn, bound of land, tilth" was not an ideal dream but a recent, and lost, reality, an actual commons.

When Governor Thomas Gates complained that the mutineers of the *Sea-Venture* retired to the woods and lived like savages, what precisely did he mean? How did savages live? For Gates and his entire generation of

Europeans, the classless, stateless, egalitarian societies of America were powerful examples of alternative ways of life. Virginia Company spokesman Robert Gray sounded an often-repeated note about Native Americans: "There is not *meum* and *tuum* amongst them." They had no conception of private property and precious little notion of work itself, as William Strachey discovered: Virginia's Indians were, he noted, "now for the most parte of the year idle." Idle, perhaps, but not starving: Sir Henry Colt wrote in 1631 that he saw in St. Christopher, in the West Indies, "many naked Indians, & although their bellyes be to great for their proportions, yett itt shewes ye plentye of ye Iland in ye nourishinge of them." Such discoveries inflamed the collective imagination of Europe, inspiring endless discussion—among statesmen, philosophers, and writers, as well as the dispossessed—of peoples who lived without property, work, masters, or kings.[25]

Tales of these alternative societies in America were carried back to Europe by sailors—the hundreds, and soon thousands, of real-life equivalents of Thomas More's Raphael Hythloday, the seafarer who returned from the New World to tell the story of *Utopia*. Members of cultures high and low depended on sailors and their "strange reports" for news of *alterae terrae*. Michel de Montaigne's personal servant was a former seaman who had lived twelve years among the Indians of Brazil; this "plain ignorant fellow" was undoubtedly a "true witness" whose stories influenced his master's conception of human possibility.[26] Through these and other tales that circulated through port cities such as London, Shakespeare had read and heard of the "golden world without toyle," of the places "without lawes, without bookes, and without judges," to be found in America. Centuries later, Rudyard Kipling would visit Bermuda and assert that Shakespeare had gotten many of his ideas for *The Tempest* from "a drunken seaman."[27] Sailors in this way brought together the primitive communism of the New World and the plebeian commonism of the Old, suggesting—at least in part—why they played such a leading and subversive role in the events surrounding the shipwreck of the *Sea-Venture* on Bermuda in 1609.

Commoning was not a single agrarian practice, nor were the commons a uniform ecological place with a fixed human tenure. Both varied from time to time and from place to place, as William Strachey and

A southern Algonquian village, 1588. Hariot,
A briefe and true report of the new found land of Virginia.

many others well knew. Strachey explained that "whatsoever God by the ministration of nature hath created on earth, was at the begynning common among men," and that the Native Americans he encountered—whom he called "the naturalls"—were much like his own ancestors, the ancient Picts and Britons who had been subdued by the Romans. There existed a particular English open-field system of agriculture, including provision for common fields, which seems to have been replicated successfully in Sudbury, Massachusetts, until it, too, was overcome by the onslaught of private accumulation.[28] Yet the commons were more than a specific English agrarian practice or its American variants; the same concept underlay the clachan, the sept, the rundale, the West African village, and the indigenous tradition of long-fallow agriculture of Native Americans—in other words, it encompassed all those parts of the Earth that remained unprivatized, unenclosed, a noncommodity, a support for the manifold human values of mutuality. Shakespeare knew the truth of the struggle for an alternative way of life on Bermuda, but he chose to turn a real place into a dreamy, literary "no-place," a utopia. His fellow investors in the Virginia Company did something similar: against those who tried to seize a life of "plenty, peace, and ease," they brutally pursued a utopia of their own.

COOPERATION AND RESISTANCE

The history of the *Sea-Venture* can be recounted as a microcosm of various forms of human cooperation. The first of these was the cooperation among the sailors, and eventually among everyone on the ship, during the hurricane, as they steered the vessel, struck sails, cleared the decks, and pumped out the water that was seeping into the hull. After the shipwreck, cooperative labor was extended and reorganized among the "hands" ashore, in part by the leaders of the Virginia Company, in part in opposition to them. This work consisted of building huts out of palmetto fronds for shelter and commoning for subsistence—hunting and gathering, fishing and scavenging. Beginning with the challenge to authority aboard ship, the commoners, led by the sailors, cooperated on the island in the planning of five distinct conspiracies, including a strike and marronage. Alongside and against that oppositional cooperation, the

Virginia Company officials organized their own project of cooperative labor: the hewing of cedar trees and the building of vessels to carry the shipwrecked on to Virginia. The tensions between the subversive and official forms of cooperation constituted the drama of William Strachey's account of life on Bermuda in 1609–1610.

Cooperation bound together many different kinds of people, with many different kinds of work experience: sailors, laborers, craftsmen, and commoners of several sorts, including two Native Americans, Namuntack and Matchumps, who were returning to the Powhatans in the Chesapeake after a voyage to England.[29] Such cooperative resistance shaped Shakespeare's conception of the conspiracy waged in *The Tempest* by Caliban the slave, Trinculo the jester, and Stephano the sailor, who combine in a plan to kill Prospero and seize control of the island (Bermuda). Caliban himself embodies African, Native American, Irish, and English cultural elements, while Trinculo and Stephano represent two of the main types of the dispossessed in Judge Popham's England. "Misery acquaints a man with strange bed-fellows," muses Trinculo as he joins Caliban beneath a gaberdine mantle, seeking shelter from a thunderstorm—but not before asking himself, "What have we here? a man or a fish?" When Stephano arrives on the scene, he surveys what he thinks is a many-legged creature and wonders if a new kind of being has been created: "This is some monster of the isle with four legs." It is not a fish, of course, nor is it a monster, nor a hybrid (a word originally used to describe the breeding of pigs and first applied to humans in 1620, when Ben Jonson referred to young Irishwomen); it is, rather, the beginning of cooperation among a motley crew of workers. Caliban promises to use his commoning skills (i.e., hunting and gathering) to show Trinculo and Stephano how to survive in a strange land, how and where to find food, fresh water, salt, and wood. Their cooperation eventually evolves into conspiracy and rebellion of the kind promoted on the island of Bermuda by the commoners of the *Sea-Venture* before they, too, were defeated.[30]

We have said that the meeting of Caliban and Trinculo under the gaberdine is the beginning of the *motley* crew. We should explain the significance of the term. In the habits of royal authority in Renaissance England, the "motley" was a multicolored garment, often a cap, worn by a jester who was permitted by the king to make jokes, even to tell the truth, to power. As an insignium, the motley brought carnivalesque expectations of disorder and subversion, a little letting-off of steam. By extension, *motley* could also refer to a colorful assemblage, such as a crowd of people whose tatterdemalion dress made it interesting. A motley crowd might very likely be one in rags, or a *"lumpen"*-proletariat (from the German word for "rags"). Although we write about and emphasize the interracial character of the motley crew, we wish that readers would keep these other meanings—the subversion of power and the poverty in appearance—in mind.

Expropriation occurred not only in England but also in Ireland, Africa, the Caribbean, and North America. The proletarians thus created worked as skilled navigators and sailors on early transatlantic ships, as slaves on American plantations, and as entertainers, sex workers, and servants in London. English participation in the slave trade, essential to the rise of capitalism, began in 1563, the year before Shakespeare was born. In 1555 John Lok brought the first Ghanaian slaves to England, where they learned English in order to return to Ghana and act as interpreters for slave traders. John Hawkyns made huge profits selling three hundred slaves in Haiti to the Spanish in 1562–1563. Queen Elizabeth loaned him a ship and crew for his second slave expedition. In Ben Jonson's *The Masque of Blacknesse* (1605), Oceanus could innocently ask of the African Niger, "But, what's the end of thy *Herculean* labors,/ Extended to these calme, and blessed shores[?]" Shakespeare, who himself admired Hercules, among other mythic figures, would help to answer that question: in 1607, the crews of the slave ships the *Dragon* and the *Hector* performed *Hamlet* and *Richard II* while anchored off Sierra Leone. Lucas Fernandez, "a converted negro, brother-in-law of the local King Borea," translated the plays for the visiting African merchants.[31] In 1618, soon after the first performance of *The Tempest,* English slave traders, chartered as the Company of Adventurers of London Trading to Gynney and Bynney by James I, built the first permanent English factory in West Africa.[32]

Shakespeare presented the conspiracy of Caliban, Trinculo, and Stephano as a comedy of low characters, but their alliance was far from laughable: Drake had depended on the superior knowledge of the cimarrons, escaped Afro-Indian slaves, in his raids on the Spanish Main.[33] And

as we have seen, the actual mutinies on Bermuda, which threw up democratic, antinomian, and communist ideas from below, were more varied,
complex, sustained, intelligent, and dangerous than Shakespeare allowed. Perhaps he had no choice. A recent law prohibited any mention of
divinity on stage and therefore made it difficult to consider the arguments of dissenters such as Stephan Hopkins, who derived their notion
of freedom from precisely such a source. The canons of 1604 also required that every English church acknowledge that each of the Thirty-
nine Articles of the Church of England was agreeable to the Word of
God. The thirty-seventh article stated that "the Laws of the Realm may
punish Christian men with death," while the thirty-eighth asserted that
"the Riches and Goods of Christians are not common, as touching the
right, title, and possession of the same, as certain Anabaptists do falsely
boast."

Like the rebels of the *Sea-Venture,* the cooperation and combination
of "strange bed-fellows" who rose up in insurrection in *The Tempest* were
represented as monstrous. Here Shakespeare contributed to an evolving
ruling-class view of popular rebellion that would be summarized by the
anonymous author of *The Rebel's Doom,* a later-seventeenth-century history of uprisings in England. Early tumults in the realm, the writer
claimed, had resulted almost entirely from the *"Disloyalty* and *Disobedience* of the most *Eminent Personages* of the Nation," but after the Peasant's Revolt of 1381, "the rabble"—as Prospero called Caliban, Stephano,
and Trinculo—"like a *Monstrous Hydra,* erecting their shapeless heads,
began to hiss against their Soveraigns *Regal Power* and *Authority."* The
strikes, mutinies, separations, and defiances against the power and authority of the sovereign Virginia Company after the shipwreck on Bermuda would play a major, even determining part in the course of colonization, as the subsequent histories of Bermuda and Virginia would show.

CLASS DISCIPLINE

Even though the *Sea-Venture* "caried in one bottome all the principall
Commissioners who should successiuelie have gouerned the Colonie" of
Virginia, all of whom were wrecked on Bermuda, and even though Sir
Thomas Gates was invested by the Virginia Company with the power to

The Hydra, supposed to be killed by Hercules.
Edward Topsell, Historie of Serpents *(1608).*

declare martial law at his discretion, the gentlemen had a terrible time establishing their authority, for the hurricane and the shipwreck had leveled class distinctions. Confronted with resistance that proposed an alternative way of life, the officials of the Virginia Company responded by destroying the commoning option and by reasserting class discipline through labor and terror, new ways of life and death. They reorganized work and inflicted capital punishment.[34]

Ever sensitive to the problems faced by his fellow investors in the Virginia Company, Shakespeare considered the issues of authority and class discipline in *The Tempest*. Aboard the ship, Gonzalo faces an uppity sailor who dares to order the aristocrats around during the leveling storm. He observes of the plain-spoken tar:

I have great comfort from this fellow: methinks he hath no drowning mark upon him; his complexion is perfect gallows. Stand fast, good Fate, to his hanging: make the rope of his destiny our cable, for our own doth little advantage. If he be not born to be hanged, our case is miserable.

Gonzalo, of course, can do nothing about the verbal mutiny as long as the ship remains in danger, so he recalls the plebeian proverb "He that's born to be hanged need fear no drowning" and takes comfort in the prospect of a hanging. Shakespeare thus suggests the importance of deep-sea sailing ships ("the Jewels of our land," as they were called by a Virginia Company official) and sailors. Both, he advises, have to be firmly controlled by the rulers overseeing the process of colonization. The ship and the sailor were necessary to the international accumulation of capital through the transport of commodities, which included, as we have seen, the expropriated workers who would create that new capital. One critical instrument of control was the public hanging.

When Gonzalo prays to fate that the rope of the boatswain's destiny may become the cable of life for the ruling class, he is making explicit a real relationship. Sir Walter Raleigh had a similar experience when exploring the waters of Venezuela: "At the last we determined to hang the Pilot, and if we had well known the way back again by night, he had surely gone, but our own necessities pleaded sufficiently for his safety." Hanging was destiny for part of the proletariat because it was necessary to the organization and functioning of transatlantic labor markets, maritime and otherwise, and to the suppression of radical ideas, as on Bermuda. In 1611, the year *The Tempest* was first performed, in Middlesex alone (which county already contained the most populous parishes of London) roughly 130 people were sentenced to the gallows and ninety-eight were actually hanged, considerably more than the annual average of about seventy. The following year Bartholomew Legate and Edward Wrightman, both followers of the Puritan separatist Robert Browne and brethren of Stephan Hopkins, were burned at the stake for heresy. Even grislier punishments were enacted at sea, where any sailor caught sleeping on watch a third time would be bound to the mainmast with a basket of bullets tied to his arms; after a fourth offense he would be hanged with a biscuit and knife from the bowsprit, forced eventually to decide whether to starve or to cut himself down to drown. A man designing to steal a ship would be hanged by his heels overboard until his brains were beaten out against the ship's sides. Shakespeare evaded such realities in his play, but he and his friends in the Virginia Company knew well that capitalist colonization depended on them.[35]

Gruesome kinds of capital punishment were not the only notions of class discipline aboard the *Sea-Venture,* and one of these would have long-term implications for the colony of Virginia and indeed for all of England's Atlantic empire. The source of it lay in the Netherlands in the late sixteenth century, in the new forms of military discipline developed by Maurice of Orange for Dutch soldiers. In what would prove to be a centerpiece of the "military revolution," Maurice redesigned military work processes, breaking soldiers' movements into component parts and recombining them to create new cooperation, efficiency, and collective power.[36] These ideas and practices were carried by Sir Thomas Gates and Sir Thomas Dale to Virginia in 1610 and 1611, and from there by future Governor Daniel Tucker to Bermuda. This new way of organizing military cooperation relied ultimately on the terror of the gallows and the whipping post (on one occasion Tucker personally whipped forty men before breakfast). Its reality and its necessity can be seen in the social and political dynamics of early Virginia, almost all of whose early leaders— Gates, De La Warr, Dale, Yeardley, and others—were officers "truly bred in that university of warre, the Lowe Countries."[37]

The resistance that first appeared on Bermuda persisted in Virginia as colonists refused to work, mutinied, and often deserted to the Powhatan Indians. Here continued the "tempest of dissention: euery man ouervaluing his own worth, would be a Commander; euery man vnderprising an others value, denied to be commanded." Here were the "license, sedition, and furie [which] are the fruits of a headie, daring, and vnruly multitude." Soldiers, sailors, and Indians conspired to smuggle guns and tools from the Virginia Company's stores and held "night marts" to sell the appropriated goods. Many of Virginia's leaders had faced the same problems in Ireland, where English soldiers and settlers had deserted the plantations to join the Irish. As an anonymous observer wrote of the year 1609 in Virginia, "To eate many our men this starveing Tyme did Runn Away unto the Salvages [sic] whom we never heard of after." Some desertions thus began with an urgent question in the native tongue: "*Mow-chick woyawgh tawgh noeragh kaquere mecher?*" ("I am very hungry, what shall I eat?"). One in every seven settlers at Jamestown deserted during the winter of 1609–10. Henry Spelman, a youth who had lived among the Powhatans in order to learn their language, returned to the tribe in 1609 "by Reason that vitals [i.e., victuals] were scarse with us." Yet hunger was not the only issue, for English colonists regularly fled to the Native Americans, "from the moment of settlement in 1607 until the all but total breakdown in relations between English and natives following the 1622 massacre." Captain John Smith knew that the principal attraction for the deserters was the opportunity "to live idle among the savages." Some of those who had lived like savages on Bermuda apparently would not be denied.[38]

This situation helped to call forth the *Laws Divine, Moral, and Martial,* sanctioned by the Second Charter of the Virginia Company (1609) with the advice of Francis Bacon, who was, according to Strachey, a "most noble fautor [favorer] of the Virginian Plantation, being from the beginning (with other lords and earles) of the principall counsell applyed to propagate and guide yt." The charter, as suggested above, empowered Sir Thomas Gates to declare martial law in order to bring the colony to discipline and thereby to make money for the new stockholders. The first nineteen articles of the new law, imposed by Gates the day after he arrived in Virginia, had likely been drawn up amid the conspiracies that challenged his rule on Bermuda and against that island's backdrop of liberty, plenty, and ease. These mostly martial laws established military discipline for labor and dispensed harsh punishments, including execution, for resistance. In all, the laws contained thirty-seven articles, promising whippings, galley service, and death galore: twenty-five of them prescribed capital punishment. Thomas Dale adapted the latter sections of the *Laws Divine, Moral, and Martial* "from a Dutch army book of ordinances which he had brought with him." One of the main purposes of the laws was to keep English settlers and Native Americans apart.[39]

The people to whom the colonists deserted in defiance of Dale's laws were a *Tsenacommacah,* or loose alliance, of thirty-odd smallish groups of Algonquians. Their paramount chief, Wahunsonacock, a Pamunkey Indian whom the English called Powhatan, was a "tall well proportioned man, with a sower look," sixty years old and possessed of "a very able and hardy body to endure any labour." The fourteen thousand allied Algonquians inhabited a rich ecological zone made up of mixed forest and Chesapeake waterways, on which they exercised an economy of collecting and horticulture. They hunted (Virginia white-tailed deer, bear, wild turkey, goose, quail, duck); they fished (herring, shad, sturgeon); they captured eels and shellfish (crabs, clams, oysters, mussels); they gathered (fruits, berries, nuts); and they practiced tillage (maize, beans, squash). They were nourished upon a better all-around diet than the Europeans. The confederation consisted of small-scale societies without ownership of land, without classes, without a state, but with all paying tribute to Wahunsonacock, "the subtell owlde foxe." They pursued little economic specialization and attempted little trade; they were self-sufficient. Their society was organized around matrilineal descent, and both men and women enjoyed sexual freedom outside marriage. There existed no political/military bureaucracy for their roughly fifteen hundred warriors. Even Wahunsonacock performed the tasks of an ordinary man and was addressed by all not by his title but by his personal name. All the items Gonzalo "would not have" in his utopia were likewise missing in Powhatan society, except one: corn, or Indian maize. In search of food and a way of life that many apparently found congenial, a steady stream of English settlers opted to become "white Indians," "red Englishmen," or—since racial categories were as yet unformed—Anglo-Powhatans.[40] One such was Robert Markham, a sailor who came to the region with Captain Christopher Newport on the first Virginia voyage (May–June, 1607) and ended up a renegade: he converted to Algonquian culture and took the name Moutapass.[41]

The defections continued, especially among soldiers and laborers compelled by harsh discipline to build fortifications to the west, at Henrico, out of which would grow Richmond. In 1611, a few of those who "did Runne Away unto the Indyans" were retaken by a military expedition. Sir Thomas Dale "in A moste severe mannor caused [them] to be executed." Of these, "Some he apointed to be hanged Some burned Some to be broken upon wheles, others to be staked and some to be shott to death." These "extreme and crewell tortures he used and inflicted upon them" in order "to terrefy the rest for Attemptinge the Lyke."

When he caught a few others pilfering goods from the Virginia Company's supplies, Dale "cawsed them to be bownd faste unto Trees and so sterved them to deathe." Terror created boundaries.[42]

Thus did popular anticapitalist traditions—a world without work, private property, law, felony, treason, or magistrate—find their perfect antithesis in Thomas Dale's Virginia, where drumbeats called settlers to labor and the *Laws Divine, Moral, and Martial* promised terror and death to any who dared to resist. Military men transformed Bermuda and Virginia from places of "liberty and the fullness of sensuality" to places of bondage, war, scarcity, and famine. By 1613 colonists on Bermuda were starving to death as their bodies, bent and blue, spent their vital forces laboring on fortifications that would make of the island a strategic military outpost in the early phase of English colonization. One unnamed man refused to give in to the new reality, preserving the older vision of Bermuda as he "hid himself in the Woods, and lived only on Wilkes [whelks] and land Crabs, fat and lusty many moneths." The destruction of the Bermudian paradise was signaled by a massive rat infestation and an ominous visitation by "a company of Ravens, which continued amongst them all the time of the mortality and then departed."[43]

CHAPTER TWO

Hewers of Wood and Drawers of Water

All I have to do in this world is to be merry,
which I shall if the ground be not taken from me.
—*Francis Beaumont,* The Knight of the Burning Pestle *(1607)*

Youth, youth it is better to be starved by thy nurse
Than live to be hanged for cutting a purse.
—*Ben Jonson,* Bartholomew Fair *(1614)*

THE ENEMIES AT COURT OF Sir Walter Raleigh, the archetypal imperialist adventurer, imprisoned him in the Tower after the accession of
James I in 1603 on insubstantial evidence that he had intrigued with
Spain to kill the king. In prison Raleigh wrote his *History of the World*
and in it mentioned Hercules and "the serpent Hydra, which had nine
heads, whereof one being cut off, two grew in the place." Raleigh, of
course, identified with Hercules, and he used the hydra to symbolize the
growing disorders of capitalism. "The amorphous laboring class, set
loose from the traditional moorings of the peasantry, presented a new
phenomenon to contemporaries," historian Joyce Appleby has noted.[1]
Combining Greek myth with the Old Testament, Raleigh developed a
historical interpretation of Hercules: "That he slew many thieves and tyrants I take to be truly written, without addition of poetical vanity," he
wrote, and "Sure it is that many cities in Greece were greatly bound to
him; for that he (bending all his endeavours to the common good) delivered the land from much oppression." Hercules helped to establish king-
ship, or political sovereignty, and commerce, under the dominance of a
particular ethnic group, the Greeks. He served as a model for the exploration, trade, conquest, and plantation of English mercantilism; indeed, a
cult of Hercules suffused English ruling-class culture in the seventeenth

century.[2] Raleigh noted, "Some by Hercules understand fortitude, prudence, and constancy, interpreting the monsters [as] vices. Others make Hercules the sun, and his travels to be the twelve signs of the zodiac. There are others who apply his works historically to their own conceits."

Francis Bacon, who as lord chancellor tried Raleigh in 1618 and was the first to inform him of his death sentence, turned the myth of Hercules and the hydra into a powerful conceit indeed. Born to a leading Elizabethan courtier and educated at Cambridge, Bacon was a philosopher who advocated inductive reasoning and scientific experimentation, and a politician who lost favor with the queen but regained it under James by betraying his erstwhile friends. He connected utopian thought with practical projects, writing New Atlantis, "Of Empire," and "Of Plantations" while investing in the Virginia Company. He drafted his essay "Of Seditions and Troubles" after the Enslow Hill Rebellion (1596), in which food and antienclosure rioters in Oxfordshire planned to march to London to join rebellious apprentices. Bartholomew Steere, a carpenter and one of the rioters, predicted, "We shall have a merrier world shortly. . . . I will work one day and play the other." Steere suffered two months of examination and torture in London's Bridewell Prison at the hands of Bacon and other officials. While Bacon claimed that he sought to enlarge the "bounds of Human Empire to make all things possible," his will to power violently crushed alternatives such as the one hoped for by Steere.

Bacon wrote about Hercules in his interpretation of Prometheus, who signified mind and intellect and thereby proved that man might be regarded "as the centre of the world." The winds sailed the ships and ran the engines just for man; plants and animals furnished food and shelter just for him; even the stars worked for him. The quest for knowledge was always a struggle for power. The voyage of Hercules to set Prometheus free seemed to Bacon to be an image of God's redeeming the human race.[3] The story of Hercules was on Bacon's mind when he came to write An Advertisement Touching an Holy War, published in 1622, a famine year and shortly after Bacon's downfall and conviction on charges of bribery. He wrote it to pay his debts and to find his way back into the corridors of power. The treatise addressed the conflict between the king and the members of Parliament over who was to hold the purse strings of govern-

Frontispiece of Francis Bacon's The Great Instauration *(1620):*
a ship of discovery returns through the Pillars of Hercules.
By permission of the Folger Shakespeare Library.

ment: Bacon advised that the only "chance of healing the growing breach was to engage the country in some popular quarrel abroad." The recent national quarrel with Catholic Spain would not qualify, since James I favored a Spanish alliance. Hence Bacon looked elsewhere for enemies adequate to his proposed jihad.

He began by comparing war to capital punishment. The justification for both must be "full and clear," in accord with the law of nations, the law of nature, and divine law, lest "our blessed Saviour" become a Moloch (i.e., an idol to whom sacrifices were made). A death sentence was justified against those unavowed by God, those who had defaced natural reason and were neither nations in right nor nations in name, "but multitudes only, and swarms of people." Elsewhere in the same essay Bacon referred to "shoals" and "routs" of people. By taking his terms from natural history—a "swarm" of bees, a "shoal" of seals or whales, a "rout" of wolves—and applying them to people, Bacon drew on his theory of monstrousness. These people had degenerated from the laws of nature and taken "in their body and frame of estate a monstrosity." In 1620 Bacon had called for the rigorous study of monsters, "of every thing . . . which is new, rare, and unusual in nature." To him, monsters were more than a portent, a curiosity, or an exoticism; rather, they comprised one of the major divisions of nature, which were: 1) nature in course; 2) nature wrought; and 3) nature erring. These three realms constituted what was normal, what was artificial, and what was monstrous. The last category bridged the boundaries of the natural and the artificial and was thus essential to the process of experiment and control.[4] These divisions are well-known features of Bacon's thought. His *An Advertisement Touching an Holy War,* by contrast, is not well known, yet it reveals the form and temper of its age.

Bacon drew upon classical antiquity, the Bible, and recent history to provide seven examples of such "multitudes" that deserved destruction: West Indians; Canaanites; pirates; land rovers; assassins; Amazons; and Anabaptists. Having listed these, he wrote,

Of examples enough; except we should add the labours of Hercules; an example which, though it be flourished with much fabulous matter, yet so much it hath, that it doth notably set forth the

consent of all nations and ages in the approbation of the extirpat-
ing and debellating of giants, monsters, and foreign tyrants, not
only as lawful, but as meritorious, even divine honour: and this although the deliverer came from the one end of the world unto the
other.

This is the crux, or crucial thought, where genocide and divinity cross.
Bacon's advertisement for a holy war was thus a call for several types of
genocide, which found its sanction in biblical and classical antiquity.
Bacon thereby gave form to the formless, as the groups he named embodied a monstrous, many-headed hydra. But who were these groups? And
why did he recommend holy war against them?

THE CURSE OF LABOR

The answers to these questions may be found by continuing the analysis,
begun in the previous chapter, of the processes of expropriation, exploitation, and colonization in the era of Raleigh and Bacon. We argue that
the many expropriations of the day—of the commons by enclosure and
conquest, of time by the puritanical abolition of holidays, of the body by
child stealing and the burning of women, and of knowledge by the destruction of guilds and assaults on paganism—gave rise to new kinds of
workers in a new kind of slavery, enforced directly by terror.[5] We also
suggest that the emergence of cooperation among workers, in new ways
and on a new scale, facilitated new forms of self-organization among
them, which was alarming to the ruling class of the day. Bacon saw the
new combinations of workers as monstrous and used the myth of the
many-headed hydra to develop his theory of monstrosity, a subtle, thinly
veiled policy of terror and genocide. The idiom of monstrosity would
gain special relevance with the emergence of a revolutionary movement
in England in the 1640s, in which the proletarian forces opposed by
Bacon would play a critical part.

We will concentrate in this chapter on the making of "hewers of wood
and drawers of water," a phrase adopted in the authorized version of the
Bible published in the year *The Tempest* was written (1611), and one that
has flourished in modern social description. The alliteration (*wood,*

water) and the assonance (*hewer, drawer*) have provided some of the attraction, but since the actual work that the phrase describes is menial, onerous, and dirty, the essential uses have revolved around dissonance and irony. Seventeenth-century London artisans used the phrase in their protests against deskilling, mechanization, cheap labor, and the loss of independence. Swift employed it in 1729 to describe the position of the Irish beneath their English lords, as did Wolfe Tone in 1790 and James Connolly almost two centuries later. In 1736 Bolingbroke, the aristocratic high Tory, added a racial spin: "The herd of mankind" constituted "another species," "scarce members of the community, though born in the country," "marked out like the Jews, a distinct race, hewers of wood and drawers of water."[6] In the nineteenth century the British Chartists gave the phrase animal connotations: "The labouring classes—the real 'people'—[have] been roused in the attempt of making the working classes beasts of burden—hewers of wood and drawers of water."[7] In *Emmanuel Appadocca* (1854), the first anglophone novel published in the British Caribbean, Maxwell Philip wrote of the Africans, who "gave philosophy, religion, and government to the world, but who must now stoop to cut wood, and to carry water." Osborne Ward noted in *The Ancient Lowly* (1888), "They were not only slaves but they formed, as it were, another race. They were the plebeians, the proletariat; 'hewers of wood and drawers of water.'"[8] The use of the phrase was extended into the twentieth century when Samuel Haynes, a follower of Marcus Garvey and president of the Newark branch of the NAACP, wrote the national anthem of Belize, which culminates, "By the might of truth and the grace of God,/No longer shall we be hewers of wood." W. E. B. Du Bois explained that the aim of the black artisan was "to escape white contempt for a nation of mere hewers and drawers of water." One of the exegetical tasks of pan-Africanism was to show that these biblical terms also applied to white people. The words were crucial to the formation of the African National Congress in South Africa in 1912 and figured again in Nelson Mandela's speech about the dismantling of apartheid in 1991. George Jackson, the black revolutionary, emphasized the concomitant state of propertylessness: "Has any people ever been independent that owned neither land or tool? . . . more of the same, the hewing of wood and the carrying of water."[9]

While hewing and drawing suggest timeless travails, the phrase in fact originated in the early era of capitalism. William Tyndale coined "hewers of wood and drawers of water" in his translation of the Old Testament in 1530. It appears in two contrasting biblical contexts. The first is in Deuteronomy 29, where Moses makes a covenant at Jahweh's command. He reminds the people of their deliverance from Egypt, the forty years in the wilderness, the battles of conquest. He calls together the captains of the tribes, the elders, and the officers and commands: "Your little ones, your wives, and thy stranger that is in thy camp, from the hewer of thy wood unto the drawer of thy water" must enter into a covenant. Jahweh then curses for a dozen or more verses. The covenant is inclusive, constituting a people or nation, under threats and in dread. The second context is in Joshua 9:21: "And the princes said unto them [the Gibeonites], Let them live; but let them be hewers of wood and drawers of water unto all the congregation." Two verses later, the punitive nature of the phrase is explained: "Now therefore are ye cursed, and there shall none of you be freed from being bondmen and hewers of wood and drawers of water for the house of my God." The Gibeonites have been punished with enslavement, yet they remain within the covenant.

For the African, European, and American hewers of wood and drawers of water in the early seventeenth century, work was both a curse and a punishment. These workers were necessary to the growth of capitalism, as they did the work that could not or would not be done by artisans in workshops, manufactories, or guilds. Hewers and drawers performed the fundamental labors of expropriation that have usually been taken for granted by historians. Expropriation itself, for example, is treated as a given: the field is *there* before the plowing starts; the city is *there* before the laborer begins the working day. Likewise for long-distance trade: the port is *there* before the ship sets sail from it; the plantation is *there* before the slave cultivates its land. The commodities of commerce seem to transport themselves. Finally, reproduction is assumed to be the transhistorical function of the family. The result is that the hewers of wood and drawers of water have been invisible, anonymous, and forgotten, even though they transformed the face of the Earth by building the infrastructure of "civilization."

The Labors of the Hewer and Drawer

The hewers of wood and drawers of water had three main functions: they undertook the labors of expropriation; they built the ports and the ships and provided the seafarers for Atlantic commerce; and they daily maintained the households.

Labors of expropriation included the clear-cutting of woods, the draining of marshes, the reclamation of fens, and the hedging of the arable field—in sum, the obliteration of the commoning *habitus*. Woodlands contained flourishing economies of forest people in England, Ireland, Jamaica, Virginia, and New England; their destruction was the first step toward agrarian "civilization," as summarized by Hercules when he gave land to the cultivators in neolithic times. This was and is the language of cultivators and "improvers," of settlers and imperialists, and even of a money-hungry government, as when the early Stuarts disafforested crown lands in a reckless search for revenues. The felled trees fueled the growing iron, glass, brewing, and shipbuilding industries, resulting in a threefold increase in the price of firewood between 1570 and 1640. In the latter year the "Act for the Limitation of Forests . . . was the signal for the beginning of widespread destruction of forests."[10] In 1649 the Parliamentary Committee for the Preservation of Timber was formed to check the depredations of the "looser and disordered sort of people" who continued to insist upon their common rights in the forests. In the year 1636 it took twenty-four oxen to drag the giant oak that would serve as mainmast to the *Sovereign of the Seas;* scores of people labored simultaneously, in precise alignment, to lift it onto wheels or wain. By the end of the seventeenth century only an eighth of England remained wooded.

Similarly, in America, settlers claimed and cleared the ground for agricultural colonies. In Virginia, "the spade men fell to digging, the brick men burnt their bricks, the company cut down wood, the Carpenters fell to squaring out, the Sawyers to sawing, the Soldier to fortifying," as cooperative labor built the first settlements. The colonists were at first unfamiliar with the broadax and the felling ax, but after the Pequot War, which opened the way westward, they soon learned to saw, fell, cleave, split, and rive, making timber and its products the basis of an export economy to Barbados and other parts of the West Indies. Servants and

An American landscape hewn and enclosed, with Native Americans canoeing by.
Patrick Campbell, Travels in the Interior Inhabited Parts
of North America in the Years 1791 and 1792 *(1793).*

slaves hacked away at the rain forest of Barbados, slowly clearing the
lands for plantations and sending home to England the new settlements'
first cash crop: timber. When the English took possession of lands overseas, they did so by building fences and hedges, the markers of enclosure
and private property.[11]

Another major work of expropriation was the draining of the fens. An
Act of Parliament of 1600 made it possible for big shareholders in the fens
to suppress the common rights that stood in the way of their drainage
schemes. New plans and works, requiring unprecedented concentrations
of labor, proliferated. King James organized hundreds in the draining
and enclosure of parts of Somerset in the early seventeenth century, turning a commoning economy of fishing, fowling, reed cutting, and peat
digging into a capitalist economy of sheep raising. Coastal lands were reclaimed and inland peat moors drained in the Somerset "warths." Some
eleven thousand workers were required to drain the fens around Ely during the 1650s, when drainage engineers from Holland, "equipped with a
literally world-changing technology," diverted rivers to create artificial

watercourses as large as any since Roman times, leaving in their wake an entirely new landscape of straight ditches and square fields. A poet of the area, Michael Drayton, described the land as "plump-thigh'd moor and full flank't marsh."[12]

The "battle of the fens" began in 1605 between capital owners such as Lord Chief Justice Popham ("covetous and bloodie Popham") and the fowlers, fenmen, and commoners. The terms of battle ranged from murder, sabotage, and village burning on the one hand to protracted litigation, pamphleteering, and the advanced science of hydraulics on the other. Sporadic outbursts of opposition to the drainage grew into a sustained campaign of action as commoners, often led by women, attacked workmen, ditches, dikes, and tools in Hatfield, on the Isle of Axholme, and elsewhere in the late 1620s and 1630s. Oliver Cromwell, who became a commissioner for draining the Great Level, sent a major of his own regiment to suppress the rioting commoners and received in return two hundred acres of drained land. A poet who equated common rights with theft celebrated the victory in verse:

> *New hands shall learn to work, forget to steal*
> *New legs shall go to church, new knees shall kneel.*

In 1663 Samuel Pepys passed through the "most sad fennes, all the way observing the sad life of the breedlings," as he called their inhabitants. The sadness was the consequence of a specific defeat. Thomas Fuller wrote in 1655, "Grant them drained, and so continuing; as now the great fishes therein prey on the less, so the wealthy men would devour the poorer sort of people . . . and rich men, to make room for themselves, would jostle the poor people out of their commons."[13] Another result of the contradictory process whereby dispossessed commoners labored to dispossess others was the creation of the idyllic "English countryside," in which, again, the toil of those who made it possible was rendered invisible.[14]

The second labor of the hewer of wood and the drawer of water was building the ports for long-distance trade, a task that, like the clearing of the land for commercial agriculture, was essential to the new capitalist order. John Merrington has drawn attention to the first political economists, who emphasized the rigid division of land into town and countryside in the transition to capitalism.[15] Of special significance within this larger division was one particular kind of city and one particular kind of countryside: the port and the plantation. The early seventeenth century was the critical formative moment for each.

In 1611 John Speed published his atlas in four volumes, *The Theatre of the Empire of Great Britain*, in which he depicted the bridges, palisades, towers, bastions, gates, walls, and outworks of the harbors and ports of England, Ireland, the Mediterranean, West Africa, the West Indies, and North America. "The pestilent marsh is drained with great labour, and the sea is fenced off with mighty barriers," wrote Adam Ferguson in explaining the progress from rude nations to the establishment of property. "Harbours are opened, and crowded with shipping, where vessels of burden, if they are not constructed with a view to the situation, have not water to float. Elegant and magnificent edifices are raised on foundations of slime."[16] London and Bristol had long been port cities, but both expanded as the hewers and drawers laid the stone and built the wharves to accommodate their new bulk trades. Liverpool, incorporated in 1626, grew quickly after the midcentury. In Ireland, Belfast (1614) was built on reclaimed land, using the giant oaks felled by Carrickfergus hewers; Dublin became a "Bristol beyond the seas" as its workers exported grain and built ships; and Cork and Waterford grew behind their channels, islands, and winding rivers, while Wexford prospered with the fishing trade. Derry, both port and plantation, was rebuilt in the early seventeenth century, after British conquest, by the labors of the conquered natives. In Scotland, Glasgow's merchants were slowly making their first connections with the tobacco fields of Virginia. Mediterranean ports also played a role in commerce, from the shallow crescent bay within the walls of Tripoli to the port of Algiers and the Sallé in Morocco, all built in part by European slaves captured upon the high seas. In West Africa, Cape Coast Castle was erected in 1610 by the Portuguese, operated by the Dutch, and finally taken by the English in 1664; the Dutch were also busy off Dakar, establishing, with the labor power of African and European workers, the slave-trading port of Goree Island in 1617. The earliest European trading factory on the West African coast, Elmina, was rebuilt in 1621. West Indian ports—Bridgetown in Barbados and Port Royal and Kingston in Jamaica—were constructed to handle the tobacco and eventually the sugar produced on the plantations. On the North American mainland, Boston flourished behind its numerous harbor islands; New York and Philadelphia evolved from Dutch and Swedish origins to become major anglophone ports; and Charlestown, founded in Carolina in 1670, became the largest port in the South.

These nodes of the Atlantic nautical networks were built by workers who hauled the rubble to create a breakwater—a mole, or jetty, or pier—to protect the anchorage; hewed the stone, transported it, and arranged it on the seabed; and piled rocks to form retaining walls, or seawalls, with drainage and weepholes. They hewed the wood, carried it, and secured it upon the stone foundations in cribworks of timber. They dug and hauled the dirt for the aprons, quays, and basins. As John Ruskin observed in *The Stones of Venice,* "There is no saying how much wit, how much depth of thought, how much fancy, presence of mind, courage, and fixed resolution there may have gone to the placing of a single stone. . . . This is what we have to admire,—this grand power and heart of man in the thing; not his technical or empirical way of holding the trowel and laying mortar."

The "grand power" thus displayed was the power of cooperation among numerous carters and diggers, spalpeens and barrowers, who used rudimentary tools such as shovels, picks, axes, spades, pots, jugs, pails, and buckets to lay the foundations of the port cities.

The third labor of the hewer of wood and drawer of water was maintaining the life supports for communities on land and at sea, from chopping and gathering to pumping and toting. On ships as on plantations, in families as in entire cities, wood and water were the basis of life. Early Jamestown, Virginia, was known for its "fresh and plentie of water springs" and its "wood enough at hand." Dixcove, an English fort in Ghana, was called in 1692 "a good place for corn and at wooding and watering."[17] Fort slaves brought these life supports to ships, which were often "in distress for wood and water." A boat a day, for example, carried water to the Dutch slavers anchored at Shama, west of Elmina; indeed, even at Elmina rainwater cisterns were not built until 1695.[18]

If the hewers of wood were male, the drawers of water were almost inevitably female. Adam Clark's biblical commentary about drawers of water (1846) drove home the point: "The disgrace of this state lay not in the *labouriousness* of it, but in its being the common employment of the *females.*" In his novel *Barnaby Rudge,* Dickens in the 1840s looked back upon the Gordon Riots, with their insurrectionary and democratic danger, and introduced a servant woman with the pronouncement that "if she were in a more elevated station of society, she would be gouty. Being but a hewer of wood and drawer of water, she is rheumatic. My dear Haredale, there are natural class distinctions, depend upon it." John Taylor wrote as truthfully in 1639, "Women are nothing but your drudges and your slaves. . . . A woman's work is never at an end." Pepys collected testimony of revolt: "Other women's husbands can rise in the morning and make their wives a fire, fetch them in water, wash shitten clouts, sweep the house, scour the Andirons, make the Bed, scrape Trenchers, make clean chooves, rub Stockings, air Apparel, and empty the Pot."[19] Bridget Hill has emphasized the drawing of water as the foundation of housework.[20] A drudge or "slavey" fetched the water and carried out the slops in the Victorian household, while "endless trips by the mother and older children with jugs, basins or buckets" provided water for daily reproduction.[21]

The drawing of water was part of state-sponsored science in the seventeenth century, not least because agriculture and mining depended on hydraulics, whether to drain the fens or to pump water from flooded mines. The latter need stimulated Thomas Savery, John Calley, and Thomas Newcomen to develop the steam engine. An eighteenth-century theorist wrote:

> Men have already invented mills for grinding of corn, by the wind or water, the sawing of boards and the making of paper; the fire engine for the raising of water, the draining of mines, etc. and thus relieving mankind from drudgery: and many more engines, of this general kind, may doubtless be constructed, and should employ the thoughts of inventive and mechanical philosophers, in order still farther to ease mankind from too severe bodily labor, and the exertion of mere brutal strength: for even hewers of wood, and drawers of water, are men in a lower degree.[22]

In actuality, mechanization increased the number of hewers and drawers of water, as did technological changes in water-delivery systems. At the end of the fifteenth century, when water was drawn to London through wooden pipes from Islington or Tyburn, the Fellowship of the Brotherhood of Saint Christopher of the Waterbearers of London did most of the hauling from the conduits. Water was free. In 1581 this changed as the first privately owned, pumped water supply was constructed at the London Bridge. "We have water companies now instead of water carryers," wrote Jonson in 1598. Indeed, in 1600 "the whole company of the poor Water Tankard Bearers of the Cittie of London and the suburbs thereof, they and their families being 4000 in number," petitioned Parliament against the private quills, as water pipes were known. Privatization nonetheless continued with the New River Company, chartered in 1619, which brought water from Hertfordshire to Clerkenwell reservoirs, through wood pipes and then from lead pipes to private subscribers. By the 1660s the era of free water by right had ended—another commons expropriated. The poor were thrown back on the wells and gravity-fed conduits to obtain water for themselves.

In summary, the hewers of wood and the drawers of water built the infrastructure of merchant capitalism. They clear-cut the forests, drained the fens, and created the fields for capitalist agriculture. They built the ports for capitalist trade. They reproduced the households, families, and laborers for capitalist work. The labors of hewing and drawing were usually carried out by the weakest members of the demographic structure: the dispossessed, the strangers, the women, the children, the people in England, Ireland, West Africa, or North America mostly likely to be kidnapped, spirited, trepanned, or "barbadosed." Terror was inherent, for such work was a curse, a punishment. The formless, disorderly laboring class had been given a new form, and a productive one: whether waged or unwaged, the hewers of wood and the drawers of water were slaves, though the difference was not yet racialized.

TERROR

In England the expropriation of the peasantry was accompanied by systematic violence and terror, organized through the criminal sanction, public searches, the prisons, martial law, capital punishment, banishment, forced labor, and colonization. Magistrates used cruel and pitiless legislation to whip, dismember, brand, hang, and burn thousands; privy searches rounded up thousands more masterless men and women. The judicial decision known as *Gateward's Case* (1607) denied common rights to villagers and propertyless commoners.[23] Despite these cruel expropriations, a residue of paternalism remained: it was still expected that, to quote from Ben Jonson's play *Bartholomew Fair* (1614), Justice Overdo would "give puddings to the poor, . . . the bread to the hungry, and custards to his children."

The real-life equivalents of Justice Overdo routinely sent the poor, the hungry, and the young to prison, an institution that was central to the regime of terror in England. Thomas Dekker listed thirteen "strong houses of sorrow" in London alone. Bridewell became a prison in 1553 for orphans, vagrants, petty offenders, and disorderly women. Houses of correction were erected across England—in Essex, for example, in 1587, 1607, and 1609. The prisons and bridewells forced labor upon thousands of the men, women, and children who passed through them. The combination of pain and work entailed was described by one inmate in 1596: "Every dayes taske is to bunch five and twenty pounds of hempe or els to have no meat. And then I was chayned nyne weekes to a blocke and a month besides with it and five monthes without it in Little Ease and one of the turretts which is as bad, and fiyve weekes I went in the myll and ten dayes I stood with bothe my handes stretched above my heade against the wall in the standinge stocks." The prison thus joined punishment to production to create work-discipline.[24]

Capital punishment embodied the ultimate, spectacular power of the regime of terror, whether expressed by the provost martial who executed summary death upon the vagabond or by the slower-moving criminal justice system. Edmund Spenser remembered the execution of Murrogh O'Brien in Limerick: "I saw an old woman which was his foster mother took up his head whilst he was quartered and sucked up all the blood running there out, saying that the earth was not worthy to drink it, and therewith also steeped her face and breast, and tore her hair, crying and shrieking out most terribly." For Spenser, the woman's behavior, far from being justified, furnished proof of Irish barbarity.

London, whose suburbs housed the unprotected, rebellious workers of the putting-out system, was itself ringed by reminders of the death penalty. To the south, the heads of malefactors were stuck on pikes and lodged for display at the southern end of London Bridge. To the east, pirates were hanged at a gallows erected at Execution Stairs, or drowned in Wapping by the rising tides of the Thames. To the north, at Smithfield, the "fires" martyred many Protestants during Queen Mary's reign, though after 1638, when the market was established, it was principally cattle that were consigned to slaughter there. Finally, to the west, standing near what is now Speaker's Corner, was the Tyburn gallows, which remained active until 1783. To "go west" became proverbial for death.

Hangings were staged throughout the realm: seventy-four persons were hanged in Exeter and another seventy-four (coincidentally) in Devonshire in 1598. In all the forty English counties, some eight hundred went to the gallows in each year of the seventeenth century, according to James Fitzjames Stephen, the Victorian historian of criminal law. Of the 436 people hanged in Essex between 1620 and 1680, 166 were burglars, 38 were highway robbers, and 110 were thieves. In the 1630s thieves were hanged for stealing goods valued at as little as eighteen pence. Edward Coke concluded in the *Third Institute*, "What a lamentable case it is to see so many Christian men and women strangled on that cursed tree of the gallows, insomuch as if in a large field a man might see together all the Christians that, but in one year throughout England[,] come to that untimely and ignominious death, if there were any spark of grace or charity in him, it would make his heart to bleed for pity and compassion." If Coke felt pity, the "water poet" John Taylor believed in "the necessitie of hanging," and wrote more than a thousand lines of verse in praise of it:

> *Of Hangings there's diversity of fashions*
> *Almost as many as are sundry Nations:*
> *For in the world all things so hanged are*
> *Than any thing unhang'd is strange and rare.*

When Taylor visited Hamburg in 1616, he was fascinated by the execution of a poor carpenter who was smashed to pieces on the wheel by an executioner. Compared to "our Tyburn Tatterdemalion or our Wapping winde-pipe stretcher," the poet exclaimed, the Hamburg executioner seemed like one of the pillars of Hercules![25] Taylor made explicit the rela-

Many poor women imprisoned, and hanged for Witches. Ralph Gardiner,
England's Grievance Discovered *(1655). Rare Books Division,*
New York Public Library, Astor, Lenox, and Tilden Foundations.

tionship between hanging and capitalism when he compared the hanged
to "dead commodities."

Women were a specific target of terror, as four thousand witches were
burned and hundreds more hanged after 1604, when the punishment for
"bewitchment" was made more severe. The terror had three peaks, in
1590–97, 1640–44, and 1660–63. Between 1558 and 1680, 5 percent of all
English indictments, and fully 13 percent in the Home Circuit, contained charges of witchcraft. James I had himself interrogated women accused of witchcraft and had written a treatise of erudite misogyny, *Daemonologie,* to assert against skeptics the reality of witchcraft and the need
for capital punishment. Silvia Federici has shown that the European
witch-hunt reached its most intense ferocity between 1550 and 1650, "simultaneously with the Enclosures, the beginning of the slave trade and
the enactment of laws against the vagabonds, in countries where a reorganization of work along capitalist lines was under way." The ducking
stool, the cart's tail, branding, the pillory, the cage, the thew, and the
branks were all used for the torture of women.[26]

In all its forms, terror was designed to shatter the human spirit. Whether in London at the birth of capitalism or in Haiti today, terror infects the collective imagination, generating an assortment of demons and monsters. If Francis Bacon conceptualized the science of terror from above, Luke Hutton's *Black Dog of Newgate,* written in 1596, expressed the folklore of terror from below. Hutton had been indicted for theft in 1589 (specifically, for stealing surgical instruments) and served a short bid in Newgate; though he composed a great ballad of banditry and remorse ("Be warned, young wantons, hemp passeth green holly"), his life would end at the gallows in York in 1598. He dedicated *The Black Dog* to Chief Justice Popham, who had probably pardoned him for an earlier conviction and for whom the poem was an ambiguous kind of payback.[27] It tells the story of Hutton's arrest, detention, and first days in Newgate. In the poem the black dog is a diabolical fury that first appears as a broom man quietly cleaning the streets, reminding us that terror often masks itself as cleanliness: the Privy Council "swept" the street of vagabonds. The sweeper is then transmogrified into a beast, like Cerberus (Hydra's sibling), a dog whose ears are snakes, whose belly is a furnace, whose heart is steel, whose thighs are wheels, and who seizes Hutton and tosses him into Newgate. The burden of the poem is to name the dog, a burden that is never lifted; the inability to name the oppressor thus becomes a first disability of terror.

The myth of the black dog originated in the Middle Ages, at a time of famine. A scholar jailed in Newgate—for conjuring which "by charms and devilish witchcraft had done much hurt"—was deemed by the other prisoners to be "passing good meat." His fellow inmates watched in horror as the scholar turned into a dog, "ready with his ravening jaws to tear out their bowels"; driven to a fearful, insane frenzy, they then killed the prison-keeper and escaped, "but yet whithersoever they came or went they imagined the black dog to follow." Some said that the black dog was a standing stone in the part of the dungeon called Limbo, "the place where the condemned Prisoners be put after their Judgement, upon which they set a burning candle in the night, against which, I have heard that a desperate condemned Prisoner dashed out his braines."[28] In certain respects the black dog of Newgate parallels the voodoo *backa,* or dog of repression, who also feeds on human beings. The *backa* is a form taken by the living dead, or zombie: "It was a walking spirit in the likeness of a black dog gliding up and down the streets a little before the time of execution." In Ireland Edmund Spenser observed zombies among the defeated Irish, who "looked like anatomies of death; they spoke like ghosts crying out of their graves."[29]

Newgate's black dog led Hutton and many others to that acme of the regime of terror, the hanging:

> Yon men which thou beholds so pale and wan,
> Who whiles look up, and whiles look down again,
> Are all condemned, and they must die each man.
> Judgment is given that cord shall stop their breath
> For heinous facts—as murder, theft and treason.
> Unworthy life! To die law thought it reason.

> The sermon ended, the men condemned to die,
> Taking their leaves of their acquainted friends,
> With sorry looks, pacing their steps, they ply
> Down to a hall where for them there attends
> A man of office who, to daunt life's hopes,
> Doth cord their hands and scarf their necks with ropes.

> Thus roped and corded, they descend the stairs:
> Newgate's black dog bestirs to play his part,
> And does not cease for to augment their cares,
> Willing the carman to set near his cart.
> Which done, these men, with fear of death o'erhanging,
> Bound to the cart are carried to be hanged.

> This rueful sight, yet end to their doomed sorrows,
> Makes me aghast and forces me bethink.
> Woe unto woe! And so from woeful'st borrows
> A swame of grief. And then I sounding sink.
> But by Time's aid I did revive again.
> Might I have died it would be lesser pain!

Overwhelming horror thus conduced to a desire for death, a second disability of terror. The black dog did the work of reason and law, using

The Blacke Dogge of Newgate :
both pithie and profitable
for all Readers.

Vide, Lege, Caue.

Time shall trie the trueth.
by Luke Hutton

Imprinted at London by *G. Simson* and *W. White*.

The Black Dogge of Newgate. Luke Hutton, The Discovery of a
London Monster called, the black dog of Newgate *(1638).*

death to elaborate a culture of fear that was indispensable to the creation of labor-power as a commodity.[30]

If the prison, house of correction, and gallows expressed one aspect of capitalism in England, military adventure, colonization, and plantation expressed another around the Atlantic. When Sir Humphrey Gilbert established the first English colony in the New World, in Newfoundland in 1583, the chronicler of the settlement compared it to the military adventures of Joshua, who conquered "strange nations," took their lands and divided them among God's people, and kept the vanquished at hand "to hewe wood and to carie water." Gilbert's hewers and drawers included not only "savages" but his own countrymen—those men, women, and children who had "live[d] idly at home" and might now "be set on worke" in America, mining, manufacturing, farming, fishing, and especially "felling . . . trees, hewing and sawing . . . them, and such like worke, meete for those persons that are no men of Art or science." Both Gilbert and Richard Hakluyt, the main propagandists for English exploration and settlement, saw an advantage in England's late entry into the European scramble for New World colonies: the expropriations that coincided with colonization meant that England, unlike Portugal, Spain, the Netherlands, or France, had a huge and desperate population that could be redeployed overseas.[31]

Authorities emptied the jails for the Cadiz expedition of 1596 and again for Mansfield's army in 1624. According to the Beggar Act of 1598, the first-time offender for begging was to be stripped and whipped until his back was bloody; second-time offenders were banished from England, beginning the policy of transportation. Several thousand soldiers were recruited from London's Bridewell between 1597 and 1601, and in 1601 and 1602 four galleys were built and then manned by felons. After 1617 transportation was extended as a statutorily permitted punishment for felons; at each assize thereafter, half a dozen men were reprieved for galley service and ten conscripted for the army. Sir William Monson expressed the relationship among expropriation, theft, terror, and slavery when he wrote:

The terror of galleys will make men avoid sloth and pilfering and apply themselves to labour and pains; it will keep servants and apprentices in awe; . . . it will save much blood that is lamentably spilt by execution of thieves and offenders, and more of this kingdom than any other. . . . And that they may be known from others, they must be shaved both head and face, and marked in the cheek with a hot iron, for men to take notice of them to be the king's labourers, for so they should be termed and not slaves.[32]

Banishment legislation was aimed at the Irish, the Gypsies, and Africans after the 1590s. The English conquest of Ireland in 1596 laid the material foundation and established the model for all conquests to follow. Land confiscation, deforestation, legal fiat, cultural repression, and chronic crises of subsistence caused the Irish diaspora, sending men and women in waves to England and America. In 1594 all native Irish were commanded to leave England. Ulstermen found in Dublin were shipped to Virginia as slaves, as were Wexford rebels in 1620. The Gypsies, a nomadic people who had brought Morris dancing to England, offered an example of life lived without either landownership or master. By an Act of Mary, any Gypsy who remained in England longer than one month could be hanged; an Act of Elizabeth expanded the capital laws to include those who "in a certain counterfeit speech or behavior" disguised themselves as Gypsies. In 1628 eight men were hanged for transgressing these laws, and their female companions transported to Virginia. In 1636 another band of Gypsies was rounded up; the men were hanged and the women drowned at Haddington. Africans, too, commanded the attention of Queen Elizabeth I, who in 1596 sent an open letter to the lord mayor of London and to the mayors and sheriffs of other towns: "Her Majesty understanding that several blackamoors have lately been brought into this realm, of which kind of people there are already too many here . . . her Majesty's pleasure therefore is that those kind of people should be expelled from the land." In the same year, she engaged a German slave dealer to confiscate black people in England in return for English prisoners of war. In 1601 she proclaimed herself "highly discontented to understand the great numbers of negars and Blackamoores which . . . are crept into this realm."

Another part of the terror was forced labor overseas, a different kind of "going west." Through the transatlantic institution of indentured servitude, merchants and their "spirits" (i.e., abductors of children and adults) shipped some two hundred thousand workers (two thirds of all those who left England, Scotland, and Ireland) to American shores in the seventeenth century. Some had been convicted of crimes and sentenced to penal servitude, others were kidnapped or spirited, while yet others went by choice—often desperate choice—exchanging several years' labor for the prospect of land and independence afterward. During the first half of the seventeenth century, labor-market entrepreneurs plucked up the poor and dispossessed in the port cities (London and Bristol especially, and to a lesser extent Liverpool, Dublin, and Cork) and sent them initially to Virginia, where the practices and customs of indentured servitude originated. In order to entice settlers to and secure labor for the infant colony, the investors of the Virginia Company of London fashioned a covenant between the company and the workers. Imperial and local rulers of other colonies, most notably Barbados, adapted the new institution to their own labor needs. Indentured servitude, Eric Williams has remarked, was the "historic base" upon which American slavery was founded.[33]

Prisons of various kinds—including the ship's hold, the tender boat, the hulk, the crimp house, the pressroom, the "cook-house" (London), the barracoon, the storehouse, the factory (Gold Coast), the trunk (Whydah), the cage (Barbados), or the city jail (almost anywhere)— were, as Scott Christianson has shown, indispensable to the various Atlantic slave trades, whether the prisoners were sailors, children, or felons, whether they were from Africa or from Europe.[34] Many indentured servants, Thomas Verney explained in 1642, came from the "bridewells, and the prisons." Sir Josiah Child claimed that "the major part" of the women servants were "taken from Bridewell, Turnball Street, and such like places of Education." It was a time when "jayls [were] emptied, youth seduced, infamous women drilled in." According to a pamphlet of 1632, the plantations they were destined for "were no better than common 'sinkes,' where the commonwealth dumped her most lawless inhabitants." Virginia's servants were said to "have no habitations, & can bring neither certificate of their conformity nor ability and are better out than within the kingdom," while Maryland's were "for the most part the scum of the people taken up promiscuously as vagrant and runaways from their English masters, debauched, idle, lazy, squanderers, jailbirds, and the like." John Donne promised in a sermon of 1622 that the Virginia Company "shall sweep your streets, and wash your dores, from idle persons, and the children of idle persons, and imploy them: and truely, if the whole Countrey were such a Bridewell, to force idle persons to work, it had a good use." He wanted America to *function* as a prison, and for many it did.[35]

Among those many were thousands of children, for the hewers and drawers were young. The Virginia Company made arrangements with the city of London for the transportation of several hundred poor children between the ages of eight and sixteen from the city's Bridewell to Virginia. London's Common Council approved the request, authorized constables to round up the children, and shipped off the first young laborers in the early spring of 1619. When a second request was made, the council was again accommodating, but the children themselves had other ideas, organizing a revolt in Bridewell and declaring "their unwillingness to go to Virginia."[36] Their resistance apparently drew attention, and it was soon discovered that the city lacked the authority to transport the children against their will. The Privy Council, of which Francis Bacon was then a member, jumped into the fray, granting the proper authority and threatening to imprison any child who continued to resist. Of the several hundreds of children shipped to Virginia at this time, the names of 165 were recorded. By 1625 only twelve of those were still alive; the other 153, or 93 percent, had died. There is little reason to assume different outcomes for the fourteen to fifteen hundred children said to be on their way to Virginia in 1627, or for the four hundred Irish children stolen "out of theyre bedds" in 1653 and sent off to New England and Virginia.[37]

The experience of seventeenth-century servitude has survived in two firsthand accounts, written by James Revel and an anonymous woman who called herself a "Trapann'd Maiden." Convicted of theft and sentenced to hang, Revel entered the land of the living dead when his execution was transmuted to fourteen years' labor in Virginia. When he arrived there after midcentury, he was purchased by a planter, given a "hop-sack frock in which I was to slave," and set to work on a plantation alongside ten European and eighteen African slaves. Emphasizing the terror of his sentence, he said he "had much rather chuse to die than go" to America. For her part, the female servant was "cunningly trapann'd" by a spirit and likewise sent to Virginia, where she suffered years of "Sorrow, Grief, and Woe." She wore rags, slept on a bed of straw, drank only water, and ate poorly, being given no meat. She hewed wood ("The Axe and the Hoe/Have wrought my overthrow") and drew water ("The water from the spring/Upon my head I bring"), all the while withstanding the abuse of "my Dame." There was "No rest that I can have,/Whilst I am here a slave."[38]

In 1609 the author of *Nova Britannia*, who saw the project of colonization as "farre excelling" the heroic deeds of Hercules, explained the connections among the dispossessed, the new penal code, and the rise of a new mode of production: "Two things are especially required herein, people to make the plantation, and money. . . . For the first, wee need not doubt, our land abounding with swarmes of idle persons, which hauing no meanes of labour to relieue their misery, doe likewise swarme in lewd and naughtie practises, so that if we seeke not some waies for their forraine employment, we must prouide shortly more prisons and corrections for their bad conditions." By 1617 ruling-class policy was to ship the expropriated to far-flung labor markets, and various slave trades grew up to accommodate and extend the policy. Thus began what in a later day would be called the middle passage. Terror was instrumental; indeed, it was a mechanism of the labor market for the hewers and drawers. They had become deracinated. This was a third disability of terror.[39]

THE SPECTER OF HERCULES

If some used the biblical concept of "hewers of wood and drawers of water" to give form to the formless, others saw the amorphous class as a many-headed hydra and conjured Hercules to terrorize and destroy the beast, especially during the revolutionary circumstances of the 1640s, when the incipient class began to find new means of self-organization. Paradoxically, the worst sites of oppression and terror offered opportunity for collaboration. For example, the prison, like the shipwreck, was something of a leveller, where the radical protestant, the sturdy rogue, the redundant craftsman, the Catholic recusant, the wild Irishman, the commonist, and the cutpurse met on roughly equal terms. Lovelace in the Westminster Gatehouse in 1642 penned the lines, "Stone walls do not a prison make, nor iron bars a cage." E. D. Pendry, a historian of Elizabethan prisons, argues that the wave of prison riots that occurred during the second decade of the seventeenth century was due less to a deterioration of conditions than to the meeting of heretics and thieves, or political and common prisoners.[40] Martin Markall, the beadle of Bridewell, stressed the association of landed offenders, such as Irish rebels, Gypsies, and Roberdsmen, with those of the sea, such as mariners and pirates. English, Latin, and Dutch were the languages of communication in prison.[41] The prison, like the ship and the factory, organized large numbers of people for purposes of exploitation, but it simultaneously was unable to prevent prisoners from organizing against *it*. Hewers and drawers helped to inaugurate the English Revolution. If we return now to Bacon's theory of monstrosity, we can see that his "holy war" was really a campaign of extirpation and genocide. To understand his murderous prescriptions of 1622, we must hold the seven heads of his hydra up to the "Satanic light" of history-from-below. The "wise man" of the scientific revolution gave original voice to Conrad's cry in the Congo in 1897: "Exterminate all the brutes."

The first target of the holy war was Caliban. Bacon called him the West Indian, an appellation that would have applied to any Native American, whether in the Caribbean or in North, South, or Central America, and especially to any group that dared, like the Caribs, to resist European encroachment. The native peoples of the Americas stood outside the law of God and nature, according to Bacon, because of their nakedness, their illiteracy and ignorance of horse riding ("thinking that horses did eat their bits and letters speak"), and their "eating of men." Imperialists had long used charges of cannibalism to justify expropriation (though of course they themselves were the cannibals: many upper-class people took medicinal "mummy," concocted from human cadavers and believed to be particularly potent when made from the hanged or from Libyans).[42] Bacon explained that "wild and savage people are like beasts and birds, which are *feræ naturæ*, the property of which passeth with the possession, and goeth to the occupant." He wrote this just after the Powhatan attack on the Virginia colony in 1622, in which 347 European settlers (nearly one quarter of the population) had been killed. In *An Advertisement Touching an Holy War*, Bacon gave the Virginia Company and other colonizers something more lasting than revenge: a theory of genocide.

A second category of person who might be exterminated was the Canaanite, he or she who had lost land to the Israelites—in short, a dispossessed commoner. This would have included the many thousands of dispossessed in England, the wild Irish beyond the pale, and Africans. Bacon wanted workers for the colonies—"work-folks of all sorts [who] will be the more continuously on work without loss of time"—and expected them to be made available by enclosure, by the wars of attrition in Ireland (where the plan was "to burn all the corn and kill all the cattle, and to bring famine," as Spenser wanted), and by the slave trade.[43] Later William Petty would estimate that some 504,000 Irish perished between 1641 and 1652, "wasted by the sword, Plague, Famine, Hardship and Banishment." Thomas Morton saw a *New English Canaan, or New Canaan,* in Massachusetts, to quote the title of his 1637 book, but he advocated acquiring the land through cooperative trade with the Native Americans. He praised their midwives, medicine men, and uses of the land. His followers, servants and fugitives of several languages and colors, hoisted the maypole and joined the round dance, earning the wrath of the Puritans, whose attitude toward the sensuality of popular culture was similar to Bacon's. The architect of empire wanted Canaanites—borderless hewers and drawers—for the plantations; indeed, Africans were already at work in Virginia. But such people had no place in his ideal society, as he explained in *New Atlantis* (1627). Here Bacon imagined a future chaste nation, the "virgin of the world," and contrasted this patriarchal dream with the "Spirit of Fornication" represented by a "little foul ugly Æthiop."[44]

A third "multitude" or "swarm" of people deserving extinction was pirates, "the common enemy of human society." In selecting this enemy Bacon was acknowledging the corsairs of North Africa, who during the reign of James I and after attacked not only English shipping (taking almost five hundred ships between 1609 and 1616 alone) but the coasts of England and Ireland in slaving raids. The men they captured from ships, a figure put at twenty thousand during the 1620s, helped to quarry the rocks for the Barbary harbors. Some northern European seamen, English and Irish included, were not captured by but rather deserted to the Algerian pirates—or "turned Turk," as they called it—bringing skill, technology (the "round ship," for example), and experience to the polyglot community of Mediterranean pirates. These renegades included Henry Chandler (later Ramadan Raïs), a former Somerset farm laborer; Peter Easton, who commanded forty vessels in 1611; and John Ward, born "a poore fisher's brat" in Faversham, Kent, who led a mutiny in 1603, stole a ship, renamed it *Little John,* and commenced pirating. The pirate port of Sallé, wrote Father Dan, the first European historian of the corsairs, was thus "made . . . into a republic," a compound culture of heretics and religious radicals (Ranters and Sufis). Bacon wished to eradicate the "receptacle and mansion" of pirates in Algiers.[45]

The fourth class Bacon marked for destruction consisted of land rovers, from highway robbers to petty thieves, the same people Hercules had slain in delivering his own land from oppression. Their existence is recorded in the coney-catching pamphlets of Thomas Dekker and Robert Greene. Dekker warned, "The abram cove is a lusty strong rogue . . . a face staring like a Saracen. . . . These walking up and down the country, are more terrible to women and children, than the name of Raw-head and Bloody-bones, Robin Goodfellow, or any other hobgoblin." This is an early description of what has since been called the *lumpenproletariat,* lazzaroni, or underclass. In the glossaries of cant or thieves' talk we are given a veritable dramatis personae of the land rovers, all those who rejected wage labor: the Abraham-men, palliards, clapperdudgeons, whipjacks, dummerers, files, dunakers, cursitors, Roberds-men, swadlers, prigs, anglers, fraters, rufflers, bawdy-baskets, autem-morts, walking morts, doxies, and dells. At the head of them all was the uprightman, of whose kind Thomas Harman, the Kentish squire, wrote, "Of these ranging rabblement of rascals, some be serving-men, artificers, and labouring men traded up in husbandry. These, not minding to get their living with the sweat of their face, but casting off all pain, will wander, after their wicked manner, through most shires of this realm."[46]

The fifth group was assassins. Stuart kings lived in deathly fear of assassination. As attorney general, Francis Bacon interrogated Edmund Peacham, an old clergyman, because a sermon had been found in his house foretelling a rebellion by the people and the death of the king. No plot was discovered, though he was "examined before torture, in torture, between tortures, and after torture."[47] John Webster wrote a play about a Roman general who did not pay his troops, an obvious reference to the

King's favorite, Buckingham, who was killed by an angry, unpaid sailor in 1625.[48] One day the general, Appius, is held in awe by the people; the next he is in prison and fettered:

> *The world is chang'd now. All damnations*
> *Seize on the Hydra-headed multitude,*
> *That only gape for innovation!*
> *O who would trust a people?*

The tyrannicides of the early Stuarts (Buckingham in 1625 and Charles Stuart in 1649) point to the insurrectionary danger caused by courtiers' and republicans' contending for state power—a sordid situation that Bacon himself knew well.[49]

The sixth group suggested for extirpation was another collective enemy of Hercules, the Amazons, whose "whole government public and private, yea the militia itself, was in the hands of women." Armed women frequently led popular disturbances in Bacon's era. The Irish pirate queen Grace O'Malley, the "nurse to all rebellions for forty years," commanded heterogeneous followers of different clans and terrorized merchants far and wide until her death, in 1603. In 1607 "Captain Dorothy" led thirty-seven women wielding knives and throwing stones against the enclosures of Kirkby Malzeard in the North Riding of Yorkshire. Bacon knew of this struggle, for as Lord Chancellor ten years later he would observe that "Clubb Lawe" had prevailed. Armed women also spearheaded food riots, in 1595 seizeing food corn at Wye, in 1605 marching on the Medway ports to prevent the export of grain, and in 1608 going so far as to board grain ships in Southampton to keep their cargo from being shipped away. During the Western Rising (1629–31), women again led food riots, thus time in Berkshire and Essex. In 1626 the Star Chamber proceeded against women who had threatened to destroy Gillingham (Wiltshire) forest enclosures. "A certain number of ignorant women" pulled down enclosures in 1628. In Braydon Forest, meanwhile, "Lady Skimington" was the alias of male rioters who disguised themselves as women.[50]

The final and perhaps most dangerous group against which holy war might be waged was the Anabaptists, who in sixteenth-century Münster had held "all things to be lawful, not according to any certain laws or rules, but according to the secret and variable motions and instincts of the spirit; this is indeed no nation, no people, no signory, that God doth know."[51] Here was the specter of communism! And Bacon wanted to "cut them off from the face of the earth." As attorney general in 1615, Bacon had sentenced to death John Owen, whose writings he deemed Anabaptist, inclined to "the pulling down of magistrates" and the binding of "Kings in chains and their nobles in fetters of iron." One of Bacon's enemies was Robert Browne, the advocate of congregational churches governed from below, by mutual consent, rather than from above, by elder, king, or nation, and organized on principles of lawful debate, dispute, protest, and questioning. Browne had directly influenced Stephan Hopkins, who had led the resistance on Bermuda in 1609. Browne's theory of self-organization had revolutionary implications, calling as it did for democratic covenants. Earlier, Thomas Nashe had written of the repression of the Anabaptists in the German peasant revolt: "What is there more as touching this tragedie that you would be resolved of? say quickly. . . . How John Leyden dyed, is that it? He dyed like a dogge, he was hanged & the halter paid for. For his companions, doe they trouble you? They troubled some men before, for they were all kild, & none escapt, no not so much as one to tell the tale of the rainbow."[52] In his work as a torturer (in 1619 he stretched a schoolmaster, Samuel Peacock, on the rack until he fainted), Bacon perhaps indulged a similar vanity, believing that "the tale of the rainbow" itself could be extirpated. He thus used Hercules and the hydra to suggest an expansion and intensification of state terror.

Bacon's theory of monstrosity and terror was carried into the middle of the seventeenth century by Thomas Edwards, who studied the heresies of revolutionary England and published *Gangraena: Catalogue and Discovery of many of the Errours, Heresies, Blasphemies and pernicious Practices of the Sectaries of this time,* in three volumes in 1646. Edwards cataloged 176 different heresies in volume 1, twenty-three in volume 2, and fifty-three in volume 3, for a total of 252. In his dedication he described his combat against the "three bodied Monster *Geryon,* and the three headed *Cerberus,* " and "that *Hydra* also, ready to rise up in their place." At the beginning of volume 2 he noted that "whilest I was writing this Reply, had even finished it, striking off this three headed Cerberus, new heads of that monstrous Hydra of Sectarism sprung up." The heads of Bacon's hydra lunge out of Edwards's work, in the shape of religious radicals, indigenous Americans, Africans, commoners, sailors, and women.

The "Anabaptists" denounced by Bacon had multiplied during the subsequent generation, posing a revolutionary challenge during the 1640s and 1650s and setting men such as Edwards to work. Some of these heretics, Edwards explained, favored communism, claiming "that all men are Commoners by right" and that "all the earth is the Saints, and there ought to be a community of goods, and the Saints should share in the Lands and Estates of Gentlemen, and rich men." An associated belief was the millenarian notion that Christ would visibly reign for a thousand years, putting down all oppressors, while Christians lived in worldly delight (though no one seemed to know when to begin the calculation of the millennium!). Many of the Anabaptists were also antinomians, believing that the "moral law [was] of no use at all to believers," that the Old Testament was not binding on God's chosen, and that faith and conscience took priority over good works and lawfully constituted authority. Indeed, some held that it was "unlawful for a Christian to be a magistrate," while others felt that secular government itself was an oppression. Skepticism toward rules, ordinances, and rituals abounded, as did revelations and visions. Some religious radicals asserted that the "body of the common people is the Earthly Sovereign."

Like Bacon, Edwards adopted an international perspective on his subject, remarking that many of the heresies had been promoted by persons "cast out of other Countries." He condemned the numerous spiritual extremists of New England:

> How many cast out of *New England* for their Antinomianisme, Anabaptisme, &c. have come over, and here printed Books for their Errors, and preach up and down freely; so that poor *England* must lick up such persons, who like vomit have been cast out of the mouth of other Churches, and is become the common shore and sinke to receive in the filth of Heresies, and Errors from all places; what was said of *Hannibals* Army, it was *colluvies omnium gentium*, the same may be said of us for all kinde of sects and sectaries, *Anglia colluvies omnium errorum & sectarum.*

The core of Hannibal's army was African, and indeed the continent to which English slave traders were flocking in the 1640s was never far from

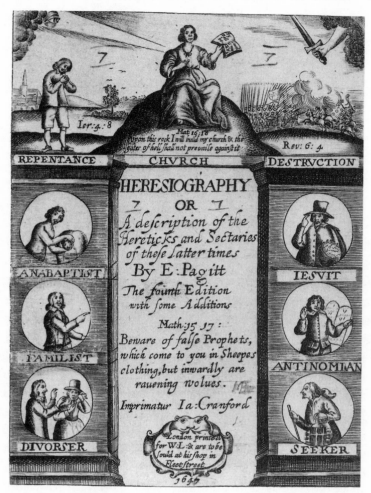

Title page of Heresiography, *by Ephraim Pagitt, 1654.*
By permission of the Houghton Library, Harvard University.

Edwards's mind. Many of the heresies of seventeenth-century England seemed to Edwards to be variations of the North African heresies of early Christianity, such as those of the Donatists.[53] He wrote, "Error, if way be given to it, knowes no bounds, it is bottomlesse, no man could say how farre *England* would goe, but like *Africa* it would be bringing forth Monsters every day."

When Edwards singled out for particular scorn those monsters he described as "hairy, rough, wilde red men," Caliban reappeared in revolutionary England, as did native America more generally. In much the same vein, the editor of an English newsbook reported in April 1649 the sayings of two "savage Indians" at the French court:

> [One Indian] observed two things which he stood amazed at. First, that so many gallant men which seemed to have stout and generous Spirits, should all stand bare, and be subject to the will and pleasure of a Child [Louis XIV]. Secondly, that some in the City were clad in very rich and costly Apparel, and others so extream poor, that they were ready to famish for hunger; that he conceived them to be all equaliz'd in the ballance of Nature, and not one to be exalted above another.

The editor denounced the natives as "two Heathen Levellers."[54] In the Americas, fear of Indian attacks and slave revolt went hand in hand with fear of "familisme [the doctrine of the sixteenth-century sect called the Family of Love], Anabaptisme, or Antinomianisme," and the many-headed hydra summarized the threat in a powerful rhetorical figure.[55] Edwards wrote that John Calvin, who attacked popish heresy as well as the heresies of libertines and Anabaptists, was a "Christian Hercules, overcoming so many monsters."

Bacon's Amazons were also animated in Edwards's account, in the heresy "that 'tis lawful for women to preach, and why should they not, having gifts as well as men?" Equally threatening were women who held it unlawful "to hear any man preach, either publickly or privately." Dispossessed commoners and land rovers were likely the ones expressing the "jubilee" heresy that Christ came into the world to preach deliverance to the captives (in prison), or the critique of capital punishment, "God doth not hang first, and judge after." Other heretics opposed Bacon's whole strategy of warfare, holy or unholy, insisting "that 'tis unlawful to give thanks for victories for one man's killing another"—that in short, " 'tis unlawful to take up arms, or to kill any man." More specifically, a "godly Citizen" had told Edwards of hearing a "great Sectary that belonged to the Army say, speaking of *Ireland,* he doubted, and so did many more in the Army, whether it were lawfull to go fight against the *Irish;* and that that Country was theirs, as well as *England* was ours."

Bacon, in sum, approached the hydra from above, identifying subjects to be acted upon: the swarms, shoals, and routs, as he called the multitude. A generation later, Edwards approached the monster from below, reactively, where it formed covenanted churches, politicized army regiments, rural communes, and urban mobs. The commoners, the vagabonds, the soldiers and sailors, the servants and the slaves, the masterless men and women, the hewers of wood and the drawers of water—all those many new slaves—came from far and wide and traveled further, preaching, interrupting, spouting, ranting, and organizing. As Edwards wondered, "How do persons cast out of other Countries for their Errours, not only live here, but gather Churches, preach publikely their Opinions! what swarms are there of all sorts of illiterate mechanick Preachers, yea of Women and Boy Preachers! What a number of meetings of Sectaries in this City, eleven at least in one Parish!" Across the ocean, on Bermuda, in 1640, an eight-year-old mulatto girl named Sarah Layfield was brought to court on charges of uttering "foolish and dangerous words touching the person of the King's majesty."[56]

During the December Days of 1641, the London crowd, or mob, assembled tumultuously at Whitehall and Westminster, lending support to the radicals in the House of Commons whose views of liberty and restrictions on kingly power were listed in the Grand Remonstrance, which was printed in the same month. The king denounced them as a "multitude of Brownists, Anabaptists and other sectaries." Two Common Councilmen for London were accused of contriving the tumult: they were said to have gone "from house to house and brought this Hydras Head to Westminster, and put in their mouths to cry out, 'No Bishops, No Popish Lords.'" The hydra, composed of sailors, mechanics, watermen, apprentices, the lowly and the base—or, put another way, the revolutionary urban proletariat—was now taking independent action.[57] Francis Bacon's sometime secretary Thomas Hobbes took notice of such new forms of organized power when, for example, mariners and 'prentices used the instruments of street warfare (a cudgel, a musket, an oar, a farmer's trine, a bill hook) to break open the prisons on Mayday 1640— and noted, as well, the king's inability to control them through the usual means, money. Hence Hobbes's interpretation of the hydra:

B. You have read, that when Hercules fighting with the Hydra, had cut off any one of his many heads, there still arose two other heads in its place; and yet at last he cut them off all.

The rising of Prentises and Sea-men, Mayday, 1640.
Thomason Tracts E116/49. By permission of the British Library.

A. The story is told false. For Hercules at first did not cut off those heads, but bought them off; and afterwards, when he saw it did him no good, then he cut them off, and got the victory.

The king would not in the end "get the victory" because, as some said, he did not deploy sufficient violence and terror against the hydra. Strafford advised hanging some aldermen who refused to loan Charles money; instead, two young rioters were hanged, one after being tortured on the rack, the last time the device was used in England.[58] After Charles I was beheaded at Whitehall on January 30, 1649, Anthony Ascham wrote *Of the Confusions and Revolutions in Government* (1649), reminding all of the need for a new Hercules "to tame Monsters." Thus was the role of Oliver Cromwell and the revolutionary bourgeoisie defined. Their task was to turn the many-headed hydra back into hewers of wood and drawers of water.

CHAPTER THREE

"A Blackymore Maide Named Francis"

Soon fugitives will come and tell you their news by word
of mouth. At once you will recover the power of speech
and speak with the fugitives; you will no longer be dumb.
—*Ezekiel 24:26–27*

I will pour out my spirit in those days even upon slaves and slave-girls.
—*Joel 2:29*

. . . If de fust woman God ever made was strong enough to
turn de world upside down all her one lone, all dese togeder
ought to be able to turn it back and git it right side up again.
—*Sojourner Truth (1851)*

THE ENGLISH REVOLUTION broke out in 1640. At first the conflict appeared to be among the kingdoms of Scotland, Ireland, and England, a contest for regional dominance and religious conformity. It was not long, however, before Parliament asserted its rights and powers against the personal and absolute rule of Charles I, introducing the slogan "No taxation without representation" and expanding the writ of habeas corpus as an instrument of individual freedom against arbitrary imprisonment. Civil war pitted king (Cavaliers) against Parliament (Roundheads). The creation of the New Model Army in 1645 resulted in a series of military victories for the parliamentary side. The increasingly successful revolutionaries did away with censorship of the press, abolished repressive courts such as the Star Chamber (where Bacon had once ruled), and executed King Charles I by decapitation in January 1649. They then dissolved the monarchy and the House of Lords and declared a republic.

Oliver Cromwell and the militant Puritans led the revolutionary forces. The Atlantic merchants, lesser gentry, and nascent industrialists who tended to back Cromwell all gained much from the economic changes encouraged by the state. The Navigation Acts protected British trade and shipping; agricultural enclosures privatized property; industrial legislation removed production from paternal restrictions on profiteering; and financial alterations in the stock market and funded debt promoted speculative capitalism. English merchants moved decisively toward the African slave trade as sugar plantations, imported from Brazil, expanded throughout the West Indies. In making their revolution, Cromwell and his propertied allies had to rely upon the radical voices of the many-headed hydra—the Levellers and the Diggers, the soldiers and sailors, the urban rioters and rural commoners—which proved to have an agenda of their own. Christopher Hill summarized the revolutionary era as a "great overturning, questioning, revaluing of everything in England"; H. N. Brailsford stated simply, "What was at stake was the ownership of England."[1] The ideas of the radicals were eventually suppressed by Cromwell and his ilk, but they were nonetheless formative, in their own day and later.[2]

Some of the more revolutionary notions of the day may be best illustrated by an extraordinary text about a woman named Francis, a "blackymore maide" who, as a member of a radical religious congregation in Bristol during the 1640s, provided leadership especially to the women of that congregation. The text was written by a church elder, Edward Terrill, which means that ours cannot be a simple story about Francis; it must also necessarily be a tale about the teller of it. She was black; he was white. She was a woman; he was a man. She was a sister in the congregation; he was an elder of the church. She was a servant; he was a master. Underlying these familiar oppositions was a basic antinomy: she lived and died during the revolution of the 1640s, while he came of age in the 1640s but thrived during the counterrevolution after the 1660s. The story of Francis and Terrill helps to illuminate the dynamics of race, class, and gender in the English Revolution and to show how the radical voices were ultimately silenced.[3] The outcome of the English Revolution might have been dramatically altered: the commons might have been preserved; values other than those of market society and commodity production might have triumphed; work might not have been seen as the condition of human salvation; patriarchy in the family might not have been saved, nor the labor of women devalued; torture and terror might not have survived in the law and its practice; popular assemblies might have proliferated and become open; mutual subsistence rather than individual accumulation might have become the basis of economic activity; and divisions between master and slave might have been abolished.

Edward Terrill was just a boy when the revolutionary wars erupted. Born in Almondsbury in 1634, he moved to Bristol in 1640 and was apprenticed to a scrivener in 1645. He was "convinced" by a religious experience in 1654 and baptized by immersion in 1658. In partnership with Thomas Ellis, a sugar trader who provided Broadmead Church with financial support, Terrill prospered, and he soon became an elder of the church. Meanwhile, the king, now Charles II, was restored to the throne in 1660, and a period of repression ensued. Terrill and the Broadmead Baptist Church (as it was called after the Restoration) suffered under the Corporation Act (1661), the Act of Uniformity (1662), and the Test Act (1673), which required all urban officials, all religious ministers, and all government officers to be communicants of the Church of England; they suffered further under the Conventicle Act (1664), prohibiting nonconformist worship even in private houses, and the Five Mile Act (1665), banning nonconformist ministers from living within five miles of a town.[4]

During this time of trial and persecution, Terrill wisely began to keep what came to be known as the "waste book," subsequently published as *The Records of a Church of Christ in Broadmead, Bristol, 1640–1687,* a collection compiled between 1672 and 1678.[5] The narrative is a composite document that includes oral history that Terrill recorded in conversation with Dorothy Hazzard, the founder of the congregation to which both Francis and Terrill belonged; selections from another manuscript notebook that is now lost to us; and finally, the author's own rewriting of history, prompted by Restoration repression.[6] Here is what Terrill had to say about Francis:

By the goodness of God they had one **Memmorable** member aded unto them namely a **Blackymore maide** named **Francis** (a servant to one that lived upon ye Back of Bristoll) which thing is somewhat rare in our dayes and Nation, to have an Ethyopian or Blackmore to be truly Convinced of Sin; and of their lost State without ye Redeemer and to be truly Converted to ye Lord Jesus Christ, as she was: which by her profession or declaration at ye time of her reception: together with her Sincere Conversation; she gave greate ground for Charity to believe she was truly brought over to Christ, for this poor **Æthiopian's** soule savoured much of God, and she walked very humble and blamelesse in her Conversation, to her end; and when she was upon her death bed: She sent a Remarkable Exhortation, unto ye whole Church with whom she walked, as her last request unto them: which argued her holy, childlike fear of ye Lord; and how precious the Lord was to her Soule; as was observed by the manner of her Expressing it. Which was this, one of the Sisters of ye Congregation coming to visit her, in her Sicknesse, She solemnly took her leave of her, as to this world: and pray'd ye Sister, to remember her to ye whole Congregation, and tell them, that she did Begg every soule, To take heed that they did lett **The glory of God to be dear unto them** a word meet for ye Church ever to remember; and for every particular member to observe, that they doe not loose ye glory of God in their families, neighbourhoods or places where God casts them: it being ye dyeing words of a Blackmoore, fit for a White heart to store. After which this Æthiopian yielded up ye Spirit to Jesus that redeemed her and was Honourably Interred being carryed by ye Elders, & ye chiefest of note of ye Brethren in ye Congregation (Devout men bearing her) to ye grave, where she must rest untill our Lord doth come who will bring his Saints with him. By this in our days, we may see, Experimentally, that Scripture made good, οὐχ ἔστ προσω πολήπτης ὁ Θεὸς. Ἀλλὰ ἐν παντὶ ἔθνει, that is God is no respecter of faces: But among all nations, &c. Acts 10: 34:35.

This is all Terrill wrote about Francis—a fragment, it might be thought. The absence of more information means that we cannot treat her in a conventionally biographical way. Alternately, we may consider her in the context of an ensemble of social relations, four of which stand out as formative. She was a "servant" at a time when that term suggested a hewer of wood and drawer of water, both in the specific tasks of her job

The Church being thus Settled as aforesaid by their Now-
Congregating, and leaving those that Sucked in Libertisme
Notions to forbear, in that manner those kept to the
Simplicity of y Gospell withdrew from them and kept
together, meeting as aforesaid Lords dayes and on y fifth day.
haueing now a Pastor, they chose mr Ingollo aforesaid (otherwise called Doctor Angell) to be their teacher and sate
under his Ministry about four or fiue years: They also
desired him to break bread unto them which accordingly he did
dureing y said time; and soe y Church walked together and
increased: And while they thus walked with Mr Ingollo
their teacher: By the Goodnesse of God they had one
Memorable member added unto them namely a
Blackymore maide named ffrancis (a servant to one
that liued upon y Back of Bristoll) which thing is somewhat rare in o dayes and Nation to haue an Ethiopian
or Blackmore to be truly convinced of Sin; and of their
lost State without y Redeemer and to be truly converted
to y Lord Jesus Christ, as she was: which by her profession
and declaration at y time of her reception: together with
her sincere Conversation; she gaue greate ground for charity
to beleiue she was truly brought over to christ; for this poore
Ethiopian's soule savoured much of God, and she walked
very humble and blamelesse in her Conversation, to her
end; and when she was upon her death bed; She sent a
Remarkable Exhortation, unto y whole Church with whom
she walked, as her last request unto them: which argued
her holy childlike feare of y Lord; and how precious the
Lord was to her Soule; as was observed by the manner
of her Expressing it: Which was thus, one of the Sisters
of y Congregation coming to visit her, in her Sicknesse; She
solemnly tooke her leaue of her, as to this world: and prayd
y Sister, to remember her to y whole Congregation, and tell
them, that she did Begg every Soule to ta,e heed that they
did set The glory of God to be dear unto them, and
most for y Church ever to remember; and for every particular
member to observe, that they doe not loose y glory of God in their
families, neighbourhoods or places where God casts them: it being y

Francis
a blacke
Woman

Edward Terrill's account of "a Blackymore maide named Francis."
"The Records of a Church of Christ in Broadmead, Bristol, 1640–1687."
Broadmead Church, Bristol.

description and in the lowly, defenseless status accorded her. She was a "blackymore" with that word's social and religious connotations of colonialism. She was a sister in a gathered congregation recently organized by and for women. She was a Baptist given to liberty and like notions at a moment in history preceding the formation of discrete denominations.

SERVANT, BLACKYMORE, SISTER, AND BAPTIST

As a servant, Francis was part of what was probably the biggest occupational category of her era. Agricultural workers were servants, as were domestic producers in the manifold handicrafts and plantation workers in the colonies. Francis, however, was a particular type of servant: a maid. The labors of a maid might include cooking, washing, doing laundry, gathering fuel, bearing water, nursing the sick, or comforting the afflicted, depending on whether she was a chambermaid, kitchen maid, housemaid, maid-of-all-work, or scullery maid.[7] The patriarchal family, itself the model of guild and kingly power, depended on such labors. Yet in the seventeenth century the occupation underwent changes with the rise of capitalism. Servants were deliberately excluded from some of the proposals for the democratic franchise, and in the cities their status declined as service became increasingly polarized and feminized.[8] "Service is a state of subjection, grounded partly in the curse of God for sin; partly in Civill constitution; it is a miserable condition," wrote a Cambridge scholar named Paul Bayne in 1643, in a thousand-page treatise on the religious justification for such service. Its basis was obedience: "I say to one, goe, he goeth, come, and he cometh, doe this, hee doth it."[9] The scholar noted that perpetual obedience could not be expected, for once unemployed, servants would try to beard their masters and would cut their throats, too, if they could. We might say Francis was a proletarian: she did not possess any means of production, and the payment for her labor was ambiguous. She was paid by the year and otherwise lived on tips and vails, or customary rights to household items, a practice Bayne denounced as "rolling another mans pigeons to their owne lockers." Against the ruling-class view of the lowliness of service, a buoyant spiritual tradition arose among servants—a glint of light captured by Professor Nell Painter in her description of the "unseen holy women . . . who performed household labor."[10]

Francis, like other servants, was thus poor, and the Bristol congregation understood that. Indeed, Terrill's text indirectly reflects discussions within the congregation about her poverty. The economic insecurity of the 1640s made the promise of material aid from the independent churches attractive to the poor, but the suppression of conventicles (on the grounds that Protestant gatherings were heretical and illegal) during the Restoration, when Terrill was writing, rendered such obligations difficult to meet. This would explain Terrill's emphasis on the religious sincerity or authenticity of Francis, his insistence that she had truly been brought over to Christ and was truly convinced of sin.

Terrill tells us that Francis was servant to one who lived upon the Back of Bristol. The Back was a specific location next to the river Avon, along the largest apron space by the wharves where the deep-water vessels— slave ships included—moored. A comparison of maps of the town between 1568 and 1673 shows intensive development. The Back of Bristol put Francis at the interface of the triangular trade and amid the human news of the continents. Exchanges of the North Atlantic—Gaelic, African, American, West Indian, and Dutch voices—would have been in her ear. Her eye would have spied the labor markets of men, women, and children; her soul, their spirits. Bristol was then England's third-largest town (with twelve thousand residents) and second-largest port. There was a wealthy mercantile elite at the top and a class of former foresters and downsized weavers living in extreme poverty at the bottom. In 1640 the established traders of the Society of Merchant Adventurers were challenged by a group of younger, aggressive dealers who were deeply involved in free trade across the Atlantic. Labor-market entrepreneurs had transformed the man-trade into a highly profitable business, since 1623 using the Bristol bridewell as a transshipment center of forced labor to the Caribbean. Peter Fryer writes that the "small speculators had their snouts in the trough alongside the big merchants." Having established a trade in labor as a transatlantic commodity, merchants now began to move into the African slave trade. This would prove to be the city's greatest source of wealth by the end of the seventeenth century, but that was by no means clear in the 1640s. Although the Dutch governor at Fort Elmina reported nineteen English ships hovering off the slave coast between 1645 and 1647, English dominance was not yet certain.

The immediate problem of Terrill's passage about Francis is that while he calls her a memorable member of the congregation, he gives us little to remember her by. He buries her voice in the middle of the paragraph, quoting directly fewer than ten words. As a scrivener, Terrill was a master of the pen, his means of expression; he knew when to use capital letters, how to spell, when to increase the size of letters for emphasis. In general such skills could lead to the profession of chronicler, or to banking, and something of those professions may be found in Terrill. Penmanship led to chronicling the church as well as to profiting from West Indian trade. In this text we note how Terrill emphasizes the ethnicity of Francis, mentioning it explicitly six times and implicitly twice more. He labels the paragraph, in the margin, "Francis, a Black Woman." He spells *blackamoor* and *Ethiopian* inconsistently, suggesting to us that something about the subject made the master scrivener nervous. The passage thus contains a mystery: why the anxiety?

Other black people had lived in Bristol before Francis. The first recorded was Cattelena, who died in 1625. But the city's numbers were growing as Bristol's slave traders carried ever larger number of Africans to Barbados, and some back to their own home port. "Blackness" in Francis's day had contradictory associations. The Geneva Bible (1560) asked, "Can the blacke More change his skin?" (Jeremiah 13:23) and commented that the cloak of hypocrisy should be pulled off, thereby associating blackness with divine truthfulness. The Leveller Sexby, who had the *Agreement of the People* translated into French, argued at the Putney Debates (where as we will see in the next chapter the common soldiers in 1647 debated the future of England), "We have gone about to wash a blackmoor, to wash him white, which he will not. . . . I think we are going about to set up the power of kings, some part of it, which God will destroy."[11] He thus associated blackness with republicanism. Differences in skin color signified something other than either sincerity or republicanism by the time Terrill wrote, but if we are to understand why the subject provoked anxiety at that later time, there is much else we need to know.

Francis was a sister and an "Anabaptist" in a group that took shape in the 1630s around Dorothy Hazzard, a seamstress, who gathered a writing-school master, a glover, a house carpenter, a countryman, a butcher, a farrier, and a young minister to worship together.[12] They assembled to "cry day and night to the Lord to pluck down the lordly prelates of the time, and the superstitions thereof." They did not permit bowing at the name of Jesus; they refused to kneel at the Sacrament; and they opposed idolatrous pictures and images.[13] Nor did they observe feast days: Hazzard kept her shop open on Christmas Day and sat there sewing in the broad daylight.[14] Terrill compared Hazzard to biblical figures such as Priscilla (a Roman who risked her neck for Saint Paul), Ruth (a gleaner who, in return for her loyalty, asked, "May I ask you as a favour not to treat me only as one of your slave-girls?"), and Deborah (who authorized resistance among the drawers of water: "Hark, the sound of the players striking up in the places where the women draw water!" [Judges 5:11]). Hazzard gathered around her pregnant women in need of assistance, traders, and workers, some on their way to New England in search of the simplicity and equality of the primitive first Christians. They formed a new covenant in 1640, "that they would, in ye Strength and assistance of ye Lord, come forth of ye world, and worship ye Lord more purely." In calling Dorothy Hazzard "a he-goat before the flock" (Jeremiah 50:8), Terrill acknowledged female leadership.[15]

When war broke out, Dorothy Hazzard was prominent among the two hundred women and girls who defended Bristol's Frome Gate against the assault of the king's nephew Prince Rupert, who nonetheless eventually captured the strategic port town and its heavily fortified royal arsenal. Hazzard and her fellow spiritual travelers then took to the roads. At first they sought succor from a Welsh church led by Walter Craddock; then they walked to London, "into a wildernesse state, passing through a Red Sea of Blood by ye wars." The assembly (as they called themselves) was separate, it was gathered, it was pure, it was militant, but it was not (yet) Baptist. This was the assembly, or gathering, that Francis joined.

The times were incendiary. Craddock exclaimed, "The Gospel is run over the Mountains between Brecknockshire and Monmouthshire, as the fire in the thatch."[16] In 1644 John Milton wrote in *Areopagitica*,

Behold now this vast city, a city of refuge, the mansion house of liberty, encompassed and surrounded with his protection. The shop of war hath not there more anvils and hammers waking, to fashion out the plates and instruments of armed justice in defense of beleaguered Truth, than there be pens and heads there, sitting by their studious lamps, musing, searching, revolving new notions and ideas wherewith to present, as with their homage and their fealty, the approaching reformation; others as fast reading, trying all things, assenting to the force of reason and convincement.

The words expressed the revolutionary hopes, the eager spirit of inquiry, and the militant search for truth that awaited Francis and her fellowship.

Meanwhile, combat continued in Bristol. Parliamentary forces, fresh from victory at Naseby and commanded by Colonel Thomas Rainborough, launched a counterattack against Prince Rupert's army in 1645, with soldiers' scaling the walls of Prior's Hill Fort amid a rain of round and case shot. When the scaling ladders proved too short, the infantry crept in at the portholes, prevailing in a two-hour battle against the push of pike. Colonel Rainborough's victory helped to preserve the city as a stronghold of religious radicals who usurped the pulpits, preached in the streets, and engaged in ruthless iconoclastic behavior, producing a revolutionary energy in militant Calvinism or libertarian antinomianism.[17] The former was the doctrine of puritanical work-discipline; the latter offered a gracious view of freedom.

Between 1644 and 1649, the peak of antinomianism, those who would later become Baptists "proved the most successful disseminators of radical religious ideas until the rise of the Quakers in the 1650s."[18] They were directly associated with the revolutionary victories of the New Model Army and with the organization and birth of the Levellers. During its sojourn to London, the small Bristol band led by Hazzard was inflamed by the reason and truth of the "approaching reformation." Once back in Bristol, Terrill reported, "the heads and minds of many of the members were filled with controversies, insomuch that every meeting almost was filled with disputes and debates: [so] that they were in great confusion, and but little order. Some of them [were] against ordinances, as having got above them, or pleading that while the church of Christ was in her wilderness state they should not use them, and so took liberty to forbear them." They formed another covenant, "leaveing those that sucked in Libertisme Notions to forbear."[19]

At their meetings, "there was liberty for any brother, and for any sister by a brother, to propose his doubt of, or their desire of understanding, any portion of scripture." The rest of the congregation would speak "one by one and then be silent, and another speak, and so a third." It was a creative moment in world history, when democracy was practiced directly; these were some of its first rules. Laurence Clarkson wrote at about this time, 1647, "Who are the oppressors but the Nobility and Gentry; and who are oppressed, if not the Yeoman, the Farmer, the Tradesman and the Labourer? then consider, have you not chosen oppressors to redeeme you from oppression? . . . your slavery is their liberty, your poverty is their prosperity; yea, in brief, your honoring of them, dishonoreth the communality. . . . Unlord those that are lorded by you."[20] The Broadmead assembly hired Nathaniel Angello to minister to its members but soon removed him for his too-great fondness for music and clothes. Walter Craddock, the itinerant antinomian, came next: he preached upon the text "All things are lawful for me" (1 Corinthians 10:23), asserting that "now the day was breaking out after a long night, and light was coming every day more than other; and there were many Gospel priviledges, and of the new Jerusalem that we should then enjoy." Craddock welcomed drunkards and adulterers into his gatherings; he encouraged preaching by "fishermen, poor men, and women sometimes."[21] In 1648, preaching on "Go ye into all the world, and preach the gospel to every creature" (Mark 16:15), he said, "We are not sent to get Galley-slaves to the Oares." He believed that the simplest people commonly understood the Gospel the best. He wrote:

> I have seen poore women in the mountaines of Wales . . . they have been so poor that when they have come to a house to beg a little whey or butter-milke, they have been faine to beg the loane of a pot, or a dish to put it in. So . . . we cannot carry one graine of grace home, unlesse God give us spirituall buckets. As that woman said, John 4, Here is water, but where is the bucket to draw? So God may say, thou wantest grace, but where is thy bucket? saith the humble soul, Lord I have none, thou must both give the water and lend the bucket to carry it home.[22]

This is the exegesis of the poor by the poor for the poor. In 1648, some eight hundred itinerant Welsh ministers were preaching; the Vagrancy Act was passed specifically against them.[23]

In Terrill's account, Francis comprehends the powerlessness that might allow the spirited, kidnapped souls of Bristol to be cast nearly anywhere. She asks a sister in the congregation to carry her message to the whole assembly, not to "loose yᵉ glory of God in their families, neighbourhoods or places where God casts them." She recognizes that a neighborhood may be international, a notion of shipmates, a family of oceanic passages. Francis understands community without propinquity. For her, neighborhood is the congregation whose existence she has nurtured in deep and unforgettable ways. She would have known about slavery and the struggle against slavery. On May Day 1638, for instance, the first African slave rebellion in English history took place on Providence Island. From the wharves, Francis would have brought Atlantic news to her congregation, recounting stories of the terrors: the man-trade at Elmina Castle, the servants' revolt in Barbados, the grinding sugar mills of Suriname, or the repression of the Boston antinomians. We do not know where Francis lived before Bristol. Was she, like Tituba of Salem in the 1690s, from Barbados? Was she from Suriname, where Aphra Behn, the novelist and playwright, passed her childhood at this time? Had she been in Boston at the time of the first legal challenge to the African slave trade? The glory of God was merely the last of her exhortations; it would be interesting to know the others.[24]

GLORY AND NO RESPECTER OF PERSONS

Terrill's paragraph concludes with a quotation in Greek. The title page of the *Records* is likewise in Greek, while the page headers alternate between Greek and Hebrew. Terrill's use of Greek calls attention to an important debate. Philology of this kind was characteristic of Protestantism. Does the quoting of Greek mask a murky purpose? Francis, Terrill asserts, is an example (he calls her an experiment) who proves Scripture, rather than the opposite, a recipient of the Bible's spiritual aid. If she emphasizes the Spirit, he emphasizes the Letter. Terrill thus subverts, or even contradicts, Francis's message. What is that message? and why does Terrill subvert it? Francis is associated in the text with two biblical ideas, one her own ("the glory of God") and the other, apparently, Terrill's ("God is no respecter of faces"). What did these signify in the midst of revolutionary civil war in England? Why should they be remembered?

Three primary meanings of *glory* may be distinguished in the Scriptures. First, found in Ezekiel and Isaiah, is an external meaning, an atmospheric sense, with secondary figures such as seraphim and cherubim surrounding the numinous Jahweh. We detect this meaning in the architecture and music of the mercantilist or Baroque state, from the Palladian Whitehall to Wren's "glorious" Saint Paul's—resplendence, beauty, and majesty expressed in Portland stone. This was the glory of Archbishop Laud, a looking-up, glory from the top down. It was not for Francis, but two other meanings of glory were. One of these emerged in three key episodes in the Gospels describing the life of Jesus, in which glory descended to Earth: when the shepherds kept watch at the birth of Jesus; at the Transfiguration (the "Son of man shall come in glory of his Father with his angels; and then he shall reward every man according to his works" [Matthew 16:27]); and during the last days in Jerusalem, when Jesus describes the end of the world. Glory was part of eschatology, the last things; it was also a time of justice. Another meaning of *glory* originated in the book of John and was developed in Paul's letters. Here glory and glorification were related to the promise of an end to bondage (Romans 8:15–17) and to an interior glory that came down to Earth and entered the spirit of the children of God. It was within: "For God, who commanded the light to shine out of darkness, hath shined in our hearts to give the light of the knowledge of the glory of God" (2 Corinthians 4:6). Glory was democratized; it became available to all.

Francis would have agreed with the Digger Gerrard Winstanley when he wrote, "The glory of Israel's Commonwealth is this, They had no Beggar among them." He explained: "What glory soever you shall be capable of to see with your own eyes or hear with your ears, it is but the breakings forth of that glorious power that is seated within for the glory of the Father is not without him."[25] Lodovick Muggleton urged in 1658, "You must not imagine the kingdom of glory to be in a global condition, as this world is. . . . The world to come is a boundless kingdom, that lieth all open."[26] In the 1640s glory was associated with the destruction of Babylon and the building of Zion, or the New Jerusalem. The historical actors, the destroyers and the builders, were often considered to be "the poorest and the meanest," the hewers of wood and the drawers of water. Glory signified the transcendental present—not a passive waiting for a future in Heaven but actions, to be taken by the dispossessed, to create

Heaven here on Earth. Glory appeared through devout expression that mediated between holy text and subjective experience. It might sound like groaning, howling, screeching, or screams of pain, but it had the power to transform persons.[27] Hence it was alarming to authority, as explained by Thomas Hobbes: "Glory, or internal gloriation or triumph of the mind, is the passion which proceedeth from the imagination or conception of our own power above the power of him that contendeth with us." Ostentation in words and insolence in action were its signs. The discourse of glory among the humble assemblies of the 1640s was synonymous with audacity and originality.[28] Glorying symbolized historical agency.

These ideas appeared in an important sermon delivered and published by Hanserd Knollys, "A Glimpse of Sion's Glory" (1641), on the Revelation text "And I heard as it were the voice of a great multitude, and as the voice of many waters, and as the voice of mighty thunderings, saying: Hallelujah, for the Lord God Omnipotent reigneth." Babylon falls and glory rises. There "shall be abundance of glorious prophecies fulfilled, and glorious promises accomplished." The "poorest and meanest of all" were called to glorious revolutionary action: "Blessed is he that dasheth the brats of Babylon against the stones." Similar ideas were expressed after the battles of Marston Moor and Naseby, which ended the first civil war, giving victory to the New Model Army of the Puritans and Parliament. Thomas Collier, a Baptist, preached a sermon at army headquarters at Putney, on September 29, 1647, on Isaiah's text "Behold I create new heavens, and a new earth." God's glory, explained Collier, appeared on Earth as the saints built a New Jerusalem, where the lion and the lamb would lie down together. "The glory of this new creation . . . consists in the execution of righteousness, justice and mercy, without respect of persons. It is to undo every yoke."[29] Glory lay, he preached, in the struggle against slavery.

Collier was not alone in connecting glory with the second idea associated with Francis, that God is no respecter of persons, or, in Terrill's translation, "no respecter of faces." The phrase was an old one (Nashe had used it in 1594 in noting that the rebels of the German peasant revolt were as poor and base in trades as the twelve apostles), but it did not become part of the English Bible until it was incorporated in the authorized version of 1611. How, we must ask, may persons be respected? By ethnicity, by nation, by race, by gender, and by class. Charles I avowed, "For the hazards of war are equal, nor doth the cannon know any respect for persons."[30] In the Americas, Captain Underhill justified the slaughter of six to seven hundred Pequot men, women, and children at Fort Mystic, Connecticut, in 1637 by invoking his God: "He hath no respect of persons."[31] The phrase thus had martial as well as egalitarian connotations, which lent it to wide use in the revolution. It is a phrase of levelling. In the quotes above, the levelling is of the dead; in contrast, it is its association with economic and social justice, or the levelling of the living, that is significant for us.

The Diggers and the Ranters associated glory with the levelling of the living. To quote from the Digger manifesto, *The True Leveller's Standard Advanced* (1649), the desired end was

that we may work in righteousness, and lay the foundation of making the earth a common treasure for all, both rich and poor. That every one that is born in the land may be fed by the earth, his mother that brought him forth, according to the reason that rules in the creation, not enclosing any part into any particular land, but all as one man working together, and feeding together as sons of one father, members of one family; not one lording over another, but all looking upon each other as equals in creation. So that our Maker may be *glorified* in the work of his own hands, and that every one may see he is *no respecter of persons,* but equally loves his whole creation, and hates nothing but the serpent. Which is covetousness. [emphasis added]

It was a fundamental concept for Winstanley; indeed, it was the "spirit of the whole creation."[32] The Ranters, for their part, published a pamphlet entitled *A Justification of the Mad Crew* (1650), "a true Testimony of that sweet and unspeakable Joy and everlasting glory that dwels in and breaks out." He who would know God must let his own glory break out, the pamphlet held. Glory kept low company, "among the rogues, theeves, whoremasters, and base persons of the world." As no respecter of persons, God "pulleth down the mighty from their Throne, and sets up men of low degree." God's refusal to respect persons thus constituted a kind of internationale of glory: "He is in England, France, and Turkey," and therefore "the people in England, France, and Turkey [must become] one people and one body, for where the one lives there liveth the other also." In the geographic terminology of the seventeenth century, "Turkey" signified both the religion Islam and the continent Africa. A person such as Francis was specifically included. "Here glory lyeth, and is concealed to the most of men, it is coming forth to some, peeping through the lattis, and looking behind the wall; it is above board to others, well, what is it?" It was no respecter of persons; rather,

> he beholds all things and persons, with the same and in the same purity, with and in the same glory, all perfect in him, compleat in him, righteous in him, children of pleasure in him: He sees dancing, lying with one another, kissing pure and perfect in him; He loves all with an everlasting love, the thief that goes to the Gallows as well as the Judge that condemns him, and the Judge with a love of and from eternity as well as the thief.

It is significant that Terrill forsook the familiar egalitarianism of the authorized version of the Bible by altering "persons" to "faces." His translation distances him and his church from some revolutionary meanings of the phrase. "Face," in this context, suggests something superficial, a mask; and in this case, the mask is that of a "blackamore." The translation calls attention to skin color. These "dyeing words of a Blackmoore" were "fit for a White heart to store," sighed Terrill, and he quotes the Greek words of Acts 10:34. His readers would have known the biblical context. The story was important to the growth of Christianity since it told of the first baptism of a non-Jew. Cornelius, a God-fearing man but a Roman or Gentile, was sent in a vision to visit Peter, before whom he prostrated himself. Peter welcomed him, saying, "Of a truth I perceive that God is no respecter of persons." Francis thus stood for Cornelius, and Terrill for Peter. The analogy points to the universalism of early Christianity and the English Revolution and to their contribution to the doctrine of human solidarity. James Nayler asked of this decisive biblical incident: "Had Cornelius sufficient light within him before Peter preached unto him? Answer: Jesus came to open blind eyes, not to give them eyes." Terrill's choice of words attenuates this meaning; in a moment we shall see why.[33]

The last part of Terrill's passage concerning Francis consists not so much of her own testimony as of the evidence of others, and in this case that evidence is the prominence and the devotion of the elder brethren of the church who carried her to the grave. The revolutionary implications of the idea associated with Francis help us to understand why Terrill felt the need to sandwich her words between the repetitive bona fides of her sincerity on one side of her prophetic exhortation and the elders, the brethren, the devout, as her pallbearers on the other. He precedes his discussion of Francis with a digression of seven or eight pages on John Canne, which is an astonishing interpolation because the latter came to Bristol in 1648, not in 1640–41, as Terrill implies. Why did Terrill make this interpolation? Canne was the scion of the ruling Bristol oligarchy, who had great influence within the Puritan movement (a relative held the contract for the transportation of Scottish and Irish prisoners to slavery in the plantations).[34] He had been the leader of an independent church in Amsterdam from 1630 to 1647, he was a major publisher of English puritanism (his fully cross-referenced Bible of 1647 was authoritative), and after his return to England in 1649 he attacked the Levellers and wielded influence with the Council of State. Terrill could not have chosen a more learned, more respected Puritan to indicate the respectability of Baptist separation. Terrill presents Canne as a confident teacher whose Twelve Steps enabled the congregation to separate under an iron rod of rule. Terrill himself preached a deep baptism by immersion, not dipping or sprinkling; the trick, however, was to avoid any suspicion of the anabaptism of a century earlier, during the German peasant revolt, when both private property and the patriarchal family had been overthrown. Not only could Canne show how the German Anabaptists had taken "some very irregular actions," he was an opponent of the Levellers. Thus, when Terrill misdates the leadership of Canne, so that Broadmead will appear to have been a Particular Baptist congregation from the beginning, the purpose of the misdating is not merely to antedate the denominational origin but also to conceal the antinomianism, or "libertism," of the period 1641–49. The interpolation seems to prove the disciplined respectability of Baptist separation, thus protecting the church in the 1670s and 1680s. It is part of the revision of history that mutes Francis.

FROM PROPHETESSES TO PROLETARIANS

By telling the story of Francis, and by telling it in the way he does, Terrill at first notes and then undermines the role of women's spirituality within the community, within the governance of the church, and within its emerging doctrines. The women of the gathered congregations were notoriously outspoken in the 1640s, and Francis, "one of the Sisters of yᵉ Congregation," was among them. Terrill responds with an assertion of male authority, male governance, and doctrine as enunciated by male ministers, stressing that upon her death Francis "was Honourably Interred being carryed by yᵉ *Elders*, & yᵉ chiefest of note of yᵉ *Brethren* in yᵉ Congregation (Devout *men* bearing her) to yᵉ grave" (emphasis added). Why was this necessary?

The millenarian Fifth Monarchist Mary Cary wrote in 1651, "The time is coming when not only men but women shall prophesy; not only aged men but young men, not only superiors but inferiors; not only those who have university learning but those who have it not, even servants and handmaids." Every saint, declared Cary, "may be said to be a prophet . . . for when the Lord hath revealed himself unto the soul and discovered his secrets to it . . . the soul cannot choose but declare them to others." Phyllis Mack writes that even more than the male "mechanick preacher," the female prophet "represented a kind of authority that was inappropriate, even monstrous, by conventional standards, but conforming to a more radical vision of human equality, on earth and in heaven."[35] Women who prophesied before Francis included the "Woman of Ely," an itinerant minister often denounced by heresy-hunters of the 1640s, and the poor woman whose prophecy converted the reprobate young soldier John Bunyan. Three others merit further discussion here: Sarah Wight, Dinah (a maid and "a Moor not born in England"), and the antinomian controversialist of Massachusetts, Anne Hutchinson. The meeting of Sarah and Dinah indicated the association between the end of slavery and the "new covenant," while the case of Anne Hutchinson shows how female prophets of this era might be branded as heretics, witches, or monsters.

When Dinah ("the Moor," as she was later described) came to visit Sarah Wight in London at the end of May 1647, "in affliction both in soul and body," Henry Jessey, a Baptist leader of a separatist congregation in Southwark, was in the room and recorded their dialogue.[36] Sarah had been fasting for two months and was confined to bed and in considerable turmoil herself. Her immediate companion and maid was Hannah Guy, an Irish Baptist of Traleigh and an associate of Craddock. Also in Sarah's circle were Richard Saltonstall, who registered the first formal protest against the slave trade in anglophone America; the future regicide Hugh Peter, who would be praised by Richard Price in 1789 and condemned by Edmund Burke; and the seeker John Saltmarsh, chaplain to the revolutionary army, a "strange genius, part poet, part whirling dervish," who advocated "the brotherhood of man."[37] It was thus a meeting of Irish, African, Welsh, English, and American.

> MAID [DINAH]: I am oft tempted against my life.
> MRS. SARAH: Why, what causeth it?
> MAID: Sometimes this, because I am not as others are: I do not look so, as others doe.

Sarah goes on to expound on the power of Christian redemption and the equality of believers before enunciating the antinomian axiom, "This is my covenant, I will be mercifull to their iniquities; *and,* Ile give you a new heart, Ile put my fear in your heart, Ile write my Lawes there." But Dinah remains in doubt: "He may do this for some few, but not to me." And Sarah replies, "He doth not this to one onely, nor to one Nation onely; for, many Nations must be blessed in him. He came to give his life for a ransome for many, to give himselfe for the life of the world. He is a free agent; and why should you exclude your selfe?"

Sarah saw the deliverance from internal and external bondage as simultaneous; she affirmed the unity between the Kingdom Within and the Kingdom Without, the new Heaven and the new Earth. John Saltmarsh wrote an introduction to the printed version of this extraordinary dialogue. Saltmarsh, a Yorkshire countryman of Jessey's, was, as we have said, chaplain to Fairfax's army, whose triumphs had just put an end to the first civil war. "There is no church," he noted in 1646, "nor ordinances yet." People were seeking, he explained, "yet they are to begin as in primitive times with gifts and miracles."[38] He, too, was confused about blackness, ethnicity, and slavery. Saltmarsh wrote of Sarah, under her legal condition, "She is in bondage, in blackness, and darkness and tempest," while asserting that under her Gospel condition, God was "making known his glory in the *dark.*" Saltmarsh's *Smoke in the Temple* argued that Christ's kingdom was a realm not of "compliancy and obedience and submission, but of consultation, of debating, counselling, prophesying, voting, &c."[39] He believed that Sara Wight could help fulfill God's "new covenant"; the "poore, low, and humble" were its instruments, and "more and more is to be revealed," he wrote with revolutionary expectation. The question was, would the abolition of the slave trades be included in the "approaching reformation," as Milton expressed the unfolding of the revolutionary program?

To help build the new Earth, Anne Hutchinson had in 1634 sailed to Massachusetts Bay, where she worked as a midwife, a healer, and, like Sarah Wight, a spiritual counselor. She prophesied and expressed her antinomian ideas as she gathered with women, drawers of water like Francis and Dinah, at the town spring on High Street. Jane Hawkins (who would later be banished from the colony for heresy) and Mary Dyer (who would later be hanged for sedition) met daily at the wellspring on High Street in Boston.[40] From these humble beginnings grew ever larger conventicles to discuss the sermons of the orthodox Puritan ministers, who began to see the meetings—and Hutchinson in particular—as affronts to their own power. To them, the reproduction of antinomian ideas was closely linked to the broader reproduction of the population of the Bay colony. Hutchinson's allies in the militia also objected to the appointment of an army chaplain, threatening to refuse to go to war against the Pequots and weakening the military power of the colony.[41] The ensuing Antinomian Controversy resulted in a major challenge to the ruling authority of Governor John Winthrop and the Puritan elders in Massachusetts Bay.

Winthrop and the Puritan elders never formally charged Anne Hutchinson with witchcraft, but the whole affair, as Carol Karlsen has noted, trembled through innuendo and insinuation on the edge of such accusations.[42] Winthrop and others considered Hutchinson's miscarriage in 1638 to be "strange to amazement": she had given "30 monstrous births or thereabouts, at once; some of them bigger, some lesser, some of one shape, some of another; few of any perfect shape, none at all of them (as

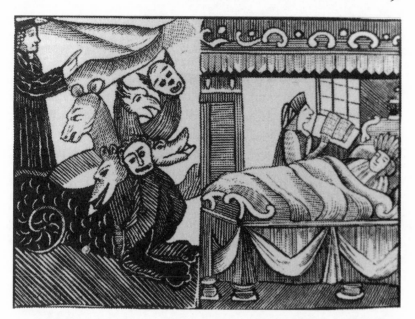

A "monstrous birth" as a many-headed hydra. The Miracle of Miracles
(n.d., but likely early eighteenth century).

farre as I could ever learne) of humane shape." Mary Dyer, for her part, was said to have given birth to a baby that had "horns like a Beast, and ears, scales on a rough skin like a fish called a *Thornback,* legs and claws like a *Hawke.*" To some it seemed clearly the work of the Devil upon typically porous and vulnerable women. Here was female power in reproduction at its most nightmarish to the puritanical patriarchs: monstrous, threatening, unregulated. With Bacon's theory of monsters behind them, and with their own notion of Satan foremost in their minds, the first reaction of the Puritans was murderous. The second was only slightly less extreme: Anne Hutchinson was banished from the colony to Rhode Island ("island of errors"). Her defeat removed opposition to the Pequot War and cleared the way for slavery. Many surviving Pequots were enslaved and shipped off to the other Puritan colony in the New World, Providence Island; the return cargo to Massachusetts was African slaves.[43] In writing about the Antinomian Controversy, Edward Johnson considered it "no Marvell then if so many Errours arise, like those fained heads of Hidra, as fast as one is cut off two stand up in the roome."[44] Cotton Mather's chapter on the same subject in his *Magnalia Christi Americana* (1702) was entitled "Hydra Decapita."

Indeed, it was during the time of Francis and the female prophets that Matthew Hopkins, in his official capacity as the English Witch-Finder General, led a terrorist hunt against so-called witches. As the authorities used witchcraft statutes to prosecute religious radicals, an estimated one thousand women lost their lives between 1645 and 1647. Hopkins, a specialist in maritime law and insurance, worried that witches interfered with trade by cursing ships; he was advised in this matter by the royal astrologer, Lilly. Inquiries came to him from Naples and Barbados. Supported not only by Parliament but by the leading "rationalists" of the day (Hobbes, Boyle, Bodin, Harvey), this misogynist obsessed about diabolical sex, "pricking" female bodies for the Devil's mark. His assistant wrote that Satan bound his witches "to imitate Christ in many things, as his Assemblies, and Sabbaths, Baptism and Covenants," implying a connection between Satan and the radical religious movements led by women in the 1640s.

Female prophecy must be situated in the crisis of reproduction in the middle of the seventeenth century. This was the peak period for the criminalization of women in England and throughout Europe, as prosecutions for infanticide, abortion, and witchcraft reached their highest rate. It was also the period in which men began to wrest control of reproduction from women (male midwives appeared in 1625 and the forceps soon thereafter); previously, "childbirth and the lying-in period were a kind of ritual collectively staged and controlled by women, from which men were usually excluded." Since the ruling class had begun to recognize its interest in increased fecundity, "attention was focussed on the 'population' as a fundamental category for economic and political analysis."[45] The simultaneous births of modern obstetrics and modern demography were responses to the crisis. Both, like the witchcraft prosecutions, sought to rationalize social reproduction in a capitalist context—that is, as the breeding of labor power.[46] A recurring motif in the ruling-class imagination was intercourse between the English witch and the "black man"—a devil or imp. The terror was not limited to an imaginary chamber of horrors; it was an actuality of counterrevolution.

By 1650, "the age of independent female prophecy was over."[47] But not without complaint. When the prophetess Anna Trapnel was arrested in

Cornwall in 1654, the "justices . . . came to fetch me out of my bed," she wrote, "and some came upstairs, crying, A witch, a witch." When the authorities requested that Anna's neighbors assist them in capturing her, "one of my friends told them, that they must fetch their silk gowns to do it then, for the poor would not do it." Women had largely been silenced; the openings of the previous decade had closed. The Leveller women had petitioned in 1649, "Considering that we have an equal share and interest with men in the commonwealth, and it cannot be laid waste, (as now it is) and not we be the greatest and most helpless sufferers therein; and considering that poverty, misery, and famine, like a mighty torrent, is breaking in upon us . . . and we are not able to see our children hang upon us, and cry out for bread, and not have wherewithall to feed them, we had rather die than see that day."[48] In Bristol, Sarah Latchett railed against Pastor Ewins at Broadmead and was imprisoned for her pains, and Mrs. Prince, who interrupted the same congregation by humming, was thrown out as a Ranter.

The fifty-second heresy described by Thomas Edwards illuminated a central contradiction of the age, "For by naturall birth all men are equally and alike born to like propriety, liberty, and freedom; and as we are delivered of God by the hand of nature into this world, every one with a naturall innate freedom and propriety, even so are we to live, every one equally and alike to enjoy his birth-right and priviledge." Freedom for the "free-born Englishman" was based on birth, but parturition was regarded as at once monstrous, liminal, and diabolical. It was during this period that the term *proletariat* entered the English vocabulary; it made a learned entrance in the sense that classical scholars borrowed it from the Servian Constitution of ancient Rome. Its pejorative meaning has lasted—referring to a member of the poorest class, the lowest and most vile—but its original sense had a more exact reference, namely, "subjects to multiplie and beget issue" (1609), "reserved only to beget children" (1610), or, as James Harrington explained in *Oceana* (1658), "such as thro their poverty contributed nothing to the Commonwealth but children." It thus reflects the devalorization of women's labor of reproduction. The currency of the term belongs to the epoch of witch-burning. The nascency of capitalism, based as it was on exploited unpaid labor, thus required control even over human parturition.

QUIETISM IN WORD AND DEED

For the male side of the movement, the repression of the counterrevolution descended more slowly, aided by squabbling among the defeated, whose growing sectarianism must be seen in the context of jockeying for power within the Cromwellian regime and competition for riches in the wars for the slave trade. Formerly, Dennis Hollister (a grocer), Thomas Ewins (a tailor), and Robert Purnel (a carpet weaver) had been elders of the Broadmead Church, the pallbearers who carried Francis to her grave. But in the new world of the Cromwellian Republic, with its Western Design, *guerre de course,* Dutch War, and African trade, the devout fell out with each other. In this way, once-common seekers and notionists became different denominations, Baptists and Quakers. It is not difficult to read their polemics in the scarcely veiled terms of antinomianism and the slave trade. As the Irish prisoners were being transported in 1652, Purnel accused his enemies of "notionism" and "anabaptism," prophesying, "You shall speedily receive a total Rout: You have gathered your selves together, but you shall be scattered, yea, you shall be broken in pieces." Hollister added ranterism to the charge of notionism and significantly charged, "You are running to the Assyrians for help, and into Ægypts land a place of darkness are ye gone, seeking to recover a vail to hide your selves from the face of the Lamb." He concluded, "Ye are the many-headed Beast in divers forms, sects, and opinions, under the name of Papist, Atheists, Independents, Anabaptist &c." Bristol, the epicenter for the movement that produced both Baptists and Quakers, ironically provided the scene for the most horrific act of repressive quietism of the counterrevolution, for it was there that "radical antinomianism made a last-ditch bid for expression before Puritan conservatism drove it underground"—or overseas. "Some of our way have shouted, and cryed Hossannah, holy, holy, King of Israel to James Nayler, &c.", upon whom was visited the most odious terror.[49]

In October 1656 James Nayler rode through the gates of Bristol, his horse guided by three women: Martha Simmonds, Hannah Stranger, and Dorcas Erbery. They trudged knee-deep in mud, sang psalms of praise, and cast flowers across the way. Nayler was a Yorkshireman who was, at the time, a more successful evangelist even than George Fox, the

James Nayler. Alte und neue Schwarm-Geister-Bruth, und Quäcker-Gruel, *part 6 of* Anabaptisticum et enthusiasticum Pantheon *(1702).*

founder of the Quakers. He wandered the countryside appealing to putting-out workers; he was thrown in prison and shared the straw on the ground with pirates. His class consciousness was well developed. Nayler wrote, "For your scoffing at the plow, I am of it, knowing it to be a lawful employment, much better than the hireling that works not at all, but lives on other man's labours, taking by violence what's other men's labours; but seeing the plow is a reproach with you, why should not the tithes be so also, which are a fruit of the plow?"[50] In 1653 he explained why he did not take off his hat or bow his knee: "The Scripture saith he that respects persons commits sin." He was a powerful preacher. He preached jubilee—the acceptable year of the lord, the liberty of the captive. He preached revolution, quoting Ezekiel, "Is not the Lord overturning, overturning, overturning?"[51] He inveighed against the oppressors for taking the commons, "getting great estates in the world, laying house to house and land to land, till there be no place for the poor. And when they are become poor through your deceits then you despise them and exalt yourselves above them and forget that you are all made of one mold, and one blood, and must all appear before one judge, who is no respecter of persons."[52] He spoke out against the slave trade: "Where can the innocent go out and not a trap laid to bring him into bondage and slavery to some of these spirits?"[53] He proclaimed, "I have fellowship with them who live in Dens, and desolate places in the Earth."

To the authorities, Nayler's entry into Bristol seemed a blasphemous imitation of Jesus' entrance into Jerusalem. A frightened Parliament, wanting to "send a decisive political message to insubordinate sectarians," tried him for violation of the Blasphemy Act, which indeed had been enacted against him. He answered the charges without removing his hat, which prompted a long and unprecedented debate about how to punish him. Only a narrow vote spared his life, though George Downing argued solemnly, "We are God's executioners, and ought to be tender of His honour." Nayler was taken from Newgate to the Black Boy Inn near the Royal Exchange, where his agony began. He suffered 310 lashes at the cart's tail, across London. On Tower Hill, he embraced the executioner, who branded his forehead and then with a red-hot iron bored a hole through his tongue.[54]

Nayler was thus silenced, and many others were meant to hear the message of terror. Thousands of Protestant radicals were imprisoned; others were shipped overseas. The Quakers and the Muggletonians rewrote their own histories during the 1660s and 1670s, deradicalizing their movements and suppressing the voices of prophets and antinomians.[55] Even Nathaniel Angello, Broadmead's first minister, found preferment and joined the mocking chorus against Nayler, publishing an allegorical romance called *Bentivoglio and Urania*.[56] Nayler, a false prophet, induced "Enthusiastical Fury" and was associated with arson, superstition, sexuality, and deceit. He remained an object of vicious fun for years. For instance, in Tom Brown's *Letters from the Dead to the Living* (1702), Nayler is imagined in hell, where amid "black spiritual janizaries" and "immortal negroes" Lucifer dresses him up "in a rainbow-coloured coat," the Renaissance symbol of the fool, called the motley. Nayler dines with hungry mechanics on a meal of scorpions, West Indian iguanas, shovel-nosed sharks, and a leviathan. Such savage ridicule, like the theories of monstrosity of Francis Bacon and Thomas Edwards, must be read with a "Satanic light" in order to see the many heads of the hydra—the sailors, clowns, Africans, mechanics, and radical sectaries.

Meanwhile, like "new age" entrepreneurs, some Baptists and Quakers began to prosper, acquiring wealth overseas, particularly in Ireland and the Caribbean. George Bishop, a Bristol Quaker who implied tyrannicide at the Putney Debates of 1647, was by 1662 offering the consolation of the afterlife for the sufferings of this one.[57] William Kiffin, a former fellow apprentice of Leveller John Lilburne and himself a powerful figure in English Baptist circles, who banished Elizabeth Poole from the congregation for opposing capital punishment for Charles Stuart, offered the restored king a gift of ten thousand pounds. Edward Terrill himself had become involved in many aspects of the sugar industry in Barbados, as a money-scrivener, a broker, a warehouseman, a creditor, a refiner, and a planter. His son, William, managed a family plantation in Barbados, Cabbage Tree Hall, and married Rebecca, heiress to two other plantations. On "A Topographical Description and Admeasurement of the Yland of Barbados in the West Indies with the M[aste]rs Names of the Severall Plantacons," published in 1657, Terrill's name appears three times adjacent to little plantation symbols.[58] His descendants would comprise one of the leading families in the eighteenth-century planter elite.[59]

We now may begin to understand the repressive anxiety within Terrill's text. At one glorious time his church had been part of a movement opposed to slavery, but the history of that era was written during a different, wicked time, after slavery had become the basis of prosperity for the same church. Could these Bristol Baptists remain at once devout Christians and eager slave traders? What solution would they find to this problem? The answer lies partly in Terrill's very anxiety, for it was racism that would begin to provide these consciences with a solution.[60] We see such race consciousness grow and flourish in the person of another radical Baptist, John Bunyan.

A tinker's son born in an open-field village, Bunyan was a revolutionary soldier who in 1644 took part in the siege of Leicester.[61] He was a roarer, ranter, swearer, and bell-ringer himself, affected by the ideas of

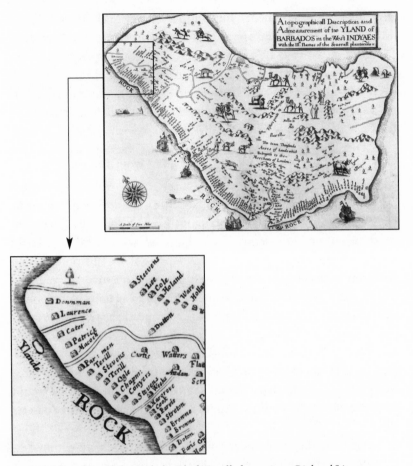

Map of Barbados with detail of Terrill plantations. Richard Ligon,
A True & Exact History of the Island of Barbados *(1657).*
Beinecke Rare Book and Manuscripts Library, Yale University.

the Ranters, Diggers, and Levellers before being converted by a poor
woman, which led him to preaching, the Baptist Church, and jail. After
the revolution, Bunyan began to look back on a period that was revolutionary, hopeful, millenarian. In his best-known allegory, *Pilgrim's Progress,* his pilgrim, named Christian, encounters "a man black of flesh" who
is a false apostle, "a man that flattereth his Neighbour [and] spreadeth a
Net for his feet." He shows a false way to the Celestial City. After this encounter Christian converses with Hope, who has found "Rioting, Revel-

ling, Drinking, Swearing, Lying, Uncleanliness, Sabbath-breaking and what not" at Vanity Fair. Bunyan thus associates the African with the activities of the Ranters, or of his own youth. Indeed, Hope says, "All our righteousness are as filthy rags, by the works of the Law no man shall be justified." This kind of antinomianism survived in English Dissent, but here Bunyan blames the victim: it is true that the riches of the time (Vanity Fair) were accumulated by the labors of slaves who were more and more African, but it is untrue that the slaves themselves were responsible for the vanity that Bunyan so profoundly denounces. This is what Marcus Garvey was able to point out in his commentary on *Pilgrim's Progress*.

Christiana, Christian's wife, meets another black man who symbolizes "the vile Person" who can never be washed clean. One of Bunyan's children's poems taught a racialized theology in which Moses, "a fair and comely man," was contrasted with his wife, "a swarthy Æthiopian." Bunyan wrote *The Holy War* (1682) as an allegory, based on his experiences as a soldier during the 1640s. It begins, "Well, upon a time there was one Diabolus, a mighty Gyant, made an assault upon this famous Town of Mansoul, to take it, and make it his own habitation. This Gyant was King of the Blacks or Negroes, and most raving Prince he was." Here Bunyan inverts the historical truth, pretending that Africans assaulted European Christendom rather than the reverse. Propaganda could not tell a greater lie: white is black, and black is white. It illustrates the value of the warning sounded by the African American theologian James Cone: "Underneath the European language of freedom and equality there is slavery and death."[62]

DEVILS BLACK AND WHITE

At the time when Francis reminded all to heed the glory of God, it was not at all clear that liberal capitalism would be created; that the sugar plantation and the Atlantic slave trade would become platforms of economic growth; that enclosed private property would become the principle of land tenure; that white supremacy would become the theory of accounting for ethnic differences; or even that the congregation of multitudes with so many different ideas would become a Baptist Church. These developments were not inevitable; they were all contested, and many of the ideas that Francis stood for were defeated. This was revolution and counterrevolution. And yet Francis and her ideas have survived. The revolutionary notion of glory reappeared more than a century and half later, at another moment of counterrevolution, when Shelley wrote his hymn to freedom:

> *Men of England, heirs of Glory,*
> *Heroes of unwritten story,*
> *Nurslings of one mighty Mother,*
> *Hopes of her, and one another*

> *Rise like Lions after slumber*
> *In unvanquishable number,*
> *Shake your chains to earth like dew*
> *Which in sleep had fallen on you—*
> *Ye are many—they are few.*

Here glory has gender and national connotations foreign to the fragment left by Francis. Nevertheless, alluding to Shelley and seeking to understand the English radical tradition, Edward Thompson wrote in *The Making of the English Working Class* (1963), "It is above all in Bunyan that we find the slumbering Radicalism which was preserved through the eighteenth century and which breaks out again and again in the nineteenth." *Pilgrim's Progress* contributed "most to the stock of ideas and attitudes which make up the raw material of the movement from 1790 [to] 1850." Written in prison during the repression of the 1660s, bitter toward the idle rich and comforting in its faith, *Pilgrim's Progress* remains an amusing, inspirational testament of survival and defeat. As Bunyan said of himself,

> *He fell suddenly into an Allegory*
> *About their Journey, and the way to Glory.*

In an Atlanta penitentiary, Marcus Garvey wrote *Vanity Fair* (1926), taking his title from *Pilgrim's Progress,* though not his subtitle, *The Tragedy of White Man's Justice.* Garvey denounced racism, saying, once again, "God is no respecter of persons." It took a Jamaican, a pan-Africanist indeed, to rediscover the radical tradition in a way that omitted Bunyan's racialism yet retained a full measure of his individualism and uplift.[63]

"Soon fugitives will come and tell you their news by word of mouth. At once you will recover the power of speech and speak with the fugitives; you will no longer be dumb" (Ezekiel 24:26–27): something like this happened in England between 1645 and 1649. Proletarians of different provenance were cast together and began to realize that together they could do more than they could separately. This is the dynamic that Francis helped to set in motion, and certainly Dinah, too, as she and Sara Wight discovered the story of deliverance from bondage. A Boston antinomian, a Yorkshire plowman, "a Moor born out of England," and mechanic preachers met and began to talk. Of course such conversations had been going on for years, as when political and common prisoners rioted in Elizabethan prisons, and they would continue after 1649, in the jail cell where Naylor was quartered with pirates, or in Newgate, where the Muggletonians found protection from the condemned highwaymen ("No, said I, it is not for Prisoners to complain of Prisoners").[64] The most remarkable pamphlet of the Diggers was entitled *A Light Shining in Buckinghamshire*. It called for equal rights, free elections, a commonwealth, and a just portion for every person. Its subtitle suggested that Diggers had a local/global consciousness, for the light found in Buckinghamshire led to *A Discovery of The Main Grounds and Original Causes of all the Slavery in the World, but chiefly in England* (1648).

"In sanctification [black women] have located a power that has made possible survival and autonomous action when all other means fail," Nell Painter has observed.[65] That Terrill did not omit mention of Francis altogether is evidence that she possessed an undeniable spiritual power. How that power would be remembered was determined first by the emergence of eloquent new voices that were raised against Atlantic slavery between 1645 and 1649, and second by the silencing of those voices at the hands of Cromwell and the Restoration, which assured the triumph of racialized slavery. Yet even the opponents of slavery, such as Sara Wight and John Saltmarsh, expressed their views in racialized imagery. The same was true of the anonymous author of *Tyranipocrit Discovered* (1649), who denounced the rich, the powerful, and the propertied; inveighed bitterly against capital punishment; advocated communism; and attacked slavery throughout the world.[66] He groped toward an understanding of the complexity of class rule, seeking to understand its moments of both force and consent. Like Bunyan, he used allegory. Satan had officiated at a marriage union between Tyranny and Hypocrisy, he wrote; one was figured as a black devil, the others as a white one:

> My black children, which are whores, and knaves, gluttons, drunkards, swearers, Sabbath-breakers, artlesse theeves, and all poor prophane persons, they shall bee all your slaves and wait and attend on Tyranipocrit, and his friends, and you may freely use, and abuse them at your pleasures, for these, although they bee my children, yet they are so unruly, and out of order, that I know not almost how to trust them. . . .

> O thou white devil, I would faine uncase thee, and discover thy vile practises, that all men may see and know that thou art an ugly, odious devil, I mean thou that wilt winne honour by thy impious practises, thou that hast God in thy mouth, but wilt not cast the devil out of thy heart, thou that commandest and teachest others to doe that good which thou praisest in thy mouth, and hatest in thy heart: thou that bindest heavy burdens, and layest them on other mens shoulders, but wilt not touch them thy selfe with one of thy fingers: O it is thou that stealest with a high hand, and yet with an impudent face, thou wilt outface the Law.

Francis embodied, to use the terms of Francis Bacon, three heads of the hydra: she was an Anabaptist, she was an independent woman, and she was a "West Indian." To emphasize these aspects of her is not, of course, to qualify her as a swarm or rout deserving of extermination, but on the contrary to help us recognize her as a fellow creature and as an Atlantean proletarian. She was not a monster, even though the attempt to erase the message she carried only ensured its multiplication, like the hydra's heads. It is impossible to accept her as the "foul little ugly Ethiop" who stained the immaculate *New Atlantis,* because in the actual Atlantic she brought an exceptional purity of word and intention. Those who held the view that God was no respecter of persons were themselves deeply disrespected during and after the political defeat of the English

Revolution, particularly the women, who were thought by capitalist patriarchy to be good for nothing but breeding. Since no mention is made of children at either her deathbed or her funeral, we may assume that Francis was a single woman, whose conception of family did not include the breeding of children, especially not as future slaves or labor power. She became the means of conveying to future generations on both sides of the Atlantic mountains[67] the message that God is a respecter of neither persons nor faces. Virginia Woolf asserted "the rights of all—all men and women—to the respect in their persons of the great principles of Justice and Equality and Liberty."[68] Not to respect persons was to find unacceptable the power relations of hierarchy based on class, gender, or race. Francis utterly confounded all three. The glorifying, disrespecting presence of the multiple figures of the Atlantic proletariat in the English Revolution can no longer be denied.

CHAPTER FOUR

The Divarication of the Putney Debates

For really I think that the poorest he that is in England hath a life to live,
as the greatest he; and therefore truly, sir, I think it's clear, that every man
that is to live under a government ought first by his own consent to put
himself under that government; and I do think that the poorest man
in England is not at all bound in a strict sense to that government
that he hath not had a voice to put himself under; . . . I should doubt
whether he was an Englishman or no, that should doubt of such things.
—Colonel Thomas Rainborough, The Putney Debates *(1647)*

As DOROTHY HAZZARD and her band of Broadmead believers made
their way to London during the mid-1640s, they crossed the river
Thames at the village of Putney. With an alluvial plain to the north and
hills to the south, Putney was a meeting place for travelers, as well as for
commoners, household servants, market gardeners, and river workers
such as the watermen, ferrymen, and fishermen who lived there. "Putney
appears to have been at all times a considerable thoroughfare," explained
Daniel Lysons, the parish incumbent and historian of the 1790s. "It was
usual formerly for persons traveling from London to many parts of the
West of England, to proceed as far as this place by water."[1]

If Hazzard crossed the Thames at Putney in the autumn of 1647 on her
return to Bristol, she would have seen the New Model Army encamped
on the heath, ordered there by Oliver Cromwell to occupy strategic
ground between the king at Hampton Palace and Parliament in Westminster. The soldiers had won great victories but now were restive, mutinous, and organized to advance their own interests. They wanted their
wages, they wanted freedom from impressment, and they wanted provision for the wounded, widows, and orphans. They did not want to go to
Ireland. Only a few months before, petitioning troops had wondered,
"Have the Souldiers only, who have been Instruments to recover the lost

Liberties of the Nation, fought themselves into Slavery?" They considered themselves to be "free commoners of England drawn together and continued in arms in judgment and conscience for defence of their own and the people's right and liberties." They had advocated an end to slavery through the biblical jubilee, saying, "Ye may be free if ye will, be free now and ever, now or never, this is the seventh year, the year of jubilee." They had sidestepped General Thomas Fairfax and elected "agitators" to represent their interests. Fairfax had tried to suppress a soldier's petitions for wages but ultimately failed: "This was only as cutting off a *Hydra's* Head," he wrote, "for they began again, not so near the Head-Quarters, but in more remote Corners of the Army." Soon they presented their petition to a highly displeased Parliament.[2] Dan Wolfe writes, "The genius of war is audacious action, that of democracy, persuasion, tentative judgment, humility of mind." These were all in balance at Putney.[3]

Crossing at Putney in late October or early November, the Broadmead group may have passed Saint Mary's church at the time of the crucial debates between Cromwell, leading the officers of the army, on the one hand, and the agitators, representing the rank and file, on the other. The latter sat around the communion table of Saint Mary's, defiantly keeping their hats on as they discussed the future of England, indeed the very meaning of "England." The most powerful advocate for the common soldier at the Putney Debates was Thomas Rainborough, a member of a maritime family and a man of the sea himself. He had served in the navy until 1643, when he took a command in the Parliamentary army and fought bravely at Naseby, Sherburne, Oxford, Worcester, and Bristol, where we earlier saw him. The most radical of the leading officers in the New Model Army, he was affiliated with rank-and-file militancy and with soldiers who had returned to England from America to wage war against the king. He had opened London Bridge to the sectaries in the crisis of August 1647. He was also the virtual leader of the Levellers, perhaps the first political party of any kind and certainly the first democratic one, advocating law in the English language (proceedings had up to then been in Latin), the right to call witnesses, the right to a speedy trial, equality under the law, no impressment, religious toleration, jury trials, no double jeopardy, the right to confront accusers, and the abolition of capital punishment for theft. He emphasized the sovereignty and rights of "the poorest he that is in England," and was aware of the "many scufflings between the honest men of England and those who have tyrannized over them." One of these scufflings concerned the denial of access to the commons, which to Rainborough was the "greatest tyranny that was thought of in the world." The gentry "turned the poor men out of doors"—that is, evicted them. Defending the popular right to the commons and the subsistence they afforded, Rainborough claimed that "God hath set down that thing as to propriety with this law of his, *Thou shalt not steal.*"[4]

Commonism and slavery defined the debate at Putney. On the other side was Henry Ireton, the learned and smoothly confident spokesman for the grandees and gentry. He, like Rainborough, was an active soldier, having fought at Naseby, Newbury, Gainsborough, Edgehill, and Bristol. After the capitulation of Oxford he married Cromwell's daughter. In the debates he admitted frankly, "All the main thing I speak for, is because I would have an eye to property." He took offense at Rainborough's words about "the poorest he that is in England," understanding clearly that they applied to people such as Francis, who were not English. Quoting the Mosaic Law to prop up the laws and authorities Rainborough attacked, he advised the assembled soldiers and indeed the entire nation, "*Honour thy father and mother,*" a maxim that "doth extend to . . . our governours." Rainborough immediately perceived Ireton's words as an argument for upper-class authority, whether kingly or Parliamentary, and answered impatiently, "The great dispute is, who is a right father and a right mother?" Since "the people of England . . . have not voices in the choosing of their fathers and mothers—they are not bound to that commandment." His view paralleled that of Winstanley, for whom the father was the spirit of the community and the mother was the Earth. Colonel Nathaniel Rich meanwhile expressed the fear that if the propertyless four fifths of the kingdom voted, they might legislate "that there shall be an equality of goods and estates." Rainborough explained the corollary: if only rich men ruled, then "the one part shall make hewers of wood and drawers of water of the other [four], and so the greatest part of the nation be enslaved."

Putney thus became not only a geographic but a historical crossroads, one that has been interpreted in many ways over the last century. Three observations may be made here about the major interpretations. First,

Meeting of the General Council of the Army, with agitators at right, 1647.
Thomason Tracts E409/25, by permission of the British Library.

following the German socialist Edouard Bernstein, who used Putney to
move revolutionary Marxism toward social democracy, one group of interpreters emphasized the origins of a broader franchise and citizenship
in the debates of 1647. The project was parliamentary democracy; its
subject was the respectable citizen worker.[5] Second, in an hour of loom-
ing military defeat, on May Day, 1942, Aneurin Bevan, a Labour M. P.
and future founder of the national health service, published an article
under the name "Thomas Rainborough," which helped to initiate the
wartime political discussion that culminated in the Labour Party's vic-

tory in 1945. The Putney Debates also held great meaning for British soldiers, including Edward Thompson, who carried in his knapsack a copy of the *Handbook of Freedom* (1939), in which Edgell Rickword and Jack Lindsay wrote, "It will be noticed how the word 'common' and its derivatives, now so strangely altered in drawing-room usage, appear and re-appear like a theme throughout the centuries. It was for the once vast common lands that the peasants took up arms; it was as the 'true commons' that they spoke of themselves when they assembled, and it was the aspiration of men not corrupted by petty proprietorship 'that all things should be in common.'"[6] Bevan summarized the debates in a single brilliant chiasmus of two breaths: "Either poverty must use democracy to destroy the power of property, or property in fear of poverty will destroy democracy." Bevan's project was the industrial welfare state; its subject was the industrial worker.[7] Third, in September 1945 Ras Tefari Makonnen hosted the Pan-African Congress in Manchester. The delegates resolved, "We are unwilling to starve any longer while doing the world's drudgery." Among the independence seekers such as Nkrumah and Kenyatta were students of the Putney Debates, notably C. L. R. James, who saw their significance within the history of the struggle against slavery and empire.[8] In this case poverty had no democracy to use in attacking property. The project of James and others was national liberation; the subject was the drudge worker.

The Putney Debates, ever patient of interpretation, have thus been useful to struggles for the vote, the welfare state, and colonial liberation.[9] But there is more. We find two neglected themes: the struggle for the commons and the struggle against slavery. The author of *A Light Shining in Buckinghamshire* wrote that "man, following his sensuality, became an encloser, so that all the land was enclosed in a few mercenary hands and all the rest made their slaves." The fork in the road at Putney pointed to either a future with the commons and without slavery, or to one with slavery and without the commons. The commons were a reality, not pie in the sky.

As soldiers at Putney gathered wood for their campfire, they knew that the debates had relevance to all commoners. Those in Putney, for example, enjoyed common pasture, furze, turf, gravel, underwood, and stones, as well as river resources of smelt, salmon, flounder, shad, roach,

Colonel Thomas Rainborough, Putney debater.
Thomason Tracts, by permission of the British Library.

dace, barbel, eel, and gudgeon. The debates had special urgency for those affected by the decision of Charles I in 1637 to enclose 236 acres of wastelands between Hampton Court and Richmond for a hunting park. Clarendon, the royalist, noted that the attack on common rights "increased the murmur and noise of the people," which would eventually grow into a revolutionary clamor and bring down a succession of tyrants: Archbishop Laud, Lord Strafford, and King Charles I. The plunder of the Putney estate of his patron probably confirmed in a young Thomas Hobbes the love of private property and the loathing of the commons that he passed on to his pupil, the future Charles II.[10]

Rainborough spoke with angry eloquence against slavery. For slavery, too, was a reality. As a military man, Rainborough was especially concerned about soldiers and sailors. "I would fain know what the soldier hath fought for all this while?" he asked. "He hath fought to enslave himself, to give power to men of riches, men of estates, to make him a perpetual slave." He added, with bitter sarcasm, "We do find in all presses that go forth none must be pressed that are freehold men. When these gentlemen fall out among themselves they shall press the poor scrubs to come and kill [one another for] them." Rainborough knew whereof he spoke. He had recruited soldiers among the mobility and 'prentices in St. Giles's–in-the-Fields, a London parish that also contained a depot for children spirited to the West Indies. As a naval officer he had seen sailors resist impressment, and as a Leveller he knew that their resistance had registered in the *Agreement of the People,* a leveller's attempt to provide a written constitution. They had warned that "the matter of impristing and constraining any of us to serve in the wars is against our freedom" and sworn that they would resist "slavish condition." Impressment was slavery.[11]

Another kind of slavery was being practiced a few miles downriver from Putney. Hardly a ship sailed for the West Indies, said a Parliamentary ordinance of 1643, without a cargo of the spirited. A specialist in the Virginia trade wrote, "The Servants are taken up by such men as we here call *Spirits,* and by them put into Cookes houses about Saint *Katherines,* where being once entred, are kept Prisoners untill a Mastter fetches them off; and they lye at charges in these places a moneth or more, before they are taken away when the Ship is ready, the *Spirits* charges and the Cooke for dieting paid, they are Shipped" to America. A precise vocabulary attended the practice: to "nab" was to take a person into custody; to "kidnap" was to seize a child; to "spirit" was to abduct and carry a person overseas; to "barbados" was to abduct someone and ship him or her to Barbados; and to "trepan" was to entrap or ensnare a person for labor. These slang terms came into existence in the 1640s and 1650s, but not without opposition: "Malitious tongues ha's impaired it much: For it hath beene a constant report amongst the ordinaries sort of people, That those servants who are sent to Virginia, are sold as slaves."[12] As late as 1660 ordinary parents pitifully followed ships carrying their children to the West Indies down river to Gravesend, "cryinge and mourninge for Redemption from their Slavery."[13]

Rainborough also spoke out against African slavery, both the slavery of Europeans imprisoned in North Africa and that of Africans imprisoned for sale in the Americas. Rainborough's father, William, had led a naval blockade of eight ships against Sallé in North Africa in 1637; he had rescued 339 prisoners and returned to London in triumph. The Grand Remonstrance presented to the king in 1641 complained of the thousands of sailors lost to slavery. Richard Overton, the Leveller pamphleteer, saw a continuum of miserable slavery extending from the "aged, sick and crippled, begging your halfe-penny Charities," through those in naval vessels and *"the poore; your hunger-starved bretheren"* and "those whom your owne unjuste Lawes hold captive in your owne Prisons," to, finally, the "Gally-slave in Turkie or Argiere."[14] Rainborough was concerned with the enslavement not only of English people; the signet ring he wore on his finger bore the image of "a Moor's head proper, wreathed argent, bearded sable." His official identity and the authority of his written word were thus represented by a symbol of liberation from slavery and an image of an African.

When Rainborough inveighed against slavery, he included mancipation of several kinds: the practice of impressment, spiriting or kidnapping to the Americas, the capture for forced labor of English people in West and North Africa, and the enslavement of Africans. Agitation against slavery was an essential element in the publications and practices of the Levellers. They fought to abolish slavery. What was at issue, then, was not a rhetorical abstraction of political propaganda, but something real, experienced, suffered, and known. A rough definition of slavery at the time would include these features: it began in an act of expropriation and terror; it affected children and young people particularly; it compelled violent exploitation; and more often than not, it ended in death. The hewers and drawers, or the laboring subjects of the Atlantic economy, met this definition in an era well before race or ethnicity came to define slavery.

Thomas Rainborough would not survive the English Revolution. He was assassinated by a royalist raiding party in 1648, to the grief of thousands of people who poured into the streets of London for his funeral. Yet what he stood for at Putney would flow down the Thames, where a hundred thousand seamen, watermen, and bargemen linked England to the Atlantic hydrographic system. For Thomas Clarkson, the abolitionist, rivers provided an image of freedom; for James Joyce, the smithy of the Irish soul, rivers transmitted languages. A recent student of rivers writes, "They are forever picking up solid matter in one place and putting it down in another."[15] Rivers divaricate. From Putney, after 1647, would flow the ideas and practices of both freedom and slavery. A man, woman, or child might there embark upon a boat and, apart from transfers to other types of vessels, not disembark until reaching the harsh estuarial waters of the Shannon or the Liffey (Ireland); Bridgetown or Port Royal (the Caribbean); the Gambia or the Niger (West Africa); the Chesapeake or the Potomac (Virginia).[16]

NAPLES, 1647

On July 7, 1647, a Neopolitan fisherman named Masaniello led a protest by the market women, carters, porters, sailors, fishermen, weavers, silk winders, and all the other poor, or lazzaroni, of the second- or third-largest city in Europe.[17] The rebellion began in the marketplace of Naples, where producers rural and urban discovered that the Spanish viceroy had levied a new gabelle, or tax, on the city's fabled fruit (Goethe believed that the Neapolitans had invented lemonade).[18] The rebels turned the world upside down: galley oarsmen became captains, students were given books, prisons were opened, and tax records were burned. Nobles were forbidden to wear expensive garments, while their palaces were marked for destruction and their furnishings burned in the streets. "These Goods are got out of our Heart's Blood; and as they burn, so ought the Souls and Bodies of those Blood-suckers who own them, to fry in the Fire of Hell," cried one of the insurgents.[19] The rebels decreed that anyone caught looting might be executed, so "that all the World may know, we have not enterpris'd this businesse to enrich ourselves but to vindicate the common liberty." The price of bread fell to rates consistent with a moral economy. This was the essence of the revolt, which Masaniello expressed in "savage eloquence." His preferred figure of speech, however, was not to be found in the rhetorical handbooks of the Renaissance; rather, it was the price list: "Look ye here, my Lads, how we are ridden, Gabel upon Gabel, 36 Ounces the Loaf of Bread, 22 the Pound of Cheese," et cetera, et cetera. "Are these things to be endured? No, my Boys; Get my Words by Heart, and sound them thro' every Street of the City."

Although it lasted only ten days, the revolt of Naples in July 1647 marked the first time that the proletariat of any European city seized power and governed alone. Michelangelo Cerquozzi, the baroque painter, recognized the gravity of the event and painted *The Revolt of Masaniello* (1648) as a battle scene. Amid the tents and booths of the crowded market, the traffic of commerce, the herded livestock, the great barrel on the water wagon, that the hundreds of people have begun to take action is shown by new gestures of men bending for rocks, of bare arms raised, of pointed fingers. His is a sober assessment of an urban insurrection, equally without condescension or heroism.[20] An eighteenth-century historian raised his eyebrows and gasped, "After Ages will hardly believe what Height of Power this ridiculous Sovereign arrived to, who, trampling bare-foot on a throne, and wearing a Mariner's Cap instead of a Diadem, in the space of four Days, raised an Army of above 150,000 Men, and made himself Master of one of the most populous Cities in the worlde."[21]

Masaniello's story had special importance for the centers of European seafaring, England and Holland. English merchants had recently eclipsed their Italian counterparts in Levant shipping and now sent as many as 120 ships and three thousand sailors to Naples each year, with attendant desertions and turnovers. Sailors were a major source of information about the revolt. Less immediately effective but more lasting were the medallions struck in Amsterdam, the drama surreptitiously produced in London, and the translations of the first history of the uprising.[22] In 1649 T. B. published a play entitled *The Rebellion of Naples or the Tragedy of Massenello commonly so called: but rightly Tomaso Aniello di Malfa Generall of the Neapolitans. Written by a Gentleman who was an eye-witness where this was really acted upon the Bloudy Stage, the Streets of Naples.* In 1650 James Howell, an entrepreneur, a royalist, and literary man with connections to the Levant Company, translated Alexander Giraffi's *An Exact History of the Late Revolutions in Naples; and of Their Monstrous Successes,* and in the same year *The Second Part of Masaniello . . . The End of the Commotions.*[23] These were dedicated to the governor of the Levant Company with the reminder that,

The people is a beast which heads hath many
England of late shew'd this more than any.

Power and solidarity were themes of the play *The Rebellion of Naples.* On the frontispiece of its published text appeared an illustration of Masaniello himself, bare-legged and bonneted, overlooking a sky with a bare forearm hurling thunderbolts at a squadron of warships; Neptune raises his trident as squares of pikemen fail to prevent a few mariners from hauling the entire city of Naples from the sea to the beach. In his first monologue, Masaniello compares himself to a galley oarsman. The first words from the crowd, meanwhile, are the sailor's abiding principle of solidarity and the particular cry heard during the mutinies of 1626: "One and all, One and all, One and all."[24] Alluding to the English Levellers and John the Baptist (whose June feast day had been canceled in Naples for fear of tumult), Masaniello's adviser promises to "level the high walls of government with the earth they stood on: The Axe is already laid to the root." The Spanish viceroy refers to the furious beast with many heads and shamelessly asks, "How will you make your sauces, if you will not squeeze your Oranges? Or Wine, if you will not presse the Grape?"

Slavery, Africa, and the women of Naples were major concerns both of the play and of the translated history. One of Masaniello's advisers had been a slave in Algeria for nineteen years, and another had been a galley slave. The slave of a duke, a Moor, was freed. Masaniello had a daughter who was a blackamoor, who sang a song in praise of blackness. During the summer-festival ritual that actually provided the flashpoint of the insurrection, Masaniello led a group of teenagers masked in blackface who attacked a mock fort in the middle of the mercato. Giraffi compared the armed women and girls of Naples and their decisive street-fighting skills to so many Amazons. Masaniello's own wife was imprisoned for failing to pay the gabelle. The women vowed "they would burn the City, and themselves and Children along with it, before they would be Beasts of Burden any longer, and bring up their Children to be Slaves and Pack-Horses to a proud and haughty Nobility." T. B. compared the women to Ursula, the symbol of disorder in Ben Jonson's *Bartholomew Fair.* An old woman observing the black daughter suggested that she and the white daughter stop scrutinizing one another and instead look elsewhere, to "see what becomes of all the Money, and all the Land." *Cui bono.*

Masaniello and his army of fisherman capturing Naples. T.B.,
The Rebellion of Naples, or the Tragedy of Massenello . . . *(1649).*
Beinecke Rare Books and Manuscripts Library, Yale University.

The Rebellion of Naples combined persons, events, and ideas from both Naples and London, demonstrating a circulation of the experience of insurrection and suggesting a unity of class conflicts in a diversity of locations. The people had discovered their own strength; this was an autonomous insurrection whose force and power had to be respected—it could not be laughed off the stage. It remained a source of fear to the emerging politics of the bourgeois state; it also remained an example of hope for actual proletarians searching for justice, such as Thomas Spence, as we shall see later. In a notebook, Spinoza portrayed himself in the guise of the fishmonger.[25] John Locke sported with Masaniello to ridicule the divine right of kings. His friend James Tyrrell argued that even when the mobile, or urban mob, murmured at grievous taxes, it could not be justified in revolting because that inevitably led to vast spoilage of property, as Masaniello had proved.[26] Authorities in Maryland, New York, Massachusetts, Virginia, and London used the name of

Masaniello to tar political opponents. Tom Paine feared the name, but the soldiers, sailors, and commoners of the English Revolution did not. In November 1647, only a few days after the debates at Putney, a speaker in London said, "The same business we are upon is perfected in Naples, for if any person stand up for monarchy there, he is immediately hanged at his door."[27]

LONDON, 1649

If the Masaniello revolt and the Putney Debates of 1647 represented a high point of revolutionary possibility, the downfall began in 1649 with two exemplary executions. One seemed to kill the old regime of monarchy and hierarchy, the other the hope of a new regime based on neither of those. The first was the beheading of King Charles on January 30. A poor woman named Elizabeth Poole, of Abington, had twice advised the General Council of the army that though God "hath a controversie with the great and mighty of the earth," they should have no "respect of persons" and therefore should not execute the king.[28] Many other radicals, Levellers included, also hesitated over the death of the king, but to no avail. An executioner disguised as a sailor decapitated him, and the Cromwellian republic was born in the bloodletting. The execution by firing squad of Robert Lockyer, a soldier, on April 27, originated in the grumblings of unpaid soldiers against what they called the "cutthroat expedition" to Ireland, which escalated into mutiny at Bishopsgate in April. Cromwell, fearing a general rising of "discontented persons, servants, reformadoes [and] beggars," rode to Bishopsgate with Fairfax to lead the suppression of the mutiny, arresting a number of men, finding five guilty, and condemning Lockyer, a leader among the soldiers, to be shot at Saint Paul's. When the moment of execution came, Lockyer disdained a blindfold and appealed to his executioners, brother soldiers, to put down their guns. They refused, fired, and killed him. Thousands, wearing green (the color of the Levellers and of Thomas Rainborough), thronged the streets of London at his funeral.

The executions of the king and the soldier came at a time when a portion of the revolutionary movement had begun to challenge capital punishment. The subject had attracted study by Thomas Browne, who in

1646 had published his thoughts concerning the biomechanics of decapitation, suffocation, crucifixion, and illagneation, and the various theatrical effects produced by each.[29] The critique offered by soldiers and religious radicals made the same connection that had been drawn in the
Putney Debates, between expropriation and slavery. Samuel Chidley, a
Leveller and a minister, once commented that if felons transported to
America were "sold as slaves," then "it is a worse slavery, yea, a great tyranny indeed, to take away their lives" by hanging.[30]

Within a month of the execution of the king, the Council of State received information from Walton-on-Thames concerning Robert Everard, who had come to George's Hill in Surrey "and sowed the ground
with parsnips, carrots, and beans," the signature action of the Diggers.
The gesture was humble, but the Diggers' hopes were not, for they saw
their commune as a solution to the problems of expropriation, imprisonment, hanging, and slavery, not to mention hunger:

> This freedom in planting the common Land, will prevent robbing,
> stealing, and murdering, and Prisons will not so mightily be filled
> with Prisoners; and thereby we shall prevent that hart breaking
> spectacle of seeing so many hanged every Sessions as they are. And
> surely this imprisoning and hanging of men is the Norman power
> still, and cannot stand with the freedom. . . . This freedom in the
> common earth is the poors right by the Law of Creation and equity
> of the Scriptures, for the earth was not made for a few, but for whole
> Mankind, for God is no respecter of Persons.

Later the Diggers asked,

> What need have we of imprisoning, whipping, or hanging Laws, to
> bring one another into bondage? and we know that none of those
> that are subject to this righteous law dares arrest or inslave his
> brother for, or about the objects of the earth, because the earth is
> made by our Creator to be a common Treasury of livelihood to one
> equall with another, without respect of person.

By taking direct action to repossess the land and by building about a
dozen communes, the Diggers delivered themselves from slavery.[31]

To the Council of State, Everard's planting seemed "ridiculous, yet that conflux of people may be a beginning whence things of a greater and more dangerous consequence may grow." Worried, Lord Fairfax interviewed Everard and Winstanley at Whitehall in April. They refused to remove their hats. Everard echoed the prophecy of Sarah and Dinah when he "said he was of the race of the Jews . . . but now the time of deliverance was at hand, and God would bring his people out of this slavery, and restore them to their freedom in enjoying the fruits and benefits of the Earth." Winstanley defended himself in court in language that echoed Rainborough's words at Putney: "I shew by the law of righteousness that the poorest man hath as true a title and just right to the land as the richest man." Fairfax concluded that the alternative example of the Diggers was too dangerous to escape destruction. He personally led a troop of horse to the most important of the communes, George's Hill, and drove the commoners off the land, breaking their spades, trampling the crops, and destroying their houses. Among the first acts of the leaders of the young English republic was thus direct military intervention on behalf of private property. They feared that rural commoners and the city proletariat might join forces in the conflux as they had done in Naples.

Winstanley and the Diggers more broadly believed that the death penalty was logically related to the enclosure movement. Kingly power "hedges the weak out of the Earth, and either starves them, or else forces them through poverty to take from others, and then hangs them for so doing."[32] Given that the poor were forced to work beneath subsistence, "this Law that frights people and forces people to obey it by Prisons, Whips, and Gallows, is the very kingdom of the Devil, and Darknesse, which the Creation groans under at this day." Robert Coster queried "whether the Lords of the mannors, do not hold their Right and Title to the Commons, meerly from the Kings Will . . . and whether the strongest point in their Law for the keeping up their Title, be not, *Take him Jaylor?*" The author of *Tyranipocrit Discovered* advanced similar arguments in 1649, and with Atlantic scope. This abolitionist tract denounced the slavery being developed in America, of both poor people and Indians. The idle rich commanded others to labor, the thieving rich commanded others not to steal, and together they made thieves by Act of Parliament and hanged them. Yet God was no respecter of persons.[33]

Samuel Chidley considered the death penalty an abomination that defiled the land with blood. He petitioned the Lord Mayor in June 1649, announcing that since the penalty is "inhuman, bloody, barbarous, and tyrannical," capital laws "are no rules for me to walk by." He also petitioned the Council of State, warning that "the foundations of the earth are out of course." He visited the Old Bailey, where he "observed that the [inmates] . . . are poor labourers, and such creatures, who stole things of a small value, peradventure, for mere necessity." The magistrates threw him out. He advised Parliament to lay the ax to the root: "Certainly the law cannot be good, that forceth all men to prefer the meanest thing before the greatest, that is, a little wicked mammon with an idolatrous badge upon it, before a man's precious life." In 1652, as lay minister at Christ Church, Newgate, he published *A Cry Against a Crying Sin*, which was printed in red ink. He tried to nail the book to the Tyburn gallows, but the crowd was too dense, so he was "forced to nail it to the tree, which is upon the bank by the gallows," where it was read by many. An anonymous writer joined Chidley in pointing the finger of shame: "For man to inclose all Lands and Creatures from his kind, is utterly unnatural, wicked, and treacherous. . . . Mark this you great Cormudgings, you hang a man for stealing for his wants, when you your selves have stole from your fellow Brethren all Lands, Creatures, &c."[34]

Following the regicide, the Levellers sought to ally with, in turn, the rural poor, the urban proletariat, and finally the soldiers in the army, but the execution of Robert Lockyer indicated the beginning of their end. Cromwell thumped the table and explained to Fairfax, "I tell you sir, you have no other way to deal with these men [the Levellers] but to break them in pieces," for "if you do not break them they will break you." Two weeks later the military power of the Levellers was tested at Burford. Levellers were rounded up and imprisoned, assassinated, executed, and exiled, but their ideas could not be contained. Despite near famine conditions, the London bourgeoisie gloated with a day of feasting. Abiezer Coppe objected in the most powerful single rant of class-war jubilee of the time, called *A Fiery Flying Roll: A Word from the Lord to All the Great Ones*. Levellers "were the cause of many turbulent commotions, which like Hydra's heads, one being lopped, others instantly sprouted up," as was observed as late as 1656.[35] So the killing of Lockyer, while not a martyrdom on the royal scale, helped to assure the survival of the ideas of the Levellers:

Their self-will is their law, stand up now, stand up now,
Their self will is their law, stand up now.
Since tyranny came in they count it now no sin
To make a gaol a gin, to starve poor men therein.
Stand up now, stand up now.

The gentry are all round, stand up now, stand up now,
The gentry are all round, stand up now,
The gentry are all round, on each side they are found,
This wisdom's so profound, to cheat us of our ground.
Stand up now, stand up now.

"The Digger's Song" ended on a Francis note: "Glory here, Diggers all."
Once the antinomian challenge had been defeated, the way was open to
conquer Ireland, to wage war against the Dutch and the Spanish, to stabilize Barbados, to seize Jamaica, and to establish slavery more broadly
than ever by linking West Africa with the Caribbean.

IRELAND, 1649–1651

On March 29, 1649, the day after the Leveller leadership had been
crushed by the arrest of John Lilburne, William Walwyn, and Richard
Overton, Cromwell agreed to take charge of the expedition to conquer
Ireland. Thus commenced "the Via Dolorosa of the Irish," as James Connolly wrote, and, its historical corollary, the beginnings of the "green Atlantic."[36] Once Cromwell's Irish expedition had been announced, opposition to it grew quickly throughout the army in April and May. The
author of *The English Soldiers' Standard* warned that the officers intended
to enslave the soldiers and advised the election of new agitators. The
newsbook *Mercurius Militaris,* published by John Harriss, explained
that "this Irish Design" was meant "to keep this nation in slavery." The
Levellers, for their part, circulated the mildly titled *Certain Queries Propounded to the Consideration of such as were Intended of the Service of Ireland,* which posed questions far from mild: "Whether Julius Caesar,
Alexander the Great, William Duke of Normandie, or anie other the
great Conquerors of the world, were anie other then so manie great and
lawless thievs?" The Levellers knew the Irish expedition was a diversion:

"If they could but get us once over into Ireland (they thinke) they have us sure enough: either we shall have our throats cut, or be famished, for they are sure we can never get back againe over the Great Pond." A Leveller leaflet questioned the right of Englishmen "to deprive a people of the land God and nature has given them and impose laws without their consent." The author wondered whether the Irish were not justified "in all that they have done . . . to preserve and deliver themselves from the usurpations of the English," and declared that it was the duty of every honest man to oppose Cromwell's campaign. While open resistance was quelled, thousands deserted.[37]

Cromwell departed Bristol in July for Dublin. His destination was Drogheda, where massacre was dealt out. Cromwell described his approach: "Every tenth man of the soldiers killed, and the rest shipped off for the Barbadoes."[38] Cromwell estimated that 2,100 were killed; Hugh Peter placed the number at 3,552. Two years later Ireton, the defender of property in the Putney Debates, laid siege to Limerick on the Shannon. "Ireton was content to rest his hopes mainly on famine and on the plague which raged within the walls," writes one historian, but we must add that he had the heavy guns and the gallows with which to enforce the famine. "One old man desired to be hanged instead of his daughter, 'but that,' says Ludlow, 'was refused, and he with the rest driven back to town.' A gibbet was then raised in sight of the walls, upon which condemned criminals were hanged, and this stopped the exodus." Thousands perished during the siege, including Ireton himself, who caught cold and died.[39] According to Gardiner, a new capital-punishment statute for Ireland put eighty thousand at risk of execution. Sir John Davis had argued a generation earlier that Ireland was barbarous precisely because, unlike other, well-governed kingdoms and commonweals, it did *not* have a death penalty.[40]

Cromwell next turned his attention to seizing land, in order to pay the soldiers and the investors in Adventures for Lands in Ireland (including, at two hundred pounds apiece, Thomas and William Rainborough).[41] The Army Council debated whether "to eradicate the Natives" or merely "to divest them of their Estates."[42] A few years later, in 1652, the preamble of the Act for the Settlement of Ireland decided the issue: the landlord system was installed. It was "not the intention of parliament to extirpate that whole nation," for the land could not be cultivated "without the

A "poore Souldier" in the New Model Army in Ireland.
The humble Petition of us the Parliaments poore
Souldiers in the Army of Ireland *(1647)*.

help of the natives." Fixed enclosures replaced open fields, single dispersed farms replaced nucleated settlements or the clachan, commercial tillage and an increase in agricultural labor replaced subsistence strips and environmental egalitarianism. This ruthless transfer of the land of Ireland to an immigrant landlord class was accompanied by a major cadastral mapping enterprise, Sir William Petty's Down survey of the 1650s, which put Ireland "down" on paper.[43] And it brought a wave of "rude persons in the country, [by] whom [the landlords] might expect often to be crossed and opposed," also known as tories, a name that was first officially applied in 1647 to masterless men living a life of brigandage.

The labor of the dispossessed Irish would now be deployed on the estates of English masters, not only in Ireland but across the Atlantic. Cromwell sent thousands of Irish to Jamaica.[44] This was not a wholly new experience, as indicated by Hugh O'Neill on the eve of the defeat at Kinsale in 1601: "We Irishmen are exiled and made bond-slaves and servitors to a strange and foreign prince." A thousand Irish slaves had been sold to Sweden in 1610.[45] Sir William Petty estimated that one sixth of the adult males, some thirty-four thousand men, were shipped out of Ireland and sold abroad in the aftermath of the 1649 conquest. By 1660 there were at least twelve thousand Irish workers in the West Indies, and nine years later, eight thousand in Barbados alone. "Though we must use force in taking them up, . . . it is not in the least doubted that you may have such numbers of them as you see fit," wrote Henry Cromwell in response to a request from Jamaica for a thousand Irish girls and a thousand boys. The poet lamented,[46]

> Tribeless, landless, nameless,
> Wealthless, hostless, fameless
> Wander now thine aimless
> Children to and fro.

In addition to the boys and girls and land, knowledge was taken, too. Robert Boyle received huge masses of Irish lands, the profits from which helped to maintain the Royal Society, which also benefited from the trade secrets that Boyle appropriated from the art and mystery of the Irish craftsman. He was impressed, for example, by "a smith, who with a hammer . . . can out of masses of iron, forge great bars or wedges, and make those strong heavy chains, that were employed to load malefactors, and even to secure streets and gates" in order to protect property in Ireland and to produce more of it overseas.[47]

BARBADOS, 1649

Irishmen were among the conspirators who plotted in 1649 to make themselves freemen and masters of Barbados. The successful cultivation of sugar, brought by the Dutch from Pernambuco, Brazil, to the island in 1640, had intensified the exploitation of plantation workers. Richard Ligon, an eyewitness, believed the conspiracy involved a majority of the servant class, which at the time numbered near ten thousand. He saw the event as a direct response to the cruelty of the masters, which caused the servants to seek freedom or die in the act. They never reached the moment of action, however, as an informer alerted the authorities to their plan. Hundreds were arrested, many tortured, eighteen executed. The leaders were "so haughty in their resolutions, and so incorrigible, as they were like enough to become actors in a second plot." Despite the executions, resistance to slavery continued, including a new plot organized by Africans.[48]

By the late 1640s the masters of Barbados had much wealth to protect from those who had produced it. After visiting the island in August 1645, George Downing wrote, "If you go to Barbados, you shall see a flourishing island, many able men. I believe they have brought this year no less than a thousand Negroes, and the more they buy, the better able they are to buy, for in a year and half, they will earn (with God's blessing) as much as they cost." When Richard Ligon first arrived in Bridgetown, in 1647, he counted twenty-two ships in the harbor, "quick stirring and numerous." The 1651 charter of Barbados noted that the principal source of "wealth of the inhabitants of the island consisteth chiefly in the labour of their servants." Barbados became England's wealthiest colony, and "one of the richest Spots of earth under the Sun."[49]

Barbados was described as "the dunghill whereon England doth cast forth its rubbish. Rogues and whores and such people are those which are generally brought here." True enough: the first cargo of convicts reached Barbados in 1642. An act of 1652 permitted English magistrates summarily to seize vagrants or beggars and ship them to the plantations. A shipload of prostitutes from the jails of London was transported to Barbados as breeders. Besides these, the island was inhabited by all sorts: English, French, Dutch, Scots, Irish, Spanish Jews, Indians, and Africans. Heinrich von Uchteritz, a German mercenary who fought for Charles Stuart, was sold to a plantation that had "one hundred Christians, one hundred Negroes, and one hundred Indians as slaves." The Native Americans were mostly Guianese Arawaks, who came to the island early on as free people but were enslaved by 1636. English servants and African slaves arrived in the first English ships in 1627, and the Irish in the 1630s; two thousand per year came from England in the 1640s, and three thousand in the 1650s. They were sometimes sold according to their weight. Many were veterans of the English Revolution—soldiers, "familists"—who became poor planters, propertyless freemen, and indentured servants. Some of them, in antinomian fashion, denied all ordinances. George Fox visited Barbados in 1671 and preached similar notions to "the *Blacks,* the *Taunies,* and the *Whites.*"[50] The planters moved against religious radicals suspected of involvement in the conspiracy of 1649 by banishing 122 men.

The sugar planters imposed a puritanical work discipline, which to the slave embodied a Satanic principle in both the physics and the economics of accumulation: "The Devel was in the English-man, that he makes every thing work; he makes the *Negro* work, the Horse work, the Ass work, the Wood work, the Water work, and the Winde work."[51] It took four decades to clear the island's xerophilous forest, with its ironwood, rodwood, tom-tom bush, and hoe-stick wood. The final phase of deforestation began in 1650, after which coal had to be imported from England to keep the sugar boiling. The successful cultivation of sugar relied upon a labor process of multiracial gangs in the canefields:

> *trash, windmill, crack bubble o vat in de fac'try*
> *load pun me head, load in de cart, de mill spinnin spinnin spinnin*
> *syrup, liquor, blood o de fields, flood o' the ages.*

The workers of the early plantation system were chattels; their labor was organized and maintained by violence. Floggings and brandings left bodies scarred beyond the imagination, or so thought Father Antoine Biet, who witnessed these punishments in 1654. Orlando Patterson has written that "the distinction, often made, between selling their labor as opposed to selling their persons makes no sense whatsoever in real human terms." The same Devil controlled all.[52]

Resistance included running away, arson, murder, revolt. The Irish, according to Governor Searle in 1657, wandered around as vagabonds, refusing to labor. James Holdip, a planter, watched cane fields worth ten thousand pounds go billowing up in flames in the year of the conspiracy, 1649. In 1634 servants had conspired to kill their masters and make them-

selves free, then to take the first ship that came and go to sea as buccaneers. Their leaders, John and William Weston, had experienced the
antienclosure riots surrounding Bristol in the 1620s and 1630s.[53] Cornelius Bryan, a redheaded Irishman, was flogged, imprisoned for mutiny,
and eventually deported. "As he was eating Meat in a Tray," he said "that
if there was so much English Blood in the Tray as there was Meat, he
would eat it, and demanded more." The cooperation between such red-
shanks and African slaves was a nightmare for the authorities. The Governor's Council announced in 1655 that "there are several Irish Servants
and Negroes out in rebellion in ye Thicketts and thereabouts," making a
mockery of a law passed in 1652, "An Act to Restrain the Wanderings of
Servants and Negroes." The first recorded group of maroons in Barbados
was interracial, as was the cage in the capital, Bridgetown, into which recaptured runaways were thrown. "What planters feared most of all was a
rebellious alliance between slaves and servants," explains the historian of
Barbados, Hilary McD. Beckles. Irish and Africans conspired together
in plots of 1675, 1686, and 1692. The "Black Irish" emerged as a regional
ethnicity in Montserrat and Jamaica.[54]

To stabilize their regime, the rulers of Barbados separated the servants,
slaves, and religious radicals from each other. This they accomplished in
the 1650s and 1660s, with inadvertent help from Oliver Cromwell, mi-
crobes, and the "spirits." In Cromwell's Western Design of 1655, a naval
squadron headed by Venables and Penn stopped off at the island and carried away some four thousand servants and former servants of Barbados
to attack Jamaica and seize it from Spain. Most of them died of yellow
fever. As servants left the island or perished, the big planters replaced
them with African slaves, who by the 1660s were being provided by slave
traders in greater numbers and at lower prices than traders of indentured
servants could offer. The upper class also used informal policy to create
division, instigating criminality and taking comfort as workers quar-
reled among themselves. Morgan Godwyn explained this as the politics
of "Tush, they can shift":

An effect of their scant allowance of Food to their Slaves [is] the
many Robberies and Thefts committed by these starved People
upon the poorer English. Of which, I should affirm their owners to

be the occasion, by thus starving of them, I think I should not hit much either beside, or beyond the Mark. That they are not displeased at it, if dexterously performed, is the general belief and sense of the Sufferers: And this is said to be the true meaning of that customary reply, Tush, they can shift, to the Stewards and Overseers requests for a supplie of the Negro's want of Provision.[55]

In this scenario, starvation produced theft, to which the poor English responded by shooting the thieves dead. The division between servant and slave was codified in the comprehensive slave and servant code of 1661, which became the model for similar codes in Jamaica, South Carolina, Antigua, and St. Christopher. The planters legally and socially differentiated slave from servant, defining the former as absolute private property and offering the latter new protections against violence and exploitation. The effort to recompose the class by giving servants and slaves different material positions within the plantation system continued as planters transformed the remaining servants into a labor elite, as artisans, overseers, and members of the militia, who, bearing arms, would be used to put down slave revolts. The policy of "Tush, they can shift" was institutionalized as a permanent structural characteristic of American plantation society. Once the abolitionism of the English Revolution was defeated, sugar production increased threefold in Barbados.[56]

THE RIVER GAMBIA, 1652

Following the executions of 1649, the Irish invasion, and the defeat of the servant rebellion in Barbados, two of the main rivals of the era, Oliver Cromwell and Prince Rupert, took different paths to same destination, West Africa—one politically, the other actually. Rupert, the opponent of Rainborough at the siege of Bristol in 1643, nephew of the beheaded King Charles I, and cousin of the future King Charles II, took to the seas as a royalist privateer with his brother, Prince Maurice. Cromwell meanwhile pursued an aggressive strategy designed to reduce Dutch might and establish England as the preeminent maritime power of the Atlantic. The two halves of the English ruling class (the "new merchants" and the old aristocrats) met and clashed at the river Gambia, where they created the triangular slave trade. The English were the major slavers in Africa at the end of the seventeenth century, but not at the beginning.[57] In fact, in 1623 one English trader, Richard Jobson, when presented in Gambia with "certaine young blacke women," made answer, "We were a people who did not deale in any such commodities, neither did we buy or sell one another." This would change by 1649.

The drama of the slave trade lies in the way the people of the river were caught between two historic forces, commonism and slavery. Léopold Senghor, the poet of Négritude, says that the "Negro African society . . . had already achieved socialism before the coming of the European."[58] W. E. B. DuBois revered the human warmth of the West African village. Walter Rodney characterized political organization as chieftancies and "ethnicities organized communally." The river Gambia is a major watercourse of Africa, navigable for five hundred miles. Jobson observed that the Mandingo agriculturalists seeded their fields using a series of iron-tipped hoes: "One leading the way, carries up the earth before him, so many others following after him, with their several Irons, doing as he leadeth, as will raise up a sufficient furrow."[59] Rice grown by Jola women in freshwater swamps was the major subsistence crop and would later form the basis for the South Carolina rice culture. The chief estuarial commodity was salt. Canoes traded in fish and the oysters of the mangroves. James Island was fortified in 1651, and rights were negotiated with the Niumi people to hew wood and draw water on the mainland. The Jola people on the southern bank would never recover from the slave trade. Nasir al-Din (d. 1674), a religious revolutionary and Berber cleric, preached naked in the villages to overthrow the dynasties corrupted by the slave trade, which would become a state enterprise by the end of the century.[60]

In the storied year of 1649, British merchants ordered the construction of a trading fort, or factory, on the Gold Coast.[61] At the same time the Guinea Company, first founded in 1618, was scrutinized by the "new merchants" and the Council of State, receiving a new charter in 1651, when ships were dispatched to West Africa. Matthew Backhouse, a representative of the Guinea Company and a triangulator of trade among England, Africa, and the West Indies, sailed to the river Gambia in September 1651 with Captain Blake aboard the *Friendship*. Their purpose was to establish regular trading relations and to obtain fifteen or twenty "young lusty Negers of about 15 yeares age" to carry to Barbados. Backhouse himself traded for twenty-five elephant teeth and African textiles, the esteemed "Mande country cloth" whose staggered bright colors influenced the visual traditions of Brazil, the Caribbean, and the United States.[62] They arrived in Gambia soon after a previous English ship had suffered a mutiny in which the slaves "got weapons in their hands, and fell upon the Saylors, knocking them on the heads, and cutting their throats so fast" that the master, in despair, "went down into the Hold, and blew all up with himself; and this was before they got out of the River." Such events caused the Guinea Company to stock its ships with "shackles and boults for such of your negers as are rebellious and we pray you be veary carefull to keepe them under and let them have their food in due season that they ryse not against you, as they have done in other ships."

After Prince Rupert was defeated by Rainborough at Bristol, he escaped to Kinsale, the Irish port, where he provisioned and manned a small fleet before setting out to roam the Mediterranean and the Atlantic, hoping to keep Barbados royalist. In December 1651 Rupert watered at Arguin, tucked under Cape Blanc, near the waters of the dreadful disaster memorialized in Géricault's *Raft of the Medusa*. Rupert hired a pilot in the Cape Verde Islands, then another in the mouth of the Gambia River, then a third, a *grometta* named Jacus. A creole population of mixed African and Portuguese, beginning in the fifteenth century and known as *lançados*, acted the part of intermediaries. For his part, Jacus served first the Cromwellians and then the royalists.[63] Upriver in a tributary on March 2, Rupert captured two English merchant ships, the *Friendship* and the *Supply*, whose crews were weakened by malaria, before sailing on March 18 for Cape Mastre and the town of Reatch.

Jacus advised a stop. "Some of them stole off in one of their canoes a sailor of Prince Maurice's, a native of that place, who lived long among Christians, and was become one himself; but upon promise of the others that he should return aboard again, he went with them to visit his parents." The muster books of the era reveal scores of absences from any given ship, so this was hardly unusual. Nevertheless, the prince, resolving to capture the sailor by force, sent a hundred men after him, who were dislodged from their boats in the surf. Two gentlemen, Holmes and Hell, were taken hostage. Of Hell we know little, but Holmes helped to form the imperial nation. Here followed a rapid series of events on sea and shore in which nautical power confronted indigenous people ("the beach of dreams, and insane awakenings," wrote Césaire). A canoe paddled out to treat. One of the men was slain. The prince ordered out another hundred musketeers. The natives "sent a considerable party of men into the sea, as high as their necks, to impede our landing who, as soon as they saw us present at them, dived under water to avoid the execution of our shot; and then appearing, gave us a volley of arrows . . . until one of their arrows unfortunately struck his Highness Prince Rupert above the left pap, a great depth into the flesh, who called instantly for a knife, and cut it forth himself."

This was enough, and thanks to Jacus, the others were rescued, rowed quickly back to their ships, and sailed away. Jacus himself remained, declining the offered rewards of Rupert, preferring the intermediating topography, the beach or estuary, between land and sea. Oral historians of the locality, the griot, remember not only Kunta Kinte and the "saga of an American family," for this was the region of *Roots* (1976), but multitudes of sagas of centuries of European violence on the beaches.[64] Why was this African sailor so important to Rupert? Was it his linguistic ability? His knowledge of the region? His skills as a mariner? Or was it his transatlantic knowledge of American slavery, which might prove dangerous to English interests in the region? The tale we tell is not a family saga but one of class forces at the critical meeeting of the sailor of the European deep-sea ship and the boatman of the African canoe. This meeting contained the possibility of cooperative resistance against a common enemy who in this case would bear the scar of it for the rest of his days.

No sooner had Rupert begun to retreat than a mutiny broke out on one of his ships and carried it away. A second mutiny then occurred in the Cape Verde Islands, led by William Coxon. With him were the cooper, the gunner, the boatswain, the master's mate. Such officers spearheaded the 1648 mutiny. Capp quotes a gunner who claimed to be "above ordnances."[65] The ship had 115 men on board—French, Spanish, Dutch, English, and many Africans. Twenty-five of this multilinguistic, multiethnic crew became active mutineers.[66] They changed the name of the ship from *Revenge of Whitehall* (Charles Stuart had been beheaded at Whitehall) to *Marmaduke,* under which name it would sail in 1655 to the Caribbean with Venables and Penn. In 1649 the tenth query to the troops going to Ireland had been "whether those that contend for their freedom (as the English now) shall not make themselves altogether unexcusable, if they shall intrench upon other's freedom; and whether it be not an especial note and characterizing badge of a true pattern of freedom, to indeavor the just freedom of all men as well as his own?"

The encounters on the river Gambia in the year 1652 continued to shape the lives of Prince Rupert and Robert Holmes, who in turn shaped the course of English Atlantic history. Robert Holmes would twice return to Gambia, first in 1661 to seize what would become James Island, the main English fortification on the river, and later, in 1663–64, to attack the Dutch factories. When he sailed by the place where he and Rupert had battled the boatmen years before, he remembered, "At this Portodally [Portudal] if it had not been for God's providence I had been murthered by some of the Blacks of the Country on shore."[67] Building his career at a time when the navy was becoming the formative institution of the nation, Holmes personally precipitated two world wars. James Island in particular and the river Gambia in general became "the main stronghold of the English in the northern part of Africa during all the history of the African Companies." Dryden praised him: "And Holmes, whose name shall live in epic song . . . who first betwitched our eyes with Guinea gold." Dryden praised Rupert, too, as an eagle, a messiah who "shook aloft the fasces of the main." Rupert became the driving force in the rechartering of the Royal African Company in 1660 and again in 1663, after the restoration of Charles II to the throne. This charter laid pompous claim to the entire maritime interface from the Pillars of Hercules to the Cape of Good Hope, "and all the singular Ports, Harbours, Creeks, Islands, lakes, and places in the parts of Africa." The weird speech-act of magical usurpation can be compared with the bat in the baobab tree who poked his head out to tell the first king (or *mansa*) of Niumi, "I do not deny your claim of having found a country, but whatever country you have found, it has an owner."[68]

So the incident of Rupert's breast wound reminds us, first, that the workers in the slave trade participated only under certain conditions—in this case, a sailor's being permitted shore leave to say farewell to his family—and second, that the fastest-growing parts of the proletariat were sailors and African slaves. The sailors were multiracial—Irish, English, African—and a center of this Afro-maritime world was London. Although Backhouse himself was unable to return to London, his cargo did, and it included "one niger boy" at a time when "Black Tom" was becoming a London stereotype. In Westminster Tom introduced himself to an old miser:. "Gwide Maystre, Me non Inglant by mine Phace, none Inglant by mine Twang: Me de grecat strawnger of Aphric, me de pherry phull of Maney." Tom, who had never been out of England in his life and spoke no other language but English, was a trickster who manipulated the Londoners' greed and prejudice against outlanders to turn the situation to his own advantage.[69]

LONDON, 1659–1660

If the Putney Debates of 1647 revealed the English Revolution as an abolitionist movement, a 1659 Parliamentary debate on slavery and the "freeborn Englishman," held on the eve of the restoration of Charles II and the Stuart monarchy, marked a counterrevolutionary reversal. Circumstances had changed since Francis and Rainborough questioned the relationship between slavery and freedom at the peak of revolutionary possibility. Domestic repression of the radicals had made possible new adventures for the English bourgeoisie in Ireland, Barbados, Jamaica, and West Africa. On March 25, 1659, Marcellus Rivers and Oxenbridge Foyle petitioned the House of Commons "on behalf of themselves as of three score and ten freeborn people of this nation now in slavery in the Barbadoes; setting forth most unchristian and barbarous usage of them." The ensuing debate made it clear that a convergence of ideas about slavery, race, and empire among Parliamentarians and royalists, former antagonists in the English Revolution and civil wars, would ease the way to the restoration of the monarchy.[70]

Rivers and Foyle had been arrested for running guns for Charles Stuart and imprisoned in the aftermath of the Salisbury rising of 1654. They protested their treatment as unbecoming "freeborn Englishmen" because they were never given a proper trial and were arbitrarily jailed for a year. They were then snatched from their prisons and hurried to Plymouth, where they were thrown aboard a deep-sea vessel. As the goods and chattels of the merchant and M. P. Martin Noell, they were locked belowdecks with the horses. Rivers and Foyle did not say how many of their fellow white slaves had died, been sewn into canvas coffins, and been thrown over the side of the ship, but if the voyage was typical, the number would have been between eight and fourteen. After several weeks the prisoners arrived in Barbados and were sold to the "most inhuman and barbarous persons, for one thousand five hundred and fifty pound weight of sugar a-piece, more or less, according to their working faculties." The slaves were forced to work, "grinding at the mills and attending at the furnace" or digging in the fields side by side with other slaves from England, Ireland, Scotland, America, and Africa.[71] They lived in pigsties, they ate potatoes and drank potato water, they were whipped, they were bought and sold. Their petition implied that there were human rights against such exploitation.[72]

The petition provoked a heated and disingenuous debate. The M. P.'s knew that the petitioners were little different from the thousands of English men and women who had been spirited away over the previous thirty years. Noell, who had spirited many of them, was forced to admit, "I trade into those parts," but he hastened to defend the planter class in Barbados by saying, falsely, that the work on the sugar plantations was not as hard as represented and, truly, that the island was "as grateful to you for trade as any part of the world." He tried to lessen the impact of the petition by denying the historic importance of indentured servants in building the plantation system and by interjecting racial distinctions: in Barbados, he reassured Parliament, "the work is mostly carried on by the Negroes."[73]

Some in Parliament treated the petition politically, as a royalist issue. But Sir Henry Vane, the millennialist radical who had supported Anne Hutchinson in the Antinomian Controversy in Boston in 1636–37, announced, "I do not look on this business as a Cavalierish business; but as a matter that concerns the liberty of the free-born people of England." Arthur Annesley added, "I am sorry to hear Magna Charta moved against this House. If he be an Englishman, why should he not have the benefit of it?"[74] Several M. P.'s began to define English freedom against

African slavery. Edward Boscawen, who had invested in the successful campaign to capture Jamaica from Spain in 1655, explained that "you have Paul's case before you. A Roman ought not to be beaten." By this he meant that Englishness should be a global citizenship that protected its owners against violence. If Parliament failed to act on the petition, he solemnly explained, "our lives will be as cheap as those negroes." Sir Arthur Hesilrige "could hardly hold weeping" when forced to think of Englishmen working alongside Africans. As the universalist claims of revolution shrank to a narrow, racialist nationalism, a few still clung to broader ideals. Sir John Lenthall worried, "I hope it is not the effect of our war to make merchandize of men." Thomas Gewen complained, "I would not have men sold like bullocks and horses. The selling of a man is an offence of a high nature." Major John Beake summarized the point: "Slavery is slavery, as well in a Commonwealth as under another form."[75]

It was a decisive moment, as explained by Hilary McD. Beckles: "Parliament felt that the Barbadians, and other West Indians, did not really need white labour any more—black slavery was fully established and proven to be very profitable." Meanwhile, military labor in the metropolis was proving itself to be troublesome again. Soon after the debate, the common soldiers of the New Model Army again grew mutinous and again elected agitators to represent them. The specter of Putney began to haunt the propertied; this time, they restored the monarchy.[76] Once back in power, the royalists acted out their conception of the "rights of the free-born Englishman" by organizing repression, including exemplary hangings, against the very people who had developed the discourse in the first place. The New Englander Thomas Venner led Fifth Monarchist workers into battle against the king in 1661, chanting, "King Jesus and the heads upon the gates"—meaning the heads of the executed regicides.[77] Venner himself was caught, hanged, and drawn and quartered, his head stuck up in public. *Hydra decapita.*

The development of the English doctrine of white supremacy thus occurred in the context of counterrevolution, the restoration of the monarchy, and the advance of the slave trade. England's rulers, led and inspired by Rupert and Holmes, began to discuss writing a new charter for the Company of Royal Adventurers into Africa and waging war against the Dutch for control of the West African man-trade.[78] The meaning of the

expression "free-born Englishman" could never thereafter be entirely innocent or hopeful for most of the people of the world. The repression of
the Restoration completed the radical diaspora. Regicides stowed away
for America and Europe; Ranters, Quakers, and Muggletonians disappeared overseas. Edward Burrough, the Quaker, told Charles II, "If you
should destroy these vessels, yet our principles you can never extinguish,
but they will live for ever and enter into other bodies to live and act and
speak."[79] *Hydra redux.*

Virginia, 1663–1676

In September 1663 a group of laborers in Poplar Spring (Gloucester
County), Virginia, met secretly at midnight in a house in the woods.
They plotted to seize arms and a drum, to march from house to house,
appeal to others in bondage, and then demand their freedom from the
governor. Several of the rebels had worn the red shirt of the New Model
Army; some had been Fifth Monarchists, others Muggletonians. At the
Restoration they had been sentenced to servitude and shipped to Virginia. They now aimed to capitalize on widespread labor discontent
within the plantation system, planning to overthrow the governor and
set up an independent commonwealth. An informer betrayed the plot.
Four were hanged, and five transported. The planters determined that
the day of the rising, September 13, should be commemorated as an annual holy day.[80] Revolutionary antinomianism had reared its head in the
tobacco fields.

The early Chesapeake tobacco proletariat consisted of Newgateers,
Quakers, renegades, sailors, soldiers, Nonconformists, servants, and
slaves.[81] In 1662 the House of Burgesses erected whipping posts and
granted masters the legal right to beat their servants. Complaining of the
"audatious unrulines of many stubborne and incorrigible servants resisting their masters and overseers," they promised beatings and extra
service to anyone who laid violent hands on his or her master, mistress,
or overseer. Summarizing the rising tensions on Virginia's eastern shore,
Douglas Deal writes that "physical violence, verbal abuse, work slow-
downs, sabotage, and running away by servants all became much more
common after 1660."[82] As in Barbados, servants and slaves often ran

away together, prompting repressive, deliberately divisive legislation in 1661 and 1662 that made the servant responsible for the time that the slave was away from his master. In 1664 Maryland's rulers passed an act against Englishwomen who were "forgetfull of their free condition and to the disgrace of the Nation doe intermarry with Negro Slaves by which alsoe divers suites may arise touching the Issue of such women and a great damage doth befall the Masters." Virginia's big men worried in 1672 that servants would "fly forth and joyne" with slaves in maroon communities. The House of Burgesses banned the entry of Quakers into the colony, called for the imprisonment of those already there, and forbade their meetings and publications. George Wilson, a former soldier in the New Model Army who in early 1662 was chained to a post with an Indian in a stinking prison in Jamestown, denounced the cruelty and oppression of a "Company of Lazy and Leud people who not Careing to worke feed upon the Swete and Labour" of others. Wilson organized interracial gatherings at which women preached heretical doctrine. The big planters attacked interracial cooperation except where it was necessary for the production of tobacco.[83]

The resistance of plantation workers exploded in 1675–76 in Bacon's Rebellion, which was actually two distinct uprisings. The first, beginning in late 1675, was a war for land by freedmen and small farmers against Indians and a portion of the colonial ruling class in Virginia. The second, beginning in September 1676, was a war against slavery, waged by servants and slaves who entered the fray after being promised their freedom by Nathaniel Bacon in exchange for military service against the forces of the Virginia governor, Berkeley. By late September, the rebel army was "sum'd up in freemen, searvants, and slaves; these three ingredience being the Compossition of Bacon's Army." Many of Bacon's other followers, especially those who were masters, soon deserted him.[84] But if the freeing of servants and slaves cost Bacon support from one quarter, it increased it from another, as poor, rugged fellows flocked to him from all around the colony. *Strange News from Virginia,* published in London in 1677, noted that Bacon's forces consisted of "Runnagado English" along with slaves and servants. The poet Andrew Marvell heard from a ship's captain that Bacon entered Jamestown "having first proclaim'd liberty to all servants and Negroes."[85] This was the language of jubilee.

The abolitionists burned Jamestown and looted the estates of Berkeley's supporters. When Thomas Grantham began to negotiate on behalf of the king the final settlement of the conflict in January 1677, he faced four hundred armed English and African servants and slaves; he promptly tried to divide them by offering a better deal to the servants. Some accepted the deal and went home; others deserted to Roanoke; still others wanted to fight on. Eighty slaves and twenty servants remained in arms, prompting Grantham to make repeated, though treacherous, promises of freedom. After the still-armed rebels boarded longboats to make their escape, he turned a ship's cannon on them, forcing them to surrender and to suffer reenslavement.[86]

Bacon was denounced as a Leveller, and his followers as antinomians. In her play *The Widow Ranter, or a History of Bacon in Virginia* (1690), Aphra Behn suggested the influence of the Ranters upon events in Virginia, seeing revolutionary continuity in the colony's seventeenth-century rebellions. She may have based the character of the Widow Ranter on any of a number of female rebels, including the prostitutes who chose to die alongside the soldiers.[87] Contemporaries saw in Bacon's army the fearful monstrosity theorized a half century earlier by Francis Bacon. Colonel Edward Hill lamented the many "brave, wise, just & inocent good men that have fallen under the lash of that hidra the vulgar," while Governor Berkeley wrote in June 1676 that a "monstrous number of the basest of the People" had declared for Bacon, who himself was another Masaniello. Virginia's rulers executed twenty-three rebels.[88]

The uprising of the plantation workers in 1675–76 shaped the subsequent evolution of the Chesapeake. Immediately after the rebellion ended, the planters charged the governor with restraining "any inhumane severity which by ill masters or overseers may be used toward Christian servants." The self-conscious segmentation of the plantation proletariat became even more evident in legislation of 1682, providing that "all servants not being christians, being imported into this country by shipping" (i.e., Africans) should be slaves for life, while those who came by land (Indians) should be servants for twelve years. European servants continued to serve only four to five years. Virginia's big planters began to substitute African slaves for European indentured servants,[89] a development that changed indentured servitude in the Chesapeake as it had done in Barbados. Fewer indentured servants were imported, and those who were tended to be given skilled supervisory and policing positions. Beginning in the late 1670s legislation was enacted throughout the British American plantation colonies to encourage and protect "Christian"—increasingly "white"—colonists.[90]

By the 1670s antinomians were tolerated by the big planters only if they distanced themselves from the experiences of plantation labor and acted the now important part of the "white" colonist, serving in the militia to defend the colony against rebellious slaves. George Fox soothed Barbadian slaveowners by explaining in 1671 that slave revolt was "a thing we do *abhor* and detest." If the first defeat of antinomianism in the English Revolution had helped to secure the slave trade and accelerate the growth of capitalism, its second defeat, in America, helped to secure the plantation as a foundation of the new system. The Chesapeake's "unruly home spirits" slowly changed their colors, from motley to black, and by 1680 the day of the indentured servant and the antinomian as primary revolutionary forces in the Atlantic had passed. The planters' fear of multiracial rebellion was replaced by fear of the slave revolt, as expressed in two acts aimed at preventing "Negro insurrections," passed in 1680 and 1682. The transition was completed with "An Act Concerning Servants and Slaves" (1705), which guaranteed the rights of servants and defined slaves as a form of property that would constitute the basis of production in Virginia.[91]

The plantation was thus made fast in Virginia and Maryland by the late 1670s, but alternatives remained, one of them especially close at hand. Some who fled slavery recovered the commons in Roanoke, located in the Albemarle Sound. To the dismal swamp flew European and African American slaves (with and without indentures), felons, landless paupers, vagabonds, beggars, pirates, and rebels of all kinds, who beginning in the 1640s lived there under the protection of the Tuscarora Indians. They all fished, hunted, trapped, planted, traded, intermarried, and formed what their main chronicler, Hugo Leaming, has called a Mestizo culture. The members of the community included Nathaniel Batts, who was also known as Secotan, war chief of the Tuscarora Empire and member of the Grand Council of the Tuscaroras; African-Americans Thomas Andover (pilot) and Francis Johnson (coastal wrecker); and John Culpeper, who had left Charleston, South Carolina, because "he was in danger of hanging for laying the design and indeavouring to sett the poore people to plunder the rich." Culpeper had also taken part in Bacon's Rebellion and yet another rising in New England before returning to Roanoke to lead armed mobs of former plantation workers, sailors, "Indians, Negros, and women" against the effort to establish proprietary government in 1677. The people of Roanoke, known for their "enthusiasm," opposition to oaths, anticlericalism, emphasis on the "inner light," and devotion to "liberty of conscience," were antinomian and abolitionist, calling for an end to slavery as early as 1675. The very existence of the multiethnic maroon state was a threat to Virginia, whose governor worried that "hundreds of idle debtors, theeves, Negros, Indians, and English servants will fly" to the liberated zone and use it as a base for attacks on the plantation system. It would take years for the colonial authorities to tame Roanoke and to constitute North Carolina as an official colony, after which the struggle for the commons would shift to the seas, with sailors and pirates the new maroons.[92]

The defeat of the servants and slaves and the recomposition of the plantation proletariat coincided with the origins of scientific racism. The cartographer and physician William Petty weighed the matter in *The Scale of Creatures* (1676): "There seem to be several species even of human beings," he wrote. "I say that the Europeans do not only differ from the aforementioned Africans in colour . . . but also . . . in natural manners and in the internal qualities of their minds." Following Francis Bacon, he was developing a new discourse, an ideological racism different in tone and methods from the racial prejudice of the overseer with a whip or the bully on the deck. The biological excuse for white supremacy would be refined by the English philosophers Locke and Hume and by English biologists, but there was nothing inevitable about its development, for alternative approaches existed even in England. In 1680 Morgan Godwyn, for example, explained the doctrine of Negro inferiority by refusal of work: "Surely *Sloth and Avarice* have been no unhandy Instruments and Assistants to midwife it into the World, and to Foster and Nurse it up." Earlier still, in April 1649, Winstanley wrote, "As divers members of our human bodies make but one body perfect; so every particular man is but a member or branch of mankind," and noted again in August of the same year that the Earth was a common treasury "for whole mankind in all his branches, without respect of persons."[93]

THE COMMONS OR SLAVERY

Gerard Winstanley was the most articulate voice of revolution during the late 1640s. He opposed slavery, dispossession, the destruction of the commons, poverty, wage labor, private property, and the death penalty. He was not the first person to come up with a rational plan for social reconstruction, but he was, as Christopher Hill has noted, the first to express such a plan in the vernacular and to call on a particular social class—the common people—to put it into action.[94] How he came to these beliefs is revealed by his experience at the beginning of the revolutionary decade, when he worked as a cloth merchant and fell victim to fraud. At a time when the cloth industry was collapsing, Winstanley personally lost £274 and was reduced to parochial charity. He thus had a hard-won, bitter knowledge of the "theeving art of buying and selling." R. J. Dalton has argued in a carefully researched article that this fraud was the "single most influential [experience] of Winstanley's life; without it he might never have developed his communist ideology."[95]

The man who defrauded Winstanley was Matthew Backhouse, the same slave-trading merchant who sailed aboard the *Friendship* to the river Gambia in 1651. Backhouse was experienced in the trade, as a decade earlier he had fraudulently gathered an operating capital of roughly seven hundred pounds from Winstanley and others "before embarking on a preplanned voyage to the Guinea coast of west Africa." Cloth, he knew, was in demand in Africa; slaves, he knew, were in demand in Barbados. After the repression of the radicals by Cromwell and the Parliamentarians in early 1649, Backhouse returned to England and renewed his relationship with the reconstituted Guinea Company, signing a five-year contract with the new merchants that led to the voyage of 1651. Backhouse had dispossessed Winstanley in 1641, pushing him toward antinomianism and communism. If Winstanley, like Rainborough at Putney in 1647, expressed a revolutionary vision of a future without slavery, Backhouse, like Ireton, helped to put into practice that vision's counterrevolutionary opposite.

Backhouse had one solution to the crisis of the seventeenth century, Winstanley another. At the beginning of the century, the worry of the ruling class had been overpopulation, hence the plantations, migrations, colonizations, and scarcely veiled suggestions of genocide; by the end of the century, the rulers were fretting about the opposite. Thus, qualitatively new policies for the creation of labor power—the mobilization of sailors, the attention to reproduction in utero, and the African slave trade—emerged as fundamental tasks of the mercantilist state. English rulers, merchants, and planters dispossessed tens of thousands more in Ireland, Barbados, West Africa, and Virginia, making slavery the foundation of Atlantic capitalism.[96] Winstanley's encounter with Backhouse helped him to formulate a new and different answer to the crisis: he took up commoning and became a theorist of the commons, but within an enlarging perspective. Just as English cloth was exported to Africa, where it would be traded for slaves to be shipped to Barbados, Winstanley saw that justice could not be a national project, nor could the commons exist in one country only: "Money must not any longer . . . be the great god that hedges in some, and hedges out others."[97] When in July 1649 he wrote, "The teeth of all nations hath been set on edge by this sour grape, the covetous murdering sword," he had Barbados and Gambia in mind. He moved toward a planetary consciousness of class: "English Christians are in a lower and worser condition than the heathens," he lamented, smarting from the old wound, that English Christians cheated and cozened. "Surely, the life of the heathens shall rise up in judgement against you, from the greatest to the least."[98] His declaration of April 30, 1649, on behalf of the common people was addressed to "the powers of England and to all the powers of the world." Deliverance from oppression would rise "among the poor common people" and "spring up to all nations," and "all the commons and waste ground in England and in the whole world shall be taken in by the people in righteousness."[99]

After being thrown off George's Hill in January 1650, Winstanley summed up, "I have writ, I have acted, I have peace: and now I must wait to see the spirit do his own work in the hearts of others, and whether England shall be the first land, or some other, wherein truth shall sit down in triumph."[100] Despite the defeats inflicted by Winstanley's enemies on London Levellers, Irish soldiers, Barbadian servants, and Virginia slaves, truth *did* sit down in other lands. It sat in swampy tri-isolate communities; it swayed on the decks of deep-sea ships; it rubbed shoulders with the poor in the taverns of the divaricated port cities; it strained for a hearing on the benches of the churches of the Great Awakening, or on stools on the dirt floors of slave cabins at night. In England, it seemed to pause: "Now the Spirit spreading itself from East to West, from North to South in sons and daughters is everlasting, and never dies; but is still everlasting, and rising higher and higher in manifesting himself in and to mankind."[101] This was the everlasting gospel, which would migrate to the western Atlantic before returning in so many words to England with Ottobah Cugoano and William Blake: the struggle against slavery, the struggle for the commons.

CHAPTER FIVE

Hydrarchy: Sailors, Pirates, and the Maritime State

When I was free once more,
I was like Adam when he was first created.
I had nothing at all, and therefore resolved
to join the privateers or buccaneers. . . .
—*A. O. Exquemelin,* The Buccaneers of America *(1678)*

All the ships crews are drawn out,
and the slaves that have deserted
to us from the plantations
are all brave determin'd fellows. . . .
—*John Gay,* Polly: An Opera *(1729)*

RICHARD BRAITHWAITE, who supported Parliament in the English Revolution and lost a son to Algerian pirates, described the seventeenth-century mariner:

He was never acquainted with much civility; the sea hath taught him other rhetoric. . . . He cannot speak low, the sea talks so loud. His advice is seldom taken in naval affairs; though his hand is strong, his headpeace is stupid. . . . Stars cannot be more faithful in their society than these Hans-kins in their fraternity. They will have it valiantly when they are ranked together, and relate their adventures with wonderful terror. Necessary instruments are they, and agents of main importance in that Hydrarchy wherein they live; for the walls of the State could not subsist without them; but least useful they are to themselves, and most needful for others supportance.[1]

Sailors telling tales belowdecks, c. 1810. Charles Napier Robinson,
A Pictorial History of the Sea Services, or Graphic Studies
of the Sailor's Life and Character Afloat and Ashore *(1911).*
Brown Military Collection, John Hay Library, Brown University.

The upper-class Braithwaite condescended to his subject, calling him
loud, stupid, even savage, but he knew him well. He knew that sailors
were essential to English expansion, commerce, and the mercantilist
state. He knew, moreover, that they had ways of their own—their own
language, storytelling, and solidarity.

In this chapter we will employ Braithwaite's term *hydrarchy* to desig-
nate two related developments of the late seventeenth century: the organization of the maritime state from above, and the self-organization of
sailors from below. As the strong hands of Brathwaite's sailors made the
Atlantic a zone for the accumulation of capital, they began to join with
others in faithfulness, or solidarity, producing a maritime radical tradition that also made it a zone of freedom. The ship thus became both an
engine of capitalism in the wake of the bourgeois revolution in England
and a setting of resistance, a place to which and in which the ideas and
practices of revolutionaries defeated and repressed by Cromwell and

then by King Charles escaped, re-formed, circulated, and persisted. The period between the 1670s and the 1730s marked a new phase in the history of Atlantic capitalism, one in which the breakthrough discussed in the previous chapter was consolidated and institutionalized amid new and geographically expanded class struggles. During the pause when revolutionary ideas and action seemed to be missing from or muted in landed society, hydrarchy arose at sea to pose the era's most serious challenge to the development of capitalism.

IMPERIAL HYDRARCHY, OR THE MARITIME STATE

The seizure of land and labor in England, Ireland, Africa, and the Americas laid the military, commercial, and financial foundations for capitalism and imperialism, which could be organized and maintained only through Braithwaite's hydrarchy, the maritime state. A decisive moment in this development was the terrifying discovery by Cromwell and Parliament in 1649 that they had only fifty naval vessels with which to defend their republic against the monarchs of Europe, who did not look happily upon the severed head of Charles I. The new rulers of England urgently (and permanently) mobilized the shipyards at Chatham, Portsmouth, Woolwich, and Deptford to build the necessary ships. They passed "Laws and Ordinances Martial" authorizing impressment and warranting the death penalty for resistance, as a means to provide the necessary labor. By 1651 the New Model Navy had defeated the royalists at sea and begun to menace, even intimidate, the still-hostile other governments of Europe. England's new men took immediate steps to extend their commercial and military power by sea, enacting two linked pieces of legislation: one for the merchant shipping industry, the Navigation Act of 1651, and another for the Royal Navy, the Articles of War of 1652. These two acts, both reaffirmed by the Restoration government after 1660, would dramatically expand the powers of the maritime state.[2]

With these acts Cromwell and Parliament signaled their intention to challenge the Dutch for maritime supremacy and to assert their own sovereignty in the Atlantic. The writers of the first act intended to displace the Dutch as primary carriers of the transatlantic trades by reserving imports for English vessels. In 1660, a new Navigation Act detailed the Atlantic commodities to be shipped by English merchants, sailors, and ships. An additional act, of 1673, established a staff to police colonial trade, enforce the acts, and make sure that the king was getting his proper share of the booty. Parliament emphasized foreign trade as the way to advance English shipping and economic power. In 1629 English merchants shipped only 115,000 tons of cargo; by 1686 that figure had tripled, to 340,000 tons, with a corresponding increase in the number of sailors who handled such immense amounts of cargo. The lucrative Atlantic trades in tobacco, sugar, slaves, and manufactures led English merchant shipping to expand at a rate of 2 to 3 percent a year from roughly 1660 to 1690.[3]

The success of the Navigation Acts depended on accompanying changes in the Royal Navy. The Articles of War of 1652 imposed the death penalty in twenty-five out of thirty-nine clauses and proved an effective means for governing English ships during the war against the Dutch. After the Press Act of 1659 (which renewed the martial law of 1649), the articles were reenacted in 1661 as the Naval Discipline Act, which established the power of courts martial and specified the death penalty for desertion. Meanwhile, Samuel Pepys set about reorganizing the English navy in other respects, professionalizing the officer corps and building more, ever bigger, and ever more powerful ships. During the second Dutch war, some three thousand sailors deserted the English navy to fight for the enemy, which moved English authorities to stage highly visible executions of deserters and to make "flogging round the fleet" a frequent form of discipline. The Articles of War were renewed yet again in 1674, during a third war against the Dutch. The transformation of the Royal Navy during these years can be summarized in terms that parallel almost perfectly the development of the merchant shipping industry: the navy had 50 ships and 9,500 sailors in 1633, and 173 ships and 42,000 sailors in 1688.[4]

If Cromwell inaugurated the maritime state and Charles II realized its promise, finally displacing the Dutch as the hegemonic Atlantic power, it was because of advisers such as Sir William Petty (1623–1687), the father of political economy or, as it was called in his day, political arithmetic. Petty, who wrote the *Political Anatomy of Ireland* for Charles II, had begun his working life as a cabin boy at sea. He was part of England's conquering army in Ireland, serving as physician general in 1652 and cartographer of confiscated lands in the Down survey of 1654 (he took fifty thousand acres for himself in County Kerry, where he organized hewers of wood, fishermen, quarrymen, lead miners, and iron workers.) Such experiences gave him a clear understanding of the primary importance of land, labor, and transatlantic connections. Labor, he believed, was the "father . . . of wealth, as lands are the mother." Labor had to be mobile— and labor policy transatlantic—because lands were far-flung. He advocated shipping felons to plantations overseas: "Why should not insolvent thieves be rather punished with slavery than death? so as being slaves they may be forced to as much labour, and as cheap fare, as nature will endure, and thereby become as two men added to the commonwealth, and not as one taken away from it."[5] He noted the increasing importance of the slave trade to imperial planning: "The accession of Negroes to the American plantations (being all Men of great labour and little expence) is not inconsiderable." He included reproduction in his calculus, projecting that the fertility of women in New England would compensate for losses in Ireland. Based on the assumption that "you value the people who have been destroyed in Ireland as Slaves and Negroes are usually rated, viz., at about £15 one with another; Men being sold for £25 and Children £5 each," he estimated the financial losses of the war in Ireland (1641–51) at £10,355,000.[6] Petty's main point, however, was that ships and sailors were the real basis of English wealth and power. "Husbandmen, Seamen, Soldiers, Artizans, and merchants, are the very Pillars of any Common-Wealth," he wrote, but the seaman was perhaps most important of all, as "every Seaman of industry and ingenuity, is not only a Navigator, but a Merchant, and also a Soldier." He concluded, "The Labour of Seamen, and Freight of Ships, is always of the nature of an Exported Commodity, the overplus whereof above what is Imported, brings home money, etc."[7] Sailors thus produced surplus value above the costs of production, including their own subsistence; the political arithmetician called this process "superlucration." Petty thus originated the labor theory of value by refusing to think of workers in moral terms; he preferred the quantifiable approach of number, weight, and measure. His method of thinking was essential to the genesis and the long-term planning of the maritime state.

Such planning emerged during the quarter century surrounding the three Anglo-Dutch wars (roughly 1651–75), when the shipping industry and the navy took on their modern forms, but it reached a new stage after the accession of William III in 1688 and the declaration of war against France the following year. Just as the theater of merchant shipping had in recent years shifted from the Mediterranean, the Baltic, and the North Sea to the Atlantic—to Africa, the Caribbean, and North America—so the theater of war followed, moving from the northern seas, where the Anglo-Dutch wars had been fought, to the Atlantic, where a broader and more forthright battle for overseas trade and territories would be waged. English rulers fought to protect their plantation economies, and not only against France and Spain. At the request of sugar planters and merchants who now wanted to trade and smuggle goods to New Spain, Sir Robert Holmes commissioned a squadron of ships in 1688 to dispatch the buccaneers who had once been based in Jamaica. The freebooters who had filled Jamaican coffers with Spanish gold were now an obstacle to a more orderly accumulation of capital, which would soon be planned from London and carried out on an Atlantic scale. "It is a sign of the growing importance of the distant colonies and oceanic trades in the estimation of all Europe," wrote J. H. Parry, "that the age of the buccaneers should be followed by the age of the admirals."[8]

The consolidation of the maritime state took place in the 1690s, by which time the Royal Navy had become England's greatest employer of labor, its greatest consumer of material, and its greatest industrial enterprise. English rulers had discovered the navy as an instrument of national policy during the 1650s, in the defense of the republic, and had expanded its function as protector of shipping and overseas markets. A pamphleteer of 1689 echoed the Articles of War and the Naval Discipline Act of 1661 in writing that the navy was "the bulwark of our British dominions, the sole fence of our Country."[9] Here were Brathwaite's "walls of the State," an enclosure built around a new field of property whose value and appreciation were expressed in a congeries of changes in the 1690s: the concentration of maritime capital in joint stock companies, which grew from eleven in 1688 to more than a hundred by 1695; the formation of the Bank of England in 1694; the growth of the marine insurance industry; the beginnings of the deregulation of the Royal African Company (1698) and the emergence of the free traders who would in the next century make England the world's greatest transporter of slaves; the increasing use of commercial newspapers; the booming importance of manufacture and the related export and reexport trades. The Act of Trade of 1696 brought all colonial affairs under the purview of the Board of Trade and generalized the admiralty court system throughout the empire. The Act of Trade consolidated the gains of the new Atlantic capitalism, but it also pointed to a threat that had not been eliminated by Holmes and the navy of 1688. One of the biggest and most worrying issues facing Parliament and the Board of Trade remained pirates: accordingly, Parliament passed an "Act for the More Effectual Suppression of Piracy" in 1698, hoping to convince colonial administrators and citizens of the necessity of the death penalty for a crime that had long been tolerated and sometimes even encouraged.[10]

THE SHIP

By the last half of the seventeenth century, capitalists had organized the exploitation of human labor in four basic ways. The first of these was the big commercial estate for the practice of capitalist agriculture, whose American equivalent was the plantation, in many senses the most important mercantilist achievement. Second was petty production such as the yeoman farmer or prosperous artisan enjoyed. Third was the putting-out system, which had, in Europe, begun to evolve into the system of manufactures. In Africa and the Americas, European merchants put out firearms, which were used by their clients to capture people (to sell as slaves), to kill animals (for their furs), and to destroy a wealth of common ecologies. The fourth means of organizing the exploitation of labor was the mode of production that united all of the others in the sphere of circulation—namely, the ship.

Each way organized human labor differently. The large-scale estate and plantation were among the first sites in modern history of mass cooperation. Petty production remained the context for resourcefulness and independent individualism. Manufacture and the putting-out system created the fragmented, detail laborer whose "idleness" would become the bane of the eighteenth-century political economist. The ship, whose milieu of action made it both universal and sui generis, provided a setting in which large numbers of workers cooperated on complex and synchronized tasks, under slavish, hierarchical discipline in which human will was subordinated to mechanical equipment, all for a money wage. The work, cooperation, and discipline of the ship made it a prototype of the factory.[11] Indeed, the very term *factory* evolved etymologically from *factor,* "a trading representative," and specifically one associated with West Africa, where factories were originally located. One trading syndicate off the Gold Coast in the 1730s would anchor a ship permanently to serve as a base for stocks, intelligence gathering, and cargoes; it was called a floating factory. By 1700 the ship had become the engine of commerce, the machine of empire. According to Edward Ward, who wrote in defense of the maritime state, it was "the Sovereign of the Aquatic Globe, giving despotic laws to all the meaner Fry, that live upon that Shining Empire." For Barnaby Slush, a defender of the skilled sailor, it was, however, "too big and unmanageable a machine to be run by novices." Sailors and the ship thus linked the modes of production and expanded the international capitalist economy.[12]

Despite the nationalism of the Navigation Acts and the Naval Discipline Act, and despite the bold declarations that English ships must be sailed by English seamen, it was nonetheless true that many of the ships were actually Dutch (having been seized in the wars) and that many of the seamen were not English. The expansion of the merchant shipping industry and the Royal Navy during the third quarter of the seventeenth century posed an enduring dilemma for the maritime state: how to mobilize, organize, maintain, and reproduce the sailoring proletariat in a situation of labor scarcity and limited state resources. Rulers discovered time and again that they had too few sailors to operate their various maritime enterprises, and too little money with which to pay wages.

One result of this situation was a fitful but protracted war among rulers, planners, merchants, captains, naval officers, sailors, and other, urban workers over the value and purposes of maritime labor. Since conditions aboard ship were harsh and wages often two or three years in arrears, sailors mutinied, deserted, rioted, and altogether resisted naval service. Over and against these chronic struggles for freedom and money, the state used violence and terror to man its ships and to man them cheaply, preying often on the poorest, most ethnically diverse populations. The press-gang, which swaggered to brutal prominence during the 1660s, swung bigger sticks in the 1690s as the demand for maritime labor continued to swell.[13] For sailors, the press-gang represented slavery and death: three out of four pressed men died within two years, with only one in five of the dead expiring in battle. Those lucky enough to survive could not expect to be paid, as it was not uncommon, writes John Ehrman, the preeminent scholar of the navy of the 1690s, for a seaman to be owed a decade's wages. The figure of the starving, often lame sailor in the seaport town became a permanent feature of European civilization, even as the motley crew became a permanent feature of modern navies.[14]

The dynamic of manning was different in merchant shipping, but the outcome was similar. As the conditions of seafaring life ebbed and flowed, as hard discipline, deadly disease, and chronic desertion thinned the ranks of the ship, the captain would take on sailors wherever he could find them. The ship became, if not the breeding ground of rebels, at least a meeting place where various traditions were jammed together in a forcing house of internationalism. Even though the Navigation Act of 1651 stipulated that three fourths of the crew importing English goods were to be English or Irish under penalty of loss of ship, tackle, and lading, English ships continued to be worked by African, Briton, quashee, Irish, and American (not to mention Dutch, Portuguese, and lascar) sailors. Ruskin was therefore correct in saying, "The nails that fasten together the planks of the boat's bow are the rivets of the fellowship of the world." Ned Coxere, who went to sea in 1648 and "served several masters in the wars between King and Parliament at sea," wrote, "Next I served the Spaniards against the French, then the Hollanders against the English; then I was taken by the English out of Dunkirker; and then I served the English against the Hollanders; and last I was taken by the Turks, where I was forced to serve then against English, French, Dutch, and Spaniards, and all Christendom." Alexander Exquemelin remarked on the mingling of cultures among the buccaneers in the late seventeenth century. William Petty also understood the international reality of the lower deck: "Whereas the Employment of other Men is confined to their own Country, that of Seamen is free to the whole world." During the 1690s, English sailors served under all colors, for, according to John Ehrman, "the interchange of seamen between the different maritime countries was too widespread and deep-rooted a custom" to eliminate.[15]

The ship was thus not only the means of communication between continents, but also the first place where working people from those different continents communicated. All the contradictions of social antagonism were concentrated in its timbers. Imperialism was the main one: the sun of European imperialism always cast an African shadow. Christopher Columbus had not only a black cabin boy but an African pilot, Pedro Niño. As soon as the *Mayflower* discharged the pilgrims, it sailed for the West Indies with a cargo of people from Africa.[16] Forced by the magnitude of its own enterprise to bring huge and heterogeneous masses of men and women together aboard ship to face a deathly voyage to a cruel destination, European imperialism also created the conditions for the circulation of experience within the huge masses of labor that it had set in motion.

The circulation of experience depended in part on the fashioning of new languages. In 1689, the same year that the two factions of the English ruling class under the constitutional tutelage of John Locke learned to speak a common language, Richard Simson wrote of his experiences in the South Seas, "The means used by those who trade to Guinea, to keep the Negroes quiet, is to choose them from several parts of ye Country, of different Languages; so that they find they cannot act joyntly, when they are not in a Capacity of Consulting with one another, and this they cannot doe, in soe farr as they understand not one another." In *The London Spy* (1697), Ned Ward described in sporting vocabulary the Wapping "salt water vagabonds" who were never at ease except at sea, and always wandering at home. To communicate, they had to develop a language of their own, which was, Ward asserted later, in *The Wooden World Dissected* (1708), "all Heathen Greek to a Cobbler." A student of seventeenth-century ships' logs has shown in sixty densely worded pages how very different was maritime phonetics from that of the landsman. Mariners spoke a "dialect and manner peculiar to themselves," said a writer in the *Critical Review* (1757).[17]

What W. E. B. DuBois described as the "most magnificent drama of the last thousand years of human history"—the Atlantic slave trade—was not enacted with its strophes and prosody ready-made. A combination

Slaves below deck, *by Lieutenant Francis Meynall, 1830.*
© *National Maritime Museum, London.*

of, first, nautical English; second, the "sabir" of the Mediterranean; third, the hermeticlike cant talk of the "underworld"; and fourth, West African grammatical construction, produced the pidgin English that became in the tumultuous years of the slave trade the essential language of the Atlantic. According to one modern philologist, "No other form of speech in the history of the English language has been so deplored, debated, and defended." The word *crew,* for example, originally meant any augmentation of a band of armed men, but by the end of the seventeenth century it had come to signify a supervised squad of workmen bent to a particular purpose, as the cooper's, gunner's, or sailmaker's crew, or even the ship's entire company—that is, all of the men of the vessel. B. Traven placed the emphasis on the collectivity, the crew, in contrast to William Dampier, Daniel Defoe, and Samuel Taylor Coleridge, for whom the sailor was an individualist. Traven asserted that "living together and working together each sailor picks up the words of his companions, until, after two months or so, all men aboard have acquired a working knowledge of about three hundred words common to all the crew and understood by all." He concluded, "A sailor is never lost where language is concerned": no matter what coast he was thrown on, he found a way to ask, "When do we eat?"[18]

Linguists describe pidgin as a "go-between" language, the product of a "multiple-language situation," characterized by radical simplification. It was a dialect whose expressive power arose less from its lexical range than from the musical qualities of stress and pitch. Some African contributions to maritime and thence standard English include *caboodle,* "kick the bucket," and "Davy Jones's locker." Where people had to understand each other, pidgin English was the lingua franca of the sea and the frontier. By the mid-eighteenth century, pidgin-speaking communities existed in Philadelphia, New York, and Halifax, as well as in Kingston, Bridgetown, Calabar, and London, all of them sharing unifying syntactic structures.[19] Pidgin became an instrument, like the drum or the fiddle, of communication among the oppressed: scorned and not easily understood by polite society, it nonetheless ran as a strong, resilient, creative, and inspirational current among seaport proletarians almost everywhere. Krio, itself a lingua franca of the West African coast, was spoken in many places, as were Cameroons pidgin, Jamaican creole, Gullah, and Sranan (Suriname). The multilinguality and Atlantic experience common to many Africans were demonstrated by a black man in the Comoros Islands of the Indian Ocean in 1694, who greeted pirate captain Henry Avery, the "maritime Robin Hood," in English. The man, as it happened, had lived in Bethnal Green, London.[20]

THE SAILORS' HYDRARCHY

As thousands of sailors were organized for collective cooperative work in the merchant shipping industry, in the Royal Navy, and in wartime privateering, the motley crew began, through its work and new languages, to cooperate on its own behalf, which meant that within imperial hydrarchy grew a different hydrarchy, one that was both proletarian and oppositional. The process was slow, uneven, and hard to trace, not least because the alternative order of the common sailor was decapitated almost every time it reared its head, whether in mutiny, in strike, or in piracy. It took a long time for mariners to get, as one man put it, "the choice in them-

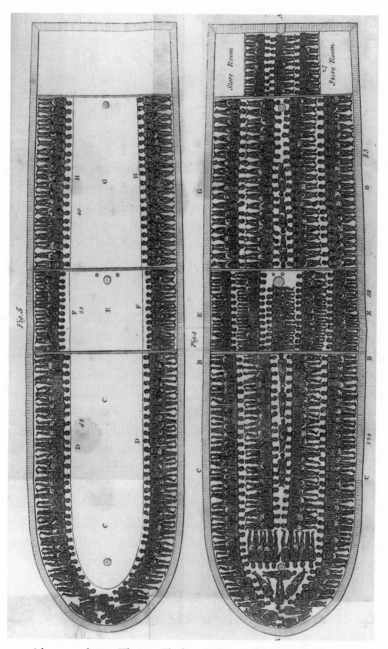

A language lesson. Thomas Clarkson, History of the Rise, Progress,
& Accomplishment of the Abolition of the African Slave Trade
by the British Parliament *(1808).*

selves"—that is, the autonomous power to organize the ship and its min-iature society as they wanted. The sailor's hydrarchy went through several stages, appearing most clearly—and, to the authorities, most threaten-ingly—when sailors organized themselves as pirates in the early eigh-teenth century.[21]

Piracy itself passed through a number of historical stages before com-mon working sailors could make it a vessel of their own. Atlantic piracy had long served the needs of the maritime state and the merchant com-munity in England. But there was a long-term tendency for the control of piracy to devolve from the top of society to the bottom, from the high-est functionaries of the state (in the late sixteenth century), to big mer-chants (in the early to middle seventeenth century), to smaller, usually colonial merchants (in the late seventeenth century), and finally to the common men of the deep (in the early eighteenth century). When this devolution reached bottom, when seamen—as pirates—organized a so-cial world apart from the dictates of mercantile and imperial authority and used it to attack merchants' property (as they had begun to do in the 1690s), then those who controlled the maritime state resorted to massive violence, both military (the navy) and penal (the gallows), to eradicate piracy. A campaign of terror would be employed to destroy hydrarchy, which was thus forced belowdecks and into an existence that would prove both fugitive and durable.[22]

The mass resistance of sailors began in the 1620s, when they mutinied and rioted over pay and conditions; it reached a new stage when they led the urban mobs of London that inaugurated the revolutionary crisis of 1640–41. In 1648 sailors aboard six vessels of the fleet mutinied in the name of the king; some would later mutiny against the king's command-ers, such as Prince Rupert. The immediate remaking of the fleet along re-publican lines brought religious radicals into the navy, though never as many as served in the army. The Cromwellian regime bought the sup-port of many sailors by promising prize money and by creating, in 1652, a new occupational category, the "able seaman," who made twenty-four shillings a month rather than the usual nineteen. Yet problems remained for the sailor, including the "turnover" (which sent a man from one vessel to another before he was paid), arrears and inflated tickets rather than money payment, and impressment, the response to which was a series of riots and mutinies in 1653 and 1654. The "Humble Petition of the Sea-men, belonging to the Ships of the Commonwealth of England," dated November 4, 1654, complained of disease, poor provisions, bloodshed, wage arrears, and most of all the "thraldom and bondage" of impress-ment, which were "inconsistent with the Principles of Freedom and Liberty."[23]

The sailors' struggles registered in the published radical discourse of the 1640s and 1650s, especially in pamphlets written by the Levellers. Richard Overton denounced impressment in 1646, decrying the need "to surprize a man on the sudden, force him from his Calling . . . from his dear Parents, Wife and Children . . . to fight for a Cause he understands not, and In Company of such as he hath no comfort to be withall; and if he live, to returne to a lost trade, or beggary." In the first *Agreement of the People,* the Levellers stated plainly, "The matter of impresting and con-straining any of us to serve in the warres, is against our freedome." In *A New Engagement, or, Manifesto* of August 1648 they expressly denied Par-liament the power to conscript men for fighting on land or sea. There was "nothing more opposite to freedom," they explained in a petition to Par-liament of September 1648. They opposed impressment again in the sec-ond *Agreement of the People,* issued ten days before the king was be-headed. The following month Parliament approved impressment, and the Levellers again denounced it, in *New Chains Discovered* (1649). Fi-nally, on May Day, 1649, even though the tide had turned against them, the Levellers wrote in the third *Agreement of the People,* "We doe not im-power them to impresse or constraint any person to serve in war by Sea or Land every man's Conscience being to be satisfied in the justness of that cause wherein he hazards his life, or may destroy an others." This would be a fundamental idea in the lower deck's oppositional tradition, even after the experience of defeat and the diaspora of thousands, sailors included, to the Americas.[24]

The struggles waged by sailors of the revolutionary era for subsistence, wages, and rights and against impressment and violent discipline first took autonomous shape among the buccaneers in America. Even as buc-caneering benefited the upper classes of England, France, and the Neth-erlands in their New World campaigns against their common enemy, Spain, common seamen were building a tradition of their own, at that time called the Jamaica Discipline or the Law of the Privateers. The tradition, which the authorities considered to be the antithesis of discipline and law, boasted a distinctive conception of justice and a class hostility toward shipmasters, owners, and gentlemen adventurers. It also featured democratic controls on authority and provision for the injured.[25] In fashioning their hydrarchy, the buccaneers drew upon the peasant utopia called the Land of Cockaygne, where work had been abolished, property redistributed, social distinctions leveled, health restored, and food made abundant. They also drew on international maritime custom, by which ancient and medieval seafarers had divided their money and goods into shares, consulted collectively and democratically on matters of moment, and elected consuls to adjudicate differences between captain and crew.[26]

The early shapers of the tradition were those whom one English official in the Caribbean called the "outcasts of all nations"—the convicts, prostitutes, debtors, vagabonds, escaped slaves and indentured servants, religious radicals, and political prisoners, all of whom had migrated or been exiled to the new settlements "beyond the line." Another royal administrator explained that the buccaneers were former servants and "all men of unfortunate and desperate condition." Many French buccaneers, such as Alexander Exquemelin, had been indentured servants and before that textile workers and day laborers. Most of the buccaneers were English or French, but Dutch, Irish, Scottish, Scandinavian, Native American, and African men also joined up, often after they had in one way or another escaped the brutalities of the Caribbean's nascent plantation system.

These workers drifted to uninhabited islands, where they formed maroon communities. Their autonomous settlements were multiracial in nature and organized around hunting and gathering—usually the hunting of wild cattle and pigs and the gathering of the king of Spain's gold. These communities combined the experiences of peasant rebels, demobilized soldiers, dispossessed smallholders, unemployed workers, and others from several nations and cultures, including the Carib, Cuna, and Mosquito Indians.[27] One of the most potent memories and experiences underlying buccaneer culture, writes Christopher Hill, was the English Revolution: "A surprising number of English radicals emigrated to the

West Indies either just before or just after 1660," including Ranters, Quakers, Familists, Anabaptists, radical soldiers, and others who "carried with them the ideas which had originated in revolutionary England." A number of buccaneers, we know, hunted and gathered dressed in the "faded red coats of the New Model Army." One of these was a "stout grey-headed" and "merry hearted old Man," aged eighty-four, "who had served under Oliver in the time of the Irish Rebellion; after which he was at Jamaica, and had followed Privateering ever since." In the New World, such veterans insisted upon the democratic election of their officers, just as they had done in the revolutionary army on the other side of the Atlantic. Another source of buccaneering culture, according to J. S. Bromley, was the wave of peasant revolts that shook France in the 1630s. Many French freebooters came, as *engagés*, "from areas affected by peasant risings against the royal *fisc* and the proliferation of crown agents." Protesters "had shown a capacity for self-organization, the constitution of 'communes,' election of deputies and promulgation of *Ordonnances*," all in the name of the "*Commun peuple*."[28] Such experiences, once carried to the Americas, informed the life ways of the buccaneering "Brethren of the Coast."

The early experiences were passed on to later generations of sailors and pirates by the hearty souls who survived the odds against longevity in seafaring work. When one privateering captain took on board four seasoned buccaneers in 1689, he designated them "to be a mess by themselves, but the advantage of their conversation and intelligence obliged him afterward to disperse them amongst the Shipps Company." Some of the old-timers had served on Jamaican privateers during the War of Spanish Succession, then taken part in the new piracies after the Treaty of Utrecht. The Jamaica Discipline and the exploits that it made possible also lived on in folktales, songs, ballads, and popular memory, not to mention the widely published (and frequently translated) accounts of Alexander Exquemelin, Père Labat, and others who knew life among the buccaneers firsthand.[29]

Therefore when sailors encountered the deadly conditions of life at sea in the late seventeenth and early eighteenth centuries, they had an alternative social order within living memory. Some sailors mutinied and seized control of their own vessels, stitching the skull and crossbones onto a black flag and declaring war against the world. The overwhelming majority of those who became pirates, however, volunteered to join the outlaw ships when their vessels were captured. Their reasons are not difficult to fathom. Dr. Samuel Johnson put the matter succinctly when he said, "No man will be a sailor who has contrivance enough to get himself into a jail; for being in a ship is being in jail with the chance of being drowned. . . . A man in jail has more room, better food, and commonly better company." Many sailors, of course, had made the comparison themselves, waking up punch-drunk or just plain drunk in the jails of the port cities or in the holds of outward-bound merchant ships. Johnson's point, though, was that the lot of the merchant seamen was a difficult one. Sailors suffered cramped, claustrophobic quarters and "food" that was often as rotten as it was meager. They routinely experienced devastating disease, disabling accidents, shipwreck, and premature death. They faced discipline from their officers that was brutal and often murderous. And they got but small return for their death-defying labors, for peacetime wages were low and fraud in payment was frequent. Seamen could expect little relief from the law, for its main purpose was "to assure a ready supply of cheap, docile labor."[30]

Merchant seamen also had to contend with the impressment unleashed by the expansion of the Royal Navy. In the navy, shipboard conditions were as harsh as, and in certain respects even worse than, the mercantile equivalents. Wages, especially during wartime, were lower than in the merchant service, while the quantity and quality of food aboard ship were consistently undermined by corrupt pursers and officers. Organizing cooperation and maintaining order among the often huge numbers of maritime workers on naval vessels required violent discipline, replete with carefully staged, spectacular executions, more severe than those on merchant ships. Another consequence of the number of sailors crowded onto ill-ventilated naval ships was the omnipresence of disease, often of epidemic proportions. In an irony that the pirates themselves would have savored, one official claimed that the navy could not effectively suppress piracy because its ships were "so much disabled by sickness, death, and desertion of their seamen." The knowledgeable anonymous author of a pamphlet entitled *Piracy Destroy'd* (1700) made it clear that impressment, harsh discipline, poor provisions and health,

The Sailor's Return, or Valour Rewarded, 1783.
By permission of the British Library.

long confinement aboard ship, and wage arrears had caused thousands of sailors to turn pirate. It was "the too great severity Commanders have used as to their backs and their bellies" that "had occasioned the Seamen to mutiny and run away with the Ships." The naval ship in this era, concludes one scholar, was "a machine from which there was no escape, bar desertion, incapacitation, or death."[31]

Life was a little better on a privateering vessel: the food was more palatable, the pay was higher, the work shifts were shorter, and the power of the crew in decision-making was greater. But privateers were not always happy ships. Some captains ran their vessels like naval craft, imposing rigid discipline and other unpopular measures that generated grievances, protests, or even outright mutinies. Woodes Rogers, the gentleman captain of a hugely successful privateering voyage between 1708 and 1711 and later the scourge of the pirates of the West Indies as royal governor of the Bahama Islands, clapped into irons a man named Peter Clark, who had wished himself "aboard a Pirate" and said that "he should be glad that an Enemy, who could over-power us, was a-long-side of us."[32] What would men such as Peter Clark do once they got off a merchant, naval, or privateering vessel and "aboard a Pirate"? How would they secure their own subsistence? How would they organize their own labor, their access to money, to power? Had they internalized the dominant ideas of the age about how to run a ship, or could these poor, uneducated men imagine better?

THE MARITIME WORLD TURNED UPSIDE DOWN

The early-eighteenth-century pirate ship was a "world turned upside down," made so by the articles of agreement that established the rules and customs of the pirates' social order, hydrarchy from below. Pirates distributed justice, elected officers, divided loot equally, and established a different discipline. They limited the authority of the captain, resisted many of the practices of the capitalist merchant shipping industry, and maintained a multicultural, multiracial, multinational social order. They sought to prove that ships did not have to be run in the brutal and oppressive ways of the merchant service and the Royal Navy. The dramatist John Gay demonstrated his understanding of all this when, in *Polly,* he had Macheath disguise himself as the black pirate named Morano and sing a song to the tune of "The World's Turned Upside Down."[33]

The pirate ship was democratic in an undemocratic age. The pirates allowed their captain unquestioned authority in chase and battle, but otherwise insisted that he be "governed by a Majority." As one observer noted, "They permit him to be Captain, on Condition, that they may be Captain over him." They gave him none of the extra food, the private mess, or the special accommodations routinely claimed by merchant and naval captains. Moreover, as the majority gave, so did it take away, deposing captains for cowardice, for cruelty, for refusing "to take and plunder English Vessels," or even for being "too Gentleman-like." Captains who dared to exceed their authority were sometimes executed. Most pirates, "having suffered formerly from the ill-treatment of their officers, provided carefully against any such evil" once they were free to organize the ship after their own hearts. Further limitations on the captain's power were embodied in the person of the quartermaster, who was elected to represent and protect the interests of the crew, and in the institution of the council, the gathering that involved every man on the ship and always constituted its highest authority.[34]

The pirate ship was egalitarian in a hierarchical age, as pirates divided their plunder equally, levelling the elaborate structure of pay ranks common to all other maritime employments. Captain and quartermaster received one and one half to two shares of plunder; minor officers and craftsmen were given one and one quarter or one and one half; all others got one share each. Such egalitarianism flowed from material facts. To merchant captains it was galling that "there is so little Government and Subordination among [pirates], that they are, on Occasion, all Captains, all Leaders." By expropriating a merchant ship (after a mutiny or a capture), pirates seized the means of maritime production and declared it to be the common property of those who did its work. Rather than working for wages using the tools and larger machine (the ship) owned by a merchant capitalist, pirates abolished the wage and commanded the ship as their own property, sharing equally in the risks of common adventure.[35]

Pirates were class-conscious and justice-seeking, taking revenge against merchant captains who tyrannized the common seaman and against royal officials who upheld their prerogative to do so. Indeed, the "Distribution of Justice" was a specific practice among pirates. After capturing a prize vessel, pirates would "distribute justice" by inquiring about how the ship's commander treated his crew. They then "whipp'd and pickled" those "against whom Complaint was made." Bartholomew Roberts's crew considered the matter so important that they formally designated one of their men—George Willson, who was no doubt a fierce and lusty man—the "Dispencer of Justice." Pirates roughed up and occasionally executed captured captains; a few bragged of their avenging justice upon the gallows. Pirate captain Howell Davis claimed that "their reasons for going a pirating were to revenge themselves on base Merchants and cruel commanders of Ships." Still, pirates did not punish captains indiscriminately. They often rewarded the "honest Fellow that never abused any Sailors" and even offered to let one decent captain "return with a large sum of Money to London, and bid the Merchants defiance." Pirates thus stood against the brutal injustices of the merchant shipping industry, with one crew's even claiming to be "Robbin Hoods Men."[36]

Pirates insisted upon their right to subsistence, the food and drink so often denied aboard the merchant or naval ship—the very shortage that led many sailors to go "upon the account" in the first place. One mutinous sailor aboard the *George Galley* in 1724 responded to his captain's orders to furl the mizzen-top by saying, "in a surly Tone, and with a kind of Disdain, So as we Eat so shall we work." Other mutineers simply maintained that "it was not their business to starve," and that if a captain was making it so, hanging could be little worse. Many observers of pirate life noted the carnivalesque quality of its occasions—the eating, drinking, fiddling, dancing, and merriment—and some considered such "infinite Disorders" inimical to good discipline at sea.[37] Men who had suffered short or rotten provisions in other maritime employments now ate and drank "in a wanton and riotous Way," which was indeed their custom. They conducted so much business "over a Large Bowl of Punch" that sobriety sometimes brought "a Man under a Suspicion of being in a Plot against the Commonwealth"—that is, the community of the ship. The very first item in Bartholomew Roberts's articles guaranteed every man "a Vote in Affairs of Moment" and equal title to fresh provisions and strong liquor. For some who joined, drink "had been a greater motive . . . than Gold," and most would have agreed with the motto "No Adventures to be made without Belly-Timber." The pirates of the Atlantic thus struggled to assure their health and security, their own self-preservation. The image of the freebooter as a man with a patched eye, a peg leg, and a hook for a hand suggests an essential truth: sailoring was a dangerous line of work. Pirates therefore put a portion of all booty into a common fund reserved for those who sustained injuries of lasting effect, whether the loss of eyesight or of any appendage. They tried to provide for the needy.[38]

The pirate ship was motley—multinational, multicultural, and multiracial. Governor Nicholas Lawes of Jamaica echoed the thoughts of royal officials everywhere when he called pirates a "banditti of all nations." Another Caribbean official agreed: they were "compounded of all nations." Black Sam Bellamy's crew of 1717 was "a mix't multitude of all Country's," including British, French, Dutch, Spanish, Swedish, Native

American, and African American, along with two dozen Africans liberated from a slave ship. The main mutineers aboard the *George Galley* in 1724 were an Englishman, a Welshman, an Irishman, two Scots, two Swedes, and a Dane, all of whom became pirates. Benjamin Evans's crew consisted of men of English, French, Irish, Spanish, and African descent. Pirate James Barrow illustrated the reality of this internationalism as he sat after supper "prophanely singing . . . Spanish and French Songs out of a Dutch prayer book." The government often told pirates that "they [had] no country," and the pirates themselves agreed: when they hailed other vessels at sea, they emphasized their own rejection of nationality by announcing that they came "From the Seas." A colonial official reported to the Council of Trade and Plantations in 1697 that pirates "acknowledged no countrymen, that they had sold their country and were sure to be hanged if taken, and that they would take no quarter, but do all the mischief they could." But as a mutineer muttered in 1699, "it signified nothing what part of the World a man liv'd in, so he Liv'd well."[39]

Hundreds of people of African descent found places within the social order of the pirate ship. Even though a substantial minority of pirates had worked in the slave trade and had therefore been part of the machinery of enslavement and transportation, and even though pirate ships occasionally captured (and sold) cargo that included slaves, Africans and African Americans both free and enslaved were numerous and active on board pirate vessels. A few of these maritime men of color ended up "dancing to the four winds," like the mulatto who sailed with Black Bart Roberts and was hanged for it in Virginia in 1720. Another "resolute Fellow, a Negroe" named Caesar, stood ready to blow up Blackbeard's ship rather than submit to the Royal Navy in 1718; he, too, was hanged. Black crewmen also made up part of the pirate vanguard, the most trusted and fearsome men who were designated to board prospective prizes. The boarding party of the *Morning Star,* for example, had "a Negro Cook doubly arm'd," while more than half of Edward Condent's boarding party on the *Dragon* was black.[40] A "free negro" cook divided provisions equally so that the crew aboard Francis Spriggs's ship might live "very merrily" in 1724. "Negroes and Molattoes" were present on almost every pirate ship, and only rarely did the many merchants and captains who commented on their presence call them slaves. Black pirates sailed with Captains Bellamy, Taylor, Williams, Harris, Winter, Shipton, Lyne, Skyrm, Roberts, Spriggs, Bonnet, Bellamy, Phillips, Baptist, Cooper, and others. In 1718, sixty out of Blackbeard's crew of one hundred were black, while Captain William Lewis boasted "40 able Negroe Sailors" among his crew of eighty. In 1719, Oliver La Bouche's ship was "half *French,* half Negroes."[41] Black pirates were so common as to move one newspaper to report that an all-mulatto band of sea robbers was marauding the Caribbean, eating the hearts of captured white men.[42] In London, meanwhile, the most successful theatrical event of the period was prevented from depicting the reality of black pirates, as the Lord Chamberlain refused to license *Polly,* John Gay's sequel to *The Beggar's Opera,* which had ended with Macheath about to be hanged for highway robbery. In *Polly* he was transported to the West Indies, where he escaped the plantation, turned pirate, and, disguising himself as Morano, "a negro villain," became the principal leader of a gang of freebooters. Polly Peachum dressed herself as a man and sought her hero and his fellow pirates by asking, "Perhaps I may hear of him among the slaves of the next plantation."[43]

Some black pirates were freemen, like the experienced "free Negro" seaman from Deptford who in 1721 led "a Mutiny that we had too many Officers, and that the work was too hard, and what not." Others were escaped slaves. In 1716 the slaves of Antigua had become "very impudent and insulting," causing their masters to fear an insurrection. Historian Hugh Rankin writes that a substantial number of the unruly "went off to join those pirates who did not seem too concerned about color differences."[44] Just before the events in Antigua, Virginia's rulers had worried about the connection between the "Ravage of Pyrates" and "an Insurrection of the Negroes." The sailors of color captured with the rest of Black Bart's crew in 1722 grew mutinous over the poor conditions and "thin Commons" they suffered at the hands of the Royal Navy, especially since many of them had lived long in the "pyratical Way." That way meant, to them as to others, more food and greater freedom.[45]

Such material and cultural contacts were not uncommon. A gang of pirates settled in West Africa in the early 1720s, joining and intermixing with the Kru, themselves known for their skill in things maritime (and, when enslaved, for their leadership of revolts in the New World). And of course pirates had for many years mixed with the native population of Madagascar, helping to produce a "dark Mulatto Race there." Cultural exchanges among European and African sailors and pirates were extensive, resulting, for example, in the well-known similarities of form between African songs and sea shanties. In 1743 some seamen were court-martialed for singing a "negro song" in defiance of discipline. Mutineers also engaged in the same rites performed by slaves before a revolt. In 1731 a band of mutineers drank rum and gunpowder, while on another occasion a sailor signaled his rebellious intentions by "Drinking Water out of a Musket barrel." Piracy clearly did not operate according to the black codes enacted and enforced in Atlantic slave societies. Some slaves and free blacks found aboard the pirate ship freedom, something that, outside of the maroon communities, was in short supply in the pirates' main theater of operations, the Caribbean and the American South. Indeed, pirate ships themselves might be considered multiracial maroon communities, in which rebels used the high seas as others used the mountains and the jungles.[46]

That piracy was not only for men was proved by Anne Bonny and Mary Read, who showed, sword and pistol in hand, that the many freedoms of the pirates' life might be enjoyed by women. Women were few aboard ships of any kind in the eighteenth century, but they were numerous enough to inspire ballads about cross-dressing female warriors that became popular among the workers of the Atlantic. Bonny and Read, whose exploits were announced on the cover page of *A General History of the Pyrates* and no doubt in many another yarn of their own day and after, cursed and swore like sailors, carried their weapons like those well trained in the ways of war, and boarded prize vessels as only the most daring and respected members of pirate crews were permitted to do. Operating beyond the reach of the traditional powers of family, state, and capital, and sharing in the rough solidarity of life among maritime outlaws, they added another dimension altogether to the subversive appeal of piracy by seizing the liberties usually reserved for men, at a time when the sphere of social action for women was narrowing.[47]

THE WAR AGAINST HYDRARCHY

The freedoms of hydrarchy were self-consciously established and defended by pirates, not least because they knew that they would aid in recruitment and therefore in the reproduction of their oppositional culture. What they perhaps did not fully understand was that these same freedoms, once recognized by the ruling class, would fuel a campaign of terror to eliminate the alternative way of life, whether at sea or, more dangerously, ashore. Some among the powerful worried that pirates might "set up a sort of Commonwealth" in areas where no power would be able "to dispute it with them." Colonial and metropolitan merchants and officials feared incipient separatism in Madagascar, Sierra Leone, Bermuda, North Carolina, the Bay of Campeche, and Honduras.[48] Colonel Benjamin Bennet wrote of pirates to the Council of Trade and Plantations in 1718: "I fear they will soon multiply for so many are willing to joyn with them when taken." And multiply they did: after the War of Spanish Succession, as working conditions in the merchant shipping industry rapidly deteriorated, seamen turned to the black flag by the thousands. Edward England's crew took nine vessels off the coast of Africa in the spring of 1719, and found fifty-five out of the 143 tars ready to sign their articles. John Jessup swore that a jovial life among the pirates was better than working at the big slave-trading fort of Cape Coast Castle. Such desertion was common between 1716 and 1722, when, as one pirate told a merchant captain, "people were generally glad of an opportunity of entring with [the pirates]."[49] The prospect of plunder and ready money, the food and the drink, the camaraderie, the equality and justice, and the promise of care for the injured—all of these must have been appealing. The attractions were perhaps best summarized by Bartholomew Roberts, who remarked that in the merchant service "there is thin Commons, low Wages, and hard Labour; in this, Plenty and Satiety, Pleasure and ease, Liberty and Power; and who would not ballance Creditor on this Side, when all the Hazard that is run for it, at worst, is only a sower Look or two at choaking. No, *a merry Life and a short one,* shall be my motto." When John Dryden rewrote *The Tempest* in 1667, he had one of his sailors announce, "A short life and a merry, I say." Two generations later, the aphorism had taken on a subversive tone that now called forth the executioner.[50]

Hydrarchy was attacked because of the danger it posed to the increasingly valuable slave trade with Africa. A series of sailors' mutinies shook the slave trade between 1716 and 1726, a logical outcome of the chronic complaints about food, discipline, and the general conditions of working life aboard the slave ships that left England for West Africa during those years. Sailors alleged in court that Captain Theodore Boucher of the slave ship *Wanstead* "did not allow victualls & liquor enough to support them & used them very barbarously and inhumanly in their diett." Other sailors accused their captains of tyrannical discipline. Those who dared to object to shipboard conditions might find themselves "as Slaves linked and coupled by chains together & . . . fedd with Yams & Water the Usuall dyett for Slaves."[51]

Some mutinous sailors, however, averted a fate of chains by seizing their vessels, raising the black flag, and establishing hydrarchy. After George Lowther and his comrades mutinied aboard the slave ship *Gambia Castle* in 1720, they renamed the vessel the *Delivery* and sailed away in triumph, not unlike the mutineers in Prince Rupert's convoy near the Gambia in 1652.[52] Lowther and his men may have been emboldened by the knowledge that the coast of West Africa had already become a favorite haunt of pirates, especially since the British government in 1718 had recaptured the Bahama Islands and reestablished royal authority in the place that had for years been the freebooters' main base of operations in the Caribbean. Hundreds of pirates had headed for the coast of Africa, attacking poorly defended ships and claiming their cargo. The greatest and most successful assaults on merchants' property had been carried out by a pirate convoy under the leadership of Bartholomew Roberts, which ranged up and down the African coast "sinking, burning, and destroying such Goods and Vessels as then happen'd in [its] Way."[53] Roberts's interest lay in capturing not ships full of slaves but rather ships *on their way* to trade for slaves—"good Sailing Shipps well furnished with Ammunition, Provisions, & Stores of all Kinds, fitt for long Voyages." He and his fellows also plundered the slave-trading forts, as a group of merchants explained: pirates "sometimes land at the chief Factories and carry off what they think fit." Many a slave ship in the early eighteenth century was captured and converted to pirate duties, including the recently recovered *Whydah*, captained by Black Sam Bellamy.[54]

As pirates with Bartholomew Roberts and other captains sailed from Senegambia to the Gold Coast and back again, disturbing the region most vital to British merchants in the 1720s, they "struck a Pannick into the Traders," in the words of naval surgeon John Atkins, who spent several months on the coast. One writer estimated in 1720 that pirates had already done a hundred thousand pounds' worth of damage on the coast of Africa. An anonymous writer to the Board of Trade asserted in 1724 that pirates had taken "near 100 sail of Ships in the space of two years" in the African slave trade.[55] Other estimates ran even higher. Merchants in Bristol, Liverpool, and London began to protest their losses, screaming to Parliament about the disorder plaguing the lucrative slave trade and demanding naval protection for their property. Their cries fell on sympathetic ears. When a group of merchants petitioned Parliament for relief in early 1722, the House of Commons ordered the immediate drafting of a bill for the suppression of piracy, which was, with Robert Walpole's assistance, quickly passed. Soon a naval squadron under the leadership of Captain Challoner Ogle was fitted out to sail to the African coast, where it arrived later in 1722, engaged the ships of Bartholomew Roberts, and defeated them. More than a hundred pirates were killed in battle, while others escaped into the jungle; scores were captured and ordered to stand trial. They were taken to Cape Coast Castle, the centerpiece of the British slave trade, where slaves awaiting ships were chained, confined, and "marked with a burning iron upon the right breast, D. Y. Duke of *York.*" Within Cape Coast Castle's brick walls, fourteen feet thick and guarded by seventy-four mounted cannons, a gang of pirates were executed, and their chained corpses distributed and hanged along the coast in order to maximize the terror: nine at Cape Coast, four on the Windward coast, two each at Acera, Calabar, and Whydah, and one at Winnebah. Thirty-one others were hanged at sea, aboard the *Weymouth.* Another forty were sentenced to slavery, forced to work for the Royal African Company on ships or in gold mines; all of them apparently died within a matter of months.[56] After his triumphant return to London, Challoner Ogle became, in May 1723, the first naval captain to be knighted for his actions against pirates. He was honored by King George I, whom Roberts and his fellow pirates had ridiculed as the "turnip man."[57]

The defeat of Roberts and the subsequent destruction of piracy off the coast of Africa represented another turning point in the history of capitalism, largely because piracy and the slave trade had long been linked, in the experiences of war, commerce, and imperial expansion. The conflict between pirates and slave traders on the coast of West Africa dated back

Pirate Bartholomew Roberts off the coast of West Africa.
Captain Charles Johnson, A General History of the Pyrates *(1724).*

to the end of the War of Spanish Succession in 1713, when thousands of sailors had been demobilized from the Royal Navy, causing wages to plummet, food to deteriorate, and the lash to fly among workers in the merchant shipping industry, which in turn moved sailors to cast their lot with the Jolly Roger. The end of the war brought a prize for British merchants: the *Assiento,* which gave these traders the legal right to ship 4,800 slaves a year (and the illegal right to ship many more) to Spanish America through the South Sea Company. This incentive, coupled with the final deregulation of the African slave trade in 1712, when the chartered Royal African Company had lost its battle against the free traders who had already begun to supply most of the slaves to American plantations, increased dramatically the importance of the slave trade in the eyes of British merchants.[58]

Pirates now had to be exterminated in order for the new trade to flourish, a point that was made by the slave-trading merchant captain William Snelgrave, who published *A New Account of Some Parts of Guinea and the Slave Trade,* dedicated to "the Merchants of London, trading to the Coast of Guinea." He divided the book into three sections, providing for his readers a "History of the late Conquest of the Kingdom of *Whidaw* by the King of *Dahomè*"; an account of the business practices and statistics of the slave trade; and "A Relation of the Author's being taken by Pirates" and the dangers posed thereby. But by the time Snelgrave published his book, in 1734, the pirate was dead, defeated by the terror of hanging and enhanced naval patrols, though occasionally the corpse would twitch with a mutiny here or an act of piracy there. In the immediate aftermath of the suppression of piracy, Britain established its dominance on the western coast of Africa. As James A. Rawley has written, "In the decade of the 1730s England had become the supreme slaving nation in the Atlantic world, a standing she occupied until 1807." There was a sharp jump of almost 27 percent in slave-trade exports over the previous pirate-infested decade.[59] If the plantation capital of the Caribbean, allied with the merchant capital of the metropolis, killed the first generation of pirates—the buccaneers of the 1670s—and if the capital of the East India Company killed the pirates of the 1690s, when the company's ships were hothouses of mutiny and rebellion, it was African slave-trading capital that killed the pirates of the early eighteenth century. Hydrarchy from below was a deadly enemy to hydrarchy from above, as pirates had ruptured the middle passage. By 1726 the maritime state had removed a major obstacle to the accumulation of capital in its ever-growing Atlantic system.[60]

It was not many years earlier that English and other, mostly Protestant European rulers had turned pirates loose on the riches of other realms. Now they and their former national enemies discovered common interests in an orderly Atlantic system of capitalism, in which trade would flow without attack and capital accumulate without disruption—unless, of course, the attacks and disruptions were the results of war declared by the rulers themselves. By the 1720s, thousands of pirates had deeply damaged world shipping. They had also self-consciously built an autonomous, democratic, egalitarian social order of their own, a subversive alternative to the prevailing ways of the merchant, naval, and privateering ship and a counterculture to the civilization of Atlantic capitalism with its expropriation and exploitation, terror and slavery. Whigs and Tories alike responded by repeating the repressions of the 1690s and erecting gallows for pirates and the waterfront folk who dealt with them. Merchants petitioned Parliament, whose members obliged them with deadly new legislation; meanwhile, Prime Minister Robert Walpole took an active, personal interest in putting an end to piracy, as did scores of other officials, newspaper correspondents, and clergymen. They denounced pirates as sea monsters, vicious beasts, and a many-headed hydra—all creatures that, pace Bacon, lived beyond the bounds of human society. Their violent rhetoric demanded and legitimated the use of the gallows. The pirates and their living alternative were clearly marked for extinction. Hundreds were hanged, and their bodies left to dangle in the port cities of the world as a reminder that the maritime state would not tolerate a challenge from below.[61]

The sailors' hydrarchy was defeated in the 1720s, the hydra beheaded. But it would not die. The volatile, serpentine tradition of maritime radicalism would appear again and again in the decades to come, slithering quietly belowdecks, across the docks, and onto the shore, biding its time, then rearing its heads unexpectedly in mutinies, strikes, riots, urban insurrections, slave revolts, and revolutions. John Place, for example, would help in October 1748 to organize a mutiny aboard the H.M.S. *Chesterfield*, off the coast of West Africa, not far from Cape Coast Castle. He had been there before. He had sailed as a pirate with Black Bart Roberts, suffered capture by Captain Challoner Ogle in 1722, and somehow escaped the mass executions. When the time came, a quarter of a century later, for know-how about mutiny and an alternative social order, Place was the man of the moment. The authorities hanged him this time, but they could not kill the subversive tradition that lived in tales, in action, in sullenly silent memory, on the lower decks of the *Chesterfield* and countless other vessels. The Martinican poet Aimé Césaire captured this survival of resistance when he wrote, "It is this stubborn serpent's crawling out of the shipwreck."[62]

CHAPTER SIX

"The Outcasts of the Nations of the Earth"

AT THE HEART of the New York Conspiracy of 1741 lay a love story. The lovers were John Gwin (or Quin), "a fellow of suspicious character" rumored to be a soldier at Fort George, and "Negro Peg," "a notorious prostitute" who lived at John Hughson's waterfront tavern on the west side of Manhattan. Gwin paid Peg's board at Hughson's and joined her there many a night, climbing on top of a shed and through her open window. During one of these late-night meetings he gave her a ring, a pair of earrings, and a locket with four diamonds. Eventually Peg bore his child, whose color was a matter of considerable gossip and debate around town. Some said the baby was white; others insisted that it was black.[1]

John Gwin had long been a regular at Hughson's, and not only because he visited Peg. He often showed up with "a good booty"—speckled linen, stockings, even a worsted cap full of silver coins—that he gave to the tall, gaunt Hughson, who in turn fenced the purloined goods. Gwin's friends at the tavern were always glad to see him, for they knew of the man's generosity. Since aliases were common along the waterfront, where strangers and their secrets came and went with the tides, they also knew that Gwin and Peg were called by other names: Gwin, an African American slave, was known as Caesar, at least to his owner, John Vaarck. "Negro Peg" was the twenty-one- or twenty-two-year-old Margaret Kerry, though she was also known as the "Newfoundland Irish beauty." Another thing taverngoers knew was that Gwin and Peg were deeply involved in plotting what was later called the "most horrible and destructive plot that was ever yet known in these northern parts of America." For it was at Hughson's that they and dozens of others planned a "general insurrection" to capture the city of New York.[2]

Saint Patrick's Day, 1741, was a day for remembering that Saint Patrick had abolished slavery in Ireland. A revolutionary arsonist named Quack set fire to New York City's Fort George, the chief military installation of

A view of Fort George and the city of New York, 1735.
*I. N. Phelps-Stokes Collection, Miriam and Ira D. Wallach
Division of Art, Prints, and Photographs, New York Public
Library, Astor, Lenox, and Tilden Foundations.*

the colony and one of the greatest fortifications in all of British America.
The fire smoldered all night and on the following day exploded into billowing bursts of ocher and orange. Violent March winds carried the
flames from the governor's mansion to the Church of England chapel,
the army barracks, and the office of the general secretary of the province.
Flying sparks and burning debris wafted above the wooden houses that
sat just beyond the walls of the fort, threatening the city with conflagra-
tion. A shift in the winds and a sudden rain shower halted the spread of
the blaze, but the damage had been done: the very heart of royal authority in this important Atlantic port now lay hollow and smoldering in
ashes.

It was the first and most destructive of thirteen fires that would terrorize the city of eleven thousand in the coming weeks. When Cuffee, a slave
owned by city eminence Adolph Philipse, was seen leaving the premises
of the tenth fire, the cry went up that "the negroes were rising." A vast
dragnet caught almost two hundred people, black and white, many of
whom would be investigated and tried over the next several months. Peg,

Hughson, and others were charged with "conspiring, confederating and combining with divers negroes and others to burn the City of New-York and also to kill and destroy the inhabitants thereof." The conspiracy had been organized by soldiers, sailors, and slaves from Ireland, the Caribbean, and Africa, whom the officials called "the outcasts of the nations of the earth."[3] Disrespected by the mercantile oligarchy of New York, they were not without a mutuality of respect among themselves.

The outcasts had met regularly at Hughson's, where they exercised "the hopes and promises of paradise." Here the dispossessed of all colors feasted, danced, sang, took oaths, and planned their resistance. The enslaved Bastian remembered a table overflowing with "veal, ducks, geese, a quarter of mutton and fowls" from the butcher shops in which several of the conspirators worked. Others recalled the raucous, joyous fiddling, dancing, and singing for which Hughson's was famous around town. Yet others emphasized the subversive conversation, followed by solemn oaths: Gwin asking a recruit "whether he would join along with them to become their own masters"; Cuffee saying "that a great many people had too much, and others too little"; Hughson announcing that "the country was not good, too many gentlemen here, and made negroes work hard." At Hughson's tavern, the rebels practiced a simple communism. Those who had no money were entertained "at free cost"; they "could have victuals and drink for nothing." Hughson told them, "You shall always be welcome to my house, come at any time." Bastian, exiled for his role in the rebellion, fondly recalled, "We always had a good supper and never wanted for liquor." Here, once again, was a world turned upside down, a place where Africans and Irish were kings, as they would be in the larger society after the uprising. In New York, they believed, "there should be a motley government as well as motley subjects."[4]

New York's people in ruffles were terrified of the conspiracy, for reasons both local and global. A severe winter had made the city's poor workers more miserable and more restive than usual. Trade, the lifeblood of New York, had stagnated in recent years, deepening divisions within the ruling class and creating an opening for revolt from below. Danger had also threatened from afar after the merchant mountebank Robert Jenkins waved his severed ear before the astonished bigwigs of Parliament, who then declared war against Spain (the aptly named War of Jenkins' Ear, 1739) and required the rulers of New York to supply both food and six hundred recruits (nearly one in six of the city's able-bodied white men) for the war effort. Imperial authorities had thus depleted New York's food supply as well as its defenses against French and Iroquois aggression from the north, Spanish privateers from the south, and domestic rebels from within.

The fires caused great damage to property, and New York's rulers made sure that there was ample human carnage to pay for it. On six afternoons and evenings between late May and mid-July, thirteen African men were burned at the stake. On six mornings between March and August seventeen more people of color and four whites were hanged, including John Gwin and Peg Kerry, whose romance came to an end on the gallows. John Hughson was also hanged, and his corpse, with Gwin's, gibbeted in chains and left to rot. Seventy people of African descent, among them Bastian, were exiled to places as various as Newfoundland, Madeira, St. Domingue, and Curaçao. Five people of European origin were forcibly sent off to join the British army, then at war against Spain in the Caribbean, where the conditions of soldiering life likely made theirs a delayed sentence of death. Sarah Hughson, the tavernkeeper's daughter, who was banished from the city for her own role in the conspiracy, took Gwin and Peg's baby to parts unknown.

The events of 1741 have long been controversial. The New Yorkers who lived through them argued fiercely about exactly what had happened and why, and since that time historians have done likewise. Indeed, the uniquely detailed record of the plot owes its existence to the dissension that surrounded the original events. After some expressed doubts about the conspiracy and the prosecutions, Judge Daniel Horsmanden of New York's Supreme Court compiled "the notes that were taken by the court, and gentlemen of the bar," and published them in 1744 as *A Journal of the Proceedings in the Detection of the Conspiracy formed by Some White People, in Conjunction with Negro and other Slaves, for Burning the City of New-York in America, and Murdering the Inhabitants.* His purpose was not only to prove the "justice of the several prosecutions" but also to sound, for the public benefit, a warning about the rebellious ways of slaves and to erect "a standing memorial of so unprecedented a scheme of villainy."[5]

The hanging of an African in New York, c. 1750.
Manual of the Corporation of the City of New York *(1860).*

Contemporary accounts of the episode expressed three basic positions in the debate, which prefigured the views taken by modern interpreters of the events of 1741. Some historians have followed an anonymous writer of 1741 who maintained that there never was a conspiracy, and that the whole affair resembled the hangings for witchcraft that had taken place in Salem, Massachusetts, in 1692.[6] Others have echoed the belief of William Smith, Jr., son of one of the prosecuting attorneys at the trial, who wrote that the conspirators wanted only "to create alarms, for committing thefts with more ease."[7] A third major interpretation, offered by T. J. Davis in *A Rumor of Revolt: The "Great Negro Plot" in Colonial New York* (1985), proved the original prosecutors right in claiming the existence of a dangerous conspiracy. This view holds that blacks and whites gathered and drank illegally, fenced their goods, and plotted against their masters at Hughson's tavern. They sought for themselves money and freedom, revenge against particular powerful people (not all "white people"), and the destruction by fire of certain areas (not the entire city). The rebels had grievances and plans to redress them, but no genuinely revolutionary objectives.[8]

This chapter argues that a revolutionary conspiracy, Atlantic in scope, did develop in New York, though it was not the "popish plot" imagined by Horsmanden, who saw the affair as having been orchestrated by a disguised priest. It was, rather, a conspiracy by a motley proletariat to incite an urban insurrection, not unlike the uprising led in Naples by the fisherman Masaniello in 1647. It grew out of the work of the waterfront, the organized cooperation of many kinds of workers, whose Atlantic experiences became the building blocks of the conspiracy. The rebels of 1741 combined the experiences of the deep-sea ship (hydrarchy), the military regiment, the plantation, the waterfront gang, the religious conventicle, and the ethnic tribe or clan to make something new, unprecedented, and powerful. The events of 1741 can thus be understood only by attending to the Atlantic experiences of the conspirators, in the villages and slave factories of the Gold Coast of Africa, the cottages of Ireland, the Spanish military outpost of Havana, the street meetings of religious revival, and the maroon settlements of the Blue Mountains of Jamaica and their surrounding sugar plantations.

THE WATERFRONT AND THE CONSPIRACY

The events of 1741 began along the city's docks. As valuable outposts of empire, New York and other Atlantic ports garrisoned soldiers to protect their cities and propertied people against enemies within and without. Soldiers such as William Kane and Thomas Plumstead, both stationed at Fort George, drilled, guarded, loafed, and grumbled their way through rounds of life endlessly governed by the soldier's quietest but most common enemy: boredom. As bustling centers of transatlantic trade, the seaports contained masses of workers who labored in the maritime sector of the economy, sailing, building, and repairing ships, manufacturing sail, rope, and other essentials, and moving commodities by boat, by cart, and by the strength of their backs. People of African descent, almost all of them enslaved, were especially important to the waterfront, representing about 18 percent of the city's population and fully 30 percent of its workers. Brash and Ben, for example, worked together on the Hudson loading timber, while Mink labored at his owner's ropewalk. Cuff's merchant master sent him down to the docks to work with a white boy to "sew on a vane upon a board for his sloop." The Spanish "negroes and mulattoes" involved in the conspiracy were all sailors, as were the slaves

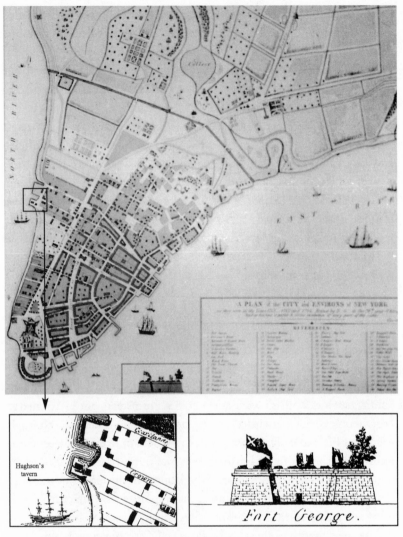

Map of Manhattan, with details of Hughson's tavern and a burned-out
Fort George. A Plan of the City and Environs of New York, 1742–4,
by David Grim. Collection of the New-York Historical Society.

Ben and London. Quack worked with soldiers on a new battery near
Fort George.[9]

After work these soldiers, sailors, and slaves retired to the dram shops,
taverns, and "disorderly" houses along the waterfront "to drink drams,

punch and other strong liquors," often staying "till two or three o'clock in the morning, . . . drinking, singing and playing at dice." Here they told tales, sometimes tall, sometimes true, among which were the stories of an uprising that had shaken New York in 1712. Here, too, they cursed, caroused, fought, danced, and created constant public disturbances, after which they often awoke in the basement of City Hall, in jail. Mutinous soldiers and sailors had been a problem for New York's rulers for several decades, prompting numerous acts of legislation to contain and punish their unruly ways.[10]

The rebels of 1741 traveled along the wharves for secret meetings, gathering at Hughson's, at Comfort's on the Hudson, and "at the house of one Saunders, upon the dock." The docks and taverns, like ships, were places where English, Irish, African, Native American, and West Indian persons could meet and explore their common interests. The authorities could not easily circumvent the flow of subversive experience, for a port city was hard to police. There were always "some strangers lurking about the city"—people such as Sambo, described as "a tall negro living at John Dewit's (a stranger)." Always there were "Vagrant and Idle persons" to be found, and "obscure people that have no visible way of subsistence," for the growth of the cities, and especially of their maritime sector, depended upon a mass of desperate but necessarily creative proletarians' being forced to work for wages in order to keep body and soul together. Everyone knew that a combination of such people was not only more likely in a port city, but more dangerous than it might be elsewhere to the concentrated, established power of a cosmopolitan ruling class.[11]

The waterfront taverns were the linchpins of the waterfront economy, the places where soldiers, sailors, slaves, indentured servants, and apprentices met to sell illegally appropriated goods and pad their meager or nonexistent wages. Tavernkeepers sometimes encouraged such trade by extending so much credit that bills could be settled only after goods were taken and submitted as payment. New York's rulers passed legislation to limit the amount of credit tavernkeepers could offer to workers, especially soldiers and sailors. The latter were especially important to illegal trade because they not only sold stolen goods but also purchased them, and conveniently disappeared when their ships set sail. Other bills were meant to halt the flow of pilfered goods ("Cloathing, or any other

Goods, Chattles, Wares, or Merchandizes"), promising double restitution or jail for offending tavernkeepers. New York's comprehensive slave code of 1730, "An Act for the more Effectual Preventing and Punishing the Conspiracy and Insurrection of Negro and other Slaves," also acknowledged the subversive potential of the waterfront economy: its first article prohibited any "trade or Traffick" with a slave without his or her master's permission, "on forfeiture of trebel the Value of the thing or things traded." Lieutenant Governor Clark noted—almost prophetically—that illicit transactions promoted "an habit of idleness, that may in time prove ruinous to the whole Province if not prevented."[12]

None of the threats against tavernkeepers who traded with soldiers, sailors, or slaves worried John Hughson. His house was the perfect place for the "caballing and entertainment of negroes" and for the fencing of stolen goods: built into it were secret compartments—in the cellar, in various rooms, and under the stairs—where hot items, slipped in through a back-alley window in the middle of the night, could be hidden. As Bastian explained, "The negroes brought what they could steal to him." In return, they, like apprentices, indentured servants, soldiers, and sailors, received money, some of which they left in the hands of the tavernkeeper, "to drink out" on credit. Other, lesser fences worked through Hughson's network. The slave Will stole a silver spoon from his mistress and carried it to the wife of soldier William Kane, who then turned it over to her husband, who in turn sold it to the silversmith Peter Van Dyke and gave Will "eight shillings of the money." Other Irish conspirators also had a hand in the illegal circulation of goods. Daniel Fagan, Jerry Corker, and John Coffin wanted William Kane "to rob houses with them and go off." But before they "went off," they would have stopped at Hughson's, as Edward Murphy had done when he wanted to cash in some purloined jewelry.[13] Indeed, so many "run goods" passed through Hughson's house, making it "a mart of so great note," that its customers had wryly begun to call the place Oswego, after the great provincial trading house where the English and Iroquois swapped their goods on the upper colonial frontier. Like the Iroquois, those who gathered at Hughson's had a special interest in guns, powder, and ammunition, which they stockpiled through the winter of 1740–41.[14]

Two of the most daring and most notorious members of the waterfront economy—and part of Hughson's "black guard"—were John Gwin and Prince, who worked along the docks, wharves, and warehouses, taking hauls big and small: fifty firkins of butter, a cache of pieces of eight, beeswax, a shirt, stockings, a coat, and whatever else came their way. According to Horsmanden, these two "very wicked idle fellows had before been detected in some robberies, for which they had been publickly chastised at the whipping-post." The authorities scarred their backs for a theft of gin, a Dutch contribution to civilization and the drink of mortal desperation of the London poor in this era. Carried by cart in a "suitable Procession round the Town," they got "at every Corner . . . five Lashes with a Cowskin well laid on each of their naked black Backs," as bystanders pelted them with "Snow balls and Dirt." Gwin and Prince took the momentary defeat in stride and in humor: in honor of the event they soon founded the "Geneva Club" and proclaimed themselves its leaders. They continued to show up at Hughson's with booty, in their pockets, on their backs, or "tied up in a large table cloth." When it came to the plot, Gwin and Prince were "two principal ringleaders in it amongst the blacks." Daniel Horsmanden made this point clear when he called the waterfront workers "brother criminals" whose thefts were the actual "ingredients of the conspiracy." Such operations along the waterfront generated leadership, connections, and solidarities that proved crucial to the conspiratorial design.[15]

As the number of committed conspirators grew, the older, smaller gangs of the waterfront economy evolved into quasimilitary forms of social organization adapted to insurrectionary purposes. A gang called the Fly Boys met at John Romme's tavern, while the Long Bridge Boys met at Hughson's. Each group had its highest leader and below him several captains, each in charge of a company. Gwin was the leader of the Long Bridge company; his equivalent in the Fly Boys was the experienced Spanish-speaking soldier Juan. Both apparently reported directly to Hughson. Other captains included Ben, a "head man or captain" and "commander of a hundred at least," and Jack, called a "head captain." Curaçao Dick, York, and Bastian rounded out those named (or self-named) in the testimony as captains, though the group should have included both Cuffee and Prince as well. All stayed in close, steady contact with Hughson. Dundee, Cook, London, and Gomez's Cuffee were lesser officers. Each company had its own drummer, such as old Tom, and its fiddler, such as Braveboy, who, Albany insisted in recruitment, was needed precisely "because he was a fiddler." Perhaps he would have been like Louis Delgres, the Martinican who led a slave revolt on the island of Guadeloupe and was last seen sitting in a cannon port in the island's Fort Matouba, fiddling madly amid the smoke and the sizzling shot to inspire his fellow rebels against the French.[16]

WEST AFRICA

The cultures and memories of West Africa figured centrally in the plan for insurrection in 1741. Several distinct groups of Africans took part, and indeed John Hughson, among others, was keenly aware of their variety and importance. Central to the plan for organizing the revolt was an inner circle of "headmen," each of whom was, as a leader within a specific community of Africans in New York, responsible for recruitment, discipline, and solidarity. Hughson instructed these most trusted men (they were all men) carefully: they were "not to open the conspiracy to any but those that were of their own country," since as Daniel Horsmanden would observe, "they are brought from different parts of Africa, and might be supposed best to know the temper and disposition of each other."[17] They worked according to plan. In making his pitch on behalf of the insurrection, Cato asked Bridgewater, "Countryman, will you help?" A slave named Ben used the same approach, saying to Jack, "Countryman, I have heard some good news." The word was that the Spanish planned to invade the city, which would support their own rising from within. Cato and Bridgewater appealed to ethnic groups such as the Papa, from the Slave Coast near Whydah; the Igbo, from the area around the Niger River; and the Malagasay, from Madagascar, who constituted the revolutionary cells of New York's movement.[18]

The leading cell was made up of Africans from the Gold Coast of West Africa, the Akan-speaking people who were known by the name of the slave-trading fort from which they were shipped: Coromantee (or, in Fante, Kromantse). Many a "Coromantee" had been an *okofokum*, a common soldier trained in firearms and hand-to-hand combat in one of the mass armies of West Africa's militarized, expansionist states (Akwamu, Denkyira, Asante, Fante), before being captured and shipped to America. Peck's Caesar was identified as "a Caromantee," as was an unnamed old woman owned by Gerardus Comfort. Moreover, five of the thirteen slaves who would be burned at the stake either had Akan daynames (Quack [Kwaku in Akan], Quash [Kwasi], and two called Cuffee [Kofi]) or were known to be Coromantee (Gwin), suggesting strong Gold Coast participation in the leadership of the plot. Yet another, Quamino (Kwamena), was hanged, while three more were transported. In the aftermath of the failed conspiracy, a slave named Warwick "cut his [own] throat," probably in the style and tradition of a defeated Asante warrior. Doctor Harry, who was almost certainly an obeah man (an Akan shaman who had deep natural and spiritual knowledge and powers) of Gold Coast origins, had produced poison—"the same sort they saw in Guinea"—for the plotters to gulp down in the event of failure.[19]

The role of the Coromantees, and of Africa more broadly, was most obvious in the administering of war oaths, which Hughson shrewdly "accommodated to their own customs." The Irish soldier William Kane testified that there existed a specific "negro oath," but in truth there were probably, as Horsmanden believed, several different oaths. The most frequent of these involved "swearing by thunder and lightning," a "terrible" oath commonly used among the Africans. Many of the slaves swore by this oath to support the revolt and never to reveal the common secret. Military oaths invoking the primal powers of thunder and lightning were in use on the Gold Coast of Africa in the middle of the eighteenth century, suggesting both the origin and the efficacy of the practice. Nanny, the legendary leader of the Windward Maroons in the 1730s, administered similar oaths, as did rebels in Antigua and elsewhere. Horsmanden sensed that the "obligation of that infernal oath" impeded the investigation in New York, but he never understood that the original source of his difficulty lay across the Atlantic, on the Gold Coast of Africa.[20]

These oaths, like African traditions of resistance more generally, were not new to New York, for they had been used a generation earlier, in 1712, in one of the bloodiest revolts ever to hit the North American mainland, when a coalition of slaves of Coromantee and Papa backgrounds set fire to a building and then killed several whites who came to extinguish the flames. Afterward, nineteen slaves were executed—burned, hanged, starved, broken on the wheel—but not forgotten.[21] Horsmanden knew the earlier history, as did attorney William Smith, who had helped to send the rebels to their "brutish and bloody" executions.[22] Now, in 1741, John Romme, it would be testified in court, encouraged the conspirators "to set them all a light fire; burn the houses of them that have the most money, and kill them all, as the negroes would have done their masters and mistresses formerly." Hughson, who himself had grown up in the environs of New York, "proposed burning the fort before anything else; because at a former rising, the white people run into the fort." The testimony of a slave named Sawney, who was only sixteen years old at the time of the second uprising, proved that he had heard the tales of 1712, perhaps from the likes of "old man" Cook or "Comfort's old Caromantee woman."[23]

THE IRISH

Another cell in New York's insurrectionary movement was Irish. These plotters, like their African counterparts, demonstrated a penchant for secret societies and conspiracy; they, too, called each other countryman. There were, in all, perhaps thirty to thirty-five Irish men and women involved in the conspiracy, though only eleven of these were recorded by name. One person testified that seventeen soldiers had attended a meeting at Hughson's tavern; more commonly an ever-changing nine or ten turned up. Most all of the Irish were soldiers—"brother soldiers," as they called themselves—stationed at Fort George. They wanted revenge against the Protestant English, expressing a desire "to burn the English church." Hatred of the army was another motivation: Jerry Corker declared, "By G-d, I have a mind to burn the fort." William Kane, whose involvement began when he told his fellow conspirators that "he would help them all that lay in his power" and ended in 1742 when he was shipped off to the Caribbean in punishment, wanted the fort in flames so that the soldiers "would have their liberty." The complicity of Corker and Kane shows just how close the conspirators got to power: both had served as "sentry at the governor's door" inside Fort George.[24]

Although little is known about the Irish individuals who took part in the conspiracy, it is possible to sketch in broad outline the historical experience that set the Irish in motion around the Atlantic in the years before 1741. A depression in the linen industry, intensified oppression by landlords and Anglican clergyman, and especially the famine of 1728–29 created new waves of Irish vagabondage and migration. Another famine in 1740–41, called in Gaelic "*bliadhain an air*" ("the year of the slaughter"), sent tens of thousands to their graves and thousands more across the seas in search of subsistence. Such vagabonds were called "Saint Patrick's vermin."[25] The traditional spalpeen migrations now moved into wider, Atlantic orbits. For many the movement led to a military experience—in the army of Britain, France, or Spain—which in turn led to a new posting at the outskirts of the empire as a soldier or military laborer. Others made their way to Irish harbors, signed on in the cod fishery, and sailed for Newfoundland, where many fell into debt and whence they traveled on as indentured servants or maritime workers to the port cities of North America.[26] Some variant of this process would appear to have been the experience of the "Irish Newfoundland beauty," Peg Kerry.

Still others fell afoul of the law and ended up in the Americas as His Majesty's seven- or fourteen-year passengers, having been sentenced as felons to long terms of punitive labor and shipped overseas. Crime and rebellion were inextricably intertwined for these Irishmen and Irishwomen, as for thousands of others in Britain who found themselves living on the wrong side of laws that were changing rapidly to protect new definitions of property. Irish felons transported to Georgia were denounced as a "Parcel of harden'd abandoned Wretches perfectly skill'd in all manner of Villainy, and who have been transported [from] their country for Committing Crimes by which they have been deemed too dangerous to be allowed to stay there." Some of the transported were rioters who had lashed out against intolerable conditions; once in America, they stole their masters' property and made "treasonable Designs against the Colony."[27]

The Irish had a history in America of betraying the English, who themselves had a history in Ireland of brutally subjugating the Irish. Several times during the seventeenth century (in 1655, 1666, and 1689), Irish indentured servants had assisted Spain or France in attacks against the English Caribbean colonies of St. Christopher, Montserrat, and Nevis.

These treacheries were well remembered among British colonial officials in the eighteenth century, especially after new calamities in Ireland sent new waves of migrants toward American shores. Governor Robert Hunter of Jamaica considered the Irish to be "a lazy useless sort of people, who come cheap and serve for deficiencies" (i.e., to expand the minority white population). On his island in the early 1730s were many—perhaps too many—Irish indentured servants and soldiers: "Many of them considering their religion might prove rather a disservice than of use to us in case of a rupture at any time with France or Spain." Hunter could only conclude, ominously, "Their hearts are not with us." The same fears gripped Hunter's counterparts in New York, particularly after war broke out with Spain in 1739 and war with France simultaneously threatened.[28]

SPANISH AMERICA

Members of a third cell within the insurrectionary plot whispered in Spanish. The leading figures here were Spanish-American sailors, "negroes and mulattoes," who had been captured on a prize vessel by Captain John Lush in the early spring of 1740, brought to New York from the West Indies, condemned with the rest of the vessel in the city's Vice-Admiralty Court, and promptly sold as slaves. A merchant testified that he had heard, while in Havana, that one of the sailors came from a family of slaves in Cartagena. The sailors themselves maintained that they were "free subjects of the King of Spain" and hence entitled to treatment as prisoners of war. Known among the conspirators as the "Cuba People," they had probably come from Havana, the greatest port of the Spanish West Indies and a center of privateering, military defense, and a free black population. Having been "free men in their own country," they felt that great injustice had been done them in New York. They "began to grumble at their hard usage, of being sold as slaves."[29]

The rage of the sailors heated many a conversation. Not surprisingly, Captain Lush, who had profited heavily from selling these prizes, was the object of special wrath. The sailors insisted that "if the captain would not send them to their own country, they would ruin all the city; and the first house they would burn should be the captain's, for they did not care what they did." Pointing to Lush's house, they said, "*D--n that son of a b---h, they would make a devil of him,"* doubtless by turning his home into an inferno. They even threatened to tie him "to a beam and roast him like a piece of beef."[30]

The Hispanic sailors had more than rage to contribute to the design to take the city, however, for they were highly skilled and knowledgeable in the ways of warfare. The tall, "very forward" Antonio de St. Bendito made no secret of their prowess. He bragged that when the time for the rising came, "while the York negroes killed one, the Spaniards could kill twenty." The sailors' reputation as experienced fighters circulated along the waterfront. John Hughson told York that "the Spaniards knew better than the York negroes how to fight"; he acknowledged their military experience by making Augustine an officer and Juan captain of the Fly Boys, one of the highest positions within the rebel command. Ben, a member of the conspiracy's inner circle, considered it good news that the "Spanish negroes" were ready to lend a hand in the rising when "the wars came." He told his skeptical countryman Jack that "those Spaniards know better than York Negroes, and could help better to take [the city] than they, because they were more used to war; but they must begin first to set the house (i.e. the houses) on fire."[31]

Here, too, the Hispanic sailors had something to offer, in particular their knowledge of the incendiary substances called fireballs that had long been used in the marauding, plundering, city-burning warfare of the Caribbean. At one of the meetings at Hughson's an unidentified Hispanic sailor "rolled something black in his hands, and broke it and gave to the rest, which was to be thrown in the houses, to set fire to the shingles in several places." Antonio and Juan were especially knowledgeable about the "stuff to put the houses on fire, by flinging it into the house." When on Monday, April 6, two fires broke out simultaneously on each side of Captain Sarly's house, the cry went up, "The Spanish negroes; the Spanish negroes; take up the Spanish negroes." Juan's knowledge, motive of revenge, and insolent bearing upon being accused raised suspicions that eventually led to his hanging.[32]

The Afro-Hispanic sailors also contributed to the plot an example of freedom based on their own maritime experience, and a means to achieve it, by coordinating an internal uprising with an external attack by Spanish forces. Of course, New York's authorities could not comprehend that news about Spanish military plans in the New World might circulate among sailors and waterfront workers. But sensing that there were real connections between the New York Conspiracy and Spanish America, they seized upon a letter written by General James Oglethorpe from Georgia in 1741 about a "popish Plot" in which secret emissaries—priests disguised as physicians, dancing masters, and the like—were inciting revolts "to burn all the magazines and considerable towns in English North America, thereby to prevent the subsisting of the great expedition and fleet in the West-Indies." Although Oglethorpe himself "could not give credit to these advices," many New Yorkers could. The real credit instead belonged to the Hispanic sailors, the human vessels who transported information and experience from one Atlantic port to another.[33]

THE GREAT AWAKENING

Another Atlantic dimension of the conspiracy of 1741 was religious, for it occurred during the Great Awakening. Beginning in the 1730s, both sides of the Atlantic witnessed an outburst of popular religious enthusiasm in which itinerant preachers traveled from place to place, testifying about their own religious experiences and encouraging working people wherever they went to become, as Gary B. Nash has put it, the "instruments of their own salvation." George Whitefield, a smallish preacher with crossed eyes, leather lungs, and burning charisma, ranged up and down the eastern seaboard of the colonies in 1739, delivering an endless succession of fiery sermons before the thousands, black and white (five to seven thousand in New York alone), who gathered to hear him.[34] The more radical itinerants preached a spiritual egalitarianism based on the biblical precept "God is no respecter of persons," and many members of the colonial upper classes hated them for it. James Davenport, for example, was accused by the conservative Charles Chauncey of Boston of acting out the communism of the Book of Acts, seeking to destroy private property and make "all things common, wives as well as goods." As the evangelicals preached justification by faith against the more traditional idea of justification by works, the specter of radical antinomianism hovered around their message and haunted their conservative adversaries. Some feared that the Levellers, Ranters, and Fifth Monarchy men of the seventeenth-century English Revolution had reappeared a century later, and they were not entirely wrong. The physician Alexander Hamilton worried that such "New Light fanatics" would strip established religion of its ritualistic powers of mystification, letting loose "the mobile, that many-headed beast," from its carefully constructed cage.[35]

Although prosecuting attorney William Smith would call New York's slave conspirators "Pagan negroes," it is clear that Christianity, much of it a result of the Great Awakening, had affected many of them. John Hughson used the Bible to administer binding oaths to a number of the slave rebels. Bastian would testify in court that he and several other slaves "were sworn on a bible." Cato agreed, claiming that Hughson took him and Albany upstairs in the tavern and "swore them upon a bible," after which they "kissed the book." Once captured, Cato would appear in court clutching his Bible to "his bosom"; "he said he read [it] in jail as often as he could." Another slave, Othello, wanted assurance that his taking part in the revolt "would not hinder him from going to heaven." Many others, black and white, fretted that by violating their sacred oath they would be "wronging their own souls." Many New York slaves had lived long enough in English-speaking colonies to comprehend and engage the Christian message of the Awakeners, and even to endow it with revolutionary meaning. As an Anglican missionary explained, "the *Negroes* have this notion, that when they are baptized, they are immediately free from their masters."[36]

Whitefield made the issue of slavery central to the Great Awakening when, in 1740, he wrote and published a letter to "the Inhabitants of Maryland, Virginia, North and South Carolina," remarking upon the slave rebellions that had recently convulsed Virginia and South Carolina and expressing his surprise that there had not been more of them. He considered rebellions past, present, and future to constitute a "judgment," a "visitation" from God. He cited the biblical story of "Saul and his Bloody House," who were subjected to famine for having enslaved the Gibeonites, "the Hewers of Wood and the Drawers of Water." God had avenged the poor slaves in the day of David and he would so again. Whitefield commanded sternly, "Go to now, ye rich Men, weep and howl for your Miseries that shall come upon you!" But he also offered the sinful masters a way out of their self-built Babylon, through a proper

Christianity that attended to the souls of both masters and slaves. Masters would cease their brutalities and avert the awful judgment at the hands of the "sons of violence." Slaves would cease to be rebellious and would naturally become better servants. Both would be conscious of their "relative Duties," to the Lord and to each other.[37]

Such words were more than many slaveowners could bear to hear. The Reverend Alexander Garden, who ministered to the slavemasters of Charleston, South Carolina, responded by accusing Whitefield of "enthusiasm and pride" and comparing him to "the *Oliverians, Ranters, Quakers, French Prophets.*" Such antinomianism, said Garden, led Whitefield to incite insurrection among the slaves. Others, such as William Smith, writing from the Caribbean, agreed: "Instead of teaching [the slaves] the *Principles of Christianity,*" enthusiasts such as Whitefield were "filling their heads with a Parcel of *Cant-Phrases, Trances, Dreams, Visions,* and *Revelations,* and something else still *worse,* which Providence forbids to name."[38]

The something worse reared its hydra head in New York in 1741, and Whitefield's poisonous influence was duly noted. John Ury, a clergyman who would be hanged in 1742 for his role in the conspiracy, believed that "it was through the great encouragement the negroes had from Mr. Whitefield [that] we had all the disturbance." Particularly pernicious, he thought, were Whitefield's views of free grace, the theological issue at the center of the antinomian heresy, the embrace of which allowed self-declared, often poor saints to take the law into their own hands. Looking back on the conspiracy in 1746, Horsmanden would also denounce the "Enthusiastical Notions" and "New Fangled Principles" of Whitefield and other "Suspicious Vagrant Strolling Preachers."[39]

An Anglican missionary in New York went further in his indictment. Whitefield, he claimed, was directly responsible for the rising, for in New York as elsewhere he had unified and encouraged the slaves as he divided and discouraged their masters. His "greatest address hath been to the *Negroes* alone": he had proposed to erect a school for slaves, which would cause many to "run away from the masters in hopes that they shall be here maintained, and have their liberty." The result would be baptism and, from the slaves' perspective, the freedom that came with it. Whitefield also inspired "feuds and animosities" everywhere he went. He knew that a "kingdom divided against itself cannot stand, but is brought to desolation." Whitefield thus "raised up a bitter spirit in the *Negroes* against their Masters." In New York as elsewhere, "all the planters are forced to be doubly upon their guard, and are not sure when they go to bed, but that they shall have their throats cut before the next morning; and it may be the overturning of several colonies."[40]

A Caribbean Cycle of Rebellion

The overturning of several colonies by insurrection seemed a real possibility in the 1730s and 1740s. During these years a furious barrage of plots, revolts, and war ripped through colonial Atlantic societies like a hurricane. No respecter of national or imperial boundaries, this cycle of rebellion slashed through British, French, Spanish, Dutch, and Danish territories, which stretched from the northern reaches of South America through the West Indies to the southern colonies and then the port cities of North America. Most of these events took place in plantation regions and were led by African Americans, but other areas (such as New York) and other actors (such as the Irish) were also involved. The magnitude of the upheaval was, in comparative terms, extraordinary, encompassing more than eighty separate cases of conspiracy, revolt, mutiny, and arson—a figure probably six or seven times greater than the number of similar events that occurred in either the dozen years before 1730 or the dozen after 1742. It was within this cycle of rebellion that the actions of the African slaves, Irish soldiers, and Hispanic sailors in New York in 1741 took on their greatest and most subversive meaning.

Scholars have studied the acts of resistance that constituted this cycle of rebellion, but almost always as isolated events; rarely have they analyzed them in relation to each other, as having both a coherence and a collective causal power. But of course both the rebels and the colonial authorities of the 1730s and 1740s were acutely aware of this profound, generative wave of struggle, even if their latter-day chroniclers have not been. Governor Mathews of the Leeward Islands in 1737 wrote of the cycle in the idiom of disease: "The contagion of rebellion is spread among these islands more than I apprehend is discovered." Governor Edward Trelawny of Jamaica, who had witnessed firsthand the numerous risings that climaxed in the Maroon War, saw clear political meaning in the rebellions, which for him expressed a "Dangerous Spirit of Liberty." Daniel Horsmanden made repeated reference to other plots and revolts in his account of New York's troubles. New York's rebels likewise knew what was going on in "the hot country," as one man called it. It had, in recent years, been hot in more ways than one.[41]

During the 1730s and early 1740s, the "Spirit of Liberty" erupted again and again, in almost all of the slave societies of the Americas, especially where Coromantee slaves were concentrated. Major conspiracies unfolded in Virginia, South Carolina, Bermuda, and Louisiana (New Orleans) in the year 1730 alone. The last of these featured a man named Samba, who had already led an unsuccessful revolt against a French slave-trading fort on the coast of Africa *and* a mutiny aboard a slave ship before the authorities of New Orleans broke his body on the wheel. The slaves of New Orleans were not intimidated by the terror, however, for they rose again in 1732. The following year witnessed rebellions in South Carolina, Jamaica, St. John (Danish Virgin Islands), and Dutch Guyana. In 1734 came plots and actions in the Bahama Islands, St. Kitts, South Carolina again, and New Jersey, the latter two inspired by the rising at St. John. In 1735–36 a vast slave conspiracy was uncovered in Antigua, and other rebellions soon followed on the smaller islands of St. Bartholomew, St. Martin's, Anguilla, and Guadeloupe. In 1737 and again in 1738, Charleston experienced new upheavals. In the spring of 1738, meanwhile, "several slaves broke out of a jail in Prince George's County, Maryland, united themselves with a group of outlying Negroes and proceeded to wage a small-scale guerilla war." The following year, a considerable number of slaves plotted to raid a storehouse of arms and munitions in Annapolis, Maryland, to "destroy his Majestys Subjects within this Province, and to possess themselves of the whole country." Failing that, they planned "to settle back in the Woods." Later in 1739, the Stono Rebellion convulsed South Carolina. Here the slaves burned houses as they fought their way toward freedom in Spanish Florida. Yet another rebellion broke out in Charleston in June 1740, involving 150 to 200 slaves, fifty of whom were hanged for their daring.[42]

Intensifying these events—and holding aloft a beacon of possibility—was the decade-long Maroon War of Jamaica. Beginning in the late

1720s, slaves escaped to the interior of Jamaica in swelling numbers, returned to the plantations in nocturnal raids, and seized livestock, tools, and sometimes other slaves to take back to their secluded and inaccessible maroon communities in the mountains. Over the next ten years the maroons created a major crisis in the plantation system, especially in the northern and northeastern regions of the island, where they repeatedly forced small, marginal planters to abandon their estates and sell off their slaves, some to New York. Writing in 1739, Charles Leslie claimed that the maroons had "increased to such a Degree, as many Times to make the Island tremble." Others agreed: Jamaica was in "a tottering state."[43]

One of the reasons that the maroons were so dangerous to the rulers of England's prize colonial possession was that they were in touch with the government of Spain by way of Cuba, which was, after all, only a canoe ride away off the northern shore of Jamaica. There were not only rumors but actual testimony that the maroons had contacted the Spanish authorities, "offering to hand over the island [of Jamaica] to Spain when they had taken it over, on condition that the Spaniards guarantee their freedom."[44] The maroons may have been confident that they would eventually take over the island themselves, but they also knew that an external attack by Spain, coupled with their own uprising from within, represented an undeniably powerful combination. The authorities of Jamaica certainly did not deny it. Indeed, in 1739 and 1740 they made peace, first with the Leeward Maroons under the firm leadership of Cudjo, then with the Windward Maroons, giving both groups land and autonomy in exchange for their promise to return all future runaway slaves and, perhaps most crucially, to fight against foreign invaders. Its primary enemy within thus neutralized, Great Britain declared war on Spain a mere three months later.[45]

A similar long-term struggle was taking place deep in the rain forests of Suriname, where maroons battled Dutch settlers who, according to Governor Mauricius, struggled to slay the hydra of resistance. A rising tide of rebellion in the Dutch colonies expressed itself in what another official called, in 1740, the intolerable "insolence of the Coloreds and Blacks, freedmen as well as slaves," and in the subversive gatherings of soldiers, sailors, and slaves in waterfront taverns to smoke, drink, gamble, trade, and plot who knew what other dreaded cooperative ventures.

Maroon leader Cudjo signs a treaty with the English authorities, 1739;
R. C. Dallas, The History of the Maroons, from their Origin to the
Establishment of their Chief Tribe at Sierra Leone *(1803), vol. 1.*

Indeed, Dutch authorities were complaining about this explosive combination of workers in the spring of 1741, precisely when the same kinds of people were making trouble in New York.[46]

The famines of 1728–29 and 1740–41 and their respective diasporas added an Irish dimension to the cycle of rebellion. Of special importance was the "Red String Conspiracy," which took place in Savannah, Georgia, in March 1736 and foreshadowed the events in New York five years later. A gang of forty to fifty transported Irish felons met in a low tippling house, where they traded in stolen goods and formed "plots and treasonable Designs against the Colony," even as the elites worried about "the Spaniards or French Instigations." Eventually they designed to burn the town, kill the white men, save their women, and then meet up with a band of nomadic Indians with whom they would make their escape, perhaps to join the German-Cherokee Christian Gottlieb Priber, who was building a "City of Refuge," a communist society for runaway African slaves and European indentured servants as well as Native Americans. The rebels in Savannah would know each other by a "Red string about the Right Wrist." The plot was foiled but nonetheless threw the young colony into "great confusion." Such events were not uncommon, as noted by Kerby A. Miller: "On numerous occasions in the late seventeenth and early eighteenth century, colonial officials in Newfoundland, Nova Scotia, New York and the West Indies feared that Irish 'papists' were plotting insurrection with negro slaves or foreign enemies."[47]

Arson was a common instrument of destruction within the cycle of rebellion, not least because fire was the most accessible of weapons among the dispossessed, especially for those who worked with it in the normal course of their daily life.[48] On the island of Danish St. John in 1733, slaves entered Fort Christiansvaern, killed several soldiers, and set fires to signal a general rising. In Somerset, New Jersey, in 1734, slaves conspired to kill their masters, torch their houses and barns, saddle their horses, and fly "towards the Indians in the *French* Interest." In the Red String Conspiracy, as we have noted, Irish workers planned to burn Savannah and escape to freedom. It was reported in October 1738 that a group of Native Americans, some of whom were whalemen, had plotted in Nantucket "to set Fire to the Houses of the English Inhabitants in the night, and then to fall upon them Arm'd, and kill as many as they could."[49] The slaves who led the Stono Rebellion in South Carolina in 1739 burned several houses as they made their way toward St. Augustine and freedom among the Spanish. More ominously still, a suspicious fire devastated Charleston on November 18, 1740, consuming more than three hundred buildings and doing, in all, several hundred thousand pounds' worth of damage. Flames continued throughout 1741 to haunt the ports and towns of New York, Boston, Charleston, and Hackensack, New Jersey.[50]

Fire also figured in prophecies, rumors, and tales. George Whitefield's friend Hugh Bryan of South Carolina wrote to his fellow slaveowners in early 1741 that the "repeated Insurrections of our Slaves" and the frequency of fires were proof of the great itinerant's dire prophecy that "God's just judgments are upon us." The big planters of South Carolina responded to this pious apostasy in their midst by arresting both Bryan and Whitefield for libel. Two weeks later—on Saint Patrick's Day, when arson was to ignite New York—a Grand Jury condemned Bryan, who taught Christianity to his own slaves, for his "sundry enthusiastic Prophecies of the Destruction of Charles-Town, and deliverance of the Negroes from their Servitude."[51] The tales would continue in 1742, with Daniel Horsmanden's reporting "several pretended prophecies of negroes, that Charles-Town in South-Carolina, and the city of New York, were to be burnt down on the twenty-fifth of March next." The timing suggested that slaves were planning new fireworks to commemorate the earlier acts of revolutionary arson. Horsmanden knew that "there were yet remaining among us, many of the associates in that execrable confederacy, who might yet be hardy enough to persist in the same wicked purposes, and make new attempts." New attempts were in fact made in February and March 1742, as some New Yorkers tried to make good the prophecies. Fire remained a weapon of liberation. If it threatened apocalypse, a new world might yet arise from the ashes.[52]

PATTERNS OF TRADE

When Dr. Alexander Hamilton arrived in New York on June 15, 1744, three years after the failed insurrection, the first thing he noticed was the forest of ships' masts in the harbor: the city truly had "a great deal of shipping." He made his way from the waterfront northward to Broad Street, where he lodged at the home of merchant Robert Hogg. This was the place where the sailor Christopher Wilson had stolen a cache of coins, the search for which by the authorities had eventually unraveled the larger conspiracy. Here Hamilton read Horsmanden's *Journal of the Proceedings*, then inspected the work of the rebels firsthand: "The castle, or fort, is now in ruins, having been burnt down four [*sic*] years agoe by the conspirators." Little did Hamilton realize that what he saw as he gazed upon the charred rubble of Fort George had its origin in what he had observed when he first entered the city: in New York's ships along the wharves and farther out at sea.[53]

A key to the events of 1741 lay in the structure of New York's commerce, which was, as Hamilton quickly understood, the driving force in this city of merchants and maritime workers. During the first half of the eighteenth century, New York's trade was not triangular but rather bilateral, a shuttling from Manhattan down the North American coast to the West Indies and back. In the half century surrounding 1740 (1715–65), roughly three out of four voyages followed the coastal/Caribbean route, plying southward to Maryland, Virginia, and Carolina and even more commonly to Caribbean destinations, especially the English and Dutch islands, Jamaica and Curaçao in particular, and to a lesser extent the French and Spanish colonies, to and from which they regularly a smuggled commodities of various kinds. Cadwallader Colden had noted in 1723 that New York's greatest remittances went to Curaçao and Jamaica.[54]

The conspiracy turned, however, not on what went out in New York's ships but rather on what came home in them. And what came home in them, again and again and again, from coastal and especially from Caribbean ports, was slaves. The primacy of the West Indies in New York's trade meant that the islands provided the vast majority of the city's slaves to achieve a balance of trade. According to statistics complied by Professor James G. Lydon from the naval officers' record lists and the inspector general's ledgers, in the dozen years before 1741, four out of five slaves (79.5 percent) came to New York from the Caribbean (the bulk of them from Jamaica), while another 6 percent came from the ports of the southern mainland colonies. They arrived in lots of three or four on small vessels of thirty to forty tons' carrying capacity, most to be sold at the Meal

Market on the lower east side of Manhattan. Fewer than one in seven of New York's slaves came directly from Africa in the big slave ships that spent months gathering a "cargo" and months more in the Atlantic crossing. Some of New York's bondmen and bondwomen had been sent from the coastal/Caribbean trade routes on special order, and some on consignment; others were what the slave traders called "refuse negroes," with physical "defects" that prevented their sale in the South.[55]

Most crucial for our purposes—and most alarming to a great many New Yorkers—was that many of the slaves who came to New York had a history, often a secret history, of making trouble. West Indian planters sold to New York's traders slaves who possessed "turbulent and unruly tempers" and often some experience in resistance. In the red wake of many a plot or insurrection in plantation America came a mini-diaspora, in which the leaders of the events were sold off, frequently away from their families and communities, to buyers in other parts of the Atlantic. Such was the practice on Antigua in 1736, when eighty-eight slaves were executed for taking part in a conspiracy, and another forty-seven sold and shipped off the island. The same program was followed on Jamaica, on Bermuda, and elsewhere, as it would be in New York after the fires of 1741.[56]

New York was hardly alone in receiving such malefactors: all of the northern seaports, including Newport and Boston, served as markets of last resort in the regional trade in slaves. The governors of both Massachusetts and Rhode Island complained bitterly of the problem in the early eighteenth century, the governor of the former claiming that the traders sent "usually the worst servants they have," including slaves who had accumulated records of violent resistance to their condition. As Edgar J. McManus has written, "Since some colonies permitted masters to export slaves convicted of major crimes, including arson and murder, the intercolonial trade involved serious risks for importing colonies like New York. How many of these slaves were channeled into New York cannot be estimated precisely, but the number was probably large." Governor Rip Van Dam cautioned in the early 1730s that a majority of the slaves imported from the South posed a serious threat to the safety of New York. Governor Cosby objected in 1734 to the "too great Importation of Negroes and Convicts"; a "Negro" and a "Convict" were often one and the same person.[57]

The New York Assembly acknowledged the problem by passing a resolution that warned the buyers of slaves against "refuse Negroes and such malefactors as would have suffered death in the places whence they came had not the avarice of the owners saved them from public justice." Indeed, the assemblymen deemed the matter so serious that they did not stop at a warning; they also imposed a special duty on slaves imported indirectly—that is, from the Caribbean and coastal America—which was twice as high as the duty on slaves imported directly from Africa. The purpose of this policy was, writes Lydon, "largely to discourage importation of recalcitrant blacks from other colonies."[58]

Daniel Horsmanden knew that rebellious slaves imported from other English colonies had played a major role in the conspiracy. In "a modest hint to our brethren in the *West Indies,* and the more neighboring English colonies," he explained how he and his fellow New Yorkers had *properly* transported seventy-seven rebels to other, non-English parts of the Atlantic. He asked other rulers within the British empire to note "how tender we have been of *their* peace and security, by using all the precaution in our power, *that none of our rogues should be imposed upon them."* Horsmanden was quietly complaining that his brother gentlemen in coastal and Caribbean America had imposed *their* rogues on New York, thereby undermining the colony's peace and security. Governor Trelawny, whose Jamaican planters had sent north many of the slaves in question, got the message. After reading Horsmanden's published account of the trial, which identified the slave named Hanover as having been involved in the plot but now being missing, Trelawny personally *found* Hanover among the 112,000 slaves in Jamaica and promptly returned him to New York. Both Trelawny and Horsmanden understood that it was impossible to import slaves without also importing the experience of opposition to slavery. It was in this literal sense that the insurrection was promoted by those whom Horsmanden called "the outcasts of the nations of the earth."[59]

One of these outcasts was a slave named Will, whose life illustrated the connections among insurrection, diaspora, trade, and new insurrection as it represented one long, Atlantic ruling-class nightmare. In 1733, Will had participated in the slave revolt on Danish St. John, in which a gang of rebels carried concealed cane bills (knives) into Fort Christiansvaern, killed several soldiers, and took control of the island's central military installation. They held the fort for seven months, until the imperial powers put aside their differences and organized a joint expedition to defeat the mostly Coromantee rebels, who had in the meantime damaged or destroyed forty-eight plantations. In the aftermath, 146 slaves were implicated in the rising, and twenty-seven of those executed. It was alleged, in New York, that during this rising Will had killed several white men with his own hands. Will was banished from St. John, sold to a planter on the island of Antigua.

Will did not wait long before beginning to plot again, for in 1735 the Akan-speaking slaves of Antigua combined with creole slaves in a plan to seize the island and make it their own. Unlike the rebels of St. John, the insurgents of Antigua never reached the stage of open action. An informer disclosed their plot, after which they were immediately rounded up and arrested. Imprisoned again and knowing that his failure to reform meant certain death, Will saved his own neck by turning state's witness, giving evidence against numerous slaves and earning, briefly, a traitor's reputation as he watched eighty-eight of his comrades be hanged, burned, and broken on the wheel. Along with forty-six others, Will was banished, sold this time to someone in New York, sold again to a new owner in Providence, Rhode Island, and then sold back once more to New York.

Will played a pivotal part in the New York Conspiracy, bringing his West Indian expertise to bear. He was, after all, "very expert at plots, for this was the third time he had engaged in them," as the court was at pains to point out. Will met, at Hughson's and other places, with the slaves and the Irish soldiers, no doubt telling the gripping, bloody tales of his earlier exploits and explaining precisely what had gone wrong. He held up the courage of the plotters on Antigua as an example, claiming that "the negroes here were cowards" and "had no hearts as those at Antigua." The plan of attack on Fort George may have owed something to Will's experience at Fort Christiansvaern. Will even showed the other rebels how to make a dark lanthorn, "a light that no body should see it," which made the nighttime work of conspiracy easier.[60]

For Will and many others, New York was a sort of penal colony in disguise; southern and West Indian planters had surreptitiously made it so. But New York's rulers found them out, discovering in their midst an unknowable but significant number of slaves who were experienced in the ways of resistance. As it happened, New York's merchants had been importing not only sugar, molasses, and slaves on their vessels but the literally explosive class relations of the slaveowning regions to the south—regions that had for several years witnessed a ferocious cycle of rebellion that featured prominently both arson and insurrection. The importation of such experience of rebellion—and the dawning recognition of its dangers—constituted the rational basis of New York's hysteria in 1741.

INSURRECTION AND IMPERIAL RIVALRY

Many of the conditions for insurrection were present in New York in 1741. The city's ruling class was divided and squabbling; a hard winter had caused misery for many; and war had broken out with Spain, increasing hardship all around and weakening military defenses when six hundred able-bodied men were shipped overseas to support the war effort. One conspirator, London, had advised some of his fellow insurrectionists that "now was the best time to do something, it being war time." Moreover, as we have seen, New York's slave traders had inadvertently brought to the city a motley crew of experienced veterans—insurrectionists such as Will, who brought their knowledge of the Caribbean cycle of rebellion of the 1730s and 1740s, *and* soldiers such as William Kane, Juan de la Sylva, and the numerous Coromantees, who brought their knowledge of war and military organization from Ireland, Cuba, and West Africa.[61]

Even though Albany believed "an hundred and fifty men might take this city" (he chose roughly the same number that had been involved in the uprising in Will's St. John), the plotters knew from the beginning that the success of their insurrection would depend on support—local (in New York), regional (in the surrounding countryside), and international (from Britain's imperial rivals, Spain and France). Hughson saw the insurrection as a rising of the mob, wherein early successes would draw more supporters to the cause. Another source of support would be people, both black and white, from the outlying areas, especially "country negroes" such as Jamaica and several sailors who had attended meetings at Hughson's. Comfort's Jack had brought his rural relatives into the plot. Peg Kerry explained that the urban rebels "were to be joined by the country negroes" after the fires were set. Arson did indeed light up the countryside on Long Island and in New Jersey after the burning of Fort George.[62]

The most important assistance would come from Britain's imperial enemies, France or particularly Spain, for like the maroons of Jamaica, the rebels in New York planned to link their uprising from within to an invasion from without. The *New York Weekly Journal* made the point clearly: "The *Spanish* Negroes (of which there are many in this Place) were deeply concerned and active in the Business; and whatever Encouragement or Assurances they might receive from abroad, or hellish incendiaries at home, they were perswaded that an Attempt on this Province would be made by the Spaniards and French, for whom they agreed to wait some Time; and if it should happen that such an Attempt should be made, and our Enemies invade us, they were to rise and join with them." A leader among the African Americans in the plot, Bastian, had the same understanding: "They had a parcel of good hands, Spanish Negroes, five or six of them (then present) who would join with the York Negroes: that they expected that war would be proclaimed in a little time against the French, and that the French and Spaniards would come here." Trial records indicate that at least ten other conspirators saw matters the same way. Primus had heard that the French and Spanish were coming and that the rebels would assist them in taking the city. Kortrecht's Caesar heard from Jack that "the Spaniards were coming here, and the negroes were going to rise, and would help the Spaniards." Scipio also expected the French and the Spanish to invade, "and then would be a fair opportunity": "they might all be free men." The fires might be the beacon of insurrection, signaling to a Spanish flotilla offshore that the time for attack had arrived; or perhaps Spain would learn about the destruction of Fort George and then decide on its own to invade. The soldiers and sailors of New Spain would help the rebels to seize the city (which had, after all, already changed imperial hands once, from Dutch to English, in recent memory), or failing that, they would "carry them off into another country, and make them a free people." In any case, the rebels would win freedom for themselves, and Spain would protect that freedom.[63]

The references to Spain, in New York and throughout the cycle of rebellion of the 1730s and 1740s, bespoke a truth well understood at the time but seldom emphasized since. The slaves of the anglophone Atlantic often saw Spain as a liberator, not least because of the tradition of Spanish abolitionism. When Bastian told other conspirators that Spain might guarantee their eventual freedom, it was no idle fantasy, for Spain had already done just that for many people of African descent in the New World. Indeed, the Hispanic sailors were, by their own claims to freedom, living, breathing instances of liberation, there to confirm the possibilities that lay in New Spain. It was widely known that the Spanish king had aggressively enticed the slaves of English masters with royal *cédulas* in 1733 and 1740, promising first limited freedom and then full freedom to anyone who escaped an English for a Spanish settlement. New Spain's officials in Florida followed through on the promise by creating an official maroon village on the northern edge of their settlement, called Gracia Real Santa Teresa de Mose, where a hundred runaways, mostly from Carolina, were settled and transformed into a first line of defense against English attacks from the north. Spain had also for years been encouraging the maroons of Britain's Caribbean colonies, as New York's many Jamaican slaves knew well. It was an accident of history, though a fateful one, that Afro-Cubans and Afro-Jamaicans conversed about freedom in New York in 1741, just as they had done when communicating across the waters between Cuba and Jamaica in the 1730s.[64]

More important still was that Spanish officials consciously planned to use agents such as the Hispanic sailors to foster slave revolt in English dominions in North America by late 1742, or perhaps even earlier. Juan Francisco de Güemes, governor general of Cuba, wrote to Manuel de Montiano, governor of Florida, to explain an imminent military action: three thousand Cuban soldiers would attack South Carolina between April and June 1742, unleashing a force of "negroes of all languages" to filter through the countryside, promising land and freedom to the slaves of English masters and inciting revolt throughout the province. The agitators and organizers of insurrection were to be not priests, as the paranoid Protestants of New York thought, but rather former slaves, who would operate through precisely the kinds of networks that existed in New York.[65]

And yet the insurrection in New York failed. It is impossible to know exactly what went wrong, but there is evidence to suggest that Quack burned the fort several weeks too early, catching everyone off guard and causing the carefully laid plans to unfold in a chaotic series of small fires, as the rebels did what they could to carry out the long-plotted uprising. Quack had been voted by his fellow conspirators "to be the person who should fire the fort" because his wife worked there as cook for the governor, which meant that he had the requisite knowledge of and access to that most strategic of places. Unfortunately for the rebels, Quack soon got into trouble with the authorities; he was prohibited from visiting his wife and banned from the fort. Acting in anger and apparently motivated by a desire for personal revenge, Quack broke discipline and set the first fire prematurely, on March 17. Several sources—including one rebel's saying to another who set a fire, "You should not have done it till we were all ready"—indicated that the fires were scheduled to be set instead in early May, at the very moment when a flotilla of five Spanish privateers arrived off the coast, having captured eight prize vessels along the way and in so doing panicked the rulers of New York. The ships' arrival coincided with the trials of John Hughson, Peg Kerry, Cuffee, and Quack.[66]

REBELLION OF THE HANGED

The multiracial waterfront posed a political problem for New York's rulers. The cooperative nature of work in the port had created dangerous insurrectionary connections between slaves of African descent—men such as Gwin and Cuffee—and "the most flagitious, degenerated, and abandoned, and scum and dregs of the white population," represented by John Hughson and Peg Kerry. The love story alluded to at the outset of this chapter was an instance of the human solidarity that developed in the plot. Colonel Thomas Rainborough had warned at Putney that care must be taken to choose the right mother and father. Solidarity was not restricted to the genetic nuclear family, nor could it be so restricted among "outcasts." As Francis spoke of the "sisters" of her spiritual community, so the Irish soldiers called one another "brother." The love of John Gwin and Peg Kerry thus paralleled a broader alliance.[67]

The authorities approached the solidarity with a trident in hand, each of its points carefully sharpened to puncture the prevailing multiracial practices and bonds of proletarian life in Atlantic New York. First they went after the taverns and other settings where "cabals" of poor whites and blacks could be formed and subversive plans disseminated. Next they self-consciously recomposed the proletariat of New York to make it more difficult for workers along the waterfront to find among themselves sources of unity. And finally, they endeavored to teach racial lessons to New York's people of European descent, promoting a white identity that would transcend and unify the city's fractious ethnic divisions. Let us treat these three major consequences of the conspiracy of 1741 in turn.

Both during and after the trials for conspiracy, New York's men in ruffles attacked the city's low tippling houses, criminalizing black-white cooperation and controlling the sites where multiracial conspiracies might unfold. Horsmanden urged "diligent inquiry into the economy and behaviour of all the mean ale-houses and tipling house within this city," especially those that entertained "negroes, and the scum and dregs of white people in conjunction." Such establishments encouraged theft and debauchery, but even worse, they provided "opportunities for the most loose, debased and abandoned wretches amongst us to cabal and confederate together, and ripen themselves in these schools of mischief, for the execution of the most daring and detestable counterprizes: I fear there are yet many of these houses amongst us, and they are the bane and pest of the city; it was such that gave the opportunity of breeding this most horrid and execrable conspiracy." Horsmanden was right: mean alehouses such as Hughson's, where the wretched of many colors and nations gathered, were indeed schools. These were places where such people told their Atlantic tales, yarns, and stories, their oral histories and lore of insurrection.[68]

The second major policy change was not a matter of governmental action but rather a series of private business decisions taken by the merchants of New York. In what may constitute the strongest evidence of the related Caribbean and insurrectionary dimensions of the conspiracy, the city's big merchants responded to the upheaval by restructuring their slave trade, sending many more of their ships directly to Africa, and many fewer down the coastal/Caribbean route, in search of slaves. Partly this was a response to a growing demand for slaves in South Carolina and

Jamaica after the economic slump of the 1730s had passed. But it was also a collective recognition by merchants that their earlier business practices had endangered their own base of accumulation. Before 1741 they had imported seven out of every ten slaves from the regions to the south, and only three of ten from Africa. After 1741 they reversed the ratio, bringing seven of ten slaves directly from Africa and only three of ten from plantation regions to their south. As James G. Lydon has written, "The full range of reasons for this shift from dependence upon indirect sources to direct importations from Africa is difficult to establish, but the slave plot at New York in 1741 appears to have been quite important." Fears about the importation of "incorrigible slaves," or "malcontents," concludes Lydon, "may well have dictated this shift in the city's trading pattern." New York merchants realized that the commodity was not always what it seemed: they had imported aboard their ships not just the scarred, beaten bodies of West Indian slaves but within those another bloody body of ideas and practices of insurrection. They would, in recognition of this fundamental fact, seek to recompose the proletariat of New York, counting at least in part on the linguistic and cultural barriers of African ethnicity to ensure social peace.[69]

The third major response to the events of 1741 was the promotion of a white identity designed to cut across and unite a variety of ethnicities. Of course many New Yorkers, people in ruffles as well as negrophobic artisans, had long taken whiteness for granted. But to those who gathered at Hughson's, the "white people" were, in code or cant, the rich, the people with money, not simply the ones with a particular phenotype of skin color. Racial typing in New York remained fluid, open, often ambiguous. The lovers John Gwin and Peg Kerry typified and exploited the ambiguity: Gwin used an Irish name, pretending to be a soldier at Fort George; "Negro Peg" complained about "that bitch" Mary Burton, who had implicated her in several thefts and thereby "made me as black as the rest." The slave Tom described his recruitment into the conspiracy in a way that would have been impossible a generation later: "The white men wanted him to join to help kill the white people."[70] The "white" David Johnson rose before an assembly at Hughson's, can of punch in hand, and pledged "to burn the town, and kill as many white people as he could."[71]

Ruling whites reacted to the racial fluidity within the conspiracy with terror and mercy, the combination of which was meant to produce new discipline and a different solidarity. First they demonized the people of European descent who were involved in the plot: Hughson and his ilk were said to be "monsters in nature," the very "disgrace of their complexion"; indeed, they were "much worse than the negroes." Hughson himself was "blacker than a negro": he was "the scandal of his complexion, and the disgrace of human nature!" Such language predicted a violent fate, and four Euramericans were accordingly hanged; others were forced into military service in the West Indies, and still others banished from the province. Another six, however, were quietly and mercifully discharged by the court, almost without comment. The decision to let them go was expressed in a simple notation in the trial records: "No person appearing to prosecute." This, too, was a message for and about "whites." New York's rulers thus divided and weakened the proletariat as they unified and strengthened a fictive community based on whiteness.[72]

And yet when Horsmanden and his like tried to use the trial and the executions to popularize lessons about race, about the unifying advantages of whiteness, the rebels, even in death, refused to cooperate. After Hughson was hanged, his corpse was gibbeted so as to offer moral instruction to anyone who dared to betray his or her race. So, too, was the corpse of John Gwin/Caesar strung up in chains, so that people of African descent would think at least twice before challenging the system of slavery in New York. Both, so the message went, would be punished into the afterlife. But curious things began to happen. Within three weeks after the hanging, Hughson's remains—his "face, hands, neck, and feet"— had turned "a deep shining black," while the hair of his "beard and neck (his head could not be seen for he had a cap on) was curling like the wool of a negro's beard and head." Moreover, "the features of his face" had assumed "the symmetry of a negro beauty; the nose broad and flat, the nostrils open and extended, the mouth wide, lips full and thick." Gwin/Caesar, in contrast, in life "one of the darkest hue of his kind," had in death undergone the opposite transformation: his face "was at the time somewhat bleached or turned whitish."

In the end, it was said, "Hughson was turned negro, and Vaarck's Caesar a white"; they had "changed colours." New Yorkers "were amazed at these appearances"—and not least of all Daniel Horsmanden, who once upon a time had described an impossible task by saying, "The Ethiopian might as soon change his skin." Word of what had happened to the bodies of Hughson and Gwin spread far and wide, "engaged the attention of many, and drew numbers of all ranks, who had curiosity, to the gibbets, for several days running, in order to be convinced by their own eyes, of the reality of things so confidently reported to be." Seeing was believing, and many accounted the transformations "wondrous phenomenons." Others spectators "were ready to resolve them into miracles." Rebels to the end, Gwin and Hughson thus took some last revenge against the white people in wigs and ruffles. Even their dead bodies were capable of subversion.[73]

CHAPTER SEVEN

A Motley Crew in the
American Revolution

In October 1765 a mob of sailors wearing blackface and masks, armed with clubs and cutlasses, visited the home of a wealthy Charleston merchant named Henry Laurens. Eighty strong and warm with drink and anger, they had come to protest the Stamp Act, recently passed by Parliament to raise tax revenues in the American colonies. Responding to the rumor that Laurens had stored in his home the stamped paper everyone would be forced to buy in order to conduct the business of daily life, they chanted, "Liberty, Liberty, & Stamp'd Paper," and demanded that he turn it over so that they could destroy it in an act of defiance. Laurens was rattled, as he later explained: they "not only menaced very loudly but now & then handled me pretty uncouthly." Finally convinced that Laurens did not have the paper, the men dispersed across the waterfront, shedding their disguises and straggling into the smoky taverns and bare boardinghouses, onto the damp wharves and creaky ships.

Their protest had consequences. Parliament, taken aback by colonial resistance, would soon repeal the Stamp Act. And in Charleston, one thing would lead to another, as another mob would meet in January 1766 to cry again for liberty. This time the protesters were African slaves, whose action caused greater fear and "vast trouble throughout the province." Armed patrols stalked the city's streets for almost two weeks, but the tumult continued. Since Charleston's harbor was crowded with ships, the seafarers were soon "in motion and commotion again," styling themselves, said a cynical Laurens, the "Protectors of Liberty." South Carolina Governor William Bull would later look back over the events of late 1765 and early 1766 and blame Charleston's turmoil on "disorderly negroes, and more disorderly sailors."[1]

Laurens and Bull identified a revolutionary subject often described by contemporaries as a "motley crew," which has rarely been discussed in histories of the American Revolution. It is a subject whose history we have traced from the hydrarchy of the 1710s and 1720s to the slave revolts and urban insurrections of the 1730s and 1740s. The defeat of these movements allowed slavery and maritime trade to expand, as gangs of slaves extended plantation acreage and gangs of sailors manned ever-growing fleets of naval and merchant vessels. Britain confirmed its primacy as the world's greatest capitalist power by defeating France in the Seven Years' War in 1763, protecting and enlarging its lucrative colonial empire and opening vast new territories in North America and the Caribbean for the hewing of wood and the drawing of water. And yet at the very moment of imperial triumph, slaves and sailors began a new cycle of rebellion.

Operations on sea and land, from mutiny to insurrection, made the motley crew the driving force of a revolutionary crisis in the 1760s and 1770s. Such actions helped to destabilize imperial civil society and pushed America toward the world's first modern colonial war for liberation. By energizing and leading the movement from below, the motley crew shaped the social, organizational, and intellectual histories of the era and demonstrated that the American Revolution was neither an elite nor a national event, since its genesis, process, outcome, and influence all depended on the circulation of proletarian experience around the Atlantic. That circulation would continue into the 1780s, as the veterans of the revolutionary movement in America carried their knowledge and experience to the eastern Atlantic, initiating pan-Africanism, advancing abolitionism, and assisting in the revival of dormant traditions of revolutionary thought and action in England and, more broadly, in Europe. The motley crew would help to break apart the first British empire and to inaugurate the Atlantic's age of revolution.

For our purposes, two distinct meanings of "motley crew" must be defined. The first of these refers to an organized gang of workers, a squad of people performing either similar tasks or different ones contributing to a single goal. The gangs of the tobacco and sugar plantations were essential to the accumulation of wealth in early America. Equally essential were the crews assembled from the ship's company, or ship's people, for a particular, temporary purpose, such as sailing a ship, undertaking an amphibious assault, or collecting wood and water. These crews knew how to pull together, or to act in unison, not least because they labored beneath the whip. The first meaning, then, is technical and specific to the plantation and maritime labor processes. The economies of the eighteenth-century Atlantic depended on this unit of human cooperation.

The second meaning describes a sociopolitical formation of the eighteenth-century port or town. The "motley crew" in this sense was closely related to the urban mob and the revolutionary crowd, which, as we shall see, were usually armed agglomerations of various crews and gangs that possessed their own motility and were often independent of leadership from above. They provided the driving force from the Stamp Act crisis to the "Wilkes and Liberty" riots to the series of risings of the American Revolution. The revolts of the eighteenth-century Atlantic depended on this broader social form of cooperation.

When we say the crew was motley, we mean that it was multiethnic. This was, as we have noted, characteristic of the recruitment of ships' crews during and after the expansion of the maritime state under Cromwell. Such diversity was an expression of defeat—consider the deliberate mixing of languages and ethnicities in the packing of slave ships—but that defeat was transformed into strength by agency, as when a pan-African, and then an African American, identity was formed from the various ethnicities and cultures. Original "ethnic" designations, such as the "free-born Englishman," could thus become generalized, as shown by our study of the African sailor Olaudah Equiano, below.

Over time, the second (political) meaning emerged from the first (technical) one, broadening the cooperation, extending the range of activity, and transferring command from overseers or petty officers to the group itself. This transition was manifested in the actions of the motley crew in the streets of the port cities: as sailors moved from ship to shore, they joined waterfront communities of dockers, porters, and laborers, freedom-seeking slaves, footloose youth from the country, and fugitives of various kinds. At the peak of revolutionary possibility, the motley crew appeared as a synchronicity or an actual coordination among the "risings of the people" of the port cities, the resistance of African American slaves, and Indian struggles on the frontier. Tom Paine feared precisely this combination, but it never actually materialized. On the contrary, as we shall see, the reversal of revolutionary dynamics, toward thermidor, shifted the milieu of the motley crew, as refugees, boat people, evacuees, and prisoners gave human form to defeat.

SAILORS

Sailors were prime movers in the cycle of rebellion, especially in North America, where they helped to secure numerous victories for the movement against Great Britain between 1765 and 1776. They led a series of riots against impressment beginning in the 1740s, moving Thomas Paine (in *Common Sense*) and Thomas Jefferson (in the Declaration of Independence) to list that practice as a major grievance. Their militancy in port grew out of their daily work experience at sea, which combined coordinated cooperation with daring initiative. Sailors engaged on board ship in collective struggles over food, pay, work, and discipline, and they brought to the ports a militant attitude toward arbitrary and excessive authority, an empathy for the troubles of others, and a willingness to cooperate for the sake of self-defense. As Henry Laurens discovered, they were not afraid to use direct action to accomplish their goals. Sailors thus entered the 1760s armed with the traditions of hydrarchy. They would learn new tactics in the age of revolution, but so, too, would they contribute the vast amount they already knew.[2]

Part of what sailors knew was how to resist impressment. This tradition had originated in thirteenth-century England and continued through the Putney Debates and the English Revolution, into the late seventeenth century with the expansion of the Royal Navy, and then on into the eighteenth with its ever-greater wartime mobilizations. When, after a quarter century's peace, England declared war against Spain in 1739, sailors battled and often defeated press-gangs in every English port. Fists and clubs flew in American ports as well, on Antigua, St. Kitts, Barbados, and Jamaica and in New York and New England.[3] Seamen rioted in Boston in 1741, beating a sheriff and a magistrate who had assisted the press-gang of H.M.S. *Portland.* The following year, three hundred seamen armed with clubs, cutlasses, and axes attacked the commanding officer of the *Astrea* and destroyed a naval barge. They rose twice more in 1745, first roughing up another sheriff and the commander of H.M.S. *Shirley,* then, seven months later, confronting Captain Forest and his H.M.S. *Wager,* but losing two of their own to the flashing cutlasses of the press-gang. Admiral Peter Warren warned in 1745 that the sailors of New England were emboldened by a revolutionary heritage: they had, he wrote, "the highest notions of the rights and liberties of Englishmen, and indeed are almost Levellers."[4]

During the 1740s sailors began to burn the boats in which the press-gangs came ashore to snatch bodies, cutting their contact with the men-of-war and making "recruitment" harder, if not impossible. Commander Charles Knowles wrote in 1743 that naval vessels pressing in the Caribbean "have had their Boats haul'd up in the Streets and going to be Burned, & their Captains insulted by 50 Arm'd Men at a time, and obliged to take shelter in some Friends House." After Captain Abel Smith of the *Pembroke Prize* pressed some men near St. Kitts, a mob of seamen "came off in the road and seized the Kings boat, hawled her up . . . and threatned to burn her, if the Captain would not return the Prest Men, which he was obliged to do to save the Boat, & peoples Lives, to the great Dishonour of Kings Authority (especially in Foreign Parts)." These attacks on the property and power of the British state were intimidating: by 1746 the captain of H.M.S. *Shirley* "dared not set foot on shore for four months for fear of being prosecuted . . . or murdered by the mob for pressing."[5]

The struggle against impressment took another creative turn in 1747, when, according to Thomas Hutchinson, there occurred "a tumult in the Town of Boston equal to any which had preceded it." The commotion began when fifty sailors, some of them New Englanders, deserted Commander Knowles and H.M.S. *Lark.* In response, Knowles sent a press-gang to sweep the Boston wharves. A mob of three hundred seamen swelled to "several thousand people" and seized officers of the *Lark* as hostages, beat a deputy sheriff and slapped him into the town's stocks, surrounded and attacked the Provincial Council Chamber, and posted squads at all piers to keep naval officers from escaping back to their ship. The mob soon faced down Massachusetts Governor William Shirley, reminding him of the murderous violence visited upon sailors by the press-

gang in 1745 and threatening him with the example of Captain John Porteous, the despised leader of Edinburgh's City Guard, who after murdering a member of the crowd in 1736 had been captured and "hanged upon
a sign post." Governor Shirley beat a hasty retreat to Castle William,
where he remained until the riot ran its course. Meanwhile, armed sailors
and laborers considered burning a twenty-gun ship being built for His
Majesty in a local shipyard, then picked up what they thought was a naval barge, carried it through town, and set it aflame on Boston Common.
Commodore Knowles explained their grievance: "The Act [of 1746]
against pressing in the Sugar Islands, filled the Minds of the Common
People ashore as well as Sailors in all the Northern Colonies (but more
especially in New England) with not only a hatred for the King's Service
but [also] a Spirit of Rebellion each *Claiming a Right* to the same Indul-
gence as the Sugar Colonies and declaring they will maintain themselves
in it."

As sailors defended liberty in the name of right, they captured the attention of a young man named Samuel Adams, Jr. Employing what his
enemies called "serpentine cunning," and understanding "Human Nature, in low life" very well, Adams watched the motley crew defend itself
and then translated its "Spirit of Rebellion" into political discourse. He
used the Knowles Riot to formulate a new "ideology of resistance, in
which the natural rights of man were used for the first time in the province to justify mob activity." Adams saw that the mob "embodied the
fundamental rights of man against which government itself could be
judged," and he justified the taking of violent, direct action against oppression. The motley crew's resistance to slavery thereby produced a
breakthrough in revolutionary thought.[6]

Adams thus moved from the "rights of Englishmen" to the broader,
more universal idiom of natural rights and the rights of man in 1747, and
one likely reason for this shift may be found in the composition of the
crowd that instructed him. Adams faced a dilemma: how could he watch
a crowd of Africans, Scotsmen, Dutchmen, Irishmen, and Englishmen
battle the press-gang and then describe them as being engaged simply in
a struggle for the "rights of Englishmen"? How could he square the apparently traditional Lockean ideas set forth in his Harvard master's thesis
of 1743 with the activities of the "Foreign Seamen, Servants, Negroes,

and other Persons of mean and vile Condition" who led the riot of 1747?[7] The diversity of the rebellious subject forced his thought toward a broader justification. Adams would have understood that the riot was, literally, a case of the people's fighting for its liberty, for throughout the eighteenth century the crew of a ship was known as "the people," who once ashore were on their "liberty."[8]

The mass actions of 1747 moved Adams to found a weekly publication called the *Independent Advertiser,* which expressed a remarkable, even prophetic variety of radical ideas during its brief but vibrant life of less than two years. The paper reported on mutiny and resistance to the press-gang. It supported the natural right to self-defense and vigorously defended the ideas and practices of equality, calling, for example, for popular vigilance over the accumulation of wealth and an "Agrarian Law or something like it" (a Diggerlike redistribution of land) to support the poor workers of New England. It announced that "the reason of a People's Slavery, is . . . *Ignorance of their own Power.*" Perhaps the single most important idea to be found in the *Independent Advertiser* appeared in January 1748: "All Men are by Nature on a Level; born with an equal Share of Freedom, and endow'd with Capacities nearly alike." These words reached back exactly a century, to the English Revolution and the Levellers' *Agreement of the People,* and simultaneously looked forward to the opening words of the Declaration of Independence of 1776.[9]

Another connection between 1747 and 1776 may be detected in Jonathan Mayhew's sermon "A Discourse Concerning Unlimited Submission and Non-Resistance to the Higher Powers," delivered and published in Boston in early 1750. The eminent clergyman preached his sermon at a time when the riot and its consequences were still on the minds of townspeople, especially the traders and seafarers who made up his own West Church. By 1748 Mayhew's preachings were considered heretical enough to get one listener, a young Paul Revere, a whipping from his father for his waywardness. By early 1749 Mayhew was tending toward what some saw as sedition, asserting that it was not a sin to transgress an iniquitous law such as the one that legalized impressment. Mayhew defended regicide in his sermon of January 30, the anniversary of the execution of Charles I, which was to him no day of mourning but rather a day for remembering that Britons will not be slaves. Like Adams before him, he argued passionately for both civil disobedience and a right to resistance that utilized force; indeed, passive nonresistance, Mayhew claimed, was slavery. Mayhew's influential defense of the right to revolution could not have been made without the action of the riot and its examination by Sam Adams and the readers of the *Independent Advertiser*.[10]

The ideas and practices of 1747 were refined and expanded during the 1760s and 1770s, when Jack Tar took part in almost every port-city riot, especially after the end of the Seven Years' War (1763), when the demobilization of the navy threw thousands out of work. For those who remained at sea, the material conditions (food, wages, discipline) of naval life deteriorated, causing many to desert. The Admiralty responded with terror: in 1764 deserters John Evans, Nicholas Morris, and John Tuffin received seven hundred lashes on the back; Bryant Diggers and William Morris were hanged. Admiral Alexander Colvill admitted that these were the "most severe punishments I ever knew to have been inflicted" for desertion. Such deadly discipline at sea imparted a desperate intensity to shoreside resistance once the press-gang resumed its work.[11]

Sailors now revived their attack on the king's naval property. When a press-gang from H.M.S. *St. John* tried in June 1764 to capture a deserter on a Newport wharf, a mob of sailors and dockworkers counterattacked, recaptured the man, roughed up the lieutenant who led the press-gang, and "threatened to haul [the king's] schooner on shore, and burn her." The crowd later went by boat to Goat Island, where it fired cannon at the *St. John*. A month later, a New York mob attacked a press-gang of the *Chaleur* and "drawed its boat before the City Hall and there burnt her." The pressed men were let go, the naval captain was forced to offer a public apology, and all efforts made in court to convict members of the mob of wrongdoing failed. Soon after, another mob of maritime workers in Casco Bay, Maine, seized a press boat, "dragged her into the middle of Town" and threatened to burn her unless a group of pressed men were freed.[12] In Newport in 1765 a mob made up of sailors, youths, and African Americans took over the press tender of H.M.S. *Maidstone,* carried it to a central location in town, and set it ablaze. As popular antagonism toward the customs service grew in the late 1760s, sailors began to attack *its* vessels as well. Thomas Hutchinson wrote that in Boston in 1768, "a boat, belonging to the custom-house, was dragged in triumph through the streets of the town, and burnt on the Common." Seamen either threatened to or actually did torch other vessels belonging to the king in Wilmington, North Carolina, and in Nevis in 1765, in Newport again in 1769 and 1772, and twice in New York in 1775. Sailors thus warned local leaders not to sign press warrants, as they twisted the longest and strongest arm of state power.[13]

In the late 1760s, sailors linked movements in England and America by engaging in revolts that combined workers' riots over wages and hours with protests related to electoral politics ("Wilkes and Liberty," in which the London mob supported John Wilkes, the journalist and ruling-class renegade, in his battles with the king and Parliament). The sailors of London, the world's largest port, played leading roles in both movements and in 1768 struck (i.e., took down) the sails of their vessels, crippling the commerce of the empire's leading city and adding the strike to the armory of resistance. Seamen's strikes would subsequently take place on both sides of the Atlantic with increasing frequency, as would struggles over maritime wages, especially after the reorganization of British customs in 1764, when officials began to seize the nonmonetary wages of seamen—that is, the "venture" or goods they shipped on their own account, freight-free, in the hold of their ship.[14] In leading the general strike of 1768, sailors drew upon traditions of hydrarchy to advance a proletarian idea of liberty. One writer, looking back on the uprising, explained, "Their ideas of liberty are the entering into [of] illegal combinations." Such combinations were "a many headed monster which every one should oppose, because every one's property is endangered by it; nay, the riches, strength, and glory of this kingdom must ever be insecure whilst this evil remains unchecked."[15]

Sailors also continued the struggle against impressment, battling the press-gangs in the streets of London in 1770 (during the war against Spain) and 1776 (during the war against the American colonies, hardly a popular cause among sailors). "Nauticus" observed the clashes between seamen and the navy in London in the early 1770s and wrote *The Rights of the Sailors Vindicated,* in which he compared the sailor's life to slavery and defended the right to self-defense. He echoed the Putney Debates more than a century earlier when he imagined a sailor's asking a magistrate, "I, who am as *free-born* as yourself, should devote my life and liberty for so trifling a consideration, purely that such wretches as you may enjoy your possessions in safety?" Like Sam Adams, Nauticus went beyond the rights of Englishmen, pitting the rights of private property against common rights and the "natural rights of an innocent subject." John Wilkes also began to argue for the right to resist impressment in 1772.[16]

The motley crew also helped to create an abolitionist movement in London in the mid-1760s by setting in motion the eccentric but zealous Granville Sharp, who became one of slavery's most implacable foes. The key moment was a meeting in 1765 in a queue at a London medical clinic between the obscure, flinty clerk and musician Sharp and a teenager named Jonathan Strong, formerly a slave in Barbados, who had been pummeled by his master into a crippled, swollen, nearly blind indigent. Sharp and his brother, a surgeon, nursed Strong back to health, but two years later his former master imprisoned and then sold him. To prevent further such inhumanity, the African sailor Olaudah Equiano pushed Sharp to study the law and the writ of habeas corpus, the most powerful legacy of the "free-born Englishman," because it prohibited imprisonment or confinement without due process of law and trial by jury, and thus might be employed against impressment and slavery alike. Sharp believed that the law should be no respecter of persons and concluded in 1769 that the "common law and custom of England . . . is always favourable to liberty and freedom of man." Especially moved by the struggles of black sailors on the waterfront, he used habeas to defend several who struggled to resist reenslavement, often by the press-gang. Sharp won a lasting victory in his legal defense of James Somerset in 1772, when the court limited the ability of slaveowners to possess and exploit their human property in England. Habeas corpus, however, was suspended in 1777, though not without opposition. The Robin Hood Club of London debated the question, "Would not suspending the Habeas Corpus Act be a proper measure at this juncture?" The negative carried the debate by a great majority. Meanwhile, a police magistrate named John Fielding founded the "Bow Street Runners," an urban metropolitan parallel to the notorious slave patrollers of the southern plantations. He paid close attention to the motley crew in London and monitored its westward circulation back to Caribbean insurrections.[17]

Sailors and the dockside proletariat attacked slavery from another angle in 1775, when they went on strike in Liverpool, as three thousand men, women, and children assembled to protest a reduction in wages.

When the authorities fired upon the crowd, killing several, the strike exploded into open insurrection. Sailors "hoisted the red flag," dragged ships' guns to the center of the city, and bombarded the Mercantile Exchange, leaving "scarce a whole pane of glass in the neighborhood." They also trashed the property of several rich slave-trading merchants. One witness to the strife in Liverpool wrote, "I could not help thinking we had Boston here, and I fear this is only the beginning of our sorrows."[18]

There was a literal truth to the observation that Boston, the "Metropolis of Sedition," was casting its long shadow on English ports on the eve of the American Revolution. An anonymous eyewitness noted that multiethnic American sailors "were among the most active in the late tumults" of London in 1768. They were "wretches of a mongrel descent," the "immediate sons of Jamaica, or African Blacks by Asiatic Mulatoes." When such seamen chanted "No Wilkes, No King!" during the river strike of 1768, they displayed the independent revolutionary spirit that informed their actions ocean-wide. An escaped indentured servant named James Aitken, better known as Jack the Painter, took part in the Boston Tea Party, then returned to England to wage revolutionary arson in 1775 against the king's ships and shipyards, for which crime he was captured and hanged. The mobility of sailors and other maritime veterans ensured that both the experience and the ideas of opposition carried fast. If the artisans and gentlemen of the American Sons of Liberty saw their rebellion as but "one episode in a worldwide struggle between liberty and despotism," sailors, who had a much broader experience of both despotism and the world, saw their own struggle as part of a long Atlantic contest between slavery and freedom.[19]

SLAVES

A new wave of opposition to slavery was inaugurated in Jamaica in 1760 by Tacky's Revolt, which was, according to sugar planter and historian Edward Long, "more formidable than any [uprising] hitherto known in the West Indies." The revolt began, significantly, on Easter, in Saint Mary's Parish, and spread like cane-fire to involve thousands islandwide. The rebels were motivated not by Christianity (Jamaican Baptism and Methodism lay in the future, and the Moravian mission, established in 1754, was tiny) but rather by the mysterious Akan religion, which, continuing despite its prohibition since 1696, stressed spirit possession, access to supernatural powers, and a lively presence of the dead. Practitioners, or obeah men, conferred immortal powers upon the freedom fighters, who shaved their heads to signify their solidarity.[20] Their idea was to seize the forts and arms and destroy the mills. One of the leaders, Aponga (aka Wager), had been a sailor aboard H.M.S. *Wager* and may have witnessed the battles between the press-gang and the mob of sailors in Boston in 1745. In Kingston, a female slave, Cubah, was dubbed "the Queen." The main leader, Tacky (whose name meant "chief" in Akan), was said to catch bullets in his hand and hurl them back at the slavemasters. The rebellion raged for several months, until a military force, which included the Scott's Hall Maroons, was organized by land and sea against the rebels. Tacky was captured and decapitated, his head exhibited on a pole in Spanish Town. After his head was recaptured by night, Edward Long admitted that "such exercises in frightfulness proved of doubtful value." Guerrilla fighting continued for a year. The carnage was among the greatest yet witnessed in a slave revolt: sixty whites killed; three to four hundred slaves killed in military action or dead of suicide once their cause became hopeless; and a hundred slaves executed. Accompanying the terror was legislation and policing, tighter control over meetings, registration of free blacks, permanent fortification in each parish, and the death penalty for those who practiced obeah.[21]

Order was reestablished on Jamaica, but apparently with little help from the merchant seamen who found themselves there when the revolt broke out and were quickly herded into the local militias to help put down the uprising. Thomas Thistlewood explained that as the sailors wandered from one plantation to another, the grog and silver spoons of the terrified sugar planters seemed to disappear. Edward Long claimed that in the middle of the revolt, a captured leader of the slave rebels told a Jewish militia guard, "As for the sailors, you see they do not oppose us, they care not who is in possession of the country, Black or White, it is the same to them." The rebel was convinced that after the revolution, the sailors would "bring us things from t'other side the sea, and be glad to take our goods in payment."[22]

Like the Knowles Riot in Boston in 1747, Tacky's Revolt revived and contributed to a tradition of revolutionary thought that stretched back to Winstanley and the English Revolution. In 1760, after the rebellion had broken out but before it was suppressed, a writer known to us only as J. Philmore wrote a pamphlet entitled *Two Dialogues on the Man-Trade*. Considering himself more a "citizen in the world" than a citizen of England, Philmore insisted that "all of the human race, are, by nature, upon an equality," and that one person simply could not be the property of another. He denied the worldly superiority of Christianity and judged the slave trade to be organized murder. Philmore had probably learned of Tacky's Revolt by way of merchant seamen, for he made it his business to frequent the docks. Much of the great deal he knew of the slave trade came "from the mouths of some sailors."[23]

Philmore supported the efforts of Tacky and his fellow rebels "to deliver themselves out of the miserable slavery they are in." His principal conclusion was clear, straightforward, and revolutionary: "So all the black men now in our plantations, who are by unjust force deprived of their liberty, and held in slavery, as they have none upon earth to appeal to, may lawfully repel that force with force, and to recover their liberty, destroy their oppressors: and not only so, but it is the duty of others, white as well as black, to assist those miserable creatures, if they can, in their attempts to deliver themselves out of slavery, and to rescue them out of the hands of their cruel tyrants." Philmore thus supported these freeborn people engaged in revolutionary self-defense, calling for immediate emancipation, by force if necessary, and asking all good men and women to do the same. Even though Philmore's ideas must have caused pacifist Quakers to shudder (Anthony Benezet drew on his writing but carefully deleted his argument about repelling force with force), they nonetheless had broad influence. He wrote that "no legislature on earth, which is the supreme power in every civil society, can alter the nature of things, or make that to be lawful, which is contrary to the law of God, the supreme legislator and governor of the world." His "higher law" doctrine would over the next century become central to the transatlantic struggle against slavery. His inclusive, egalitarian conception of "the human race" was inspired by the mass actions of rebellious slaves.[24]

Tacky's Revolt may also have helped to generate another breakthrough in abolitionist thought, in the same seaport where Sam Adams had earlier learned to oppose impressment. When, in 1761, James Otis, Jr., made his oration against the writs of assistance that allowed British authorities to attack the trade carried on between New England and the French West Indies, he went beyond his formal subject to "assert the rights of the Negroes." Otis delivered his electrifying speech immediately after Tacky's Revolt, which had been covered in a series of articles in Boston newspapers. John Adams would later recall that Otis was, that day, "a flame of fire," a prophet with the combined powers of Isaiah and Ezekiel. He gave a "dissertation on the rights of man in a state of nature," an antinomian account of man as "an independent sovereign, subject to no law, but the law written on his heart" or lodged in his conscience. No Quaker in Philadelphia ever "asserted the rights of negroes in stronger terms." Otis called for immediate emancipation and advocated the use of force to accomplish it, causing the cautious Adams to tremble. When Otis published *The Rights of the British Colonies Asserted and Proved* (1764), he claimed that all men, "white or black," were "by the law of nature freeborn," thereby broadening and deracializing the idiom of the "free-born Englishman."[25] Whether Otis had actually read Philmore's pamphlet or simply drawn similar conclusions from Tacky's Revolt, abolitionist thought would never be the same. Otis, whose echoes of the 1640s caused some to compare him to Masaniello, "was the first who broke down the Barriers of Government to let in the *Hydra* of Rebellion."[26]

Tacky's Revolt initiated a new phase of slave resistance. Major plots and revolts subsequently erupted in Bermuda and Nevis (1761), Suriname (1762, 1763, 1768–72), Jamaica (1765, 1766, 1776), British Honduras (1765, 1768, 1773), Grenada (1765), Montserrat (1768), St. Vincent (1769–73), Tobago (1770, 1771, 1774), St. Croix and St. Thomas (1770 and after), and St. Kitts (1778). Veterans of Tacky's Revolt took part in a rising in British Honduras (to which five hundred rebels had been banished) as well as three other revolts on Jamaica in 1765 and 1766.[27]

On the North American continent, the reverberations of rebellion intensified after 1765, as slaves seized the new opportunities offered by splits between the imperial and colonial ruling classes. Runaways increased at a rate that alarmed slaveholders everywhere, and by the mid-1770s a rash of slave plots and revolts had sent white fears soaring. Slaves organized uprisings in Alexandria, Virginia, in 1767; Perth Amboy, New Jersey, in 1772; Saint Andrew's Parish, South Carolina, and, in a joint

A Negro hung alive by the Ribs to a Gallows

A Negro hung alive by the Ribs to a Gallows, c. 1773, by William Blake.
Stedman, Narrative of a Five Years Expedition.

African-Irish effort, Boston in 1774; and Ulster County, New York, Dorchester County, Maryland, Norfolk, Virginia, Charleston, South Carolina, and the Tar River region of North Carolina in 1775. In the last of these, a slave named Merrick plotted with a white seafarer to make arms available and the intended revolt possible.[28]

Slave resistance was closely related to the development of Afro-Christianity. In Saint Bartholomew Parish, South Carolina, an insurrectionary plot terrified the white population in the spring of 1776. Its leaders were black preachers, including two female prophets. A minister named George claimed that England's "Young King . . . was about to alter the world, & set the Negroes Free." Further south, in Savannah, Georgia, Preacher David was almost hanged after he expounded upon Exodus: "God would send Deliverance to the Negroes, from the Power of their Masters, as he freed the Children of Israel from Egyptian Bondage." Meanwhile, a new generation of evangelical leaders emerged in the 1760s and 1770s, including George Liele and David George (Baptists) and Moses Wilkinson and Boston King (Methodists). Liele, a slave from Virginia who founded the first Baptist church in Georgia, was evacuated by the British to Kingston, Jamaica, where he established another church.[29]

As we have noted, revolutionary ideas circulated rapidly in the port cities. Runaway slaves and free people of color flocked to the ports in search of sanctuary and a money wage and took work as laborers and seamen. Slaves also toiled in the maritime sector, some with ships' masters as owners, others hired out by the voyage. By the middle of the eighteenth century, slaves dominated Charleston's maritime and riverine traffic, in which some 20 percent of the city's adult male slaves labored. The independence of these "Boat negroes" had long worried the city's rulers, especially when subversive activities were involved, as was alleged against Thomas Jeremiah, a river pilot, in 1775. Jeremiah was arrested for stockpiling guns as he waited for the imperial war that would "help the poor Negroes." "Two or three White people," probably sailors, were also held, then released for lack of evidence, and finally driven from the province. Black pilots were a "rebellious lot, particularly resistant to white control."[30]

The political effects of slave resistance were contradictory, fueling fear and repression (police and patrols) on one side and new opposition to slavery on the other. This was especially true in the years leading up to the American Revolution, which marked a new stage in the development of an abolitionist movement. Benezet, America's leading Quaker abolitionist, chronicled slave uprisings around the world and tirelessly disseminated news of them through correspondence, pamphlets, and books. His work, in tandem with resistance from below, led to new attacks on the slave trade in Massachusetts in 1767 and in Rhode Island, Delaware, Connecticut, Pennsylvania, and the Continental Congress by 1774. The first formal antislavery organization in America was established in Philadelphia in 1775.[31]

Two of the revolution's most popular pamphleteers were moved by the militancy of slaves in the 1770s to attack slavery as they expanded the arguments for human freedom. John Allen, a Baptist minister who had witnessed the riots, trials, hangings, and diaspora of London's Spitalfields silk weavers through the 1760s, delivered (and then published) "An Oration on the Beauties of Liberty" after the burning of the revenue cutter Gaspee by sailors in 1773. In the fourth edition of his pamphlet, which was read to "large Circles of the Common People," Allen denounced slavery, not least for having caused the frequent and recent revolts of slaves, which "so often occasion streams of blood to be shed." Thomas Paine, another man fair of pen and smitten with liberty, wrote against slavery immediately upon his arrival in America in 1774. He repeated in diluted form Philmore's argument for self-liberation: "As the true owner has a right to reclaim his goods that were stolen, and sold; so the slave, who is proper owner of his freedom, has a right to reclaim it, however often sold." Paine signaled his awareness of the upswing in African American resistance by referring to slaves as "dangerous, as they are now." The struggles of African American slaves between 1765 and 1776 increased the commotion and the sense of crisis felt in every British colony in the years leading up to the revolution. Within the Baptist Allen and the half-Quaker Paine, they awakened an antinomian abolitionism from a previous revolutionary age.[32]

MOBS

The trajectories of rebellion among sailors and slaves intersected in seaport mobs, those rowdy gatherings of thousands of men and women that created the crisis in the North American colonies. Like the New York conspirators of 1741, sailors and slaves fraternized in grogshops, dancing cellars, and "disorderly houses," in Philadelphia's Hell Town and elsewhere, despite efforts by authorities to criminalize and prevent such meetings.[33] They had been gathering together in Boston's northside and southside mobs since the 1740s. Indeed, perhaps the single most common description of the mob in revolutionary America was as a "Rabble of boys, sailors, and negroes." Moreover, on almost every occasion when a crowd went beyond the planned objectives of the moderate leaders of the patriot movement, sailors and often slaves led the way. Motley mobs were central to protests against the Stamp Act (1765), the Quartering Acts (1765, 1774), the Townshend Revenue Act (1767), the increased power of the British customs service (1764–74), the Tea Act (1773), and the Intolerable Acts (1774). As multiethnic mobs helped to revive old ideas and to generate new ones, they were denounced as a many-headed hydra.[34]

Multiracial mobs helped to win numerous victories for the revolutionary movement, especially, as we have seen, against impressment. The heterogeneous rioters of Boston, as we have also seen, inspired new ideas in 1747. In 1765, "Sailors, boys, and Negroes to the number of above Five Hundred" rioted against impressment in Newport, Rhode Island, and in 1767 a mob of "Whites & Blacks all arm'd" attacked Captain Jeremiah Morgan in a press riot in Norfolk. A mob of sailors, "sturdy boys & negroes" rose in the *Liberty* Riot in Boston in 1768. Jesse Lemisch has noted that after 1763, "armed mobs of whites and Negroes repeatedly manhandled captains, officers, and crews, threatened their lives, and held them hostage for the men they pressed." Authorities such as Cadwallader Colden of New York knew that royal fortifications had to be "sufficient to secure against the Negroes or a mob."[35]

Why did African Americans fight the press-gang? Some probably considered impressment a death sentence and sought to avoid the pestilence and punishment that ravaged the men of the Royal Navy. Others joined anti-impressment mobs to preserve bonds of family or some degree of freedom that they had won for themselves. And many may have been drawn to the fight by the language and principles of the struggle against impressment, for on every dock, in every port, everywhere around the

Atlantic, sailors denounced the practice as slavery plain and simple. Michael Corbett and several of his brother tars fought against being forced on board a man-of-war in the port of Boston in 1769, claiming that "they preferred death to such a life as they deemed slavery." The Baptist minister John Allen reiterated what countless sailors had expressed in action and what Sam Adams had written years before: The people "have a right, by the law of God, of nature, and nations, to reluct at, and even to resist any military or marine force." Allen then compared one form of enslavement to another. The press-gang, he insisted, "ought ever to be held in the most hateful contempt, the same as you would *a banditti of slave-makers on the coast of Africa.*" Salt was the seasoning of the antislavery movement.[36]

The motley crew led a broad array of people into resistance against the Stamp Act, which taxed the colonists by requiring stamps for the sale and use of various commodities. Since the act affected all classes of people, all were involved in the protests, though sailors were singled out by many observers for their oppositional leadership and spirit. The refusal to use stamped paper (and to pay the tax) slowed commerce, which meant that idle sailors, turned ashore without wages, became a volatile force in every port. Royal officials everywhere would have agreed with the customs agent in New York who saw the power of the "Mob . . . daily increasing and gathering Strength, from the arrival of seaman, and none going out, and who are the people that are most dangerous on these occasions, as their whole dependence for subsistence is upon trade." Peter Oliver noted that after the Stamp Act riots, "The *Hydra* was roused. Every factious Mouth vomited out curses against *Great Britain,* & the Press rung its changes against Slavery."[37]

Boston's mob took angry action against the property of stamp distributor Andrew Oliver on August 14, 1765, then twelve days later turned an even fiercer wrath against the house and refined belongings of Thomas Hutchinson, who cried out at the crowd, "You are so many Masaniellos!" Others who detested the mob later singled out its leader, Ebenezer MacIntosh, as the incarnation of the shoeless fisherman of Naples. Sailors soon carried the news and experience of the tumults in Boston to Newport, where loyalists Thomas Moffat and Martin Howard, Jr., suffered the same fate as Hutchinson on August 28. In Newport, where the mer-

Stamp Act riots in Boston, 1765. Matthias Christian Sprengel,
Allgemeines historisches Taschenbuch . . . enthaltend für 1784
die Geschichte der Revolution von Nord-America *(1783).*

cantile economy depended upon the labor of sailors and dockworkers, the resistance to the Stamp Act was spearheaded by John Webber, probably a sailor and according to one report a "deserted convict." A band of sailors known as the Sons of Neptune then led three thousand rioters in an attack on New York's Fort George, the fortress of royal authority. They followed the example of the insurrection of 1741 when they tried to burn it to the ground. In Wilmington, North Carolina, a "furious Mobb of Sailors &c." forced the stamp distributor to resign. Sailors also led mass actions against the Stamp Act in Antigua, St. Kitts, and Nevis, where they "behaved like young Lions." Mob action continued in resistance to the Townshend Revenue Act and the renewed power of the British customs service in the late 1760s and early 1770s. Seamen drew on maritime custom to add a weapon to the arsenal of justice, using tar and feathers to intimidate British officials. The clunk of the brush in the tar bucket echoed behind Thomas Gage's observation in 1769 that "the Officers of the Crown grow more timid, and more fearfull of doing their Duty every Day."[38]

The burning of the customs schooner *Gaspee* in Newport in 1772 proved to be another decisive moment for the revolutionary movement. "Lawless seamen" had often taken direct action against customs men, in Newport and elsewhere. After the *Gaspee* ran aground, sixty to seventy men swarmed out of three longboats to board the ship, capture the despised Lieutenant William Dudingston, take him and his crew ashore, and set the vessel afire. The troublemakers were subsequently charged with "high treason, viz.: levying war against the King," which sailors' burning of the king's vessels had long signified. Merchants, farmers, and artisans may have been involved in the *Gaspee* affair, but sailors were clearly the leaders, as concluded by Daniel Horsmanden, who brought his experience in presiding over the trials of the New York conspirators of 1741 to bear as head of the king's commission to investigate this new incident. The act of burning the vessel, he wrote, had been "committed by a number of bold, daring, rash enterprising sailors." Horsmanden did not know if someone else had organized these men of the sea or if they had simply "banded themselves together."[39]

Seamen also led both the Golden Hill and Nassau Street Riots in New York City and the King Street Riot in Boston, better remembered as the

Boston Massacre. In both ports, sailors and other maritime workers resented the British soldiers who labored for lower-than-customary wages along the waterfront; in New York they also objected to the soldiers' attacks on their fifty-eight-foot liberty pole (a ship's mast). Rioting and street fighting ensued. Thomas Hutchinson and John Adams believed that the events in New York and Boston were related, perhaps through common participants. Adams, who defended the British soldiers at trial, called the mob that assembled on King Street on "the Fatal Fifth of March" nothing but a "motley rabble of saucy boys, negroes and molattoes, Irish teagues, and out landish Jack Tarrs." Their leader was Crispus Attucks, a runaway slave of African American and Native American descent whose home was the small free black community of Providence in the Bahama Islands. Seamen also took part in the direct actions of the several Tea Parties, after which Thomas Lamb exclaimed in New York, "We are in a perfect Jubilee!"[40]

By the summer of 1775, seamen and slaves had helped to generate an enthusiasm described by Peter Timothy: "In regard to War & Peace, I can only tell you that the Plebeians are still for War—but the noblesse [are] perfectly pacific." Ten years of insurrectionary direct action had brought the colonies to the brink of revolution. As early as during the Stamp Act protests of 1765, General Thomas Gage had recognized the menace of the mob: "This Insurrection is composed of great numbers of Sailors headed by Captains of Privateers," as well as many people from the surrounding area, the whole amounting to "some thousands." Late in 1776, Lord Barrington of the British Army claimed that colonial governments in North America had been "overturned by insurrections last summer, because there was not a sufficient force to defend them." Sailors, laborers, slaves, and other poor workingmen provided much of the spark, volatility, momentum, and sustained militancy for the attack on British policy after 1765. During the Revolutionary War, they took part in mob actions that harassed Tories and diminished their political effectiveness.[41]

"I found myself surrounded by a motley crew of wretches, with tethered garments and pallid visages," wrote Thomas Dring as he began his imprisonment in 1782 aboard the notorious hulk *Jersey*, a British man-of-war serving as a prison ship in the East River of New York.[42] Many thousands, especially sailors, were charged with being "pirates" and "traitors" and herded into British prisons and prison ships after 1776. Philip Freneau, who spent two months in the *Scorpion* hulk, "doom'd to famine, shackles and despair," composed "The British Prison Ship," one of the era's greatest poems, in 1780:

> *Hunger and thirst to work our woe combine,*
> *And mouldy bread, and flesh of rotten swine,*
> *The mangled carcase, and the batter'd brain,*
> *The doctor's poison, and the captain's cane,*
> *The soldier's musquet, and the steward's debt,*
> *The evening shackle, and the noon-day threat.*

Amid the hunger, thirst, rot, gore, terror, and violence, and the deaths of seven or eight thousand of their fellow inmates during the war, the prisoners organized themselves according to egalitarian, collectivist, revolutionary principles. What had once functioned as "articles" among seamen and pirates now became "a Code of By-Laws . . . for their own regulation and government." Equal before the rats, the smallpox, and the guard's cutlass, they practiced democracy, working to distribute food and clothing fairly, to provide medical care, to bury their dead. On one ship a common sailor spoke between decks on Sundays to honor those who died "in vindication of the rights of Man." A captain who looked back with surprise on the self-organization of the prisoners remarked that the seamen were "of that class . . . who are not easily controlled, and usually not the most ardent supporters of good order." But the sailors drew on the tradition of hydrarchy as they implemented the order of the day: they governed themselves.[43]

The motley crew thus provided an image of revolution from below that proved terrifying to Tories and moderate patriots alike. In his famous but falsified engraving of the Boston Massacre, Paul Revere tried to render the "motley rabble" respectable by leaving black faces out of the crowd and putting in entirely too many gentlemen. The South Carolina Council of Safety complained bitterly of the attacks of sailors—both "white and black armed men"—in December 1775.[44] Elite colonists reached readily for images of monstrosity, calling the mob a "Hydra," a "many-headed monster," a "reptile," and a "many-headed power."

The Fatal Fifth of March, by Paul Revere. The Bloody Massacre;
perpetrated in King-Street, Boston, on March 5th, 1770,
by a party of the 29th Regiment *(1770).*

Many-headedness implied democracy run wild, as Joseph Chalmers explained: A government that is too democratic "becomes a many-headed monster, a tyranny of many." Against the revolutionary soldiers and sailors who fought beneath the banner of the serpent and the motto "Don't Tread on Me," John Adams proposed Hercules as the symbol for the new nation.[45]

Multiracial mobs under the leadership of maritime workers thus helped simultaneously to create the imperial crisis of the 1770s and to propose a revolutionary solution to it. The militancy of multiracial workers in Boston, Newport, New York, and Charleston led to the formation of the Sons of Liberty, the earliest intercolonial organization to coordinate anti-imperial resistance. Richard B. Morris wrote that New

York's sailors "were organized as the Sons of Neptune, apparently ante-dating the Sons of Liberty, for whom they may well have provided the pattern of organization." The commotion around the *Gaspee* incident of 1772 set in motion a new round of organization, for in the aftermath of this bold action, another revolutionary institution, the committee of correspondence, was established throughout the colonies. To loyalist Daniel Leonard, such committees were the "foulest, subtlest, and most venomous serpent ever issued from the egg of sedition."[46] But if the motley crew shaped the organizational history of the American Revolution, it had, as we have seen, an even greater impact upon its intellectual history, influencing the ideas of Samuel Adams, J. Philmore, James Otis, Jr., Anthony Benezet, Thomas Paine, and John Allen. Action from below taken in Boston, in Saint Mary's Parish, Jamaica, and in London perpetuated old ideas and generated new ones that would circulate around the Atlantic for decades to come.

One of the main ideas kept alive by multiracial seaport crowds was the antinomian notion that moral conscience stood above the civil law of the state and therefore legitimized resistance to oppression, whether against a corrupt minister of empire, a tyrannical slaveowner, or a violent ship's captain. David S. Lovejoy has convincingly shown that a levelling spirit and an antinomian disdain of laws and government lay within the rising "political enthusiasm" of the revolutionary era. Explosive mobs consistently expressed such enthusiasm, moving Benjamin Rush to name a new type of insanity: *anarchia,* the "excessive love of liberty." The higher-law doctrine historically associated with antinomianism would appear in secular form in the Declaration of Independence, denounced in its own day as an instance of "civil antinomianism."[47]

In its struggle against impressment in the 1760s and 1770s, the motley crew drew on ideas dating from the English Revolution, when Thomas Rainborough and the revolutionary movement of the 1640s had denounced slavery. In the second *Agreement of the Free People of England* (May 1649), the Levellers had explained the antinomian basis of their opposition to impressment: "We the free People of England" declared to the world that Parliament had no power to press any man into war, for each person must have the right to satisfy his own conscience as to the justice of such war. The Levellers thus made man and his conscience (not the citizen) the subject of declaration, and life (not the nation) its object.

Peter Warren was correct when he claimed that the sailors of New England were "almost Levellers"; as such, they expressed their opposition to impressment and to slavery more broadly, influenced Jefferson, Paine, and a whole generation of thinkers, and showed that revolutionary confrontation between upper and lower classes in the 1640s—and not the compromises of 1688 within the ruling orders—was the true precedent to the events of 1776.[48]

When the Tory Peter Oliver complained that the press rang the changes against slavery, he was referring to bell-ringing, and to all the permutations in which a peal of bells might be rung. He suggested a dreary drone, but we can posit a campanology of freedom. When a single bell among a tuned set is struck, its reverberations cause its neighbors to emit harmonious overtones, and when several are struck rapidly, the result is a rhythm of cascading excitement. What were the "changes against slavery" in the age of the American Revolution? There were patriot bells, clamoring with mounting insistence, and there were the loud, long reverberations struck by the distinctive notes—Tacky's Revolt, the Stamp Act crisis—of the motley crew. The patriots struck against several meanings of slavery: taxation without representation, denial of free trade, limitations on the press, ecclesiastical intolerance, and the expense and intrusions of a standing army. Sailors and slaves, meanwhile, opposed other meanings: impressment, terror, working to death, kidnapping, and forcible confinement. Both groups objected to arbitrary arrest and judgment without peers or juries. These tolling bells revived distant, deeper memories from the English Revolution. Hence the importance of habeas corpus, or freedom from imprisonment without due process of law, the deepest tone in freedom's peal and fundamental to sailor, slave, and citizen. In the cycle of the American Revolution, Tacky struck the tocsin of freedom's uprising, and the Philadelphia Convention sounded the knell of its death, though the murmuring undertones would continue, in diminuendo, and in San Domingue.

COUNTERREVOLUTION

If the motley crew's audacious actions gave motion to the multiclass movement toward independence, they also generated commotion *within* it—fear, ambivalence, and opposition. In New York, for example, the Sons of Liberty came into being as a reaction against the "threatened anarchy" of autonomous risings against the press and the Stamp Act in 1764 and 1765. Everywhere the Sons began to advertise themselves as the guarantors of good order, as the necessary counterpoint to the upheaval within which they themselves had been born. By 1766 the propertied opponents of British policy had declared themselves for "ordered resistance." In the aftermath of the Boston Massacre in 1770, John Adams defended the redcoats and made an explicitly racist appeal in court, claiming that the looks of the Afro-Indian sailor Crispus Attucks "would be enough to terrify any person." But in 1773 he wrote a letter about liberty, addressed it to Thomas Hutchinson, and signed it, "Crispus Attucks." Adams dreaded the motley crew, but he knew that it had made the revolutionary movement.[49]

Similar contradictions haunted Thomas Jefferson, who acknowledged the motley crew but feared its challenge to his own vision of America's future. Jefferson included in the Declaration of Independence the complaint that King George III had "constrained our fellow Citizens taken Captive on the high seas to bear Arms against their Country, to become executioners of their friends and Brethren, or to fall themselves by their Hands." He (and Congress) included sailors in the revolutionary coalition but tendentiously simplified their history and role within the movement, leaving out the war of classes and emphasizing only the war of nations. The passage also lacks the graceful wording and lofty tone of the rest of the Declaration: it seems awkward, confused, especially in its indecision about how to classify the sailor (citizen, friend, brother?). Jefferson employed the "most tremendous words," as Carl Becker said of the draft prose concerning African slavery, but "the passage somehow leaves us cold." There is in it a "sense of labored effort, of deliberate striving for an effect that does not come." As it happened, Jefferson added the words about impressment as an afterthought, squeezing them into his rough draft of the Declaration. He knew that the labor market was a serious problem in that mercantile age and that commerce would depend on sailors, whether America remained within the British Empire or not.[50]

Thomas Paine knew it, too. He also denounced impressment, but he was more concerned in *Common Sense* to reassure American merchants about the maritime labor supply after the revolution: "In point of manning a fleet, people in general run into great errors; it is not necessary that one fourth part should be sailors. . . . A few able and social sailors will soon instruct a sufficient number of active landmen in the common work of a ship." This had been his own experience aboard the *Terrible,* a privateer, during the Seven Years' War, which led him to argue that sailors, shipbuilders, and the maritime sector as a whole constituted a viable economic basis for a new American nation. (He failed to mention that the crew of the vessel had been motley and mutinous.) The only question remaining was how to obtain independence: should it be done from above, by the legal voice of Congress, or should it be done from below, by the mob? Here Paine shared the attitudes of others of his station: he feared the motley mob (though he would think differently in the 1790s). The multitude, he explained, was reasonable in 1776, but "virtue" was not perpetual. Safeguards were necessary lest "some Massanello may hereafter arise, who laying hold of popular disquietudes, may collect together the desperate and the discontented, and by assuming to themselves the powers of government, may sweep away the liberties of the continent like a deluge." His greatest fear lay in a concurrence of the struggles of urban workers, African slaves, and Native Americans.[51]

The motley crew had helped to make the revolution, but the vanguard struck back in the 1770s and 1780s, against mobs, slaves, and sailors, in what must be considered an American Thermidor. The effort to reform the mob by removing its more militant elements began in 1766 and continued, not always successfully, through the revolution and beyond. Patriot landowners, merchants, and artisans increasingly condemned revolutionary crowds, seeking to move politics from "out of doors" into legislative chambers, in which the propertyless would have no vote and no voice. Paine, for his part, would turn against the crowd after Philadelphia's Fort Wilson Riot of 1779. When Samuel Adams helped to draw up Massachusetts's Riot Act of 1786, designed to be used to disperse and control the insurgents of Shays' Rebellion, he ceased to believe that the mob "embodied the fundamental rights of man against which government itself could be judged," and detached himself from the creative democratic force that years before had given him the best idea of his life.[52]

The moderate patriots had, since the beginning of the movement, in 1765, sought to limit the struggle for liberty by keeping slaves out of the revolutionary coalition. The place of slaves in the movement remained ambiguous until 1774, when Lord Dunmore, governor of Virginia, attacked the patriot tobacco planters by offering freedom to servants and slaves willing to join His Majesty's army to reestablish order in the colony. The news of the offered liberation ran like wildfire through slave communities, and thousands deserted the plantations, inaugurating a new, mobile slave revolt of huge proportions. Some of these slaves would be organized as Lord Dunmore's Ethiopian Regiment; those who were not permitted to bear arms would seek the protection of the British army. American leaders, infuriated by the move, tried to preserve slavery, announcing in 1775 that recruiters should take no deserter, "stroller, negro, or vagabond," and reaffirming over the next year that neither free blacks nor slaves would be eligible for military service. Scarcity of labor would force reconsideration of this edict, however, especially later in the war. While five thousand African Americans fought for liberty, the American political and military leadership battled the British and some of its own soldiers to protect the institution of slavery.[53]

The sailor would be encouraged to serve in the Continental Navy, but he was not, according to James Madison, a good citizen for a republic. What little virtue he may have had was deadened by his life as a dumb drudge at sea: "Though traversing and circumnavigating the globe, he sees nothing but the same vague objects of nature, the same monotonous occurrences in ports and docks; and at home in his vessel, what new ideas can shoot from the unvaried use of the ropes and the rudder, or from the society of comrades as ignorant as himself." Madison's own ignorance, arrogance, or denial caused him to invert the truth, but he was right about something else: the greater the number of sailors in a republic, as he suggested, the less secure its government. Madison was joined in these attitudes by many, including the "Connecticut Wits" (David Humphreys, Joel Barlow, John Trumbull, and Dr. Lemuel Hopkins) who in 1787 wrote a poem entitled "The Anarchiad," in response to Shays' Rebellion and in memory of the cycle of revolt in the 1760s and 1770s. The poets expressed their hatred for mobs and their ideas. They sneered at "democratic dreams," "the rights of man," and the reduction of all "to just one level." One of their darkest nightmares was what they called a "young DEMOCRACY from *hell.*" They had not forgotten the role of sailors in the revolution: in their imagined state of anarchy, the "mighty Jacktar guides the helm." He had been "Nurs'd on the waves, in blust'ring tempests bred,/ His heart of marble, and his brain of lead." Having sailed "in the whirlwind" as a part of his work, this hard-hearted, thick-headed man naturally "enjoys the storm" of revolution. The poets alluded to the revolutionary acts of sailors when they referred to "seas of boiling tar."[54]

During the 1780s, such thinking came to prevail among those who made up the emerging political nation—merchants, professionals, shopkeepers, artisans, slaveowners, and yeoman farmers. Sailors and slaves, once necessary parts of the revolutionary coalition, were thus read out of the settlement at revolution's end. Of the five workingmen killed in the Boston Massacre in 1770, John Adams had written, "The blood of the martyrs, right or wrong, proved to be the seed of the congregation." Yet had Crispus Attucks—slave, sailor, and mob leader—survived the fire of British muskets, he would not have been allowed to join the congregation, or new nation, he had helped to create. The exclusion of people like Attucks epitomized the sudden, reactionary retreat from the universalistic revolutionary language that had been forged in the heat of the 1760s and 1770s and permanently emblazoned in the Declaration of Independence. The reaction was canonized in the U.S. Constitution, which gave the new federal government the power to suppress domestic insurrections. James Madison worried in 1787 about a "levelling spirit" and an "agrarian law."[55] The Constitution also strengthened the institution of slavery by extending the slave trade, providing for the return of fugitive slaves, and giving national political power to the plantation master class.[56] Meanwhile, an intensive debate about the nature and capacity of "the negro" raged between 1787 and 1790. Many Baptists and Methodists backed away from antislavery positions and sought instead a "gospel made safe for the plantation."[57] The new American ruling class redefined "race" and "citizenship" to divide and marginalize the motley crew, legislating in the 1780s and early 1790s a unified law of slavery based on white supremacy. The actions of the motley crew, and the reactions against it, help to illuminate the clashing, ambiguous nature of the American Revolution—its militant origins, radical momentum, and conservative political conclusion.[58]

VECTORS OF REVOLUTION

And yet the implications of the struggles of the 1760s and 1770s could not easily be contained, by the Sons of Liberty, Jefferson, Paine, Adams, or the new American government. Soldiers who fought in the war circulated the news, experience, and ideas of the revolution. Several veterans of the French regiments deployed in North America, including Henri Christophe and André Rigaud, would later lead the next major revolution of the western Atlantic, in Haiti, beginning in 1791. Other veterans returned to France and may have led a series of revolts against feudal land tenure that accelerated revolution in Europe during the 1790s. The news carried by Hessian soldiers back to their homeland eventually propelled a new generation of settlers toward America. But it was the motley crew, the sailors and slaves who were defeated in America and subsequently dispersed, that did the most to create new resistance and to inaugurate a broader age of revolution throughout the world.[59]

Sailors were a vector of revolution that traveled from North America out to sea and southward to the Caribbean. The sailors of the British navy grew mutinous after 1776, inspired in part by the battles waged against press-gangs and the king's authority in America; an estimated forty-two thousand of them deserted naval ships between 1776 and 1783. Many who went to sea in this era got a revolutionary education. Robert Wedderburn, born to a slave woman and a Scottish plantation owner in Jamaica, joined the mutinous navy in 1778 and thereafter worked as a sailor, a tailor, a writer, and a preacher of jubilee as he took part in maritime protests, slave revolts, and urban insurrections. Julius Scott has shown that sailors black, white, and brown had contact with slaves in the British, French, Spanish, and Dutch port cities of the Caribbean, exchanging information with them about slave revolts, abolition, and revolution and generating rumors that became material forces in their own right. It is not known for certain whether sailors carried the news of the American Revolution that helped to inspire slave rebels in Hanover Parish, Jamaica, in 1776, but there is no doubt that a motley crew of "fifty or sixty men of all colors," including an "Irishman of prodigious size," attacked British and American ships in the Caribbean in 1793, apparently in league with the new revolutionary government of Haiti.[60]

The slaves and free blacks who flocked to the British army during the revolution and who were then dispersed around the Atlantic after 1783 constituted a second, multidirectional vector of revolution. Twelve thousand African Americans were carried out of Savannah, Charleston, and New York by the army in 1782 and 1783, while another eight to ten thousand departed with loyalist masters. They went to Sierra Leone, London, Dublin, Nova Scotia, Bermuda, eastern Florida, the Bahamas, Jamaica, the Mosquito Shore, and Belize. Free people of color from North America caused problems throughout the Caribbean in the later 1780s, especially on Jamaica and in the Windward Islands, where they created new political openings and alignments in slave societies and helped to prepare the way for the Haitian Revolution. By 1800 Lord Balcarres, governor of Jamaica, would write of the "Pandora's Box" that had been opened in the West Indies: "Turbulent people of all Nations engaged in illicit Trade; a most abandoned class of Negroes, up to every scene of mischief, and a general levelling spirit throughout, is the character of the lower orders in Kingston." Here, he explained, was a refuge for revolutionaries and a site for future insurrection, a place that might "in a moment . . . be laid in ashes."[61]

A third powerful vector of revolution hurtled eastward toward the abolitionist movement in England. Granville Sharp, whose work in the late 1760s and early 1770s included opposition to impressment in the American Revolution, went on to become one of the leading figures in the transatlantic antislavery movement. After Olaudah Equiano told him in 1783 about the slave ship *Zong*, whose captain threw 132 slaves overboard in order to save supplies and then tried to collect insurance money for the dead, Sharp publicized the mass murder effectively. He also worked to establish the free black state of Sierra Leone in 1786, and served on the Committee for Effecting the Abolition of the Slave Trade in 1787. F. O. Shyllon and Peter Fryer have conclusively demonstrated the independent existence of a black population in London whose self-organization sustained and encouraged the abolitionist Sharp and, also in the 1780s, a young scholar-activist named Thomas Clarkson.[62]

After the American war, Clarkson began to gather evidence about the slave trade. Especially interested in the effects of the trade on sailors, he wanted to talk to the men who had sailed on the slave ships and to inspect those ships' crew lists in order to gauge mortality. To accomplish this, the young Cambridge scholar disguised himself as a sailor and walked the docks. But how would he get men who were terrified of the slave trade, and terrified to talk about it, to speak to a stranger? He found John Dean, a free black sailor and his first informant, in a boardinghouse kept by one Donovan, an Irishman. Dean, like thousands of others, had entered the slave trade through the rough netherworld of proletarian recruitment— the squalid sailor's tavern where, in Liverpool, Bristol, or London, slaving crews were often assembled between midnight and two in the morning. Dean had a personal tale to tell: "For a trifling circumstance for which he was in no-wise to blame, the captain fastened him with his belly to the deck, and that, in this situation, he had poured hot pitch upon his back, and made incisions in it with hot tongs." Dean and countless other sailors like him provided the personal knowledge and information that gave the middle-class antislavery movement its ballast.[63]

The relationship of sailors to the abolitionist movement, on the one hand, and to the ambiguities between the condition of slavery and sailoring, on the other, are nowhere better personified than in the life of that éminence grise of the abolitionists, the Igbo slave and sailor Olaudah Equiano. Enslaved in West Africa, he was hardly aboard the slave ship before he saw a white sailor flogged to death. In later years he would see a sailor hanged from a yardarm, a soldier hung by his heels, a man on the gallows at Tyburn; he himself was twice suspended, though not by his neck. Terror, he understood immediately, was the fate of both sailors and slaves. Aboard the *Aetna* man-of-war, he learned to read and write, to shave, to dress hair. A messmate, the Irishman Daniel Quin, taught him to read the Bible and to think of nothing "but being free." At the conclusion of the Seven Years' War, when the *Aetna* was anchored in the river Thames, his master, worried that Equiano's recent promotion to able-bodied seaman would make it harder to maintain him in slavery, forced him into a barge at the point of his sword. The Igbo sailor plucked up his courage: "I told him I was free, and he could not by law serve me so." Sold to Captain Doran of the West Indiaman *Charming Sally,* Equiano explained, "I told him my master could not sell me to him, nor to anyone else. 'Why,' said he, 'did not your master buy you?' I confessed he did. But I have served him, said I, many years, and he has taken all my wages and prize money, for I only got one sixpence during the war; besides this

Olaudah Equiano, The Interesting Narrative of the
Life of Olaudah Equiano *(1790). Rare Books Division, New York
Public Library, Astor, Lenox, and Tilden Foundations.*

I have been baptized; and by the laws of the land no man has a right to sell me." Confronted with these economic, religious, and legal arguments, Doran told him, Equiano reported, that "I talked too much English." Meanwhile, Equiano's shipmates promised to do what they could, which, apart from getting him some oranges, was nothing.

Equiano now entered the sugar economy of the West Indies. "I now knew what it was to work hard; I was made to help to unload and load the ship." His own situation began to improve, but he witnessed the intense sufferings of others—the rapes, whippings, brandings, mutilations, cuts, burnings, chains, muzzles, and thumbscrews. He wondered of the rulers of England, "Are you not hourly in dread of an insurrection?" He then quoted the speech of Beelzebub in *Paradise Lost,* written by John Milton and published exactly one hundred years earlier. Much of Equiano's evolving conception of freedom, and hence part of his own self-definition, were derived from other sailors—from his keen sense of the rights of the accused to his belief in the jury system, from his reference to his "fellow creatures" to his study of the Bible, from his quotations from Milton to his detestation of those "infernal invaders of human rights," the slavers, impressers, and trepanners.

Equiano was in Charleston during the demonstrations of joy that followed the repeal of the Stamp Act in 1766. It is easy to imagine his participating in them, and equally easy to understand why he might not want to admit it to his British readers. Many of the sailors in that demonstration went in blackface. Some years later Equiano himself had occasion to put on whiteface in an episode that was by his own account a turning point, the source of a suicidal and spiritual crisis. In 1774 he helped to recruit a black sea-cook, John Annis, onto a ship bound for Turkey. Annis, formerly a slave to one Kirkpatrick of St. Kitt's, was soon impressed by his former master and a gang of bullies on the Thames. Equiano rushed to obtain a habeas corpus but before handing it over, whitened his face to escape suspicion. He then contacted Granville Sharp, but his attorney ran off with the money, and Annis was carried to St. Kitt's, where he was staked to the ground, cut, and flogged to death. Equiano took Annis's death as a personal defeat; it plunged him into the depths of despair. Yet slowly he began to discover the rich spiritual resources of proletarian London in the 1770s—the love-feasts of a silk weaver, the evening singing of hymns. A prison reformer, a Dissenter, pointed out to him that "faith is the substance of things hoped for, the evidence of things not seen." An antinomian ("an old sea-faring man") referred him to the Isaiah of William Blake: "The wolf and the lamb shall feed together." He was guided to the Book of James and its "So speak ye, and so do, as they that shall be judged by the law of liberty." The Scripture of Isaiah, James, John, and Acts—the prophetic, the social gospel, and the persecuted—began to provide him with convincement. He went back to sea and continued to study. He identified with the condemned criminal, the needy, the poor; he moved from personal redemption to liberation theology. He wrote his own verses of despair, imprisonment, and enslavement, concluding with an allusion to the Gospel of Mark, "The stone which the builders rejected has become the main cornerstone." He thus answered Jefferson and Paine and their fears of the motley crew. But whether the disenfranchised, the enslaved, the imprisoned, the sailor—in short, the many-headed hydra—could become a "cornerstone" would be a story for the 1790s.

The failure of the motley crew to find a place in the new American nation forced it into broader, more creative forms of identification. One of the phrases often used to capture the unity of the age of revolution was "citizen of the world." J. Philmore described himself this way, as did others, including Thomas Paine. The real citizens of the world, of course, were the sailors and slaves who instructed Philmore, Paine, Jefferson, and the rest of the middle- and upper-class revolutionaries. This multiethnic proletariat was "cosmopolitan" in the original meaning of the word. Reminded that he had been sentenced to exile, Diogenes, the slave philosopher of antiquity, responded by saying that he sentenced his judges to stay at home. And "asked where he came from, he said, 'I am a citizen of the world' "—a cosmopolitan. The Irishman Oliver Goldsmith published in 1762 a gentle critique of nationalism entitled *Citizen of the World,* featuring characters such as a sailor with a wooden leg and a ragged woman ballad singer. Goldsmith praised the "meanest English sailor or soldier," who endured days of misery without murmur. He was "found guilty of being poor, and sent to Newgate, in order to be transported to the plantations," where he would work among Africans. He returned to London, was press-ganged, sent to fight in Flanders and India, beaten by the boatswain, imprisoned, taken by pirates. He was a soldier, a slave, a sailor, a prisoner, a cosmopolitan, a citizen of the world. James Howell, historian of the Masaniello Revolt, wrote in the seventeenth century that "every ground may be one's country—for by birth each man is in this world a cosmopolitan."[64]

A fourth and final vector pointed toward Africa. The African Americans in diaspora after 1783 would originate modern pan-Africanism by settling, with the help of Equiano and Sharp, in Sierra Leone. Their dispersal after the American Revolution, eastward across the Atlantic, was similar to that of radicals after the English Revolution, a century and a half earlier, westward across the Atlantic. Both movements had posed challenges to slavery and been defeated. The earlier defeat permitted the consolidation of the plantation and the slave trade, while the later defeat allowed the slave system to expand and gather new strength. Yet the long-term consequences of the second defeat would be a victory, the ultimate undoing of the slave trade and the plantation system. The theory and practice of antinomian democracy, which had been generalized around the Atlantic in the seventeenth-century diaspora, would be revived and deepened in the eighteenth. What went out in whiteface came back in blackface, to end the pause in the discussion of democratic ideas in England and to give new life to worldwide revolutionary movements. What goes around, comes around, by the circular winds and currents of the Atlantic.

CHAPTER EIGHT

The Conspiracy of Edward and Catherine Despard

ACCORDING TO NEWSPAPER accounts of February 22, 1803, Colonel Edward Marcus Despard, "dressed in boots, a dark brown great coat, his hair unpowdered," ascended the gallows "with great firmness." He had played an important role in clandestine efforts in England and Ireland to organize a revolutionary army whose goal was to seize power in London and declare a republic. He now faced hanging and beheading as a traitor. The sheriff had warned that the platform would drop instantly if he said anything "inflammatory or improper." Facing the assembled twenty thousand with "perfect calmness," Despard spoke these words:

> Fellow Citizens, I come here, as you see, after having served my country,—faithfully, honourably, and usefully served it, for thirty years and upwards, to suffer death upon a scaffold for a crime of which I protest I am not guilty. I solemnly declare that I am no more guilty of it than any of you who may be now hearing me.— But, though his MAJESTY's Ministers know as well as I do, that I am not guilty, yet they avail themselves of a legal pretext to destroy a man, because he has been a friend to truth, to liberty, and to justice. [At this, one newspaper reported, "the crowd issued forth loud huzzas."] Because he has been a friend to the poor and the oppressed. But, Citizens, I hope and trust, notwithstanding my fate, and the fate of those who no doubt will soon follow me, that the principles of freedom, of humanity, and of justice, will finally triumph over falsehood, tyranny, and delusion, and every principle inimical to the interests of the human race.

A hanging at Horsemonger's Gaol, c. 1805. Robinson,
A Pictorial History of the Sea Services. *John Hay Library.*

At this significant phrase—"the human race"—the sheriff admonished him for using such incendiary language. "I have little more to add," Despard continued, "except to wish you all health, happiness, and freedom, which I have endeavoured, as far as was in my power, to procure for you and for mankind in general." As his fellow conspirator John MacNamara was brought up to the scaffold, he said to Despard, "I am afraid, Colonel, we have got into a bad situation." Despard's answer, the newspapers noted, was characteristic of the man: "There are many better, and some worse." His last words were, " 'Tis very cold, I think we shall have some rain." Undoubtedly, he had looked up hoping to behold that little patch of blue which the prisoner calls the sky.[1]

Despard had been arrested on November 16, 1802, as he attended a meeting of forty workingmen in the Oakley Arms tavern. Those arrested included eight carpenters, five laborers, two shoemakers, two hatters, a stonemason, a clockmaker, a "plaisterer not long from the sea," and "a man who cuts wood and sells it in penny bundles." Many of them also worked as soldiers. These men had organized among common laborers, dockworkers, soldiers, and sailors—especially soldiers stationed at the Tower and "Irishmen who had served on board the Kings Ships & had been used to Cannon." Several of the Irish laborers "had been united in Ireland," a phrase showing that the mass terror of killing, torture, and deportation following the Irish Rebellion of 1798 had not extinguished the oath of the United Irish or the brotherhood of affection and communion of rights it expressed. Five thousand workers recently discharged from the wet docks were expected to join the cause: despite a period of intense shipping, they had been rendered either unemployed, as a direct result of hydraulic civil engineering, or homeless, by neighborhood clearances.

The Oakley Arms lay only a few yards from William Blake's residence, Hercules Buildings in Lambeth on the south side of the river Thames. That same year the epic visionary asked the questions

And did the Countenance Divine
Shine forth upon our clouded hills?
And was Jerusalem builded here
Among these dark Satanic Mills?

Blake's "Satanic Mills" were the Albion Mills, the first London steam-powered factory, just down the road from Hercules Buildings. Erected in 1791, this flour mill had been burned to the ground that same year, as part of the anonymous, direct resistance to the industrial revolution. Despard's conspiracy was a continuation of that resistance, occurring amid widespread machine-breaking in the west of England and martial organizing against starvation and technological redundancy in the north. Blake had left London two years earlier during the famine of 1800. Until then, the visionary and the insurrectionary had walked the same streets.

Despard described the revolutionary force as comprising "Soldiers, Sailors, and Individuals." They had been recruited in the pubs of three parts of London: in St. Giles'-in-the-Fields, virtually an autonomous zone of the motley proletariat; south of the river, where the soldiers were concentrated; and in the East End river parishes, the neighborhood of sailors and dockers. These men had joined the movement in order "to burst the chain of bondage and slavery" and "to recover some of those liberties which we have lost." They called Parliament the "Den of

Thieves" and the government the "Man Eaters." One thought "Windsor Castle was fit to teach the Gospel and maintain poor people's Children in." During their trial, the lord chief justice and presiding judge, Ellenborough, explained that "instead of the ancient limited monarchy of this Realm, its established free and wholesome laws, its approved usages, its useful gradations of rank, its natural and inevitable as well as desirable inequalities of property," Despard and his fellow revolutionaries had sought "to substitute a wild scheme of impracticable equality."[2]

Despard himself had claimed that "the people were every where ripe and anxious for the moment of attack." The plan was therefore to fire upon the king's carriage with cannon shot as he made his annual way to Parliament, then to seize the Tower and the Bank of England, to master Parliament, and to stop the mail coaches at Piccadilly as a signal for the rest of the country to rise. Despard was expert in ordnance and military strategy and tactics. But the scheme was foiled by the arrests at the Oakley Arms. Fifteen men were indicted for treason, on the grounds that they "did conspire, compass, imagine, and intend" the king's death. Their convictions were the first instances of the prosecution of imagined crimes. Eleven were found guilty. Although the jury recommended mercy, Despard and six others were executed on February 21, 1803.

Two wings of established authority, chaplain and magistrate, hovered over Despard in his last days. Like a bird of prey, the Reverend Mr. Wirkworth visited Despard to attempt to learn more about the plot, to offer spiritual services, and to urge his "public acknowledgment of God as the supreme governor." The main purpose was unfulfilled, as Despard said, "Me—no never—I'll divulge nothing. No, not for all the treasure the King is worth." To the religious request Despard "replied he had sometimes been at eight different places of worship on the same day, that he believed in a Deity, and that outward forms of worship were useful for political purposes, otherwise he thought the opinions of Churchmen, Dissenters, Quakers, Methodists, Catholics, Savages, or even Atheists, were equally indifferent." Despard then "offered some criticisms on the words *Altar* and *Ecclesia,*" which reminded Wirkworth of Thomas Paine's *Age of Reason.* The Reverend "then presented Dr. Dodderidge's *Evidences of Christianity* and begged as a favor that he would read it." Despard "requested that I would not 'attempt to put shackles on his mind, as on his body (pointing to the iron on his leg) was under so painful a restraint, and said that he had as much right to ask me to read the book he had in his hand (a treatise on Logic) as I had to ask him to read mine,' and before I could make a reply Mrs Despard and another lady were introduced, and our conversation ended."[3]

The chief magistrate, Sir Richard Ford, wrote to the home secretary the night before the execution to express his concern over the "very considerable Crowds [that] assembled during the Day and this Evening near the Gaol." He noted the difficulty of procuring workmen to build the scaffold. He mentioned the fears of the gaoler, his own decision to sleep near the prison, and his deployment of one hundred armed soldiers through the night. Since handbills "calling on the People to rise" and to rescue "these unfortunate Men" had been distributed, Ford quite naturally dreaded the possibility of a riot the following day and was prepared to subdue it.[4] The public houses were being watched. The lord mayor checked and double-checked the security of Newgate and the prison hulks. Yet amid the continued resistance of the prisoners, threats of armed rescue, and prospects of spontaneous rioting, the chief of police was most troubled by Mrs. Despard. Ford concluded his letter with unconcealed irritation: "Mrs. Despard has been very troublesome, but at last she has gone away."[5] Thus both wings of tyrannical government, chaplain and magistrate, went a-flutter at the presence of Despard's wife. Who was this woman who so scared the powers-that-be?

Catherine Despard was an African American woman who had accompanied Edward when he sailed from Central America back to London in 1790. British imperial officers often attached themselves in the Caribbean to women of color, but they usually left them behind when they returned to England. Not Despard. Catherine came along but was shunned by her husband's family as a "poor black woman, who called herself his wife."[6] She was especially active in the prisoners'-rights movement of the 1790s, later linking Edward and other incarcerated revolutionaries with activists outside the prisons. She was refused a last visit on the eve of Despard's doom and indignantly expressed a "strong opinion with respect to the cause for which her husband was to suffer." The word *cause* has two meanings, physical and moral. There was an efficient cause of which the conspiracy was an effect, and there was an ideal to be struggled for, and to both of them Catherine was as committed as her hus-

band. She had worked tirelessly to expose and improve prison conditions, writing and petitioning for the "common necessaries of life"—
warmth, fresh air, food, space, books, pen, ink, and paper and access to
family, friends, and comrades. Her work as a courier worried the nation's
attorney general and solicitor general, who believed that "so extensive
and Voluminous a correspondence" as she carried out of the prison could
have no other purpose than publication. They also feared, however, that
any attempt to search Catherine as she left the prison would inspire an
outcry. So they recommended to the home secretary that Despard's writings be seized for inspection and censorship before Catherine was permitted to take them.[7]

Catherine also worked boldly at the highest levels of society and government. She approached Lord Nelson, who had spoken generously at
the trial, to make "further application to government." The nation's
hero, victor over Napoleon at the Nile, now testified on behalf of the nation's villain, noting that twenty-three years earlier, "we went on the
Spanish Main together; we slept many nights together in our clothes
upon the ground; we measured the height of the enemies wall together.
In all that period of time no man could have shewn more zealous attachment to his Sovereign and his Country, than Colonel Despard did." Nelson in turn had a word with Lord Minto, the former governor of Corsica,
who later wrote, "Mrs. Despard was violently in love with her husband,
which makes the last scene of the tragedy affecting indeed. Lord Nelson
solicited a pension, or some provision for her, and the Government was
well disposed to grant it; but the last act on the scaffold [when the Colonel referred to the human race] may have defeated any chance of indul-
gence to any member of his family." Catherine also forfeited the pension
due her as the widow of an army officer. She assisted Edward in composing his last words, helping to define the "cause," or "the principles of freedom, of humanity, and of justice." She was thus more than just an organizer and courier. "Much of his time," it was noted of his last days, "was
employed in writing, some in reading, and the greater part with Mrs.
Despard."[8]

The struggles for freedom, humanity, and justice in 1802 were Atlantic: accounts of the conspiracy were quickly published in Paris, Dublin,
Edinburgh, and New York. Yet recent historical interpretations have

confined their compass to England, Ireland, and France. They have ignored Catherine Despard, who has remained a shadow (a woman)
within a shadow (a *black* woman) within a shadow (a *revolutionary* black
woman)—or, as Blake wrote in "Visions of the Daughters of Albion"
(1793), a poem precisely concerned with the liberation inherent in Anglo-
American–African unions, "a solitary shadow wailing on the margin of
non-entity." Sexism and racism have *kept* her in the shadows. The African American slave experience at the end of the eighteenth century was
distinguished, as C. L. R. James noted, not by race but by the collective
"extensive cultivation of the soil, which eventually made possible the
transition to an industrial and urban society." The mass cultivators of the
soil also provided mass experience in the freedom struggle against slavery, and that experience was conveyed to Albion's industrial and urban
society by folks like Catherine Despard. Our view of the conspiracy
must be broadened to include Jamaica, Nicaragua, and Belize, where
Despard lived and met Catherine, as well as Haiti and mainland America, where the freedom struggle shook the Atlantic mountains. An Atlantic perspective is likewise needed to understand Despard's own biography, because he passed his childhood, or the first sixteen years of his
life, in Ireland; he spent his manhood, or the next twenty-four years, in
the Americas; and he lived out his maturity, or his last twelve years, in
London. The union and the conspiracy of Catherine and Edward Marcus Despard may stand for a new cycle of rebellion that began in the
1790s, from which emerged not only the race and class themes in the age
of revolution but also a new definition of the human race.

IRELAND

Edward Marcus Despard was an Irishman. His conspiracy, as James
Connolly correctly insisted, was tied to that of Robert Emmet, also of
1803; and like Emmet, he was an "Irish apostle of a world-wide movement for liberty, equality and fraternity."[9] Born in 1750 on his family's estate at Donore, near Mountrath, amid the Slieve Bloom Mountains, in
what was then Queen's County, Ireland (now county Laois), he was the
youngest of six brothers. Mountrath lay within the pale of the Tudor
plantations. In the early seventeenth century, the area had been settled by

Colonel Edward Marcus Despard, c. 1803.
Courtesy of the National Library of Ireland.

Emanuel Downing, John Winthrop, and other Puritans before they moved across the Atlantic to Massachusetts Bay, selling out to Sir Charles Coote, a ruthless soldier and entrepreneur who aggressively dominated the plantation, against the claims of the Fitzpatrick sept. Despard's ancestors planted themselves in Mountrath in the 1640s, as part of the

Coote entourage.[10] Despard's secretary, James Bannantine, claimed in a memoir of 1799 that an ancestor had been an engineer at the Battle of the Boyne. By the middle of the eighteenth century, there were clerks, weavers, joiners, and carpenters in Mountrath bearing the name Despard. Edward's own immediate family produced soldiers, sheriffs, and priests for the established church.[11]

The subtle landscape of Mountrath today hides the woodlands that once covered it, which now are suggested only by townland names: Derrylahan ("the wide oak-wood"), Ross dorragh ("the dark wood"), and Derrynaseera ("the oak-wood of the freeman"). Large enclosed tracts, drained bogs, several rivers, and the forge and mill of proto-industry were all signs of that capitalist mobilization of collective labor that Arthur Young, the agricultural "improver," likened to the richness of an English scene.[12] This landscape, represented on neat eighteenth-century maps of orderly roads and tracts, concealed the squalid hovels and habitations of the dispossessed peasantry and cotters, whose living conditions during this period were even worse than those of West Indian slaves or Russian serfs. Restrictions on the export of Irish cattle to England were lifted in 1759, moving landlords to enclose the commons, destroy the ancient clachan (the unit of communal agriculture), and turn arable land into pasture. The land was well bounded by quick hawthorne hedges, among the most notable of which were those at the Despard estate at Donore, where they were said to be "extremely neat, with saddle copings." In 1761 agrarian rebels known as the Whiteboys rose against the "improvers." A cry went up: "Betwixt landlord and rector the very marrow is screwed out of our bones. . . . They have reduced us to such a deplorable state by such grievous oppressions that the poor is turned black in the face, and the skin parched on their back."[13] Nocturnal bands of hundreds of people, dressed in flowing white frocks and white cockades, pulled down the fences enclosing the commons. They were led by fairies and mythic figures such as "Queen Sieve," who wrote in 1762,

We, levellers and avengers for the wrongs done to the poor, have unanimously assembled to raze walls and ditches that have been made to inclose the commons. Gentlemen now of late have learned to grind the face of the poor so that it is impossible for them to live. They cannot even keep a pig or a hen at their doors. We warn them

not to raise again either walls or ditches in the place of those we destroy, nor even to inquire about the destroyers of them. If they do,
their cattle shall be houghed [hamstrung] and their sheep laid open
in the fields.[14]

Despard thus grew up a country of intense social antagonism. Charles
Coote complained of the "irreclaimable barbarity and uncivilization of
the peasantry"; Arthur Young found the people there more impertinent
than elsewhere, and wrote that "stealing is very common."[15] During
the 1790s, a Ribbon Society (a secret peasant association) was formed in
Slieve Bloom; sixteen of its members were eventually hanged. At the
same time and in the same region, regiments of loyalists were formed
from above, including Mountain Rangers and a regiment raised by Despard's brother.[16] Years later, his niece Jane would recall, "Living one Winter in terror, we were driven away by rebel whitefeet or blackfeet; lost all
our plate which had been placed in a neighbouring town for safety; the
house we lived in set fire to and burnt and my poor father received only
£50 damages from the country. We were moved then to Mount Mellick
for protection and afterwards to Mountrath." The Despards were, if not
great landlords, landlords still, and part of the military junta that dou-
bled the size of its army between 1792 and 1822. The Despard family was,
in short, on the front line of the class struggle between the colonizer and
the oppressed.

How was Edward the boy affected by all this? His niece's memoirs,
composed in the 1820s and preserved in the Despard family papers, provide information about him that could be relevant. By nature mild tem-
pered and mild mannered, he was said to have soaked up the contradiction with equanimity. He listened raptly to the fantastic "lies" of the
Gaelic storyteller brought in at holidays. He detested the afternoon an-
nouncement "Master, the coffee is ready" because it meant he had to read
Scriptures aloud to his grandmother.[17] According to family tradition,
even in childhood he loathed the Bible and coffee equally. At the age of
eight, "Ned" was placed as page to Countess Hertford, whose husband
at the time was lord lieutenant of Ireland, a member of "the proudest
and least moral family of any in the British dominions then as now."
Despard was known as a Latin and French scholar and a "great belle letter person."[18]

At fifteen, Ned entered the Fiftieth Regiment of the British army. Since Cromwell's time Ireland had nourished the army and navy with salt beef and butter, and so, too, was it the army's and navy's nursery, providing such manpower or cannon fodder as was needed. (In 1798 the "hibernicization" of the British regular army would almost backfire, as some regiments would not be considered "English" enough to be trusted to suppress the rebellion.)[19] All of the Despard brothers joined the British army, except for the eldest, who inherited the family estate. Ned's formative years in his native land had been passed in a period of renewed and violent class struggle over the common lands and their associated culture. Any seeds of sympathy that may have been sown in him would lie dormant for decades.

JAMAICA

In January 1766, Despard's regiment landed on Jamaica. The young Irishman disembarked into one of the world's preeminent slave societies, in which a small class of sugar planters and their overseers lived off the labor of some two hundred thousand African slaves. Despard would have seen immediately that this society was based on terror, for he arrived in the aftermath of Tacky's Revolt. Three more slave revolts soon followed it, one in 1765 and two in 1766; hangings and gibbetings marked the island landscape. Within six years Despard would be promoted to lieutenant and entrusted to help design the shore batteries and fortifications of Kingston and Port Royal, the headquarters of the British navy in the Caribbean. During his near-twenty-year residence in Jamaica, three experiences were decisive: Despard learned to survive in a deadly land; he learned to be a strategic thinker in matters military; and he learned to organize and lead motley crews, multiethnic gangs of laborers.

The health of the English officer in the Caribbean depended on the nursing he received from Jamaican women. "A soldier should be nursed," declared the senior physician to the British military in Jamaica, Dr. Benjamin Moseley, adding that the drudgery "should be performed by negroes."[20] J. B. Moreton, a planter of Clarendon Parish, advised the recently arrived English officer or gentleman to find an African American woman as quickly as possible: "If you please and humour her properly, she will make and mend all your clothes, attend you when sick, and when she can afford it will assist you with any thing in her power." The informal domestic-service sector of the Caribbean economy, from which the internationally esteemed tradition of Jamaican nursing would grow, did not neatly distinguish at this time among housekeepers, lovers, and nurses. The West Indian boardinghouse was something of a hospital as well as a restaurant and dance hall, as R. R. Madden, the Irish historian, attested after living in such a lodging in Barbados.[21] Such establishments, and the relations they assumed, could arouse color prejudice, fear of sexuality, and revolutionary fright even among Anglo reformers such as John Thelwall, who was terrified by the lascivious and riotous dancing, as described in his 1801 novel largely set in Haiti, *The Daughter of Adoption; A Tale of Modern Times*. A Kingston woman might well have adopted the free and easy approach expressed in one Jamaican ballad, which concludes on a note characteristic of the antinomianism of the 1650s. It was to be sung to the air of "What Care I for Mam or Dad":

> *Me know no law, me know no sin,*
> *Me is just what ebba them make me;*
> *This is the way dem bring me in;*
> *So God nor devil take me!*

It is likely that Despard relied on the ministrations of such a woman of African descent, though we do not know for a fact that he met his future wife at this time. Significantly, the women slaves of Jamaica, no less than the men, were freedom fighters: "The head Negro Women about Lucea, even those kept by white men, were concerned" in the slave revolt of Hanover Parish in 1776, for example.[22]

Despard's military career depended on military production by men of African descent, enslaved and free, as well as by European soldiers, who were themselves poor and multiethnic—English, Welsh, Scottish, and Irish. This labor had two strategic objects, as set forth in a treatise on the fortification of Jamaica, written in 1783: "1st Security against Insurrections" and "2nd Security against Foreign Invasion." Thereby, a "General Security of the Settlements against enemies, whether intestine or foreign, is the fundamental principle."[23] It was assumed that any invading force would encourage slave revolt, against which the authorities pursued a policy of dividing the black population, promising freedom to slaves who joined the militia. Five thousand black pioneers were to be instantly mobilized upon alarm. Despard studied cooperation, division, and the relationship between insurrection and invasion.[24]

"The unfortunate Edward," his niece wrote years after his death, "was an accomplished draughtsman, mathematician and engineer."[25] Like other engineers, he supervised the labor that built roads and bridges, he conducted sieges, he maintained fortifications, he prepared maps and sketches, and he kept financial accounts.[26] In Jamaica, twenty-one locations, with tracery, hornwork, redoubts, or glacis, required attention. "It was here in these material arrangements," wrote E. K. Brathwaite, referring to the roads, bridges, aqueducts, churches, burial grounds, great houses, and forts erected in the last quarter of the eighteenth century, "that the white contribution to the island's cultural development lay." This was architecture, "invented," said John Ruskin, to make "slaves of its workmen, and sybarites of its inhabitants." To this we must add its military function, which indeed made possible the other two characteristics.[27]

Much of the work Despard organized was like the hewing of wood and the drawing of water, for which thousands of people were mobilized. Sappers, miners, and pioneers did the pick-and-shovel work. The sapper executed fieldworks; he built and repaired fortifications. The pioneer worked with others in small squads. The work was carefully coordinated: "A pickaxe breaks the ground, two shovels following, throw the earth towards the scarp, whence two other shovels throw it up the berm; from thence again two shovels throw it upon the profile." It took seven men to transport as much dirt as one horse. The work included blasting, grubbing, mucking, hacking, bending, thrusting, straightening, and hauling—suggesting why the word *fatigue,* with its double meaning as "punishment for military misdemeanors" and "physical exhaustion," entered the English vocabulary at this time.[28] (On the other side of the Atlantic, meanwhile, in addition to "Vomiting and Diarrhoea, Shivers and Shakes and Heartaches," the Gaelic poet in his curses wished upon the English ["Sud An Nidh Ghuidhimsi Saxonig"] "Digging the Drains and Making Ditches.")[29] Despard himself had come to Jamaica from a spade culture, and moreover one in high mobilization in the 1760s as Ireland embarked on the most intensive land cultivation of its history. The spade combined many of the functions of the mattock, ax, crowbar, mallet, shovel, and hoe. It was essential to large-scale drainage projects and lazy-bed cultivation alike. Despard and his crews worked on a variety of sites, from marsh to mountain. He shared in the dangers of the work: slip-pages, irregularities, falling boulders, shifting earth, flooding trenches, falling objects, collapsing pilings, and weak shoring.[30]

During his time on Jamaica, Despard saw his military career advance. His work as an engineer helped to save both Kingston and the island as a whole—as Britain's headquarters in the Caribbean—from Spanish attack during the American War of Independence. His success was built upon the slavery and terror of island society, as he was part of a privileged class and dependent on the wealthy sugar planters for preferment and promotion, which came to him in 1783 with the award of the rank of colonel in a provincial regiment. With the help of African women, he survived the tropics. He could not have organized the polyglot motley crews had he not developed some sympathy, intellect, and lucidity in forming and co-ordinating the gangs of workers whose labor was his triumph. In that way, he was creolized.

NICARAGUA

Since Despard's regiment was disabled by disease and at less than full strength in 1776, he was not assigned to join General Howe in the British military campaign against the American colonies, but rather appointed later, in 1779, to be one of the commanding officers in an expedition against the Spanish Main. The goal was to sever North from South America by sending an expedition across Nicaragua to cut the Spanish Empire in half, at the same time connecting the Atlantic and Pacific Oceans. Governor John Dalling of Jamaica conceived the expedition while dreaming over Thomas Jefferys's *Atlas of the West Indies,* and he believed that success would produce a "new order of things." Yet the plan posed problems of logistics and communication. Troops, ships, and provisions had to be mobilized in Jamaica and then transported across a thousand miles of sea, and a base of operations had to be established on an unknown coast. The troops would disembark and reassemble on river

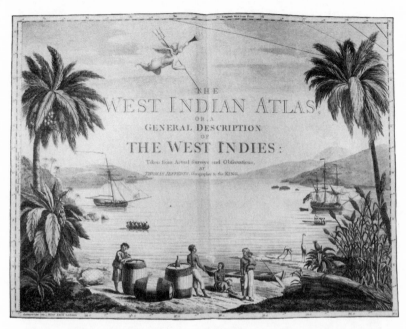

Thomas Jeffreys, The West Indian Atlas; Or, a General Description of the
West Indies Taken from Actual Surveys and Observations *(1777).*
William L. Clements Library, University of Michigan.

craft, carrying materiel and provisions sixty miles upriver, surmounting
rapids, shoals, and blind tributaries. They would then lay siege to Fort
Inmaculada, which had been built in 1655 to defend against buccaneers.
Once in command of all the strong points along the river, the men would
build vessels and outfit a fleet for operations in Lake Nicaragua. All of
these operations were, moreover, to be carried out in a debilitating milieu
of tropical heat and, after May, torrential rains.

The expeditionary force was raised in Kingston in February 1780 under martial law. Despard and other officers would lead several squadrons
of soldiers (from the Sixtieth Loyal Americans, the Seventy-ninth or Liverpool Blues, and the Royal American Foot) as well as a larger group of
irregulars from Jamaica—the Legion (composed mostly of sailors), the
Black Regiment, the Loyal Irish Company, the Royal Batteaux Corps,
and a motley contingent of Royal Jamaica volunteers. Lieutenant Governor Archibald Campbell took the farewell salute. The irregulars were

drawn up, he wrote, "in a ragged line, half-clothed and half-drunk, they seemed to possess the true complexion of buccaneers and it would be illiberal to suppose their principles were not in harmony with their faces. A hundred of them were collected together and seemed so volatile and frolicsome, I thought it good policy to order ten guineas for them to be drunk in grog on board their transports and embarked them with three cheers to the great satisfaction of the town of Kingston."

Twenty years earlier, Molyneux, the first published British authority on amphibious warfare, had described the technical/military potential of the motley crew: "Wonderful things have been done, even with little Boats, with an handful of bold and cunning men." "We [the British Empire] call ourselves the Neptune of the Sea, without knowing how, in many parties, to sway the trident,"—admitting, in other words, that their command of the "handful of bold and cunning men" was less than perfect.[31] He soberly noted that in North America and the West Indies ten such amphibious efforts had succeeded, and thirteen failed. The 1780 expedition fell into two phases. The first, lasting from February to the end of April, the dry season, culminated in the defeat of the garrison at the castle up St. Johns River. The second phase, during the rainy season, was characterized by disease, huge mortality, and, finally, retreat in December. The first was a westward movement upriver, and the second an eastward one, downstream. In the first we see Despard as a bold and daring soldier, in the second as a survivor. He was the first to arrive and the last to leave. Usually shoulder to shoulder with Despard, the young Horatio Nelson here got his boots mired in the mud and fell behind. In the first phase, Despard reconnoitered, he planned the attack, he led the first party and took fire. On April 30, Commanding Officer John Polson wrote to Governor Dalling that "nearly every gun fired was aimed either by Nelson or Despard." Despard organized parties of sappers to begin mining the ramparts. The siege was successful: the garrison surrendered, and prisoners were taken.[32]

There was a political economy to the operation: war was work, and Despard commanded. He put the men to work, set their hours, and created a wage and skill hierarchy, offering extra money to those "who really understand their business," as one of his lieutenants observed. He contended with broken and missing tools, a problem that made it difficult

Despard's drawing of Fort Inmaculada, 1780. Robinson,
A Pictorial History of the Sea Services. *John Hay Library.*

for the party to blow up the Spanish fort before retreating. He searched
for skilled masons, carpenters, sawyers, and most of all boatmen. He was
part of a military system in which authority and discipline were maintained by providing food to the soldiers. They were discouraged from
providing for themselves, especially in woods that abounded "in game,
such as warrus, or wild Hogs, guanas, Ducks, Pigeons, Currasoa Birds,
Quams, both as big as Turkeys," because that would encourage their independence. The officers refused to allow the soldiers to barter, to exchange clothing for provisions, or to hunt in the woods without permission. Troops were soon put on short allowance; then their provisioning
fell in arrears. The sick had no fruit or vegetables.[33] By the beginning of
June, the "melancholy effects of famine" were beginning to be felt at the
castle, and so, too, because of the scarcity and deteriorating conditions,
the effects of resistance: pilferage, theft, and desertion.[34] The sailors, soldiers, artificers, boatmen, and laborers had to be continually replaced as
the original complement succumbed or ran away. The soldiers who remained at the fort were soon too weak to crawl. At Greytown, downriver,
the soldiers were too sick to bury the dead.

The "gray-eyed people," as the Mosquitos called the English, increasingly depended upon native people for transportation and food.[35] Those who knew the local ecology were a product of three continents: they were American, African, and European. In the seventeenth century, the Mosquito Indians had incorporated European buccaneers and escaped or shipwrecked African slaves into their communities. By the eighteenth, they had become an advanced maritime people with major settlements at Blewfields, Pearl Key Lagoon, Boca del Toro, Corn Island, St. Andres, and Old Providence. Olaudah Equiano spent a year with them; they helped build his house south of Cape Gracias á Dios, "which they did exactly like the Africans, by the joint labor of men, women, and children."[36] They celebrated with a *dryckbot,* or drinking bout (a buccaneer custom), "without the least discord in any person in the company, although it was made up of different nations and complexions." Equiano sailed to Jamaica from London with four Mosquito chiefs, with whom he studied Foxe's *Book of Martyrs,* the mammoth sixteenth-century Protestant text of struggle and persecution. Charles Napier Bell grew up among the Mosquitos in the early nineteenth century and learned their lore from an ancient Mandingo woman, a Muslim from the headwaters of the Niger. He described the amplitude of the cockles, the plenty of the seas, the simplicity of plantain cultivation, and how the flowers, the birds, and the cricky jeen supplied all the information of an almanac. The Mosquitos, wrote another observer, "have no interest in the accumulation of property, and therefore do not labour to obtain wealth. They live under the most perfect equality, and hence are not impelled to industry by that spirit of emulation which, in society, leads to great and unwearied exertion. Content with their simple means, they evince no desire to emulate the habits or the occupations of the colonists; but on the contrary, seem to regard their toils and customs with a sense of pity or contempt."[37]

Whether out of pity, contempt, or ill health of their own, the Mosquitos grew impatient with the St. Johns expedition. Since river transport had depended upon their "spirited exertions and perseverance," and since their hunting, fishing, and turtling had helped to feed the soldiers, things soon began to fall apart.[38] Alexander Shaw, commissary of provisions, negotiated for their continued work, which they would agree to only on their own terms: "If any Mosquito men are employed in any laborious work it is only to be upon condition they chuse themselves to be so employed but they are not to be compelled, and are to be paid for their labour the same as other persons employed in such labour and are to be at liberty to return either to the Army or to their homes without Mollestation." Officers were also ordered to "take every Step that the Soldiery have little connection with them [the Indians] in Order to avoid the possibility of Disgust on their Side."[39] The Indians nonetheless decided to go home, and they took their boats with them. Those who returned to Jamaica, meanwhile, "propagated reports among the lower class of the white people" that it was unsafe to go to the St. Johns River. The Indians "have the highest ideas of freedom," wrote one of the officers in April.

Once the Indians had deserted, the expedition relied almost entirely on the "Black River Negroes"—boatmen from the Mosquito Shore—for supplies. But when one of the leaders of their contingent fell ill, "almost all these Negroes deserted, and carried off with them the smallest and most suitable boats, so that the distresses of the Troops were greatly heightened, and there remained hardly any other prospect than that of being obliged to retire." The desertions continued through May and June. By September, Despard wrote, the garrison was "so extremely weak that there are not Men sufficient to keep up the necessary Guards. The Negroes of the Corps, I have been obliged to keep in the Fort constantly to prevent their desertion, as well as to have them ready to work when necessary, & for some time past they have not had much spare time—five Men deserted one night four of the Volunteers & one of the Legion & took a Dory with them." A captain soon reported a strike, as soldiers made "an absolute Refusal of their Labour." In July, the resistance from below had taken an even more serious turn when the slaves on the Mosquito Shore revolted and captured the main town on the Black River.

Two thousand soldiers went up the St. Johns River between February and November, and a hundred returned. Another thousand sailors also perished. Writing in 1780, Lord George Germain, Britain's secretary of war, chastised Governor Dalling, "I lament exceedingly the dreadful havoc Death has made among the troops." Unlike sixty-nine other officers, Nelson and Despard survived—Nelson only because he was carried downriver in a delirium and out of the country, then nursed back to health by the Afro-Caribbean woman Cuba Cornwallis. Despard remained. In July 1780 the governor of Jamaica indulged himself and his superiors in an apologetics of wishful, xenophobic praise of British regular troops: "It is by the superiority of their discipline we are to reap the greatest advantages. Impressed with this Idea, he flatters himself each Soldier will strive to distinguish himself, and show how superior disciplined and well-bred Troops are to a motley Crew of Indians and Mulattoes."[40] Despard owed his survival to precisely such a crew.

After the catastrope of the St. Johns expedition, Dr. Moseley wrote that "the failure of that undertaking has been buried, with many of its kindred, in the silent tomb of government."[41] Despard's personal triumph was made possible by his cooperation with the motley crew, including the Mosquito Indians, the black boatmen, and the miners, sappers, and builders with whom he lived and worked for nearly eighteen months. Driven by misplaced duty to imperial arrogance, forced to deny the plenitude of a tropical commons, and surrounded by a slaughter of men whose motley origins alone prevent us accurately from calling it genocide, Despard nonetheless formed an attachment to a people—the Mosquitos—whose knowledge of the commons was seminal, whose origins among buccaneers were held in pride, and whose ideas of freedom were lofty. Was Catherine one of them?

BELIZE

Between Despard's departure from Nicaragua and his appointment as the Crown's leading official in British Honduras in 1784, the cycle of rebellion initiated by the motley crew in the 1760s resulted in American independence. Mutinies at sea, revolts on the plantations, and riots in the port cities generated an imperial crisis and a revolutionary movement to answer it, but as we have seen, at war's end many were excluded from the political settlement. Among these were the thousands of African Americans who had liberated themselves—often, after Dunmore's Proclamation (1774), by running away to the British army.[42] Military formations such as Leslie's Black Dragoons and Brown's Rangers advanced multiracial military organization and anticipated the West Indian regiments of the 1790s. Twenty thousand African Americans were carried out of North America after 1782, to Canada, the West Indies, Central America,

England, and Africa. The people in diaspora expressed their journey, or exodus, in a discourse of deliverance that owed much to the renewal of liberation theology of the English Revolution, newly fortified by African American preachers such as Sambo Scriven, who traveled to the Bahamas, George Liele, who went to Jamaica, and John Marrant, who preached in London and Nova Scotia.[43] Aboard men-of-war, in the harbors and ports of the northern Atlantic, in prisons afloat and ashore, they carried the message of jubilee as they searched for the New Jerusalem. This movement of people and ideas would come to affect Despard in Belize.

Belize was a dense tropical forest protected by the largest coral barrier reef in the Western Hemisphere. Even on Despard's and his associate David Lamb's maps, the boundaries of private property showed as unconvincing geometric lines amid the prolific rendering of forest.[44] For nearly two hundred years the region had been home to Indian, African, and European mariners, renegades, and castaways, including buccaneers, pirates, and sailors, millenarian dissidents from the former Mayan milpas, transported Jacobite rebels from the Fifteen and the Forty-Five, survivors of wrecked slave ships, and transported Jamaican rebels. They cut logwood in the mangrove swamps, often at night, by the light of pitch-pine torches, to escape the heat.[45] They sold the logwood to Jamaican traders, who in turn shipped it to Europe, where it was used as a mordant in dyeing textiles. They lived "generally in common," for whenever they used up a "stock of provisions & Liquors, they go to live with their neighbors." Although they appeared to outsiders to be lawless, they in fact had "certain rules of their own making," wrote the merchant encyclopedist Postlethwayt. Belize was a landed extension of hydrarchy in compound with Mayan milpas: it provided mankind with an example of collective self-reliance in a commons, self-government without the principle of hierarchy, and multiethnic solidarity, which had already shaped local historical consciousness by the time Despard arrived and which was to remain so powerful that when Lewis Henry Morgan visited, years later, he would coin the expression "primitive communism" to describe it.[46]

By the time Despard landed there in 1786, much of the Belize littoral had been transformed into private property. The Treaty of Paris had concluded the Seven Years' War in 1763, giving British settlers more secure land tenure and opening the way to mahogany cutting. Wealthier settlers had moved to the region, bringing with them slaves and the aggressive cupidity of a new mode of production. The magnificent trees were felled by axmen who belonged to slave gangs of cattle drovers, rafters, teamsters, cooks, providers. The mahogany was sold to European furnishers, of whom Thomas Chippendale was merely the most enterprising. His publication of *The Gentleman and Cabinet Maker's Director* (1754), with its four hundred designs and 160 folio copper plates, represented a step toward standardization, moving the industry from handicraft production to manufacture. The European ruling class now ate off of mahogany tables, clothed itself from mahogany dressers, gazed upon itself in mahogany-framed mirrors, wrote letters on mahogany écritoires, sang in choir stalls of mahogany, and so on. Meanwhile, Admiral William Burnaby had arrived with naval warships in Belize in 1765 to establish a formal legal code and to announce that land would no longer be held in common. The same year brought the first slave revolt; others followed in 1768 and 1773. By 1780, slaves outnumbered the free by six to one. Fifteen "Baymen," as the ambitious planters termed themselves, had engrossed all mahogany production.[47]

Despard's assignment there in 1786 coincided with a new agreement between Britain and Spain, called the Convention of London, whose implementation would trigger armed conflict in Belize over land and labor and decisively alter the colonel's life. The Convention required Britain to evacuate more than two thousand of its settlers from the Mosquito Shore to Belize in exchange for new mahogany-cutting rights there. In February 1787, 514 immigrants arrived from the Mosquito Shore. Most of them, Despard observed, were "indigent people of colour" of the American exodus. In May another 1,740 people joined the suddenly crowded settlement. Despard was charged with providing subsistence for the new settlers while integrating them into the colony.[48] Who were these people who came to the bay to be "Hewers of Wood and the Drawers of Water"?[49] In the first group were members of the Loyal American Rangers, who had been recruited in New York among deserters and prisoners of the Continental Army in 1780 and posted to Jamaica in 1781, when Despard "had the honor of commanding most of them" in the routing of the Spanish on the Black River in 1782.

While treaty arrangements with Spain forbade the cultivation of food, in practice this prohibition was impossible to enforce. Fishing and tur-

tling provided the staple diet of the Mayas, the Mosquitos, and the buccaneers, but not so the settlers; as their numbers grew, the rapacious
among them began to privatize the commons, and the colony thus became increasingly dependent on food imports from North America. In
order to ensure subsistence for the "poorer sort of people," Despard allowed the cultivation of plantains, yams, corn, pineapples, and melons,
disregarding the terms of the treaty. He set aside certain areas "to be enjoyed in common by all the settlers" and strengthened his alliance with
the people who knew the local ecology. He waged a bitter struggle
against American merchants who charged exorbitant prices for food-
stuffs, thereby "keeping the people poor and totally dependent upon
them." When, in 1788, such merchants violated trading regulations, he
did not hesitate to impound and even to sell their vessels.[50]

Despard also had to decide how the new settlers would "get the means
of subsistence by their labor and industry." His allocation of land from
the newly ceded territory caused the established mahogany men to howl
in protest. Earlier, the Baymen had opposed his decision to permit the
landing of a ship of convicts, suspected his motives in granting manumission from slavery, and felt insulted when he showed lenience to a Negro charged with the murder of a white man. Now Despard ignored their
pressure and proposed to hand out land by lottery, which he deemed the
"most equal and impartial mode of distribution." The Baymen responded angrily that this would give the "lowest Mulatto or free Negro"
an "equal chance" with the wealthiest. One of them could not understand how "a person of his extensive property should be placed on a footing with fellows of the lowest class and have no more land allowed him
than . . . a fellow as Able Tayler (this is a man of Collour)." The lottery,
they complained, would distribute land "without any distinction of
Age, Sex, Character, Respectability, Property, or *Colour.*" Despard, they
charged, was no respecter of persons: he insisted "that he cannot & will
not know any distinction between these very different classes of men."
He assigned lots to all classes and colors of men as well as to sixteen
women.[51]

Tensions escalated when a "free man of Colour," Joshua Jones, drew
town lot number 69 and, on Despard's authority, tore down the cook-
house of a wealthy settler that had been built on the land. Jones was arrested by magistrates representing the Baymen and clapped into jail.

Soon a "few white people of the very lowest class, a number of Mustees, Mulattos, and Free negroes," began drumming, "playing the Gambia," and "running about the streets and assembling under arms," threatening to free Jones. Despard intervened on their side and demanded Jones's release. It was one of those flashpoints of history that illuminate an epoch. The Baymen expressed a doctrine of racial supremacy combined with class superiority, arguing that the "mode of distribution adopted by the Superintendent, was equally unjust and unpolitic in putting Negroes and Mulattoes (a set of persons who, in all the West India Islands, were considered in a very inferior light to the whole Inhabitants) upon a footing with Gentlemen and Mahogany Cutters, who were the supporters of the Country." Maintaining an egalitarian view that was nonetheless still consistent with the mixed constitution of king and Parliament, Despard replied that "the legislative powers of these Islands made, it is true, some distinctions between white people and Negroes and mulattoes; but that there being no legislature in this Country, it must be governed by the law of England, which knows no such distinction, that even in those parts of the British Colonies where any such distinctions took place, it by no means did so in the distribution of the King's land; and that these people of colour were as much entitled to places to live as the first Mahogany Cutters in the Country."[52] The Baymen continued to assault the new claimants, prompting the "people of colour" to petition in 1787 against their exclusion from land by reason of race:

We your Petitioners the Inhabitants of the Mosquito Shore humbly sheweth that the many circumstances that immediately occur to us gives the most assured reason to expect that it will be really impossible for us to procure a livelihood in this Country, as we are not allowed the privileges of British subjects, and as Colored persons treated with the utmost disrespect, even threatened of being deprived of the Laws and privileges of this Country in case we do not sign and agree to a certain resolution made by a Committee appointed by persons for that purpose, which are of opinion is contrary to the proposals of Colonel Despard Superintendent of this Country and to any British Constitution whatever.

Among those signing this petition was Joshua Jones.

In the same year, Despard stood for election as magistrate. He won with more than 80 percent of the vote. His enemies claimed that some of the ballots had been cast by "ignorant turtlers" and "men of colour, possessing no species of property or any fixed residence." Robert White, the agent of the Baymen, wrote to Lord Sydney in London in 1788 that Despard's lottery "breaks into pieces all the Links of Society, and destroys all Order, Rank, and Government"; to this Despard responded by noting the partiality of the Baymen's laws to rich people.[53] Their law of naturalization excluded people of color, seeking to prevent them from independent subsistence and to force them to become servants or slaves. By September 1789 the Baymen's complaints had expanded to include the full chorus of the North Atlantic bourgeoisie. Lord Grenville, Britain's secretary of state, announced in October of that year that Despard had been suspended from office.

Race was not the only issue here: how the classes were constituted in relation to subsistence and to the commons was also in question, and inherent in that was the matter of reproduction. In the slave and military society of plantation Jamaica, reproduction was made possible by the creolized group living and nursing of the boardinghouse. In the Nicaraguan expedition of 1780, it had depended on the rigid command of scarcity in the midst of fecundity, which had led inevitably to catastrophe. Only in Belize did Despard attempt a third solution: accommodation with the commons and union with the motley crew. But Despard did not so much organize a motley crew as he was organized *by* one. While it is conceivable that Despard met Catherine in either Jamaica or Nicaragua, it is perhaps more likely that they formed their alliance in Belize. Having arrived in the settlement unmarried, Edward had a wife and a son by the time he sailed back to England in April 1790.[54] Our story, then, is of a woman of the African American revolutionary diaspora who married an Irish officer amid the egalitarian modification of a Central American commons, only to be defeated by a commercial concupiscence of empire that they now sought to face squarely in the midst of revolution.

THE HUMAN RACE

Edward and Catherine Despard reached London in the spring of 1790, one year after the storming of the Bastille and the beginning of the French Revolution, and one year before the stormy night of voodoo in the Bois Caiman that would launch the Haitian Revolution. They arrived to find a movement afoot in England to abolish slavery. The middle-class educational program about West Indian slavery promoted a sympathetic, if false, impression. Josiah Wedgwood's seal of the kneeling Negro, captioned "Am I not a Man and a Brother?" (1787), presented a posture of individual supplication, while the Plymouth Committee's image of the plan of a slave ship (1788) conveyed a sense of reiterated passivity (see page 155). Edward and Catherine knew the truth, which would become obvious to others only after the Haitian Revolution. The Despards would use this truth as they organized in London "to burst the chain of bondage and slavery," as they advocated the "principles of freedom, of humanity, and of justice," and as they developed their conception of the "human race."

In England, Edward and Catherine found a country where workers had embraced the cause of abolition. Seven hundred sixty-nine Sheffield cutlers had petitioned Parliament in 1789 against the efforts of the pro-slavery lobby: "The cutlery wares made by the freemen . . . being sent in considerable quantities to the Coast of Africa, and disposed of, in part, as the price of Slaves—your Petitioners may be supposed to be prejudiced in their interests if the said trade in Slaves should be abolished. But your petitioners having always understood that the natives of Africa"—and here they would have remembered Olaudah Equiano's talks with them as he lectured on the abolition circuit—"have the greatest aversion to foreign Slavery." Claiming to "consider the case of the nations of Africa as their own," and putting principle before material interest, the cutlers took an unusual public stand against slavery, something no English workers had done in almost a century and a half. Joseph Mather, the poetic annalist of proletarian Sheffield, sang,

> *As negroes in Virginia,*
> *In Maryland or Guinea,*
> *Like them I must continue—*
> *To be both bought and sold.*
> *While negro ships are filling*
> *I ne'er can save one shilling,*
> *And must, which is more killing,*
> *A pauper die when old.*

Sheffield was a steel town, manufacturing the sickles and scythes of harvest, the scissors and razors of the export markets, and the pike, implement of the people's war. The secretary of the workers' organization, the Sheffield Constitutional Society (formed in 1791), explained its purpose: "To enlighten the people, to show the people the reason, the ground of all their complaints and sufferings; when a man works for thirteen or fourteen hours of the day, the week through, and is not able to maintain his family; that is what I understand of it; to show the people the ground of this; why they were not able." The Constitutional Society also declared itself against slavery, much like the London Corresponding Society, which, as we shall later see, was founded early in 1792 in discussion of "having all things in common" and committed to equality among all, whether "black or white, high or low, rich or poor."

The unity of race and class concerns, however, soon began to fragment. When the Corresponding Society stepped politely into the civic realm on April 2, 1792, its official statement made no mention of slavery, the slave trade, or the commons—and this on the very day of the "April Compromise," when Parliament agreed to abolish slavery, but only "gradually"! By August 1792, the L.C.S. was defining its constituency and its aims among inhabitants of Great Britain: "FELLOW CITIZENS, Of every rank and every situation in life, Rich, Poor, High or Low, we address you all as our Brethren."[55] No more "black or white" here: equality of race had disappeared from the society's agenda. What had happened? The answer, in a word, is Haiti. In April 1792, in France, the assembly decreed full political rights for people of color, while in Haiti Hyacinth was leading fearless slaves to besiege Port-au-Prince, and Toussaint L'Ouverture had begun to organize degraded slaves into an independent military force of freedom fighters that would defeat the armies of three European empires over the next decade. Similarly, Absalom Jones and Richard Allen, expelled from the white church, founded their own African Church in Philadelphia in order to lift up former slaves whose experiences had been abject—to transform, as they put it, thorns into grapes and thistles into figs.[56] Race had thus become a tricky and, for many, in England, a threatening subject, one that the leadership of the L.C.S. now preferred to avoid.

In this confused and rapidly changing situation, what could Edward and Catherine Despard contribute? We have seen that during his last days in prison Edward would be frequently and intensively communicating with Catherine, even under the eagle eye of power. We see their conspiracy as a "breathing together" in conversation, which included the wording of the speech he would give from the scaffold (should he say "the human race"?) and the conveyance of information, if not instructions, to co-conspirators in several lands. Did they anticipate a coup d'état (Napoleon's 18 Brumaire had been in 1799), or a diversion for a French landing in Ireland, or an insurrection to provoke a general rising, or an extension of the Atlantic slave revolts? To answer these questions, we must first consider the circumstances of the conspiracy, or the social forces from which it sprang and to which it appealed: this is the *thèse de circonstance.* Then we must explore the ideas and the ideals that motivated the conspirators: that is the *thèse de complot.*

Slaves, industrial workers, sailors and dockworkers, and the Irish would provide the main insurgent force behind the conspiracy of the Despards. In the international conjuncture of 1800–1803, slaves were especially active. In 1800, the black Eighth West India Regiment mutinied in Dominica, slaves plotted on the island of Tobago, and Gabriel organized a slave insurrection in Richmond, Virginia, in which French revolutionaries and perhaps United Irishmen were implicated. A New York property holder wrote that year, "If we will keep a monster in our country, we must keep him in chains"; in Jamaica, the governor contemplated genocide. Slaves fought against the expeditionary army under Leclerc (Napoleon's son-in-law), which invaded Haiti in March 1802, and they rioted against the resumption of slavery in Guadeloupe. In the summer of 1802, many who felt betrayed by their leadership (Toussaint had been captured; Dessalines was still fighting for the French) rose in rebellious combinations of soldiers, peasants, maroons, dockers, and sailors that by February 1803 captured several cities. That same month, a jailbreak by African Americans, coupled with a rash of urban arson, nearly destroyed York, Pennsylvania. Cases heard at the Old Bailey in London in late 1802 involved several black sailors whose transatlantic experience had included sojourns in Providence, New York, Charleston, Kingston, Bridgetown, and Belize City.[57] Such men brought news of what Herbert Aptheker called a decade-long wave of slave plots and uprisings in the

United States, which culminated in 1802. Arthur, a black rebel in Virginia, appealed in that year to "both black and white which is the common man or poor white people, mulattoes will join with me to help free country."[58]

A second force was the lost commoners of England, those who sought through the Despards' conspiracy to rise against the "Den of Thieves" (Parliament) and the "Man-eaters" (the government) and "to recover some of those liberties we have lost." The Board of Agriculture had advocated the abolition of the commons in 1795. Thomas Malthus considered the woodland ecology to be an obstacle to civilization: the woods gave cover to the barbarians, the "hydra-headed monster" that had invaded and destroyed Rome. Hence, to abolish the commons was to slay the hydra, but this was no easy task. Expropriation often seemed to mobilize the disenfranchised. Thomas Spence made the point with Atlantic range: "Abroad and at Home, in America, France, and in our own Fleets, we have seen enough of public spirit . . . to accomplish Schemes of infinitely greater difficulty. . . . The People have only to say 'Let the Land be ours' and it will be so." Despard himself had witnessed violent enclosure and resistance in Ireland and had angered factions by his redistribution of land in Belize.[59]

A substantial number of the men arrested with Despard at the Oakley Arms tavern in November 1802 were craftsmen, whose degradation in the 1790s was manifested in increased hours of employment, fewer holidays, and intensified labor across the whole of their collective working day. These were accomplished by the introduction of machinery and by policing. The cotton gin and the steam engine, introduced in the 1790s, gave the plantation and the factory their lease on life by demonstrating that machines, far from abridging labor, actually increased *unpaid* work. In 1802, wage cuts caused two thousand Thames shipbuilders to "down" their tools. Then the croppers struck in Yorkshire, and the "spirit of Levelling" in Wiltshire was joined to nocturnal attacks upon textile machinery.[60] Common rights were criminalized, the workers divided. In the winter of 1802–3, the struggle to retain customary income on the London docks was bitter. Colquhoun, a Scots merchant, Jamaican planter, and founder of the London police, advocated enclosure of the docks and the construction of inland waterways. His system of preventive policing attacked the customary rights of the "aquatic labourers," or, as he explained, "the hydra in all the different forms it assumed."[61] To slay the hydra was thus to criminalize customary income.

Despard considered sailors and dockworkers, the third main group, to be especially important to his plan to capture London. There were, after all, some one hundred thousand of them, many Irish and African, and they had been rebellious for years. The mutiny on H.M.S. *Bounty* took place on a planetary voyage of 1789 to collect food (breadfruit) from the Pacific to feed people imported from Africa who slaved on West Indian plantations, where they made sugar to provide empty calories to the proletarians in Europe. In 1797, H.M.S. *Hermione* suffered its own mutiny off the coast of Haiti, led by a Belfast republican and a New York African American. At the Nore and Spithead in May and June 1797, when dozens of ships mutinied in home waters, the imperial edifice shook but did not topple, though the Bank was forced to suspend gold payments. Hundreds were court-martialed, but thereafter sixteen ounces, not the purser's fourteen, comprised the pound. In January 1802 thirteen mutineers of Admiral Campbell's squadron were tried and sentenced to death; in the same month, sixteen others were executed at Portsmouth. On Christmas Eve, 1802, several ships in Gibraltar mutinied. At the end of January 1803, Yarmouth sailors struck.

Despard's future fellow prisoner Thomas Spence wrote a commonist plan, *The Marine Republic* (1794), addressed specifically to his audience among the aquatic laborers. Spence also serialized a seventeenth-century account of Masaniello's Revolt, whose conclusion he modified to emphasize the autonomous power of an "injured and exasperated people."[62] Organizing continued on the waterfront even in the face of repression: "Be no longer SLAVES," enjoined a printed card passed silently from calloused hand to calloused hand. The L.C.S. membership card of 1797 depicted a cartoon of a man's being escorted to a boat, with a ship anchored in the distance. "Come along thou black Lubber," says the bully sailor. "O Heavens! can Christians traffic in human Blood?" is the astonished reply.[63] Despard was known among the deckhands and dockers as a "person who had been a Governor somewhere and whose Men had been mutinous and he would not punish them, so was turned out of his place."[64]

The Exact Manner of Executing the Mutineers . . . at Portsmouth, 1802.
Robinson, A Pictorial History of the Sea Services. *John Hay Library.*

Fourth were the Irish. The Despards' conspiracy was in one sense a continuation of the Irish Rebellion and its expansion into England, as Irish sailors, soldiers, and laborers figured centrally in it. Slavery and race became a common cause: a parade of Belfast reformers in 1790 featured an antislavery banner depicting a "Negro boy, well-dressed and holding high the cap of liberty." The United Irish song book *Paddy's Resource* (1795) included "The Captive Negro" and "The Negro's Complaint."[65] In 1795, Irish regiments mutinied against service in the West Indies.[66] Thomas Russell inveighed against slavery and landlordism in his *Address to the People of Ireland* (1796). Blunt and didactic, the United Irishman had as his goal to politicize popular culture rather than to valorize it.[67] Still, this worked harmoniously with Gaelic, the language of the oldest traditions of history from below, in which prophecy, millenarianism, and the world turned upside down helped to form *saoirse*. The United Irish walked and walked. To boxing matches, hurling games, funerals, and collective potato diggings they carried the messages found in *Christ in Triumph Coming to Judgment* (1795), *The Cry of the Poor for Bread*

(1796), and *The Poor Man's Catechism* (1798). This was a "communal store of knowledge, accessible to all," even to vagabonds such as Vladimir and Estragon *en attendant Godot:* "You have been told that politics is a subject upon which you should never think: that to the rich and great men of the country you should give up your judgement in the business of government. . . . Who gives this advice? . . . The men who profit by your ignorance and inattention. . . . Why not think of politics? Think of [it] seriously; think of your rulers; think of republics; think of kings."[68]

After the rebellion of 1798, the slaughter was vast: thirty thousand, far in excess of the number dead in Robespierre's Terror. A large number of United Irish, estimated Castlereagh, were transported to Jamaica, where they were drafted into the regiments: "As soon as they got arms into their hands they deserted, and fled into the mountains, where they have been joined by large bodies of the natives and such of the French as were in the island. There have already been some engagements between this part and the King's troops: several have been killed and wounded on both sides."[69] William Cobbett reported in 1798 the belief that in Virginia and the Carolinas, "some of the free negroes have already been admitted into the conspiracy of the United Irishmen."[70] These latter were conscious that one reason for their defeat in Ireland had been their failure to seize the capital, Dublin.[71] Despard, who in Jamaica had studied the relationship between internal insurrection and external attack, applied the same strategic thinking to London at a moment when invasion by revolutionary France loomed large. But London was saturated with armed shopkeepers—the Volunteers—a fact that Despard acknowledged by saying he needed fifteen hundred men to take the city but fifty thousand to hold it. A leader of buccaneers, husband to an African American, friend to Central American Indians, and an officer of the army of the United Irish, Despard put his hand to the helm of a revolutionary vessel manned by an Atlantean crew.

How had Despard met the motley crew? Some contacts he had made during his travels, and others through political organizations such as the United Irishmen and the L.C.S. He was active in street demonstrations—for example, in 1795 he was "among the Mob that was breaking Mr Pitt's Windows" at 10 Downing Street, chanting "No war, No Pitt, Cheap Bread."[72] Others he met in the taverns where the plans for the up-

Portal of the Kilmainham Gaol, c. 1796. Photograph by Peter Linebaugh.

rising were laid. But probably the most important meeting place of insurrectionists was the prison, the hydra's lair in which Despard spent much
of the decade of the 1790s. Between 1792 and 1794, he was immured in
King's Bench Prison for debt. He was detained for sixteen months in
Cold Bath Fields in 1798 after the suspension of habeas corpus. In 1799
he was removed to Shrewsbury Gaol. In 1801, he was incarcerated in the
Tower and then later in the Tothill Fields Bridewell. While he "was confined so long in the Bastille," he met mutinous soldiers and sailors,
Spenceans, artisans, Jacobins, and democrats.[73] Despard was in King's
Bench when Joseph Gerrard collected signatures on a petition supporting universal manhood suffrage.[74] Several mutineers from the Nore were
locked up with Despard in Cold Bath Fields Prison; in fact, seven mutineers had earlier escaped from the cell he occupied. Lord George Gordon
paid for dinners in Newgate attended by "all ranks . . . the jew and gentile, the legislator and the labouring mechanic, the officer and soldier, all
shared alike." Included in these occasions was James Ridgway, who published books and pamphlets on abolitionism, Ireland, and the rights of
women, as well as Bannantine's memoir of Despard in 1799.[75] Of the
boom in building prisons, Burke gloated, "We have rebuilt Newgate and

tenanted the mansion." In contrast, Lord George Gordon, who was compared to Masaniello, wrote, "We have reason to cry aloud from our dungeons and prison-ships, in defense of our lives and liberties, in this advanced period of the world."[76] Despard heard the cries and got to know the criers.

Catherine Despard heard the cries, too. She worked with the wives and friends of the habeas corpus prisoners and fought to improve the conditions that her husband and many others suffered in prison. She organized a defense campaign in Parliament and in the newspapers. In December 1802, prisoners' wives wrote to Home Secretary Pelham, "By the Command of our Husbands we Write to Petition your Lordship that their Grievances may be redressed. They being confin'd in Separate Cells & Nearly dead with Cold & Hunger we pray your Lordship that their Irons being heavy Double & exceeding Grievous may be taken off or Lightened."[77] Conditions were cruel, as revealed by John Herron's suit in 1801 against Thomas Aris, warden of King's Bench Prison: Herron's cell measured six by eight feet; he was not provided with a chamber pot; "the dirt" was removed from his cell only once a week; he was kept on a diet of fourteen ounces of bread and two draughts of water "through the spout of a tin can."[78]

What were the ideas and ideals of the Despards' conspiracy? When Judge Ellenborough summarized the state's case in 1803, he chastised Despard for his "wild scheme of impracticable equality," echoing the Baymen's accusation in 1789 that he held the "wild and Levelling principle of Universal Equality." The suggestion that Despard's ideas were utopian (in the sense that utopia = no place) was, however, false. It would be more accurate to say that they arose from many places; they were polytopian. The conception of freedom emphasized in Despard's gallows speech owed something to those who had the "highest ideas of freedom": the Mosquito Indians of the Nicaraguan coast. His notion of equality owed something to the struggles of the motley crew in the American Revolution. His commitment to justice owed something to the United Irishmen. In another version of his gallows speech, Despard was reported to have said, "Although I shall not live to experience the blessings of the godlike change, be assured, Citizens, that the period will come, and that *speedily,* when the glorious cause of Liberty shall effectually triumph."

He thus compared the revolutionary struggle of the human race with divine agency. Although averse to the Bible as a child, Despard had since studied theology and sought out other seekers of such truth. Upon his return to London, he had met the shoemaker and rabbi David Levi in Finsbury and immediately commenced millenarian biblical discussion with this well-known scholar and advocate of jubilee.[79]

Despard's interest in comparative religion would have offended William Hamilton Reid, who in 1800 wrote *The Rise and Dissolution of the Infidel Societies in this Metropolis,* a work of heresiography comparable to Thomas Edwards's *Gangraena* of 1646. Worried about plebeian clubs of atheists and deists, as well as millenarians and antinomians, Reid sounded the alarm, "This hydra had too many heads to be crushed at once." The ideas of these heterodox thinkers of Reid's nightmares went back to the English Revolution a century and a half earlier: they discredited established church authority; they made the human form divine ("The whole godhead is circumscribed in the person of Jesus Christ," as Muggleton put it); and they did not respect persons, allowing apprentices to preach in the 1790s as in the 1640s. The theological sign of seventeenth-century antinomianism was the "everlasting gospel," which was defined this way: "That by Christ's death, all the sins of all men in the world, Turks, Pagans, as well as Christians committed against the moral Law and the first covenant, are actually pardoned and forgiven, and this is the everlasting gospel."[80] African American refugees preached this "everlasting gospel" in London after 1783. One such was John Jea, a sea-cook and preacher from Old Calabar (1773), who married an Irishwoman and spread the word in New York, Cork, Liverpool, and Manchester. Richard Brothers prophesied in 1794, "All shall be as one people . . . The *Christian,* the *Turk,* and the *Pagan.*" William Blake wrote in his *Songs of Innocence* (1789):

> And all must love the human form
> In heathen, turk, or jew.
> Where Mercy, Love & Pity dwell
> There God is dwelling too.

Blake had participated in the Gordon Riots in 1780, when Newgate was besieged under the leadership of former American slaves, and he knew

Ottobah Cugoano, a London servant originally from the Gold Coast who had slaved in Grenada.

Cugoano was an abolitionist, an experienced preacher and writer, a powerful voice of freedom, and a devout believer in the "everlasting gospel." Written in the copious style of prophetic condemnation, his *Thoughts and Sentiments on the Evil of Slavery* (1787 and 1791) referred to the many shades of the rainbow, rather than to different human races. Cugoano welcomed the "world turned upside down"; he defended American Indians; he opposed the expansion of the death penalty; he insisted that Africans were as "free-born" as English; he repeatedly referred to his "fellow creatures." He believed that avarice, stock-jobbing, and private property tended to slavery. Further, he preached that "church signifies an assembly of people; but a building of wood, brick or stone, where the people meet together, is generally called so; and should the people be frightened away by the many abominable dead carcases which they meet with, they should follow the multitudes to the fields, to the vallies, to the mountains, to the islands, to the rivers, and to the ships."[81] Despard followed the people to exactly these places, and after he planned the "godlike change" he anticipated in his last speech, the people followed him to the gallows atop Horsemonger Lane Gaol. This was their conception of "church," appropriate to their conception of the "human race."

Despard's idea of the human race took much of its power from its opposition to a contrary conception of race that had emerged in the 1790s. The Orange Order had been formed in Ireland as a terrorist church-and-king mob, creating religious bigotry. Dundas had organized massive expeditions to the West Indies between 1795 and 1797 to protect and secure British interests in slavery; he had succeeded in these goals, as "commerce, finance, and seapower . . . were triumphantly secured," but only at the price of one hundred thousand British casualties.[82] The expeditions thus touched, directly or indirectly, a high proportion of the population of England, Wales, Scotland, and Ireland, as for every casualty, grieving relations or friends might pause to wonder what purpose his death had served. John Reeves, head of the Alien Office and of the Association for Preserving Liberty and Property against Republicans and Levellers, used the experience to impart lessons of racism,[83] while Hannah More's "cheap repository tracts" taught condescension, dumbing down, and racial stereotypes:[84]

> TOM: Pooh! I want freedom and happiness the same as they have got it in France.
> JACK: What, Tom, we imitate them? . . . Why, I'd sooner go to the Negers to get learning, or to the Turks to get religion, than to the French for freedom and happiness.

The Association in Saint Anne's Parish (Westminster) kept in 1794 a house-to-house register that noted the "complexion, age, employment, &c. of lodgers and strangers." Elizabeth Hamilton wrote in her novel *Memoirs of a Modern Philosopher* (1800) that radicals believed that new, unthought-of revolutionary energies belonged to the Hottentots.

After each major uprising, the racist doctrine of white supremacy took another step in its insidious evolution. After Tacky's Revolt (1760), Edward Long lavished pages of attention in his *History of Jamaica* (1774) to what Joan Dayan calls "surreal precision in human reduction."[85] After the American Revolution, Samuel Smith helped to reconfigure racism in *An Essay on the Causes of the Variety of Complexion and Figure of the Human Species* (1787). Racial investigations were conducted with scientific pretension, and human beings analyzed by logic-chopping speciation, classification, and racialization. In April 1794, a Manchester physician named Charles White, who had heard John Hunter lecture on the differential mortality rates of the St. Johns expedition, measured various body parts of Africans at the Liverpool lunatic hospital. He then examined the breasts of twenty women at the Manchester lying-in hospital, conjoining lascivious expression with racial superiority.[86] White gave the doctrine of white supremacy "scientific" legitimacy in a lecture of his own in 1795, wherein he concluded that black people belonged to a different gradation of the human race.

From Price's celebrated sermon of 1790 affirming the right to cashier governors, to Edmund Burke's powerful rhetorical riposte in his *Reflections on the Revolution in France* of 1791 (in which he labeled the people a "swinish multitude"), to Tom Paine's equally rhetorical, if plainer, *Rights of Man,* public debate seemed to be largely "an English agitation . . . for an English democracy," as E. P. Thompson emphasized. It seemed to remain so as it was developed further in Mary Wollstonecraft's *The Vindication of the Rights of Women* (1792), Thelwall's *The Rights of Nature* (1796), and Spence's *The Rights of Infants* (1796). Yet there were also other important voices. Wolfe Tone published *An Argument on Behalf of the Catholics of Ireland* in 1791; Olaudah Equiano's *Interesting Narrative* first appeared in 1789 and went through nine English editions over the next five years; and C. F. Volney's *The Ruins; Or, Meditation on the Revolutions of Empires* became available in English and Welsh translations in 1792. What was most vigorous in the debate did not come from any single national experience, English or otherwise. Much came from outsiders, and in this Edward and Catherine Despard were not alone in the cosmopolitan shaping of revolutionary ideals. In 1789 Joseph Brand, the Iroquois leader, provided Edward Fitzgerald, the Irish patriot, with a lesson in the brotherhood of man as they journeyed together through the forests of the Great Lakes; Fitzgerald had served in the West Indies after the Battle of Eutaw Springs (1780), in which his life had been saved by an African American named Tony Small. John Oswald (1760–1793) wrote for the *Universal Patriot.* At Joanna Isle in the Mozambique Passage, an Abyssinian oracle informed him that "Englishman, Joannaman, were all one brother."[87] In 1791, as a result of a spiritual experience that she expressed as "Room, Room, Room, in the many Mansions of eternal glory for Thee and for everyone," Jemima Wilkinson changed her name to "Universal Friend." On Seneca Lake in 1791 at a gathering of the Council of the Iroquois Six Nations, she preached on "Hath Not God Created Us All?" Questions on one side of the Atlantic raised very similar questions on the other. "Which Character is the most truly amiable, the FRIEND—the PATRIOT—or, the CITIZEN OF THE WORLD?" debated the speakers at Coachmakers Hall in 1790.[88] The Despards helped to advance a "universalism" from below.

Other contributors included Lord George Gordon, who discussed slavery as a midshipman in 1772 with the governor of Jamaica. Joseph Gerrard, the Scottish delegate to the convention of 1792 and himself a political prisoner, was born in St. Christopher, the son of an Irish planter. The great barrister Thomas Erskine had danced with Negro slaves and English seamen as a sailor in the West Indies.[89] In Portland, Maine, in 1790, a Bristol sailor was hanged in the first capital punishment carried out by the federal government of the United States of America. He had been found guilty of assisting a mutiny aboard a slave ship off the coast of West Africa. Richard Brothers, the contemporary of Despard and Blake, was twelve years with the navy as a midshipman, off the coast of Africa and in the West Indies, before resigning his commission in "Disgust!" because, as he was to tell the workhouse board that would incarcerate him, "I could not *conscientiously* receive the wages of *Plunder, Bloodshed,* and *Murder!*" He prophesied that London would be destroyed by an earthquake on the king's birthday, June 4, 1795. The king clapped him in an Islington madhouse, where he spent the rest of his life.

Despard was executed in February, Toussaint L'Ouverture died in an Alpine dungeon a few months later, and Robert Emmet "ran his race" in September, asking us to wait before writing his epitaph. These men were peaks of the Atlantic mountains, whose "principles of freedom, of humanity, and of justice" belonged to a single range. When the ideal was corrupted and the insurgents were defeated, the vanquished again fled; the beautiful pamphlet was stowed in someone's sea chest; the fighting hymns got anodyne words; the incendiary gesture appeared only eccentric elsewhere. The revolution moved on. What was left behind was national and partial: the *English* working class, the *black* Haitian, the *Irish* diaspora. Edward and Catherine Despard's conspiracy for the human race thus temporarily failed.

CHAPTER NINE

Robert Wedderburn and Atlantic Jubilee

ROBERT WEDDERBURN was born in Jamaica in 1762, just after Tacky's Revolt, to an enslaved woman named Rosanna and a slavemaster named James Wedderburn, a doctor whose estates in Westmoreland (Mint, Paradise, Retreat, Endeavor, Inverness, Spring Garden, Moreland, and Mount Edgcombe) were worth precisely £302,628 14s. 8d. at his death.[1] His father "insulted, abused and abandoned" his mother, as Wedderburn wrote in his autobiography. "I HAVE SEEN MY POOR MOTHER STRETCHED ON THE GROUND, TIED HANDS AND FEET, AND FLOGGED IN THE MOST INDECENT MANNER THOUGH PREGNANT AT THE SAME TIME!!! her *fault* being the not acquainting her mistress that her master had *given her leave to go to see her mother in town!*"[2] When his father sold his mother in 1766, Robert was sent to Kingston to live under the care of his maternal grandmother, who worked on the waterfront selling cheese, checks, chintz, milk, and gingerbread and smuggling goods for her owner. Wedderburn would later recall, "No woman was perhaps better known in Kingston than my grandmother, by the name of '*Talkee Amy.*'" When Wedderburn was eleven, he watched in horror as the seventy-year-old woman was flogged almost to death. Her master had died after he and one of his ships, smuggling mahogany, had been captured by the Spanish in 1773. Before the voyage, he had liberated five of his slaves, but not Talkee Amy; his nephew (and heir), convinced that she had bewitched the vessel, punished her savagely in revenge.

What Wedderburn witnessed was discipline typical of the era. The factory overlooker carried a stick. The plantation overseer brandished a whip. Schoolmasters and parents wielded the birch against children. The master and boatswain used the cat or the rattan cane on sailors; indeed, to be whipped around the fleet was a pageant of cruelty. Soldiers were flogged by officers, drummers, and sometimes even other soldiers. The triangle (a tripod composed of three halberds upon which the person to be flogged was bound) was notorious as a means of imperialist repression in Ireland. Disciplinary violence was carefully studied: a surgeon in the British army, whose duty it was to keep torture victims alive, published seventy pages on the subject in 1794.[3] In Haiti, meanwhile, a manual on the theory and practice of female flagellation appeared in 1804.[4] Cutting, bruising, penetrating, tying, squeezing, holding, and lacerating were all techniques applied by the powerful in the formation of labor power. When William Cobbett complained about the five hundred lashes administered to soldiers protesting for bread (*"Five hundred lashes* each! Aye, that is right! Flog them, flog them; flog them!" Cobbett cried), he was imprisoned in Newgate.[5]

The terror visited upon his mother and upon Talkee Amy would stay with Wedderburn for the rest of his life.[6] At the age of seventeen (in 1778), Wedderburn joined the Royal Navy during the American Revolution. He took part in the Gordon Riots of 1780, led by the African Americans Benjamin Bowsey and John Glover. Years later, in 1797, he would be connected to the naval mutiny at the Nore.[7] Between these two events, Wedderburn, along with thousands of other workers, joined the Methodist Church.[8] In the early years of the nineteenth century he would meet Thomas Spence and, with other veterans of the London Corresponding Society, enlarge Spence's circle of revolutionists. He also knew the struggles of poor craftsmen: though he had acquired the skills of the tailor, these were dishonored by the prohibition against trade-union activity in the Combination Act (1799), and would be sweated by the repeal of the apprenticeship clauses in the Elizabethan Statue of Artificers (1814). He did time in Cold Bath Fields, Dorchester, and Giltspur Street Prisons for theft, blasphemy, and keeping a bawdy house. He saw many of his comrades hanged, and he himself lived much of his life as "though a halter be about my neck."[9] Wedderburn thus knew the plantation, the ship, the streets, the chapel, the political club, the workshop, and the prison as settings of proletarian self-activity.

Wedderburn has been a neglected figure in historical studies, or at best a misfit. He has not seemed a proper subject for either labor history or black history. In the former field he appears, if at all, as a criminal and

Robert Wedderburn. Robert Wedderburn,
The Horrors of Slavery *(1824).*

pornographic character, and in the latter, as a tricky and foolish one.[10] In contrast to such views, we argue that Wedderburn was in fact a strategically central actor in the formation and dissemination of revolutionary traditions, an intellectual organic to the Atlantic proletariat. We shall explore his major notion for freedom, the biblical jubilee, in the context of a remarkable correspondence he carried on with his half-sister Elizabeth Campbell, a Jamaican maroon. We shall also consider his understanding of history and his analysis of the people and forces that would, in his view, make a transatlantic revolution. We shall see how Wedderburn overcame the dualities of religion and secularism by synthesizing radical Christianity and Painite republicanism, combining both with a proletarian abolitionism. Wedderburn continued the liberation theology that had originated in the English Revolution, then spread west to the plantation and African America, and finally returned to London in the 1780s and 1790s.

JUBILEE

One of Wedderburn's main ideas lay in the biblical tradition of jubilee, which represented an attempt to solve the problems of poverty, slavery, the factory, and the plantation. A plan for liberation, jubilee appeared both in the Old Testament, as a legal practice of land redistribution, and in the New Testament, as part of the fulfillment of a prophecy in Isaiah. The concept comprised six elements. First, jubilee happened every fifty years. Second, it restored land to its original owners. Third, it canceled debt. Fourth, it freed slaves and bond servants. Fifth, it was a year of fallow. Sixth, it was a year of no work.

In writing about jubilee in his correspondence with Elizabeth Campbell, Wedderburn joined a wide-ranging debate. George III was to organize a royalist jubilee for himself, marking the fiftieth anniversary of his reign, that would have nothing to do with debt forgiveness, manumission, or land redistribution. Samuel Taylor Coleridge advocated a deceptive jubilee that transformed active liberation into "figurative language"—rhetoric, allegory, and pedantic and cynical criticism that took the revolutionary tooth out of the scriptural bite. In 1794, as a youthful radical, Coleridge had written in "Religious Musings,"

> . . . the vast family of Love
> Raised from the common earth by common toil
> Enjoy the equal produce. Such delights
> As float to earth, permitted visitants!

When in some hour of solemn jubilee
The massy gates of Paradise are thrown
Wide open . . .

which vision, while hopeful, lacked the specificity of the Mosaic agrarian law. Wedderburn asserted a proletarian version of jubilee that had its modern origins in the written and practical work of Thomas Spence on the one hand, and in the anonymous oral tradition of African American slaves on the other. As James Cone has written, "It matters little to the oppressed who authored scripture; what is important is whether it can serve as a weapon against oppressors."[11] Wedderburn, the Methodists, and the Baptists brought these two traditions together, challenging the aristocratic and literary jubilees. Since Wedderburn's jubilee was a mainstay in the intellectual history of the Atlantic proletariat, leading in one direction to the general strike and Chartist land policy of the 1830s and in another direction to the abolition of slavery in America, we would do well to explore it closely.[12]

The Leviticus was written at the end of the sixth century, after the Babylonian captivity, when rabbis collected, copied, and edited laws, songs, poems, cultic practices, traditions, and oral memories to create the Torah, the first five books of the Old Testament. The twenty-fifth chapter of Leviticus preserved the memory of an earlier, more egalitarian time, when people lived by agriculture (producing grain, oil, and wine) and a pastoral economy (tending bovine herds, sheep, and goats) amid a process of accelerating class differentiation. Jubilee was important to the visionary politics of the prophets, especially Isaiah, Jeremiah, and Ezekiel, who sought to turn people away from idolatry and greed and looked to the past for a more virtuous life. Thus Isaiah denounced landlords:

Shame on you! you who add house to house
and joining field to field until not an acre remains,
and you are left to dwell alone in the land. (5:8)

The meaning of jubilee lay in the experiences and struggles of the oppressed, as explained in Isaiah:

The Spirit of the Lord God is upon me,
because the Lord has anointed me

> *to bring good tidings to the afflicted;*
> *he has sent me to bind up the broken-hearted,*
> *to proclaim liberty to the captives,*
> *and the opening of the prison to those who are bound;*
> *to proclaim the year of the Lord's favor*
> *and a day of the vengeance of our God*
> *to comfort all who mourn. (61:1–2)*

Isaiah thus enlarged jubilee's meaning from the ameliorist management of Leviticus to a day of vengeance on behalf of the afflicted, the bound, the brokenhearted, the captive, and the grieving. Isaiah gave voice to a class that no longer begged for reforms but rather demanded justice. When he returned to Nazareth and began preaching, Jesus opened the scroll in the synagogue to this passage in Isaiah. Then Jesus said, "Today this scripture has been fulfilled in your hearing." Jubilee was therefore not a question of interpretation but a matter of action. From law (Leviticus) to poetics (Isaiah) to fulfillment (Luke), the liberation of jubilee was retained, calling for restitution of land, manumission of the bonded, remission of debt, and cessation of work.

In the modern era, jubilee was employed by the English revolutionaries of the 1640s, including James Nayler and the early Quakers and Gerard Winstanley and the Diggers, as a means of resisting both expropriation and slavery. It remained a living idea after the revolution, to be carried forward by John Milton, John Bunyan, and James Harrington (*Oceana*). Revived in the late eighteenth century, it appeared occasionally in the era of the American Revolution (one Janet Schaw, in the West Indies in 1775 to observe Christmas festivities, reported that slaves called the holiday "an universal Jubilee") and took on broad transatlantic power in the 1780s.[13] In 1769, *Trinculo's Trip to the Jubilee* was presented on the London stage. In 1782 Thomas Spence wrote "The Jubilee Hymn; Or, A Song to be sung at the Commencement of the Millennium, If Not Sooner." It was set to the tune of the national anthem, "God Save the King" (or later, in America, to "America"):

> *HARK! how the trumpet's sound*
> *Proclaims the land around*
> *The Jubilee!*

The sceptre now is broke,
Which with continual stroke
The nations smote!
Hell from beneath doth rise,
To meet thy lofty eyes,
From the most pompous size,
Now brought to nought!

Since then this Jubilee
Sets all at Liberty
Let us be glad.
Behold each man return
To his possession
No more like drones to mourn
By landlords sad!

Spence was born in 1750 in Newcastle. Growing up on the waterfront as one of nineteen children in his family, young Spence joined the congregation of John Glas (1695–1773), a Presbyterian schismatic who followed the tenets of the primitive Christians as he understood them, advocating simple law, no penal code, no accumulation of property, love feasts, Scotch broth, the gift of speech, and plenty of song. Spence's mentor was Dr. James Murray, who supported the American Revolution, opposed enclosure, and asked in his "Sermons To Asses" (1768), "Do people ever act contrary to any divine law, when they resume their rights, and recover their property out of the hands of those who have unnaturally invaded it?" Moreover, "Was the jewish jubilee a levelling scheme?" These questions were particularly relevant in Newcastle, where the bourgeoisie was then seeking to sell or lease eighty-nine acres of the town common, a plan thwarted by commoners, who pulled down the lessee's house and fences and drove his cattle away. Inspired by the victory, Spence in 1775 wrote a lecture that he delivered before the Newcastle Philosophical Society, wherein he proposed the abolition of private property: "The country of any people . . . is properly their common," he explained. Taking the historical view, he continued, "The first landholders [were] usurpers and tyrants," as were their heirs. Everyone else had become a stranger in the land of their birth. He advised appointing a day on which the inhabitants of each parish would meet "to take their long-lost rights into possession." Spence would soon call that day jubilee; the Philosophical Society would denounce him for his "ERRONEOUS and dangerous levelling principles."[14]

Jubilee lay at the heart of what came to be known as Spence's Plan, which was chalked on walls, minted on tokens, published in halfpenny tracts that were hawked in the streets, and sung in taverns. Spence was arrested four times in the 1790s as a seditious author and a "Dangerous Nuisance." Despite the jailings and imprisonments, the insults and death threats from members of the Association for Preserving Liberty and Property against Republicans and Levellers, he persisted. He struck a token to commemorate the death of Lord George Gordon, the insurrectionist of 1780. In *The End of Oppression; Or, a Quartern Loaf for Two-Pence; being a Dialogue between an Old Mechanic and a Young One*, he wrote that revolution could be accomplished by a "few thousand of hearty determined fellows well armed." By 1802 the prime minister of England would be informed that there was scarcely a wall in London that did not have chalked upon it the slogan "Spence's Plan and Full Bellies."

After moving to London in 1792, Spence took an interest in Atlantic affairs, and especially in what sailors, Native Americans, and African Americans might contribute to a worldwide revolutionary movement. He wrote about hydrarchy in *The Marine Republic* (1794), in which a dying man gives a ship to his sons. It is, the man specifies, to be "COMMON PROPERTY. *You all will be* EQUAL OWNERS, *and shall share the profits of every voyage equally among you.* " His injunctions are drawn up as a constitution, like the articles of pirates. When his sons, the marine republicans of the title, grow weary of England's oppressive government, they "set sail for America, where they [expect] to see government administered more agreeably to their notions of equality and equity." After their ship is wrecked on an uninhabited island, they establish the Republic of Spensonia, which "looks backward to the medieval commune and forward to the withering away of the state."[15]

In *The Reign of Felicity* (1796), Spence constructed a dialogue in which one character remarks that American Indians are the "only free-

Thomas Spence. Robert Robinson, Thomas Bewick:
His Life and Times *(1887).*

men remaining on the face of the earth"; another explains that the Indians, unlike European workers, are "unwarped by slavish custom."
Spence, like Christian Gottlieb Priber earlier in the century, believed
that the Native Americans would attract the slaves and disenfranchised
laborers created by European imperialism and help lead them to libera-

tion. He knew of the triracial communities among the Seminoles and in the southeastern United States. In 1814 he would offer a spirited defense, in *The Giant Killer*, of the Cherokee lands; that same year, during a sacred revolt (which owed much to the federation attempts of Tecumseh, on the one hand, and to the inspiration of the African American struggle for emancipation, on the other), the Muskogees would be destroyed at the Battle of Horsehoe Bend. Apocalyptic teachings ("when the moon would be turned into blood"), the presence of numerous métis people, the earthquakes of 1811, the leadership of Paddy Walch and Peter McQueen, and a new dance had all united the Muskogee against the *ecunnaunuxulgee* ("people greedily grasping lands") in a desperate defense against the forces that were to bring the cotton plantation.[16]

Spence also understood the African-American interest in jubilee:

> *For who can tell but the Millennium*
> *May take its rise from my poor Cranium?*
> *And who knows but it God may please*
> *It should come by the West Indies?*

His question brings us back to the West Indian Wedderburn and the African American tradition of jubilee, which began in a subversive reading of the Bible and continued that way for generations. Similar readings had earlier inspired or been manifest in the revolutionary Christianity of the "blackymore maide" named Francis and the conversation between Sarah Wight and Dinah "the moor" about the biblical deliverance from Egyptian slavery; the use, by slaves, of the radical message of itinerant ministers of the Great Awakening to formulate their own, new designs for freedom; and the creativity of slaves and their allies, in the era of the American Revolution, in citing the Bible not only to predict an end to bondage but to justify the use of force in ending it. The resistance of slaves during the 1760s and 1770s moved many to take public positions against "man-stealing" and slavery itself. One of these was the founder of Methodism, John Wesley, who in 1774 published *Thoughts on Slavery*. He concluded (not unlike the revolutionary J. Philmore) that "liberty is the right of every human creature as soon as he breathes the vital air. And no human law can deprive him of that right which he derived from a law of nature." These sentiments would inform the evangelical and missionary work of the Methodists over the next fifty years. Baptists took a similar stand.[17]

That such churchmen were not, however, unqualified abolitionists is shown by a look at Wesley's right-hand man, Thomas Coke, the founder of the Methodist missions in the 1780s, who made eighteen transatlantic voyages during his lifetime. He took pride in the Irish Methodists who betrayed the United Irishmen's attempts to take Dublin in the spring of 1798, and he believed that Methodists played a key role in preventing West Indian slaves from rising on an English island during the 1790s ("If they have Religious Liberty, their Temporal Slavery will be comparatively but a small thing"). He reported to the government on the seditious activities of obscure, humble churches in the north of England in 1800–1.[18] And yet so broad was the discussion of jubilee that he devoted considerable, if equivocal, attention in his *Commentary on the Holy Bible* (1801) to Leviticus 25. Coke's view started with the point that land required rest. Jubilee would demonstrate the "fructifying influences of divine power," it would curb avarice, and it would prevent the ambitious designs of individuals to procure estates in order to oppress others. Coke did not advocate jubilee from below, or approve of an agrarian law, or associate the practice with the English commons or the American lands. He seemed to approve the interpretation of Maimonides, that jubilee led to saturnalia in which "everyone put a crown upon his head."[19]

Methodist and Baptist ministers—some formally educated, others penniless, self-appointed "tub preachers"—began in the 1780s to preach jubilee to largely poor congregations in Britain, the Caribbean, and North America. A growing number of these preachers were African Americans: in addition to Wedderburn, their number included Moses Baker, George Liele, Moses Wilkinson, John Marrant, Thomas Nicholas Swigle, Richard Allen, Absalom Jones, John Jea, and George Gibb. The story of Moses, the flight from Egyptian slavery, and jubilee were all important to these ministers and their followers. The Baltimore Conference of Methodists declared to its mixed-race congregation in 1780 that "slavery is contrary to the laws of God, man, and nature" (though in five years it would suspend this belief in practice, permitting slaveholders to join the congregation). Baptists also preached an end to slavery in general and jubilee in particular. Several ministers spread the message far and wide.

Liele, for example, left Savannah for Kingston, Jamaica, in 1782 and formed that island's first Baptist church two years later. "Preaching took very good effect with the poorer sort, especially the slaves," among whom he worked as a wagoner. Other ministers left North America with the British army and carried their revolutionary heritage to Nova Scotia, British Honduras, London, and Sierra Leone.[20]

Within these Atlantic circuits, jubilee was taught by sermon but also by song, especially during the revivals and camp meetings of the early nineteenth century, in what has been called the Second Great Awakening. Ministers, exhorters, and obeah men taught a call-and-response style of singing. Rhythmic complexity, gapped scales, body movements, and extended repetitions of short melodic phrases characterized the singing, which has also been called the "shout." Musicologists have noted the influence in the shout of African songs, work songs, and Indian dances. The practice of teaching the song and the Scriptures by lining out (wherein someone who could read sang one line, then those who could not read sang the same line, and so on) ensured a close, enthusiastic relationship between leader and chorus. The contrast with stiff, hierarchical upper-class religious ceremony and singing could hardly have been greater.[21]

Slaves and free people of color such as Wedderburn adopted biblical passages such as jubilee from Baptist and Methodist preachers and took them in new, rebellious directions. Gabriel organized a slave revolt in Richmond, Virginia, in the jubilee year 1800. He and his fellow militants were emboldened by the success of the Haitian Revolution, encouraged by the preachings of abolitionist Quakers, Methodists, and Baptists, and assisted by French revolutionaries and perhaps also by United Irishmen. Mingo, a preacher and exhorter, read the stories of Moses and Joshua. Gabriel was especially fond of Judges 15, in which Sampson "smote them hip and thigh with great slaughter," slaying "a thousand men" with "the jawbone of an ass." Gabriel's insurrectionary plan was ruined by a storm, after which thirty-five were hanged, religious congregations were further segregated, and laws were passed forbidding prayer meetings between sundown and sunup.[22]

Closer in age and experience to Wedderburn was Denmark Vesey, born in 1767 in the Caribbean (St. Thomas, Virgin Islands), skilled as a sailor, and converted to Methodism. A cosmopolitan, he had slaved in St. Domingue, studied with the Moravians, and learned several languages. He settled with his master, a sea captain, in Charleston, South Carolina, where during the turbulent decade of the 1790s the Methodist Francis Asbury preached on Isaiah 61 and its promise "to proclaim liberty to captives." Vesey became a leader in the free black community and the Methodist church. He, too, took inspiration from the victory in Haiti, and possibly more direct assistance as well, as one of his fellow conspirators, Monday Gell, may have corresponded with the president of the black republic. In 1809 the Negro steward of the ship *Minerva* smuggled insurrectionary pamphlets into Charleston; Vesey read them aloud, as he did the Bible. In 1820 the planters passed a law against "incendiary publications." Two years later, Vesey himself led thirty people into open insurrection, including Jack Glenn, a painter, who spoke of deliverance from bondage; Monday, an Igbo from the lower Niger; "Gullah Jack," a conjuror; and Peter Royas, a ship's carpenter who believed the group would get help from England. Vesey's organizing thus brought together a coalition of different workers—agrarian, artisan, and nautical—from the different traditions of Africa, England, the West Indies, and America. The revolt, which expressed the power of transatlantic pan-Africanism, frightened the slaveowning ruling class; in response, Charleston's rulers immediately passed the 1822 Negro Seaman Act, which permitted the sheriff to board any incoming vessel and to arrest any black sailor for the duration of the ship's stay in the port of Charleston.[23]

Less than a decade later, sailors would begin smuggling David Walker's *Appeal to the Coloured Citizens of the World, but in particular, and very expressly, to those of The United States of America* (1829) into the ports of the South. Walker invoked the legacies of the American and Haitian Revolutions as he exposed the butcheries, cruelties, and murders of slavery, as he railed against avaricious oppressors and hypocritical Christians, as he refuted the racist arguments of Thomas Jefferson, and as he called, with unassailable logic, for an armed war of liberation. His *Appeal,* which drew strongly on the apocalyptic prophetic tradition of Ezekiel and Isaiah, quickly became the manifesto of pan-African freedom.[24]

William Lloyd Garrison was another singer of jubilee, and another product of the waterfront. His maternal grandparents had sailed as bonded laborers from Liverpool; his father was a drunken sailor and his mother a flinty, New Light Baptist. His brother was a seafaring man, too. Although his mother warned him against the "hydra of politics," he would enter the political arena and transform it forever, bringing to it the antinomian spirit of 1649. Taught by David Walker and Benjamin Lundy (who escorted freedmen to Haiti), Garrison spoke on July 4 in the year of Walker's *Appeal* at the Park Street Church in Boston, proclaiming "liberty to the captives and the opening of the prison to them that are bound." It was a turning point in the abolitionist alliance. Garrison called on Atlantic strengths—the motley crew, the fellow creatures, God as no respecter of persons—and inveighed against capitalists, slavemasters, and tyrants alike. He reprinted Bunyan's *Vanity Fair,* declared that the world was his country, wrote "with the finger of God on the hearts of men," and promised to "bind up the broken-hearted, and set the captive free!"[25]

By the 1830s, African American children were singing hymns such as "Don't You Hear the Gospel Trumpet Sound Jubilee?" Despite the repression and terror that rained down on its efforts to implement jubilee, African American Christianity remained a religion of action, characterized by shouting, dancing, singing, weeping, jerking, and speaking in tongues. The movement to abolish slavery sang its way to freedom. Spence began this jubilee singing, which continued in tavern *and* chapel in Kingston, Charleston, New York, Boston, Providence, and Dublin, in the multitude of joyful hymns following August 1, from the classics of the Wesley brothers, through the marches of the Civil War, to Henry Work's "popular" sheet music of "Kingdom Coming"—

> *Oh, the master run, ha ha!*
> *And the darkies stay, ho ho!*
> *So now must be the Kingdom comin'*
> *And the year of Jubilo*

—finally reaching a kind of conclusion with the postwar Fisk Jubilee Singers.[26] Robert Wedderburn, a Methodist and Spencean, was perfectly situated to understand and advance the Atlantic revolutionary tradition of jubilee.

THE WEDDERBURN-CAMPBELL CORRESPONDENCE

Wedderburn wrote about jubilee to Elizabeth Campbell, his half-sister and a maroon in Jamaica. His main purpose was to discuss with Campbell the freeing of her own slaves as a prelude to an island-wide emancipation. First published in *The Axe Laid to the Root, or a Fatal Blow to Oppressors, Being an Address to The Planters and Negroes of the Island of Jamaica*, a newspaper written and edited by Wedderburn in London in October 1817, the correspondence is a unique source of knowledge about the Atlantic proletariat.[27] The arrival of thousands of slaves and free blacks in the aftermath of the American Revolution and the outbreak of the Haitian Revolution in 1791 had created a new impulse for agitation and organization among Afro-Jamaicans, who by 1792 had begun to form secret societies and engage in correspondence such as the Wedderburn-Campbell letters. By the early nineteenth century, explained Campbell, "the free Mulattoes [were] reading Cobbett's Register, and talking about St. Domingo." Revolution in America and St. Domingue opened the way for other movements, as the motley crew carried its news and experience to Europe and Latin America. The letters between Wedderburn and Campbell crossed divides of continents, empire, class, and race.[28]

The *Axe* might be compared to another radical publication of 1817, Thomas Wooler's *The Black Dwarf*. Did the title refer to the European sage or the Indian savage? Wooler teased, "We are not at liberty to unfold all the secrets of his prison-house." Here was the motley in both its forms, rags and fooling. The black dwarf was a trickster against throne and altar, "secure from his invisibility, and dangerous from his power of division"— Wooler might be describing the hydra—"for like the polypus, he can divide and redivide himself, and each division remains a perfect animal." (Linnaeus had given the name Hydra to a genus of freshwater polyps in 1756.) The *Black Dwarf* was international and multiethnic, featuring reviews of *Oroonoko*, news of the wild abolitionist dances of Barbados, the latest on struggles in South America. The dwarf of the frontispiece had his right hand raised in a fist of victory, and his left firmly on his hip in a further gesture of determination. A barrel-chested Pan clasped the dwarf's arm in comradely alliance and pointed to the symbols of vanquished powers—a royal scepter, a stack of money, a lord chancellor's periwig—while the handcuffs and shackles of slavery lay open in the dust. The paper symbolized a tricontinental coalition of profane figures against the Holy Alliance. The worst fears of the prude and the proper-tied, the royalist and the rich, were realized in the allegory of sexuality, Africa, and monsters. Two other journals, the *Medusa* and the *Gorgon,* likewise invoked invisible and dangerous many-headedness.

Two rebellions—one in the Caribbean, the other in England, both against slavery—provided the background for Wedderburn's correspondence. On Easter, 1816, Bussa's Rebellion engulfed Barbados. Nanny Grigg, a domestic worker on the Simmons plantation, read newspapers and informed the other slaves of developments in Haiti and England. One important piece of news concerned the Imperial Registry Bill of 1815, actually passed by Parliament to prevent the smuggling of slaves into British colonies but transformed by slave rumor into an act of emancipation: "high buckra" (the king), the rumor had it, had sent a "free paper," but the local planters were refusing to obey it. Hundreds rose up, burning almost a quarter of the sugar-cane crop and demanding their freedom. A planter alleged that William Wilberforce and the abolitionist African Institute had "pierced the inmost recesses of our island, inflicted deep and deadly wounds in the minds of the black population, and engendered the Hydra, Rebellion, which had well nigh deluged our fields with blood." Horace Campbell has written that "the widespread nature of the revolt and the organizational skills which went into the planning [were] the result of a new kind of leadership; this was the leadership of the religious preacher, literate in the English language and in the African religious practices, who combined the ideas of deliverance and resistance." Deliverance from slavery was not to be realized in Barbados in 1816, however, as almost a thousand slaves were killed in battle or executed after the rising.[29]

A few months later, the Spa Fields Riots in England were led by Spenceans and waged by canal diggers, porters, coal and ballast heavers, soldiers, sailors, dockworkers, and factory workers. Among the leaders was Thomas Preston, a Spencean who had traveled to the West Indies and considered himself an "unregistered slave." James Watson the younger, another Spencean, argued with a servant wearing the livery of Chancellor Leach just before the riots: "He was like a negro," said Wat-

Frontispiece to the First Volume of the Black Dwarf.

The Black Dwarf, *1819. The Carl H. Pforzheimer Collection of Shelley and His Circle, New York Public Library, Astor, Lenox, and Tilden Foundations.*

son, "that had run away, and had a mark of disrespect; and that very soon the time would come, when his master might lose his estate, and that he might be as good a man as his master." At Spa Fields, Watson asked the ten thousand assembled, "Will Englishmen any longer suffer themselves

Universal Suffrage or the Scum Uppermost—!!!, by George Cruikshank.
Private collection. Photograph by Rodney Todd-White.

to be trod upon, like the poor African slaves in the West Indies, or like
clods or stones?" The riots simultaneously raised the issues of the "abolition and regulation of machinery" and the abolition of slavery.[30] These
were Luddite years, when, on the one hand, steam engines and textile
machinery were introduced to abridge and cheapen labor, and on the

other hand, the workers who were degraded as a result protested by direct, violent action against the mechanical means of their oppression. Like Byron before 1816 and Shelley afterward, Wedderburn opposed mechanization when it was employed to dehumanize work. Lord Byron's maiden speech in the House of Lords (on February 27, 1812, when he was twenty-four) was on a bill providing the death penalty for Luddites: "You call these men a mob," he said, "desperate, dangerous, and ignorant; and seem to think that the only way to quiet the 'bellua multorum capitum' is to lop off a few of its superfluous heads." He reminded the peers that those heads were capable of thought. Moreover, "it is the mob that labour in your fields and serve in your houses,—that man your navy, and recruit your army,—that have enabled you to defy the world, and can also defy you when neglect and calamity have driven them to despair."

Bussa's Rebellion and the Spa Fields Riots helped Wedderburn to see that the circulation of information had become dangerous to West Indian planters—hence his decision to publish the *Axe Laid to the Root,* which apparently reached both of its intended audiences, planters and slaves. A merchant had warned the Jamaican Assembly about such publications, "in which were found doctrines destructive of the tranquillity of this island, containing direct incitement to the imitation of the conduct of the slaves of St. Domingo, and loading the proprietors of slaves with every odious epithet." In his first letter to Campbell, Wedderburn responded to the news that she had manumitted his aged mother and his brother with an enthusiastic denunciation of slavery, an exhortation to his half-sister to free her remaining slaves, a recollection of history—of the Hebrew flight from Egyptian slavery, of the early Christians, of the freedom-loving maroons—and an endorsement of the more recent ideas of Thomas Spence. In reply, Campbell described her freeing of her slaves, their restitution to the land, and her efforts to record these transactions with the governor's secretary, who had referred the matter to the governor himself, who had in turn dismissed her with mutterings about Haiti. In the third letter, Campbell explained that the governor had taken the news of her emancipation to the Jamaican Assembly, where one Macpherson had risen to speak against the doctrines of Thomas Spence and to recommend revolt against the authority of the Crown unless the licenses of Dissenting missionaries were revoked. He moved that Campbell be treated as a lunatic and that the government confiscate her slaves and lands. He also suggested that Jamaican planters import "starving Scotchmen to manage the slaves" and servants "dying for want" in England to be used "against the Blacks." The assembly then nullified Campbell's manumission, since "slaves and lands set free by an Spencean enthusiast should not be entered on the records"—but neither should the record of the assembly itself be published, for fear that "it should fall into the hands of the slaves." Worry that the *Axe Laid to the Root* had already reached the wrong hands impelled the rulers of the island to offer rewards for copies turned in: for slaves, freedom; for freemen, a slave from the estate of Elizabeth Campbell. The Wedderburn-Campbell correspondence ended with the words "To be continued," as the *Axe Laid to the Root* ceased publication.[31]

Wedderburn prophesied that "the slaves shall be free, for a multiplied combination of ideas," which the *Axe Laid to the Root* was meant to embody. Although lacking the urbane tone of Wooler's *Black Dwarf* or the confident command of Cobbett's *Political Register,* Wedderburn's newspaper nonetheless gave life to a transatlantic intellectual dialogue that synthesized African, American, and European voices. "The axe laid to the root" had special meaning for the hewers of wood and drawers of water. The words came from the books of Luke and Matthew, where they were part of the curse that John the Baptist invoked against class arrogance. They were also part of his annunciation of the Messiah and of the coming baptism by fire. The phrase was readily appropriated in the English Revolution; for example, Abiezer Coppe, having commanded the great ones to deliver their riches to the poor, answered his critics by laying "the Axe to the root of the Tree."[32] The revolutionary meanings of John the Baptist and "the axe laid to the root" were revived in the 1790s on both sides of the Atlantic, among both evangelicals and secular radicals. In Jamaica, the American preacher Moses Baker taught African slaves the Baptist version of Christianity, emphasizing John the Baptist and the inspiration of the Holy Spirit, which proved congenial to Akan and Yoruba practices of riverine spirits and their mediumship. The resulting religion, called myalism, became a "hotbed of slave rebellion" and a means of transmitting the memory of resistance.[33] In New York, George White, who had run away from slavery, heard a sermon on John the Baptist and "the axe is laid to the root." He fell prostrate on the floor, had night visions of the torments that would befall the rich, and converted to Methodism. Thomas Paine wrote *The Age of Reason* in prison in 1794 in order to "lay the axe to the root of religion." Thomas Spence repeated the phrase in *The Restorer of Society* in 1801 and at the beginning of his last publication, *The Giant Killer, Or, Anti-Landlord* (1814). Also in the former year, the American Baptist minister John Leland expressed his opposition to slavery in *A Blow to the Root*.[34] And Shelley explained in *Queen Mab*,

> *From kings, and priests, and statesmen, war arose,*
> *Whose safety is man's deep unbettered woe,*
> *Whose grandeur his debasement. Let the axe*
> *Strike at the root, the poison tree will fall;*
> *And where its venomed exhalations spread*
> *Ruin, and death, and woe, where millions lay*
> *Quenching the serpent's famine, and their bones*
> *Bleaching unburied in the putrid blast,*
> *A garden shall arise, in loveliness*
> *Surpassing fabled Eden.*

The American-born former slave George Liele had in the 1790s introduced into Jamaica the class-leader system, in which the black ministers washed the feet of their disciples.[35] "Slaves who could read the Bible . . . had thrust into their hands the sanction and inspiration of English protest movements from Wycliffe to the Levellers, and some found lessons there the missionaries did not teach," wrote historian Mary Turner. Methodists and Baptists taught scriptures aloud, by means of hymn singing and lining out. Wedderburn wrote and published hymns of his own in his early pamphlet *Truth Self-Supported* (1802); John Jea wrote a book of hymns in 1817. Methodist hymnody in particular was rich with references to jubilee. Moses Baker, the Baptist, was arrested on a charge of sedition in 1796 for including in his sermon the hymn

> *We will be slaves no more,*
> *Since Christ has made us free,*
> *Has nailed our tyrants to the cross,*
> *And bought our liberty.*

One black Baptist in Jamaica was hanged and another transported for fomenting rebellion in 1816. A Jamaican king of the Igbos was elected and celebrated in song:

> *O me good friend, Mr. Wilberforce, make we free!*
> *God Almighty thank ye! God Almighty thank ye!*
> *God Almighty make we free!*
> *Buckra in this country no make we free:*
> *What Negroe for to do? What Negroe for to do?*
> *Take force by force! Take force by force!*

The singer of the song explained that "he had sung no songs but such as his brown priest had assured him were approved of by John the Baptist . . . [who] was a friend to the negroes, and had got his head in a pan." The Spenceans in England had a similar penchant for subversive singing, matching revolutionary lyrics with popular tunes such as "Sally in the Alley" or, inevitably, "God Save the King."[36]

In his letters to Campbell, Wedderburn presented a radical account of early Christianity. In this he was much influenced by his fellow Spencean Thomas Evans, who himself had witnessed "the effect of enclosure after enclosure, and tax after tax; expelling the cottager from gleaning the open fields, from his right to the common, from his cottage, his hovel, once his own; robbing him of his little store, his pig, his fowls, his fuel; thereby reducing him to a pauper, a slave." In *Christian Policy, the Salvation of the Empire* (1816), Evans maintained that the answer to expropriation and slavery lay in the communism of the early Christians; a new era must now be "HAILED AS A JUBILEE." Wedderburn wrote, "The Christians of old, attempted this happy mode of living in fellowship or brotherhood, but, after the death of Christ and the apostles, the national priests persuaded their emperor to establish the Christian religion, and they . . . took possession of the Church property. . . . They have taken care to hedge it about with laws which punish with death all those who dare attempt to take it away." For her part, Campbell signified the broadbased approval of the ideas of Evans by saying that she knew that he and his son had been imprisoned and that the freed slaves "are singing all day at work about Thomas Spence, and the two Evans' in Horsemonger Lane prison, and about you too, brother, and every time they say their prayers, they mention the Evans', they say that God Almighty will send the angels in his time, and let them out, in answer to our prayers."[37]

The last of the letters between Wedderburn and Campbell contained a discussion about the Methodists. Campbell had argued with the governor's secretary, who accused her of having listened to the Methodists. Behind his worries lay secret nightly meetings held on estates in eastern Jamaica in 1815 by brown Methodists, who taught that the regent and Wilberforce wanted the slaves to be free. Some years earlier between (1807 and 1814), authorities had closed the Wesleyan Chapel in Kingston. The British and Foreign Bible Society had been formed in 1804, and its Jamaican branch in 1812, but just a month before the first issue of the *Axe Laid to the Root*, a Baptist missionary had spoken out in favor of the slaves and been dismissed from his position. It thus took courage for Campbell to reply to the secretary, "I say, God bless the Methodists, they teach us to read the bible." They helped to make jubilee possible.[38]

The Bible was one source of the "multiplied combination of ideas" that would lead to freedom; others were the maroons in Jamaica and the Spenceans in England. The Jamaican maroons were important to Wedderburn personally, as his extended family, but even more so historically, as a force for freedom. He began his first letter to Campbell by appealing to her ancestors: "You have fallen from the purity of the Maroons, your original, who fought for twenty years against the Christians, who wanted to reduce them again to slavery, after they had fled into the woods from the Spaniards." Here Wedderburn was referring to the first Maroon War, which he conceived as an equivalent to the movement for freedom promoted by the Diggers and Levellers, whose defeat in the English Revolution had made the Cromwellian conquest of Jamaica possible and the struggle of the maroons necessary. Cromwell and his supporters had asserted a limited "rights of man at home," Wedderburn told his half-sister, but had busied themselves "destroying your ancestors then fighting for their liberty."[39]

The recounting of this history served as a practical introduction to the acts of manumission—the jubilee—that Campbell was to perform:

Then call your slaves together, let them form the half circle of a new moon, tell them to sit and listen to the voice of truth, say unto them, you who were slaves to the cruel Spaniards stolen from your country, and brought here, by Cromwell, the great, who humbled kings at his feet, and brought one to the scaffold, sent a fleet out, whose admiral dared not return without performing something to please his master, came here and drove the Spaniards out; the slaves, my people, then fled to the woods for refuge, the invaders called to them to return to bondage, they refused; they contended for twenty years, and upwards; bondage was more terrific than death.

The history of the maroons was a necessary prelude to freedom, which had been won and renewed in three wars, in the 1650s, the 1730s, and the 1790s.[40]

"I, who am a weak woman, of the Maroon tribe, understood the Spencean doctrine directly: I heard of it, and obey, and the slaves felt the force directly," wrote Campbell. It is not clear why she referred to herself as a "weak woman." She may have been ill, or perhaps she was being ironic, malingering, signifying. It may have been a pose that she had to assume with the governor, who condescendingly answered her by saying, "Well, child, I will hear you on this head at a more convenient time." Campbell and the governor both knew, however, that the women workers of Jamaica never submitted without a fight. Indeed, within very recent memory was a strike in (1816) in which the women of one plantation had, "one and all, refused to carry away the *trash*"—that is, the crushed sugar cane whose removal was essential to the operation of the "factory in the field." The mill stopped, the driver drove, and "a little fierce young devil of a Miss Whaunica flew at his throat and endeavoured to strangle him: the agent was obliged to be called in, and, at length, this petticoat rebellion was subdued."[41]

How could a woman of the maroon tribe "underst[and] the Spencean doctrine directly"? The answer lay in the provisioning, or agricultural production for immediate use, that was common to both the maroons and the Spenceans. The maroons practiced a subsistence agriculture that was much admired by the agrarian communists in England: "Fruit and vegetables were to be found in every band, for the first thing every Maroon group did, as a prerequisite of survival, was to plant provision ground" with plantains, cocoa, bananas, pineapples, sweet corn, and cassava. Both maroons and Spenceans advocated strict, collectively set limits on individual accumulation. Cattle grazed in communal pastures, and the allotted lands were held in common. Wedderburn thus emphasized a commonality of interest between the workers of Jamaica and those of England, one that had begun a century and a half earlier in a common history.[42]

How would a woman such as Campbell have learned about the Spencean doctrine in the first place? And how, in turn, could the Spencean in England have learned the history of the maroons? The governor of Jamaica knew that the Spencean doctrine circulated via the printed word, by pamphlet and by newspaper. Robert Southey wrote about Spence's Plan in the *Quarterly Review* of October 1816; the *Courier* and the *Political Register* also published the plan, with the former source's claiming that the Spenceans had some three hundred thousand people ready to revolt. Campbell had read, with some surprise, newspaper accounts opposed to the Spenceans; she asked Wedderburn for the opinion of the Parliamentary reformer Sir Francis Burdett.[43] Throughout this period, the most important and most subversive news networks were maritime. When the governor's secretary tried to dissuade Campbell from freeing her slaves, she explained that word of her intentions had already got around: "I told them [her slaves] not to speak of it, but they talked of it the more. The news is gone to Old Arbore and St. Anns, to the Blue Mountains, to North Side, and the plantain boats have carried the news to Port Morant, and Morant Bay." Thomas Thistlewood described such coastal communication in greater detail: "The way to go was by water, along the trenches, canals and rivers, and along the coastline, from one estate's barcadier or jetty to another, in all manner of small craft, manned by slaves who heard and carried news."[44]

In fact, the strategic link in Wedderburn and Campbell's own correspondence was a sailor. Campbell explained the protocol: "I send this letter by a black cook: I dare not trust it to the Post, for they open people's letters." By the end of the Napoleonic Wars, roughly a quarter of the Royal Navy was black, and the proportion was probably only a little smaller in both the English and American merchant shipping industries.[45] John Jea, born in Calabar before being enslaved to a New Yorker, was himself working as a ship's cook aboard the *Iscet* of Liverpool when it was captured by the French in 1810. The black cook was so common as to become a stereotype in nautical fiction, reaching its apogee in Frederick Marryat's *Mr. Midshipman Easy* (1836). This figure, who was as important to pan-African communication in the age of sail as the sleeping-car porter would be in the age of rail, carried the news of jubilee.[46]

In his first letter to Elizabeth Campbell, Wedderburn assured her that a jubilee would come to Jamaica, and he assumed that she would know exactly what he meant: "The slaves begin to talk that if their masters were Christians they would not hold them in slavery any longer than seven years, for that is the extent of the law of Moses." Some of the Mosaic law of jubilee was already part of transatlantic labor policy.[47] Many servants who emigrated to America indentured themselves for a period of seven years, for example, and manumitted people of color were issued certificates of freedom that were valid for seven years.

Wedderburn quoted Isaiah in condemning those who were "adding house to house, and field to field, that is turning little farms into great ones, swallowing up widows' children and their heritage." Campbell freed her slaves as required by jubilee, then took the next step toward liberation by redistributing her land: it was reported that "Miss Campbell then cried, the land is yours . . . for I have read the word of God, and it says, the Lord gave the earth to the children of men." She added, "I am now instructed by a child of nature, to resign to you your natural right in the soil on which you stand, agreeable to Spence's plan." She stressed that her deed was not unique, merely neighborly: "I will manage it myself, as your steward, my brother will assist us, we shall live happy, like the family of the Shariers in the parish of St. Mary's, who have all things common." Perhaps she was referring here to a family name (according to the *Almanac for Jamaica* for 1818, three plantations were owned by the Shreyers), or perhaps she was thinking simply of unnamed "sharers." In either case, there was at least one other jubilee practiced on Jamaica in 1817, when "Monk" Lewis implemented a jubilee from above on his sugar estates in Westmoreland to prevent inequitable accumulation of property among his slaves: "I made it public, that from henceforth no negro should possess more than one house with a sufficient portion of ground for his family, and on the following Sunday the overseer by my order looked over the village, took from those who had too much to give to those who had too little, and made an entire new distribution according to the most strict Agrarian law."[48]

The period from 1790 to 1820 was one of social engineering and reorganization of villages and provision grounds by Jamaica's big planters. The actions taken by Lewis and by Elizabeth Campbell were consistent with themes of Jamaican agrarian history in this era, as shown by Barry Higman in his study of maps and plans of estates, which were largely regular and linear until 1810 and more irregular thereafter because of struggles over space between slaves and planters. Spence and Wedderburn anticipated the postemancipation transformation of agriculture to smallholding settlements in free villages, either founded by missionaries within the north coast estate zone or formed by squatters on abandoned estates or underutilized back lands. Some of these free villages even predated emancipation, establishing customary practices that lasted into the twentieth century as "family land." Claud McKay's novel *Banana Bottom* is about jubilee in just such a village.[49]

HISTORY AND REVOLUTION

Having explored the Wedderburn-Campbell correspondence and the history of jubilee that lay at the heart of it, let us now pose some questions about Wedderburn as a theorist of the Atlantic proletariat. First, what was his understanding of history? Second, how did he conceive of the revolutionary tradition? Third, what constituents did he see as composing the social and political force that would make the revolution? And finally, how did he combine Christianity, republicanism, and abolitionism? Wedderburn understood, perhaps as well as anyone of his day, that the fates of workers on the two sides of the Atlantic were linked. He would be a lifelong teacher of this truth, through his actions, his sermons, and his writings, including *The Axe Laid to the Root*. He was part of the postwar radical milieu and was thus familiar with both Shelley's *Queen Mab* and Volney's *Ruins*.

Wedderburn saw history as an international process of expropriation and resistance. The rich of all countries used their economic and political power first to steal the land and then to crush the people who had once occupied it, using terror to set them to work in circumstances of slavery. Wedderburn wrote that "the great majority in every nation are dispossessed of their right to the soil throughout the world." The resulting resistance he called "universal war." In 1819, at Wedderburn's Hopkins Street Chapel, the question for discussion was, "Which of the two parties are likely to be victorious, the rich or the poor in the event of Universal War[?]" Wedderburn opened with the proposition that "there were but two classes of people in England." He then extended to the assembled an invitation to historical analysis: "How did this happen?" How, we may ask, would Wedderburn have answered his own question?[50]

In his first address to the slaves of Jamaica, Wedderburn explained the centrality of the struggle over the land:

> Above all, mind and keep possession of the land you now possess as slaves; for without that, freedom is not worth possessing; for if you once give up the possession of your lands, your oppressors will have power to starve you to death, through making laws for their own accommodation; which will force you to commit crimes in order to obtain subsistence; as the landholders in Europe are serving those that are dispossessed of lands; for it is a fact, that thousands of families are now in a starving state; the prisons are full: humanity impells the executive power to withdraw the sentence of death on criminals, whilst the landholders, in fact, are surrounded with every necessary of life. Take warnings by the sufferings of the European poor, and never give up your lands you now possess, for it is your right by God and nature, for the "earth was given to the children of men."

The starting point for Wedderburn was the idea that the Earth belonged to God, who gave it to "the children of men," allowing "no difference for colour or character, just or unjust." Then came the violence and terror, as the encloser and engrosser turned the land into private property and created slavery: "He that first thrust his brother from his right [to the soil] was a tyrant, a robber, and a murderer; a tyrant because he invades the rights of his brother, a robber, because he seized upon that which was not his own, a murderer, because he deprives his brother of the means of subsistence. The weak must then solicit to become the villain's slave." The system of terror was perpetuated as landowners, who possessed no "title deed . . . consistent with natural and universal justice," nonetheless sold or willed "that which was first obtained by force or fraud" to their children. Wedderburn's message to his brothers and sisters in Jamaica was based on his own generation's experience of massive theft in England, where between 1801 and 1831 alone, 3,511,770 acres of common land were legislated from the agricultural population, an instance of class robbery by the Parliament of landlords. Arthur Young likened the process to a man's stealing another's handkerchief and then employing him to embroider the new owner's initials on it.[51] Conditions of rural life were so terrible in 1816 that the government attempted to suppress the annual report entitled *The Agricultural State of the Kingdom*. Many were actually hanged for protesting the enclosures and the high price of bread. (At the sentencing of twenty-four of them at a special assizes in Ely Cathedral, Handel's *Air* was played, with its lyric "Why do the Heathen so furiously rage together?")

Wedderburn considered it wrong that "a few should have the power to till or not to till the earth, thereby holding the existence of the whole population in their hands. They can cause a famine, or create abundance." The travesty was perhaps clearest among the Irish: "How can anyone account for the gigantic strides that death has taken through Ireland, a country that was able to supply your navy and army, all your colonies? And now the inhabitants are dying for want?" He exclaimed, "Oh! ye poor of Ireland, your death, through starvation, will be a perpetual, yea, and eternal monument of disgrace to the landholders, it will be an immortal book, wherein will be read the wicked system of private property in land." In answer to the new science of demography, which tried to disguise such murder, Wedderburn wrote, "Malthus has said, to please the rich, that the superabundant population is doomed to perish by the laws of nature, which are the laws of God. The Spenceans say the Deity gave the earth to the children of men, he is no respecter of persons"![52]

Wedderburn emphasized that tyrants, robbers, and murderers operated not only in England and Ireland but also in Africa and America, seizing not only land but also labor. African slaves, he insisted, were "Stolen Men," "stolen persons," "stolen families," people who were then "sold, like cattle, in the market." He quoted Exodus 21:16: "He that stealeth a man and selleth or if he be found in his hand, he shall surely be put to death." He condemned "all potentates, governors, and governments of every description with felony, who does wickedly violate the sacred rights of man—by force of arms, or otherwise, seizing the persons of men and dragging them from their native country, and selling their stolen persons and generations." A spy reported that Wedderburn denounced the slave traders, who "would employ blacks to go and steal females—they would put them in sacks and would be murdered if they made an alarm. Vessels would be in readiness and they would fly off with them." This, he explained, "was done by Parliament men—who done it for gain," just as they made slaves in their cotton factories, which was how they had got the "money to bring them into Parliament" in the first place.[53]

Wedderburn wanted the slaves of Jamaica to know that as the rich swept the people off the land, they made laws to protect themselves and to criminalize the dispossessed, whose efforts to subsist would now earn them the lash, the prison, or the gallows. English prisons were full of the expropriated and the criminalized. In the *Axe Laid to the Root*, he warned the slaves who would be emancipated to "have no prisons" as they organized a better society, as "they are only schools for vice, and depots for the victims of tyranny." He went on to compare the prison to the slave experience, warning the planters, "I will inform you for your present safety, and for the future good of your offspring, to let the slaves go free immediately, for in their prison house a voice is heard, loose him and let him go." As for the prisons that already existed in England, Wedderburn favored opening them. He would have agreed with the sentiment addressed by a member of the "Tri-Coloured Committee" to "Our Fellow Countrymen suffering Incarceration" in 1816, as reported by a government spy: "The prison doors will be opened [and] your lofty Bastiles be reduced to Ashes."[54]

Wedderburn also stressed the role that hanging played in the crushing of proletarian movements and the establishment of class discipline. He remembered three militants on whom the hangman's noose had tightened: Edward Marcus Despard; the Irish sailor Cashman, executed for his part in the Spa Fields riots; and John Bellingham, the assassin of Spencer Perceval, the prime minister.[55] He learned from Elizabeth

Campbell the latest news about hangings in Jamaica: "There is a law made by the assembly to hang a slave. One has been hung for preaching, teaching, or exhorting, another has been hung for throwing up his hoe and blessing the name of King George, through mistaking the abolition of the slave trade for the abolition of slavery." Wedderburn expressed his own fears at the end of his autobiography: "I should have gone back to Jamaica, had I not been fearful of the planters; for such is their hatred of any one having black blood in his veins, and who dares to think and act as a free man, that they would most certainly have trumped up some charge against me, and hung me."[56] Despite the claim that the planters "can do little, for the leaven is laid too long in the dough, and as the slaves are their bread, they must not hang them all," British policy remained murderous, on a large scale if necessary, as a private and confidential message from Downing Street to a previous governor, Sir George Nugent (1801–6), had made clear in 1804: "The influence of a Free Black Government in Saint Domingo may be always dangerous, the extinction therefore of that class of slaves in whose fidelity there is no reason to rely, and the propagation of those alone who by the habits of infancy childhood and education are susceptible of the attachment, appear to be the securest system."[57]

A new stage in the historical process was suggested by Wedderburn's pamphlet *Cast-Iron Parsons, or Hints to the Public and the Legislature, on Political Economy* (1820). During a visit to Saint Paul's Church, Shadwell, on the London waterfront, he had asked the parson whether the church was built of brick or stone. "Of neither," came the reply, "but of CAST-IRON." An old apple woman who overheard the conversation added, "*Would to God the Parsons were of Cast-Iron too.*" Wedderburn considered this to be an excellent idea: "Finding that the routine of duty required of the Clergy of the *legitimate* Church, was so completely mechanical, and that nothing was so much in vogue as the dispensing with human labour by the means of machinery, it struck me that it might one day be possible to substitute A CAST-IRON PARSON." It could be oiled and kept fresh in a closet, to be rolled out on Sundays. In fact, the idea had broader application, as it might also be possible to make a clockwork schoolmaster to teach the sciences. This invention Wedderburn called a "TECHNI-CATHOLICAUTOMATOPPANTOPPIDON." As a postscript, he suggested making a cast-iron king and cast-iron members of Parliament, and was promptly jailed for his blasphemy. He understood machinery, politicians, and the source of all wealth: "Slaves and unfortunate men have cultivated the earth, adorned it with buildings, and filled it with all kinds of riches. And the wealth that enabled you to set these people to work, was got by hook or crook from society.—Pray, was ever a solitary savage found to be rich? No; all riches come from society, I mean the labouring part of it."[58]

If Wedderburn viewed the capitalist side of history as expropriation, he saw the proletarian side as resistance. He had had the history of resistance burned into his consciousness at an early age, and it was this history that he most wanted to impart to workers in England and the Americas. This autodidact who called himself a "poor disinherited earth-worm" reached back to antiquity and brought history forward to his own day: jubilee was central to it, as were radical Christianity, peasant rebellion, slave revolt, mob action, urban insurrection, military mutiny, and strike. Within Wedderburn's own lifetime, these were the sources of proletarian power and the elements of revolution, the means by which he and others would "convert the world from a charnel-house to a paradise."[59]

Wedderburn and Campbell belonged to a tradition in which the memory of struggle was maintained through oral tradition, passed along by mnemonic devices governed by strict canons of secrecy. One of the values of the *Axe Laid to the Root* lay in Wedderburn's willingness to bring this knowledge into print in order to expand the understanding of workers in both Jamaica and England. He worked to establish common origins, connections, and parallels between the struggles in these two parts of the world, starting with the primitive Christians. The beginning, like the end, of Wedderburn's history was thus communist, a pattern set by the "Christians of old" who had "attempted this happy mode of living in fellowship or brotherhood." An interim heir to this tradition had been Wat Tyler, the leader of the Peasant's Revolt in England in 1381, who had opened the prisons and negotiated with the king to abolish serfdom before being assassinated by the magistrates of London. The resistance and the treachery were both important for the maroons and other rebels in Jamaica to remember.[60]

The English Revolution also occupied a central place in Wedderburn's thought. In the year of Despard's conspiracy (1802), Wedderburn elected to place on the title page of his *Truth Self-Supported* lines from 1 Corinthians 1:27: "God hath chosen the foolish things of the world, to confound the wise; and God hath chosen the weak things of the world, to confound the things that are mighty." Wedderburn also made a place in his pantheon for the "primitive Quakers."[61] Of sugar production in the West Indies he wrote in seventeenth-century diction:

> *The drops of blood, the horrible manure*
> *That fills with luscious juice the teeming can*
> *And must our fellow-creature thus endure,*
> *For traffic vile, th' indignity of pain?*

He understood that the imperialism and slavery visited upon Jamaica by Cromwell after 1655 had been made possible by the defeat of the radicals, whose battle had then been carried on, overseas, by the maroon ancestors of Elizabeth Campbell. The colonization of Jamaica was closely linked to England's greedy rush into the slave trade.

Although Wedderburn never directly mentioned Tacky's Revolt in his writings, he was undoubtedly influenced by it. Living his early life in Westmoreland and Hanover Parishes, where much of the fighting had taken place, he would have heard surviving veterans tell the tale. Wedderburn carried on one of the ideas that came out of the revolt, the argument first expressed in print by J. Philmore, that slaves had the right to deliver themselves to freedom by rising up and slaying the tyrants. One of Wedderburn's handbills of 1819 asked, "Can it be Murder to KILL A TYRANT?" to be followed by discussion of the allied question "Has a Slave an inherent right to slay his Master, who refuses him HIS LIBERTY?" One of the spies who attended the meeting reported that at the end of the debate, "Nearly the whole of the persons in the room held up their hands in favour of the Question." Wedderburn "then exclaimed well Gentlemen I can *now write home and tell the Slaves to murder their Masters as soon as they please.*" Another spy was sure that the meeting had a double meaning: those assembled "avow their object to be nothing short of the assassination of their Rulers & the overthrow of the Government of England."

The Haitian Revolution, the first successful workers' revolt in modern history, made a deep impression on Wedderburn. Even though he warned his brothers and sisters in Jamaica against the kind of bloodletting that had transpired in Haiti, he knew that rage was an inevitable response to terror and exploitation, and he was not unwilling to use it in a war of nerves against Jamaica's rulers, advising them, "Prepare for flight, ye planters, for the fate of St. Domingo awaits you." Wedderburn also took note of the defeat in 1798 of the United Irishmen, but he scorned their military tactics at the Battle of Vinegar Hill: maroons and rebels in Jamaica, he explained, "will not stand to engage organised troops, like the silly Irish rebels." Jamaican rebels did not depend on technology (they used "billhooks" as weapons), nor on the transport of troops by turnpike, nor on the logistics of food supply.

The rising of hundreds of slaves in Bussa's Rebellion to deliver themselves from bondage in Barbados was surely part of the Wedderburn's report on the "Insurrections of the Slaves in some of the West India Islands" at a meeting in 1819. Speakers at the rally made the connection between slavery in the Caribbean and bondage in England, proposing the abolition of both. After this event and the Peterloo Massacre of 1819, Wedderburn called for the arming of the English proletariat. Some were ready, like the Halifax weavers who in 1819 carried a banner that read, "We groan, being burdened, waiting to be delivered, but we rejoice in hopes of a Jubilee." One outcome of the proposal for armed struggle was the Cato Street Conspiracy, in which the idea was to attack the cabinet at dinner and kill particular tyrants: the lord chancellor, the lord of the treasury, the secretary of war, Castlereagh at the Home Department, the chancellor of the exchequer, the master of the mint, the president of the India Board, and the Duke of Wellington. This action would then spark other attacks in London, at the Mansion House and the Bank of England, and insurrections in the north. Wedderburn might have taken part if he had not been in prison, convicted of blasphemy. In any case, the events of 1816 made Wedderburn see that slave revolt and urban insurrection could produce a great jubilee, the apotheosis of resistance, which would be inaugurated by a work stoppage that would "strike terror to your oppressors." By 1820, jubilee had become international and pan-ethnic: it was part of the self-activity of the proletariat, associated with insurrectionary prophecy and deeds. It became the basis of the general strike, as articulated by William Benbow.[62]

Wedderburn's conception of the proletariat arose from the experiences of a life spent in the port cities of Kingston and London. James Kelley would write in 1838 that in Wedderburn's native Jamaica, "sailors and Negroes are ever on the most amicable terms." Slaves, he noted, had "a feeling of independence in their intercourse with the sailor. . . . In the presence of the sailor, the Negro feels as a man." In the island's demography, "coloured births were most common amongst slaves employed on wharves." R. R. Madden recorded these unions with understanding. In the sailoring districts of East London, "every *cove* that put in his appearance was quite welcome: colour or country considered no obstacle. . . . All was *happiness*—every body free and easy, and freedom of expression allowed to the very echo. The group motley indeed;—Lascars, blacks, jack tars, coal-heavers, dustmen, women of colour, old and young, and a sprinkling of the remnants of once fine girls, &c., were all *jigging* together."[63] Everyone knew Tom Molyneux, the black American sailor and heavyweight boxing champion. *Othello* was performed by African American sailors in Dartmoor Prison in 1814.[64] London, certainly, and other parts of England, Scotland, and Ireland as well, were already motley, or free and easy, by 1820. The authorities watched the combinations carefully, but they could not control them. In the Americas, New Orleans at Congo Square (1817) and New York at Catherine Market (1821) were two spots among many where all jigged together.[65]

Sailors were, to Wedderburn, a leading revolutionary force; indeed, he was familiar with Masaniello's Revolt of 1647. Many of his comrades had dockside or seafaring experience. The Irish Cashman had worked as a fisherman and a sailor and been nine times wounded; the account of his wages at the conclusion of the wars was described by a friend to the *Black Dwarf* (March 19, 1817), as follows:

Four *years' pay*, at the rate of one pound per month, was due to him from the owner of a transport, in which he served; that *seven months' pay*, at the rate of three pounds ten shillings per month, was due him from a ship in which he afterwards served; from another ship, *five months' pay*, at five pounds ten shillings per month; that he afterwards served on board the Sea-horse and Maidstone frigates; that he was entitled to prize money from the Sea-horse, but lost all his papers in a schooner, in which he was taken in an action off the coast of America, and carried to Philadelphia; on which occasion he was wounded, and under the surgeon's hands for a long time.

His father was killed at sea, and his mother had to beg for bread, as the pound a month that he requested be sent her from his wages never was. His hanging in March 1817 for participation in the Spa Fields Riots, when a gunsmith shop was looted, occasioned cries of "murder" and "shame."

William "Black" Davidson, born in Kingston, Jamaica, in 1786, had also been a sailor, as well as a cabinetmaker, a secretary to the shoemakers' trade union, and a teacher in a Wesleyan Sunday school. Almost six feet tall, he was admired for his courage and his strength. At a demonstration he protected one of the symbols of hydrarchy, a black flag with skull and crossbones and the words "Let us die like Men and not be sold like Slaves." He was hanged after the Cato Street Conspiracy, as was Arthur Thistlewood, who "had much of the air of a seafaring man." A city constable testified that during the Spa Fields Riots, the black American sailor Richard Simmonds was "harranguing the mob for half an hour; during the whole time he was the most active man among them." Apprehended a week later on an outward-bound East Indiaman, he explained that several blacks and mulattos had been involved in the riots; for this reason, city authorities had arrested strangers and detained both "foreign and black sailors."[66] Other men with maritime experience in Wedderburn's wide circle included the Irishman John "Zion" Ward and Richard Brothers. (Indeed, Wedderburn wondered whether Brothers's fate of being confined in a madhouse might also be his own.) Government spies noted the prominence of sailors and salty language at Wedderburn's Hopkins Street Chapel.

Wedderburn was but one link in a long chain of Atlantic antinomians. By 1802 he had already ascended "from a legal state of mind, into a state of Gospel Liberty." He had experienced "a deliverance from the power or authority of the law, considering himself not to be under the power of the law, but under Grace." Once in this state, he was free: "Being thus secure, he was enabled with boldness to examine the various doctrines he heard advanced at different times." He denied the power of Parliament to make laws that would contravene divine sovereignty in the ownership or distribution of land, and he insisted that there was godly legitimacy in resistance to oppressive laws. He asked his half-sister, "Oh Elizabeth, who first sanctioned the inhuman traffic, canst thou take away my guilt? No, cried a voice from some invisible being, the people should have resisted inhuman laws when proposed." In *High-Heel'd Shoes for Dwarfs in Holiness*, written from his dungeon in 1820, he argued for the "*armour of grace, the sword of the Spirit, and the* SHIELD OF FAITH, to enable us *to overcome the world.*" Wedderburn may have helped in the 1810s and 1820s to encourage antinomian thinking among Afro-Protestants in Jamaica. To the Native Baptists (sometimes thought of as "Christianized obeahs"), conversion "meant not embracing a strict code of Christian morality but being above morality." It followed, wrote Mary Turner, that John the Baptist "replaced Christ as the savior figure." Wedderburn distinguished himself from conservative Baptist and Methodist missionaries by asking, in discussion on Hopkins Street, "Which is the greater crime, for the wesleyan Missionaries to preach up passive obedience to the poor Black Slaves in the west Indies," or to extort their money?[67]

Wedderburn, like almost all of those whom he called, even as late as 1819, "us Jacobins," had studied the writings of Paine. These made a lifelong impression. "Glory be to Thomas Paine," he railed at the Hopkins Street Chapel: "His Rights of Man have taught us better" than "that ignorant smock faced stupid fool," the king. Wedderburn defied the government when he vowed that though Paine's books "may burn by the hand of the common Hangman," yet "they cannot burn [them] out of my head."[68] Still, Wedderburn, like Spence, pushed republican revolutionary thought beyond the positions taken by his fellow Jacobin artisanal radicals, who accepted capitalist redefinitions of property and the wage relation and considered *The Rights of Man* to be their manifesto. Mary Wollstonecraft exposed one limit of those positions in *The Rights of Women*, and Spence another in *The Rights of Infants; Or, the Imprescriptable Right of MOTHER'S to such a Share of the Elements as is Sufficient to Enable them to Suckle and Bring up their Young* (1796). Writing in a female voice, Spence attacked Paine as he shamed the men of the English proletariat: "We have found our husbands, to their indelible shame, woefully negligent and deficient about their own rights, as well as those of their wives and infants, [and] we women, mean to take up the business ourselves."

In 1817 Wedderburn debated the question "Is the American Government to be applauded or Condemned for the means they have taken to civilize the Indians by giving them a Portion of Land?" Wedderburn argued that "barbarism was better than Christianity. . . . If there was a God he would prevent Christianity from getting among the Indians give us Nature and we don't want to know God, we can worship the Sun." Making allowances for the unsympathetic, unpunctuated reporting of a spy, readers of Volney will recognize his ideas in this passage, for it was Volney who gathered the religions of the world in a semicircle (as Mrs. Campbell had gathered her slaves prior to their emancipation) for a mass debate of religious contradiction, before brilliantly demonstrating that Christianity, once its symbols and doctrines were explained by syncretic filiation, was the "Allegorical Worship of the Sun." Moreover, the origin of heliocentric theology was the Upper Nile, "among a black race of men."[69] Wedderburn summarized Christ's teaching in three commands: "Acknowledge no King—Acknowledge no priest. Acknowledge no Father." Wedderburn's own bitter, lifelong struggle with his wealthy Scottish father over the issues of paternity and inheritance thus broadened his political vision. The same, of course, was true of his transatlantic experiences of slavery and dispossession, which disinclined him to think of white, male, propertied citizenship as a means to revolutionary ends.[70]

Wedderburn demanded "in the name of God, in the name of natural justice, and in the name of humanity, that all slaves be set free." He knew that the most important abolitionists were the slaves themselves, who, like all other Atlantic workers, would of necessity deliver themselves from slavery and oppression by any means necessary. The most important means was direct action, and most emphatically not, he insisted, petitioning: "It is degrading to human nature to petition your oppressors." Wedderburn was a living testimonial to "the horrors of slavery," a phrase that served as the title of his autobiography. The power of this link was acknowledged in 1820 by William Wilberforce, who visited Wedderburn in prison and suggested that he write an account of his life for the movement, and earlier by the middle-class abolitionists who climbed up the

A peep into the City of London Tavern, *by George Cruikshank, 1817:*
Wedderburn (at right) confronts Robert Owen.
By permission of the British Library.

ladder and into Wedderburn's poor loft of a chapel to hear his denunciation of slavery.[71]

Like the linchpin, a small piece of metal that connected the wheels to
the axle of the carriage and made possible the movement and firepower
of the ship's cannon, Wedderburn was an essential piece of something

larger, mobile, and powerful. He linked through time the communist Christian in the ancient Near East with the Leveller in England and with the Native Baptist in Jamaica. He linked through space the slave and the maroon with the sailor and the dockworker, with the commoner and the artisan and the factory worker; he linked the evangelical with the Painite; he linked the slave with the working-class and middle-class opponent of slavery in the metropolis. He was the kind of person for whom "the idea of abolishing the slave trade is connected to the levelling system and the rights of man." He linked the trumpet of jubilee in the enclosed commons of England with the "shell-blow" jubilee of Jamaica. He had been a ship's gunner, and he knew exactly how a linchpin worked. He knew that without human linchpins like himself, Sam Sharpe and the Baptist War in Jamaica in 1831 might never have been possible. Sharpe, writes Mary Turner, "had formulated justifications for action inspired by the ideology that informed the radicals of the English Revolution and their descendants in the antislavery movement."[72] These justifications—and direct actions—helped to bring first the promise (on August 1, 1834) of jubilee and then its reality (on August 1, 1838): an end to slavery in the British Caribbean. Wedderburn lived long enough to witness (and no doubt to celebrate) the first, but not the second.

CONCLUSION

Tyger! Tyger!

ADAM SMITH (1723–1790), the first comprehensive theorist of capitalism, and Karl Marx (1818–1883), its profoundest critic, agreed in their approach to globalization. Both understood its maritime origins, arguing that the discovery of the sea routes to the Americas and the East Indies marked a new stage in human history. And both understood its social consequences, the fact that the expansion of commodity production (Smith called it the extent of the market, Marx the social division of labor) resettled the globe and transformed the experience of work. Smith noted that the accumulation of wealth depended on an increasing division of labor, which in turn caused workers to become "as stupid and ignorant as it is possible for a human creature to become." Marx, for his part, argued that the colonial system and the extension of the world market converted "the worker into a crippled monstrosity." He considered the imposition of factory discipline to be a "Herculean enterprise."[1] In other words, the despotism of the workplace and the anarchy of the global market developed together, intensifying work and redistributing workers in what Marx called a "motley pattern." This book has shown that the monster had a head—indeed, many heads—of its own, and that those heads were truly motley.

In the preceding pages, we have examined the Herculean process of globalization and the challenges posed to it by the many-headed hydra. We can periodize the almost two and a half centuries covered here by naming the successive and characteristic sites of struggle: the commons, the plantation, the ship, and the factory. In the years 1600–1640, when capitalism began in England and spread through trade and colonization around the Atlantic, systems of terror and sailing ships helped to expropriate the commoners of Africa, Ireland, England, Barbados, and Virginia and set them to work as hewers of wood and drawers of water. During the second phase, in 1640–1680, the hydra reared its heads against English capitalism, first by revolution in the metropolis, then by servile war in the colonies. Antinomians organized themselves to raise up a New Jerusalem against the wicked Babylon in order to put into practice the biblical precept that God is no respecter of persons. Their defeat deepened the subjection of women and opened the way to transoceanic slaving in Ireland, Jamaica, and West Africa. Dispersed to American plantations, the radicals were defeated a second time in Barbados and Virginia, enabling the ruling class to secure the plantation as a foundation of the new economic order.

A third phase, in 1680–1760, witnessed the consolidation and stabilization of Atlantic capitalism through the maritime state, a financial and nautical system designed to acquire and operate Atlantic markets. The sailing ship—the characteristic machine of this period of globalization—combined features of the factory and the prison. In opposition, pirates built an autonomous, democratic, multiracial social order at sea, but this alternative way of life endangered the slave trade and was exterminated. A wave of rebellion then ripped through the slave societies of the Americas in the 1730s, culminating in a multiethnic insurrectionary plot by workers in New York in 1741.

In 1760–1835, the motley crew launched the age of revolution in the Atlantic, beginning with Tacky's Revolt in Jamaica and continuing in a series of uprisings throughout the hemisphere. The new revolts created breakthroughs in human praxis—the Rights of Mankind, the strike, the higher-law doctrine—that would eventually help to abolish impressment and plantation slavery. They helped more immediately to produce the American Revolution, which ended in reaction as the Founding Fathers used race, nation, and citizenship to discipline, divide, and exclude the very sailors and slaves who had initiated and propelled the revolutionary movement. The liberty tree, however, sprouted branches elsewhere in the 1790s—in Haiti, France, Ireland, and England.

The proletariat has appeared throughout our book in a double aspect. First, when docile and slavish, it was described as the hewers of wood and drawers of water. The Irish revolutionary Wolfe Tone feared in 1790 that Ireland would forever be a "subordinate nation of hewers of wood and drawers of water."[2] Similarly, Morgan John Rhys, a remembrancer of the revolutionary 1640s and an abolitionist, asked in the first political periodical published in the Welsh language, *Cylchgrawn Cymraeg* (November 1793), whether the Welsh were condemned always to be hewers of wood and drawers of water.[3] John Thelwall, a poet and leading speaker for the London Corresponding Society (L.C.S., England's first independent political working-class organization), worried in the face of government repression in England in 1795 that "nine out of ten of the human race (it will, anon, be nineteen out of twenty) are born to be beasts of burthen to the remaining tythe: to be hewers of wood and drawers of water."[4] The African abolitionist Ottobah Cugoano knew that the Canaanites had been enslaved—that is, made hewers of wood and drawers of water—but he showed that slavery in the West Indies was even worse.[5] Irish, Welsh, English, and Africans alike struggled to liberate the hewers and drawers.

Conversely, when the proletariat was rebellious and self-active, it was described as a monster, a many-headed hydra. Its heads included food rioters (according to Shakespeare); heretics (Thomas Edwards); army agitators (Thomas Fairfax); antinomians and independent women (Cotton Mather); maroons (Governor Mauricius); motley urban mobs (Peter Oliver); general strikers (J. Cunningham); rural barbarians of the commons (Thomas Malthus); aquatic laborers (Patrick Colquhoun); free thinkers (William Reid); and striking textile workers (Andrew Ure). Nameless commentators added peasant rebels, Levellers, pirates, and slave insurrectionists to the long list. Fearful of the energy, mobility, and growth of social forces beyond their control, the writers, heresy hunters, generals, ministers, officials, population theorists, policemen, merchants, manufacturers, and planters offered up their curses, which called down Herculean destruction upon the hydra's heads: the debellation of the Irish, the extermination of the pirates, the annihilation of the outcasts of the nations of the Earth.

Hercules had been known since the time of Diodorus as an executioner. Hangings, burnings, mutilations, starvings, and decapitations have filled our every chapter in this black book of capitalism. What was to become of Despard's head, for example? It was reported that "the Cabinet was called at the request of the Lord Chancellor to consider what advice should be given to His Majesty respecting the disposal of the Heads of the Prisoners."[6] Dessalines, the ferocious, uncompromising leader of the Haitian revolt, tried to widen the ownership of land in Haiti, an aspiration that led to his death by mutilation in 1806. He embodied a revolutionary *lwa* or *lao,* spoke Congo, and called his people the Incas of the Sun. Défilé carried away the remains of his body, seeking to piece them together for the cemetery.[7] Masaniello, leader of the galley slaves, fishwives, prostitutes, weavers, students, and lazzaroni of Naples during their ten days of proletarian revolt, was killed and chopped up on July 16, 1647. The following day his supporters gathered up the pieces, reattached the skull to the corpse, and gave his body a funeral befitting a martial commander.[8] Walt Whitman would write a story about Richard Parker's widow and her search for his body after he was hanged for leading the mutiny at the Nore in 1797. Thus our first step has been to remember the proletarian body. We have had to translate it out of the idiom of monstrosity.

By the late eighteenth and early nineteenth centuries, some workers wanted to turn the tables on their class enemies, representing themselves as having the strength to win *and* the authority to impose a new order. They assumed the mantle of Hercules and commenced to battle a different many-headed monster. Coleridge in the 1790s referred to the counterrevolutionary forces as a hydra. The L.C.S. predicted to a similar society in Newcastle-upon-Tyne that "the Hydra of Tyranny and of Imposition will soon fall under the Guillotine of truth and reason." In November 1793, the French revolutionary artist David proposed that the convention erect a colossal statue of Hercules to represent the French people, replacing Marianne, the feminine personification of liberty. By 1795 the coins of the French Republic were divided between silver pieces bearing the figure of Hercules and bronze ones bearing that of Liberty. In November, during the Festival of Reason, held in Notre Dame Cathedral, the radical deputies again introduced Hercules: "The Terror was the people on the march, the exterminating Hercules." Charles Lamb wrote in the early nineteenth century that gorgons and hydras and chimeras were "transcripts, types,—the archetypes are in us, and eternal. These terrors—date beyond body—or, without the body, they would have been the same."[9]

In England, tribunes of the radical working class were likewise fascinated by Hercules and the hydra. "All things are sold," began Shelley in *Queen Mab,* a catalogue of human corruption through the commodity form. Light, liberty, love—each had a price,

> . . . *whilst the pestilence that springs*
> *From unenjoying sensualism, has filled*
> *All human life with hydra-headed woes.*

Richard Carlisle called his penny weekly newspaper the *Gorgon,* arguing in its first issue (1818) that "although the hydra of corruption still rears its accursed head amongst us, we are persuaded, that it must ultimately fall beneath general indignation and contempt." Henry Hunt issued a weekly entitled the *Medusa; Or, Penny Politician;* the first number, which appeared on February 20, 1819, under the motto "Let's Die like Men, and not be Sold like Slaves," was addressed "To THE PUBLIC, *alias,* the *ignorantly-impatient Multitude.*" In an attempt to provide national leadership by skilled male trade unionists over the burgeoning female and Irish textile proletariat of the northern factories, John Gast, a London shipwright, formed the Philanthropic Hercules in December 1818, just before the massacre at Peterloo in England (1819). Before the Haymarket Massacre (1886) in America, the "Revenge" circular called on the working class to rise like Hercules. Defining moments in the labor histories of England and America thus hinged on working-class references to this mythical hero.

The embrace of Hercules reflected a deepening fissure between skilled artisans—who, upon close inspection, often proved to be foremen or small managers—and the mass of migrants to the city, including young orphaned workers, female proletarians, discharged soldiers, and casualties of factory, workshop, and ship. The technological changes wrought by the steam-driven screw propeller and the substitution of iron and steel for wood in ship construction undermined the material basis of the motley crew and intensified the fragmentation of Atlantic dockside and maritime labor. The artisan, by contrast, was often a property holder, a temperate, prudent, punctual, literate citizen. His patriotism easily became nationalism. He was frequently a disciplinarian, an advocate of police. The fissure had cultural and political significance. Asa Briggs noted that in the early nineteenth century, "the gulf between skilled and unskilled workers was so great that one acute observer spoke of them as two separate races."[10] Tom Paine, Karl Marx, and Edward Thompson (who held that "working people were thrust into a state of *apartheid*") wondered if the poor were becoming a race unto themselves.

The emphasis in modern labor history on the white, male, skilled, waged, nationalist, propertied artisan/citizen or industrial worker has hidden the history of the Atlantic proletariat of the seventeenth, eighteenth, and early nineteenth centuries. That proletariat was not a monster, it was not a unified cultural class, and it was not a race. This class was *anonymous, nameless*. Robert Burton noted in *The Anatomy of Melancholy* (1624), "Of 15000 proletaries slaine in battle, scarce fifteene are recorded in history, or one alone, the General perhaps, and after a while his and their names are likewise blotted out, the whole battle it selfe is forgotten." It was *landless, expropriated*. It lost the integument of the commons to cover and protect its needs. It was *poor*, lacking property, money, or material riches of any kind. It was often unwaged, forced to perform the unpaid labors of capitalism. It was often hungry, with uncertain means of survival. It was *mobile, transatlantic*. It powered industries of worldwide transportation. It left the land, migrating from country to town, from region to region, across the oceans, and from one island to another. It was *terrorized, subject to coercion*. Its hide was calloused by indentured labor, galley slavery, plantation slavery, convict transportation, the workhouse, the house of correction. Its origins were often traumatic: enclosure, capture, and imprisonment left lasting marks. It was *female* and *male*, of *all ages*. (Indeed, the very term *proletarian* originally referred to poor women who served the state by bearing children.) It included everyone from youth to old folks, from ship's boys to old salts, from apprentices to savvy old masters, from young prostitutes to old "witches." It was *multitudinous, numerous*, and *growing*. Whether in a square, at a market, on a common, in a regiment, or on a man-of-war with banners flying and drums beating, its gatherings were wondrous to contemporaries. It was *numbered, weighed*, and *measured*. Unknown as individuals or by name, it was objectified and counted for purposes of taxation, production, and reproduction. It was *cooperative* and *laboring*. The collective power of the many rather than the skilled labor of the one produced its most forceful energy. It moved burdens, shifted earth, and transformed the landscape. It was *motley*, both dressed in rags and multiethnic in appearance. Like Caliban, it originated in Europe, Africa, and America. It included clowns, or cloons (i.e., country people). It was without genealogical unity. It was *vulgar.* It spoke its own speech, with a distinctive pronunciation, lexicon, and grammar made up of slang, cant, jargon, and pidgin—talk from work, the street, the prison, the gang, and the dock. It was *planetary,* in its origins, its motions, and its consciousness. Finally, the proletariat was *self-active, creative;* it was—and is—alive; it is onamove.[11]

What does the experience of this proletariat have to offer us today? To answer this question, we turn to a story about three neglected friends of the human race: Thomas Hardy, founder of the L.C.S.; his wife, Lydia Hardy; and Olaudah Equiano, whom we have met in previous chapters. We conclude with reflections on the lives and works of the revolutionary savant C. F. Volney and the poetic visionary William Blake. All three— the forgotten, the utopian, and the visionary—illustrated the transatlantic circulation of experience and the effect of struggles in Africa/America upon social and political developments in Europe, and all expressed an egalitarian, multiethnic conception of humanity, which, we wish to argue, represented the grandest possibility of both their age and ours. The defeat of their common idea in the pivotal years of the early 1790s gave rise to two narratives of class, race, and nation that have served to hide the history we have attempted to recover in this book.

The first is the story of the Working Class. London artisans, faced in the 1790s with the economic pressures of rising prices, outsourcing, and mechanization, were inspired by the French Revolution and their own Dissenting and craft traditions to enter into correspondence with the emerging factory proletariat in the north of England, where the first steam-driven cotton factory opened in Manchester in 1789. They proposed the common purpose of Parliamentary reform. Despite domestic repression and the prohibition of trade-union organizing, the English working class emerged after the Napoleonic Wars (1815) with a vibrant intellectual, political, and moral culture (radicalism) and became a distinct and enduring class formation, able to force its industrial and constitutional opponents first to admit trade unions and then to expand the franchise. A defining document of this story was the "Address of a Journeyman Cotton Spinner," published in the *Black Dwarf* in 1819, which described class relations in the cotton factories in terms of the length of the working day, the child labor, the gruel, the steam engine, and the blacklist.[12] The "Address" contrasted the factory worker with the plantation slave: "The Negro slave in the West Indies, if he works under a scorching sun, has probably a little breeze of air sometimes to fan him: he has a space of ground and time allowed to cultivate it. The English spinner slave has no enjoyment of the open atmosphere and breezes of heaven." This view—opposite to the pledge of solidarity expressed by the Sheffield journeymen cutlers thirty years earlier—shows working-class insularity and its vulnerability to racist appeal.

The second is the narrative of Black Power. The people of the African diaspora fought against American slavery and the deliberate degradation, dehumanization, and destruction of name, lineage, culture, and country. Organized in mass in the mine or on the plantation (the cotton gin was invented in 1793), black or pan-African consciousness arose from resistance of blood and spirit, which achieved historic successes in the 1790s. The resistance of the spirit encompassed obeah, voodoo, and the black church (including the African Baptist Church of Savannah, Georgia, founded in 1788; the Free African Society of Philadelphia, 1787; and the Abyssinia Baptist Church of New York, 1800). The resistance of blood comprised revolts in Dominica, St. Vincent, Jamaica, and Virginia, and most significantly, the Haitian Revolution of 1791–1804. Haiti was the original Black Power. If the distinctive accomplishment of the English working class was its labor press, the singular achievement of the black freedom struggle was its music. Ideological resistance would lead to David Walker and William Lloyd Garrison, and armed resistance to Denmark Vesey and Nat Turner. An ideology of providence, called Ethiopianism because it located redemption in Africa, was nurtured in opposition to the racist myths of the ruling class and the racial exclusions of the working class.[13] Even if we wished to bring these two narratives together, it would be impossible because they are true stories of their time and since. But we can remember a time before they separated.

Three Friends of the Whole Human Race

Olaudah Equiano, Lydia Hardy (née Priest), and Thomas Hardy lived together at Taylors Building, Chandos Street, Covent Garden, London, from August 1790 to February 1792. Every morning in season fruits and vegetables—parsnips, carrots, peas, apples, and strawberries—arrived from the nurseries and gardens up the river Thames, and every evening piles of rubbish were collected. The three friends shared an experience of separation from the earthly commons, so they either had to buy commodities in the market or scavenge food. None was paid much, and prices were rising. Even if they shifted for goods (people then depended upon the customary wastes of urban manufactures), they lived an insecure life, if not one of constant destitution. The three friends belonged to the "swinish multitude," as Edmund Burke had recently called the people in his diatribe against the French Revolution.[14] They were pigs in the eyes of the upper class, and motley ones at that, for Olaudah was an African, Lydia was English, and Thomas was a Scot.

Olaudah had been both a plantation slave and a sailor. Lydia's social role was parturition, hence she was a proletarian, a mother and a childraiser. Thomas was an artisan, a shoemaker. The slave/sailor, proletarian, and artisan—to identify them crudely by their economic types—were friends and would seek freedom together in 1792. Olaudah had been kidnapped at the age of ten with his sister and sold into slavery, torn from a "nation of dancers, musicians, and poets." He described the West African commons: "Our tillage is exercised in a large plain or common . . . and all the neighbours resort thither in a body." He noted that "every one contributes something to the common stock."[15] In Lydia's native Buckinghamshire, acts of Parliament had enclosed the common lands. An anonymous ditty summed up the loss and the crime:

> *The law locks up the man or woman*
> *Who steals the goose from off the common*
> *But lets the greater villain loose*
> *Who steals the common from the goose.*

Resistance to expropriation was strong in her home region, dating back to Captain Pouch and the Midlands Revolt of 1607 and to the Digger colonies of the English Revolution. Thomas, for his part, had been forced to leave his ancestral tenancy as capitalist farmers enclosed fields, consolidated runrig strips, and took in the commons, leaving the "gudeman" and cottar to join the landless.[16] "Ah, man was made to mourn!" sighed the Scottish poet Robert Burns.

Having lost the commons, all three then saw their labors undergo devaluation. Olaudah experienced the terrors of merchant capitalism aboard the slave ship that transported him (among some 1.4 million other Igbo) across the Atlantic. He labored at sea, amid the cane fields, and in the tobacco rows. He observed but could not stop the terror against his fellow creatures, off whose labors the Bank of England, the Houses of Parliament, and much of the nation thrived. Lydia, meanwhile, became pregnant six times in London, where 74 percent of all children died before the age of five.[17] She attempted to nurture five infants to childhood, but amid circumstances of penury, dearth, insecurity, and infestation, they all died young. Thomas found work as a brickie at the Carron armaments works not far from his birthplace. The "carronades" that gave the men-of-war of merchant capitalism their destructive firepower were produced amid volcanic conditions of darting flames, glowing coals, and molten iron. Severely injured when some scaffolding collapsed beneath him, Thomas recovered and sailed to London in 1774 with eighteen pence in his pocket.

Thus grounded in common experiences of expropriation and exploitation, the three friends shared rooms and ideas. Olaudah reached back to the antinomian abolitionism of the English Revolution to express through Milton's *Paradise Lost* (2:332–40) his own experience of American slavery:

> . . . *for what peace will be giv'n*
> *To us enslaved, but custody severe,*
> *And stripes, and arbitrary punishment*
> *Inflicted? and what peace can we return,*
> *But to our power hostility and hate;*
> *Untamed reluctance, and revenge though slow,*
> *Yet ever plotting how the Conqueror least*
> *May reap his conquest, and may least rejoice*
> *In doing what we most in suffering feel?*

Wherever Olaudah carried this "untamed reluctance," miracles of social alliance followed, for he played a catalytic role in the making of the United Irishmen, the English working class, and the Scottish convention movement. His life story, *The Interesting Narrative of Olaudah Equiano or Gustavus Vassa the African*, was "the most important single literary contribution to the campaign for abolition."[18] While living with Lydia and Thomas, he prepared the fourth edition of the book, which he took with him on a journey to Ireland in May 1791. The sixty Irish subscribers to the *Interesting Narrative* included a large number of radicals who would become United Irishmen later in that year.[19] Wolfe Tone came to Belfast about the same time as Olaudah and wrote his *Argument on behalf of the Catholics of Ireland,* which shared common ideas with Equiano's *Interesting Narrative.*[20]

Lydia Hardy was, like other women, active in the abolitionist movement, not in lobbying members of Parliament or participating in the deliberations of the national committee of the abolitionists, but at the parish pump or kitchen hearth. On April 2, 1792, she would write to Thomas and report on the progress of abolitionism in her hometown of Chesham: "Pray let me no how you go on in your society and likewise we [illegible word] as been donn in the parlement house concurning the slave trade for the people here are as much against it as enny ware and there is more people I think hear that drinks tea without sugar than there drinks with. . . ." The inclusive "we" here refers to the sugar boycott, one of the movement's most effective campaigns, which had been launched the previous autumn. In the same letter, Lydia would ask Thomas to give Olaudah her best wishes for "a good jorney to Scotland" (he had been working in their common quarters on the fifth edition of his book, which he would carry with him). Her acquaintances in Chesham, she bid Thomas to pass on, were "very fond of Vassa book."

Thomas Hardy had arrived in London when the unfolding American Revolution was the subject of every political discussion. Influenced by the organizational and intellectual innovations of the motley crew (the committees of correspondence and abolitionist literature), Thomas explained that "his heart always glowed with the love of freedom, and was feelingly alive to the sufferings of his fellow creatures." He developed a concern for the "future happiness of the whole human race." By 1790 he kept a shoemaker's shop located just a few yards from their rooms in Covent Garden, in Piccadilly, the embarkation point for coaches going to the west—to Bath or Bristol—and from there for ships headed for the West Indies. Here he formed the London Corresponding Society, which was egalitarian by income (membership cost one penny) and by status (titles were forbidden), though it excluded people "incapacitated by crimes." After the first meeting, in January 1792, Hardy and the other founders repaired to a tavern, the Bell in the Strand, for supper, and listened to a parable by William Frend about "certain brethren dwelling together in one house and having all things in common." Thus, at the very beginning of its deliberations, the L.C.S. considered the commons and slavery, the ideal of the one and the evil of the other. It began to seek out similar societies elsewhere for correspondence. But where? Olaudah suggested Sheffield—"a damn bad place," according to George III.[21]

Thomas pursued the suggestion. On March 8, 1792, he wrote to the Reverend Thomas Bryant of Sheffield, "Hearing from Gustavus Vassa that you are a zealous friend for the Abolition of that accursed traffick denominated the Slave Trade I inferred from that that you was a friend to freedom on the broad basis of the Rights of Man for I am pretty perswaded that no Man who is an advocate from principle for liberty for a Black Man but will strenuously promote and support the rights of a White Man & vice versa." Equiano opened for Hardy the doors to the steel and cutlery workers of Sheffield. The Reverend Bryant led a congregation that would soon be labeled the "Tom Paine Methodists," and many of its members were up in arms. In June 1791, six thousand acres of land in Sheffield and its vicinity had been enclosed by an act of Parliament. The commoners, the colliers, and the cutlers reacted in fury, releasing prisoners and burning a magistrate's barn.[22] A witness at Hardy's 1794 trial for treason laid the ax to the root: "The original cause of discontent was the inclosing a Common, which was opposed by the populace."[23] The struggle for customary rights was common to both field and manufacture; a song of 1787 illustrated the interrelationship between expropriation and criminalization. Jonathan Watkinson and the masters of the Cutlers Company calculated their compensation and decreed that thirteen knives thenceforth be counted to the dozen, since among the twelve "there might be a *waster,*" a customary taking for the workers. The people sang in protest,[24]

> *That offspring of tyranny, baseness and pride,*
> *Our rights hath invaded and almost destroyed,*
> *May that man be banished who villainy screens:*
> *Or sides with big W——n and his thirteens.*

The reference was, of course, to common rights. The ballad thumped along, comparing Watkinson to Pharoah:

> *But justice repulsed him and set us all free,*
> *Like bond-slaves of old in the year jubilee.*
> *May those be transported or sent for marines*
> *That works for the big W——n at his thirteens.*

Jubilee thus meant the restoration of manufacturing rights.

When Hardy wrote to Bryant, he mentioned the "broad basis of the Rights of Man," referring to Tom Paine's book, whose second part had just been published. *The Rights of Man* demonstrated the economic feasibility of public education for all children, social security for those over fifty, and health care for everyone. The rights encompassed by the phrase "rights of man" were growing; they would soon include the rights of women and the rights of infants. Dr. William Buchan, a physician in Sheffield, considered air, water, and sunshine to be "among the most essential articles of the knowledge and rights of man."[25] Hardy's own "vice versa" suggested that any advocate of workers' rights to bread, commons, fresh air, clean water, and representation in Parliament must stand against slavery and advocate the same for the black person.

In April, Hardy wrote, "There is an absolute necessity for us to unite together and communicate with each other that our sentiments and determinations may center in one point, viz., to have the Rights of Man reestablished especially in this nation but our views of the Rights of Man are not confined solely to this small island but are extended to the whole human race, black or white, high or low, rich or poor."[26] Like J. Philmore before him and the Despards after, he sought the liberation of the whole human race. The idea arose from his roommates, from his reading, from London Dissent, and from his knowledge of the gathering slave revolts in the Caribbean.

April 2, 1792, was a historic day. It was announced that "the LONDON CORRESPONDING SOCIETY with modesty intrudes itself and opinions on the attention of the public." The delicately worded proclamation, however, said nothing about slavery, the slave trade, or the commons. On the same day, Lydia, visiting family, wrote Thomas her letter from Chesham, politely inquiring about his society but emphasizing abolition and her news for Olaudah. Early the next morning, Parliament agreed to what, in the history of English abolitionism, is called the April Compromise. Wilberforce had asked Parliament on April 2 to resolve that the slave trade "ought to be abolished"; after midnight, the home secretary moved to amend the resolution by adding the word *gradually*. In the wee hours, the prime minister waxed eloquent. Then, after debating all night, not least about levelling principles, the members of Parliament went to breakfast, one or two of them perhaps blithely humming the hit tune of the year, "Oh, Dear! What Can the Matter Be?"[27] The way was now clear for an *expansion* of the slave trade.[28]

The coincidence of these events suggested a betrayal, which became more obvious with the passage of time. In May, Olaudah, who had joined the L.C.S., wrote to Thomas and expressed "my best Respect to my fellow members of your society." The confusion of pronouns indicated a deepening problem. By summer Hardy had begun to worry that the abolitionist movement might sidetrack the society from its main objective, parliamentary reform. Looking back on the history of the organization from the vantage point of 1799, Hardy omitted any mention of the equality of race in observing of the society's charter, "There was a uniform rule by which all Members were admitted high and low, rich and poor." The three friends soon separated. Olaudah married and dropped out of the movement; Lydia died in childbirth after being harassed by a church-and-king mob; Thomas was attacked by the government, went to prison, was acquitted, and survived to publish, in 1832, his memoirs, which minimized Olaudah's role as midwife to the birth of the L.C.S.

As we have seen when considering Despard's situation, the ramifications of the Haitian revolt undermined the revolutionary possibilities epitomized by the three friends, because it divided the abolitionist movement. In November 1791, a debate took place at Coachmakers' Hall on the Haitian slave insurrection. "People here are all panic-struck with the transactions in St. Domingo," wrote Wilberforce, but to him "people" meant the middle class.[29] The idiom of monstrosity sanctioned violent, steady repression. In debate in the House of Lords, Abingdon argued that "the order and subordination, the happiness of the whole habitable globe is threatened" by abolition: "All being equal, blacks and whites, French and English, wolves and lambs, shall all, 'merry companions every one,' promiscuously pig together; engendering . . . a new species of man as the product of this new philosophy."[30] Abolish the slave trade, he warned, and other abolitions will pop out of Pandora's box: the transporting of felons to Botany Bay, the flogging of soldiers, the pressing of seamen, the exploiting of factory workers. London bankers and merchant houses embraced the Baconian argument of monstrosity, urging the government fully to prosecute the attempt to repress the Haitian Revolution and eagerly supporting the exiled French planters in their city. Seventeen banking firms soon petitioned the Duke of Portland to annihilate and exterminate the insurgent slaves.[31] Meanwhile, the poor mechanics of Leeds acknowledged the effects of propaganda in 1792: "We are behald more like Monsters than Friends of the People," they wrote to the L.C.S. in 1792.[32] Henry Redhead Yorke, who had been born in the West Indies, spoke against slavery at a mass meeting in Sheffield in the spring of 1794. The speech got him arrested, imprisoned, and tried. At his trial he brilliantly defended himself by turning the rhetoric of monstrosity back against the authorities, promising, "The more sacrifices, the more martyrs you make, the more numerous the sons of liberty will become. They will multiply like the hydra, and hurl vengeance upon your heads."[33]

VOLNEY'S MOTLEY CROWD

In 1791 the revolutionary savant Constantin François Volney published his *Ruins; Or, Meditations on the Revolutions of Empires,* a learned, sensible, and rhapsodic work of religious anthropology and world history.[34] Its most famous passage is a dialogue between the "People" and the "Privileged Class":

PEOPLE: And what labor do you perform in our society?
PRIVILEGED CLASS: None; we are not made to work.
PEOPLE: How, then, have you acquired these riches?
PRIVILEGED CLASS: By taking the pains to govern you.
PEOPLE: What! is this what you call governing? We toil and you enjoy! we produce and you dissipate! Wealth proceeds from us, and you absorb it. Privileged men! class who are not the people; form a nation apart, and govern yourselves.

The Privileged Class sends its lawyer, its soldier, and its priest to plead their characteristic arguments with the People, but none prevails. Then it plays the race card: "Are we not men of another race—the noble and pure descendants of the conquerors of this empire?" But the People, who have studied the historical genealogy of the Privileged, burst out in gales of laughter. Finally, the Privileged Class concedes, "It is all over for us: the swinish multitude are enlightened."

Written in an accessible, liberating style, Volney's *Ruins* was as important to the age of revolution as Paine's *Rights of Man*. First published in Paris, it was translated into German and English in 1792, with American editions appearing shortly after, and numerous fly-sheets, pamphlets, and abridged editions distributed elsewhere. It was printed in Sheffield, and in Welsh translation. Its fifteenth chapter, a vision of a "New Age," was reprinted often. On the very day in May 1794 when habeas corpus was suspended and Tommy Spence was dragged off to Newgate, he included "The New Age" in the second volume of his *Pig's Meat; Or, Lessons for the Swinish Multitude*. The L.C.S. reprinted chapter 15 under the title *The Torch*, a circumstance "made use of to countenance the report of an intention to set *London on fire*."[35] In Bahia, Brazil, a copy was found in the hands of a mulatto in the midst of the 1797 conspiracy of whites, browns, and blacks.[36] The United Irishmen reworked it as a chapbook and distributed it to Belfast mill workers.[37] A second or third English translation, prepared by Joel Barlow with anonymous assistance from Thomas Jefferson, came out in 1802, when Volney may have been visiting England.[38]

Volney voted in the French revolutionary assembly to abolish slavery. He foresaw a new age, and like Tom Paine and the United Irishmen, he saw it dawning in the west: "Turning towards the west . . . a cry of liberty, proceeding from far distant shores, resounds on the ancient continent." He assailed the ruling logic of nationalism, having his Privileged Class say, "We must divide the people by national jealousies, and occupy them with commotions, wars, and conquests." He critiqued the patriarchal family: "The King sleeps or smokes his pipe while his wife and daughters perform all the drudgery of the house." He stood against the cupidity that "fomented in the bosom of every state an intestine war, in which the citizens, divided into contending corps of orders, classes, families, unremittingly struggled to appropriate to themselves, under the name of supreme power, the ability to plunder every thing." From this "arose a distinction of castes and races, which reduced to a regular system the maintenance of disorder" and perfected the science of oppression.[39]

Volney explained that civilization had begun in Africa: "It was there that a people, since forgotten, discovered the elements of science and art, at a time when all other men were barbarous, and that a race, now regarded as the refuse of society, because their hair is woolly and their skin is dark, explored among the phenomena of nature, those civil and religious systems which have since held mankind in awe."[40] Volney was a planetary wanderer who observed the variations inherent in humankind: "I contemplated with astonishment this gradation in color, from a bright carnation to a brown scarcely less bright, a dark brown, a muddy brown, bronze, olive, leaden, copper, as far as to the black of ebony and jet." He wondered "who causeth his sun to shine alike on all the races of men, on the white as on the black, on the Jew, on the Mussulman, the Christian, and the Idolater"? He believed in a grand family of the human race. He wrote,

A scene of a new and astonishing nature then presented itself to my view. All the people and nations of the globe, every race of men from every different climate, advancing on all sides, seemed to assemble in one inclosure, and form in distinct groups an immense congress. The motley appearance of this innumerable crowd, occasioned by their diversity of dress, of features and of complexion, exhibited a most extraordinary and most attractive spectacle.

Volney raised the motley crowd to a universal ideal.

Although he escaped the guillotine under Robespierre, Volney, like Tom Paine, landed in prison. He was released, along with Paine, on 9 Thermidor 1794. He soon sailed to America, taking his first English lessons from a Venetian sailor. In the winter of 1795–96, he lived in Philadelphia, across the street from the African Church, which was crowded with refugees from revolutionary St. Domingue. Volney admired the inscription over its portal, "The people that walked in darkness have seen a great light" (Isaiah 42). He made contacts in "enlightened" circles, but his behavior apparently transgressed the norms of white supremacy. He visited Thomas Jefferson at Monticello in the summer of 1796 and later wrote about a personal encounter he had there with slavery:

After dinner the master [Jefferson] and I went to see the slaves plant peas. Their bodies dirty brown rather than black, their dirty rags, their miserable hideous half-nakedness, these haggard figures, this secretive anxious air, the hateful timorous looks, altogether seized me with an initial sentiment of terror and sadness that I ought to hide my face from. Their indolence in turning up the ground with the hoe was extreme. The master took a whip to frighten them, and soon ensued a comic scene. Placed in the middle of the gang, he agitated, he grumbled, he menaced, and turned far and wide (on all sides) turning around. Now, as he turned his face, one by one, the blacks changed attitude: those whom he looked at directly worked the best, those whom he half saw worked least, and those he didn't see at all, ceased working altogether; and if he made an about-face, the hoe was raised to view, but otherwise slept behind his back.[41]

William Cobbett denounced Volney as an infidel and a cannibal, while Joseph Priestley accused him of Hottentotism. John Adams probably had him in mind when he complained that the United States was becoming a "receptacle of malevolence and turbulence, for the outcasts of the universe." Jefferson himself believed that Volney was the principal object of the Act Concerning Aliens of 1798, which was designed to promote "purity of national character" and forced the Frenchman to sail back to Europe.[42]

BLAKE'S AFRICAN ORC

William Blake wrote his prophecy *America* in 1793. Its preludium was illuminated, like the initial letter of a medieval manuscript, by the image of an outstretched figure—Orc, the symbol of revolution—pinioned spread-eagled to the ground, straining to be free. Blake derived the image from Captain John Gabriel Stedman, a mercenary soldier who had fought four years in Suriname against the maroons—escaped slaves who shared the tropical rain forest with Indians and other state-of-the-art forest dwellers—and lived to tell the tale. Stedman wrote a "narrative" and painted a hundred watercolors that he submitted in 1790 to Joseph Johnson, a publisher, who in turn hired Blake to help engrave the plates.[43]

Orc, by William Blake. William Blake, America, a Prophecy *(1793).*

From 1791 to 1794 Blake bore down, elbow grease mixing with the burin and copperplate, on these images of an American slave revolt. His poetry of this period—*Visions of the Daughters of Albion, The Marriage of Heaven and Hell, Songs of Experience, America a Prophecy, The Four*

The Execution of Breaking on the Rack, c. 1776, by William Blake.
Stedman, Narrative of a Five Years Expedition.

Zoas—and his politics (he paraded in a red liberty cap, the symbol of the emancipated slave) were deeply colored by Stedman's text, pictures, and friendship. One of the plates, entitled *The Execution of Breaking on the Rack,* provided the basis of his depiction of red Orc.

In the summer of 1776, Stedman had followed a crowd to the savannah to watch the execution of three African Americans. One of them, Neptune, had killed an overseer. He was pinioned to a rack on the ground. The executioner, a fellow African, chopped off his left hand, then used an iron rod to break and shatter his bones. Neptune lived. He fell from the rack "and Damn'd them all for a Pack of Barbarous Rascals, at the Same time Removing his right hand by the help of his Teeth, he Rested his Head on Part of the timber and ask'd the by Standers for a Pipe of Tobacco Which was infamously Answered by kicking & Spitting on him"—a final insult that Stedman and some American sailors intervened out of sympathy to stop. Neptune begged for the coup de grace, but it was denied him. He sang a song to take leave of his friends, and a second to tell his deceased relations that he would soon join them. He asked the sentinel on guard "how it came that he a White Man should have no meat." The soldier answered, "Because I am not so rich." Neptune responded, "Then I will make you a Present first pick my Hand that was Chopt off Clean to the Bones Sir—Next begin to [eat] myself till you be Glutted & you'll have both Bread and Meat which best becomes you." He laughed. When Stedman returned to the site of execution later in the day, he observed Neptune's skull on the end of a stick, nodding at him. Frightened out of his wits, Stedman recovered only when he saw that a pecking vulture had set the skull in motion.

Reflecting fourteen years later on the experience, Stedman quoted the prophet Daniel in passages that referred to the island slave trade and prophesied deliverance by a prince. Blake conjoined the redeeming warrior of Daniel with the rebellious African American Neptune to create a revolutionary symbol of energy, desire, and freedom: Orc. In contrast to Neptune's fate, in Blake's *America,* a dark virgin brings food and drink to Orc and inspires him to break free. They make love. She exclaims,

> *I know thee, I have found thee, & I will not let thee go;*
> *Thou art the image of God who dwells in darkness of Africa.*

And with that ecstatic shout, Blake began his praise-song of the American Revolution, in which the meaning of "America" was no more restricted to the thirteen states of the U.S.A. than the meaning of "revolution" was restricted to the mutilating Constitution, which treated each African American as three fifths of a human being. Blake's America was

Aftermath of the Demarara slave revolt, 1823. Joshua Bryant, Account of an Insurrection of the Negro Slaves in the Colony of Demarara *(1824).*

an African America, and his revolution included the emancipation of the whole person:

> *Let the slave grinding at the mill, run out into the field:*
> *Let him look up into the heavens & laugh in the bright air;*
> *Let the inchained soul shut up in darkness & in sighing,*
> *Whose face has never seen a smile in thirty weary years;*
> *Rise & look out, his chains are loose, his dungeon doors are open,*
> *And let his wife and children return from the oppressors scourge.*

Blake's vision was further compressed into a single, powerful symbol: the tiger. Stedman had written about the tigers and other wild cats of Suriname, where he and his fellow soldiers had once captured a jaguar in a chicken coop and drowned it. He described the cougar and the "Tiger-Cat Which is Extremely Beautiful . . . a Very Lively Animal With its Eyes emitting flashes of Lightning;—But ferocious, Mischievious, and not Tameable like the rest." Of the "Red Tiger" he wrote, "the head is small the Body thin the Limbs Long with tremendous whitish Claws The Teeth are Also Very Large, the Eyes prominent, and Sparkling like Stars." These observations inspired Blake's "The Tyger," part of *Songs of Experience,* published in 1793.[44]

Tyger Tyger, burning bright,
In the forests of the night;
What immortal hand or eye,
Could frame thy fearful symmetry?

It lived in the forest, ferocious and untamable, a creature of the commons. In the poem's trochaic rhythm we hear hammer blows or the march of soldiers, or perhaps the blows upon Neptune's body:

And what shoulder, & what art,
Could twist the sinews of thy heart?
And when thy heart began to beat,
What dread hand? & what dread feet?

What the hammer? what the chain,
In what furnace was thy brain?
What the anvil? what dread grasp,
Dare its deadly terrors clasp?

Stedman respected the creature, but only with the hunter's wish to kill it. Blake also wondered about the relation between hunter and hunted, but he widened it to include the larger social forces of oppressor and oppressed.

Stedman's *Narrative* concluded with *Europe supported by Africa & America,* a plate depicting three idealized nude women—white, black, and brown—standing arm in arm upon a green, with mountains in the distance. Stedman called it an emblematical picture "accompanied by an ardent wish that in the friendly manner as they are represented they may henceforth & to all eternity be the prop of each other; and I might have included *Asia* but this I omitted as having no Connection with the Present Narrative—we all only differ in the Colour but we are Certainly Created by the same hand & after the Same Mould"—lines that echoed Blake's own belief about the "everlasting gospel" and that helped him to compose his first draft of "The Tyger," which asked,

In what clay & in what mould
Were thy eyes of fury roll'd?

Stedman himself had fought against freedom, but he nonetheless brought the revolution of the Americas to Blake in a way that was consis-

Europe supported by Africa & America, by *William Blake.*
Stedman, Narrative of a Five Years Expedition.

tent with what Blake would have learned during the same period from Ottobah Cugoano and other abolitionists. Blake discovered in the revolts of the slaves of the Americas a revolutionary energy, politics, and vision.

After 1795, Blake would continue to write poetry that drew on American struggles, but he would not publish another line for ten years. In 1797 he wrote *Vala, or the Four Zoas,* describing child labor at grinding wheels and workers in brick kilns:

> *Then All the Slaves from every Earth in the wide Universe*
> *Sing a New Song drowning confusion in its happy notes.*

The New Song would be sung by an African, wrote Blake. The phrase referred either to Revelation 4, in which the scroll is opened by the harp players and the Lion of Judah, or to Isaiah 42, where justice will shine on every race, "a beacon for the nations, to open eyes that are blind, to bring captives out of prison." Blake continued, "The good of all the Land is before you, for Mystery is no more." He meant that ideological manacles were to be cast away.[45] Isaiah 42 was the most well-thumbed part of the Hebrew Bible for the Atlantic proletariat; these passages would have been instantly recognizable to the Afro-Baptists of Savannah, the Iroquois followers of Joseph Brant, the worshipers of the Free African Society in Philadelphia, George Liele's congregation in Kingston, or the "Tom Paine Methodists" of Sheffield. They would have known about jubilee, universalism, and Isaiah's appeal to "you that sail the sea, and all the sea-creatures, and you that inhabit the coasts and islands." These people had affected Blake himself, who in 1793 had expressed his hopes of freedom through an African torture victim in a South American colony. Yet ten years later he could ask in the song "Jerusalem," an unofficial anthem in the English-speaking world,

> *And did those feet in ancient time*
> *Walk upon England's mountains green?*
> *And was the holy Lamb of God*
> *On England's pleasant pastures seen?*

The world had been different ten years earlier, when freedom was not merely *English.*

"Seize the Fire"

The years 1790–1792 were a revolutionary moment. Egalitarian, multi-ethnic conceptions of humanity had not evolved in isolation, but rather through solidarity and connection, within and among social movements and individuals. Blake had certainly crossed paths with Equiano (perhaps their mutual acquaintance Cugoano introduced them). The L.C.S. published a cheap edition of the *Ruins,* which Hardy carried in his pocket. Blake studied Volney. The friendship of Olaudah Equiano and Thomas and Lydia Hardy proved that Atlantic combinations—African and Scot, Englishwoman and African American man—were powerful and of historic significance. Volney demonstrated the power of laughter and the centrality of Africa, to civilization in general and to the struggle between Privileged Class and People in particular. Blake embodied the anamnesis of seventeenth-century radicalism and insisted that the liberation of the imprisoned and the enslaved was necessary to all freedom struggles. All showed that the early 1790s were an expansive time for redefining what it meant to be a human being. But that time would not last.

When casualties began to mount after the British expeditions against Haiti in 1795–96, panic—and racism—spread through society. This was, as we have seen, the very moment when the biological category of race was being formed and disseminated in Britain and America, and no less the moment of the formation of the political and economic category of class. Organizations such as the L.C.S. would eventually make their peace with the nation, as the working class became national, *English.* With the rise of pan-Africanism, the people in diaspora became a noble *race* in exile. The three friends became unthinkable within ethnic and nationalist historiography. Volney disappeared from radical scholarship, except among the pan-Africanists and "Ethiopianists" who kept him in print.[46] What began as repression thus evolved into mutually exclusive narratives that have hidden our history.

English sailors and commoners wanted to stay in Bermuda rather than sail on to Virginia, and some, after they got there, deserted to Algonquian villages. Diggers built communes upon the "earthly treasury" on George's Hill as the light shone in Buckinghamshire. Resistance to slavery extended from Putney Common to the estuarial waters of the river

Gambia. Renegades who fought with Bacon against slavery in Virginia escaped to the swampy commons of Roanoke. Pirate rovers of the deep hindered the advance of West African slaving and offered occasional refuge. The outcasts gathered at John Hughson's tavern in New York for laughter and hospitality. Black preachers searched the Atlantic for a place to build a new Jerusalem. Sheffield cutlers pocketed the "wasters." Colonel Edward Marcus Despard redistributed land in Belize. Elizabeth Campbell staged a little jubilee in Jamaica. The mutineers escaped the regimen of the *Bounty* for the beautiful ecology and people of Tahiti. One of them, Peter Heywood, his legs covered with tattoos, composed a poem, "Dream," in praise of the "beauteous morals," simplicity, and generosity of the friendships he formed in Tahiti, contrasting them with the expropriation, exploitation, and possessive individualism of his own civilization. He would have gazed at the sky to see the southern constellation of stars known as the Hydra, the ancient sign of navigators, preceding even the agrarian signals of the Nile for the wanderers of the planet. To do this he would have sat not quite on the ground, but upon the root of the breadfruit tree, the nourishing commons of the Pacific. He would have meditated, in that hopeful moment of 1791, like Thomas and Lydia Hardy, Toussaint L'Ouverture, Wolfe Tone, Constantin François Volney, Edward and Catherine Despard, and William Blake—but only Heywood sat in the Pacific. Captain William Bligh used Pacific breadfruit to support Atlantic slavery, and he had Heywood captured and tried for his life. The globalizing powers have a long reach and endless patience. Yet the planetary wanderers do not forget, and they are ever ready from Africa to the Caribbean to Seattle to resist slavery and restore the commons.

Tyger Tyger, burning bright,
In the forests of the night,
What immortal hand or eye,
Could frame thy fearful symmetry?

In what distant deeps or skies
Burnt the fire of thine eyes!
On what wings dare he aspire?
What the hand, dare seize the fire?

*Detail from "A New Map of the World According to Mercators projection,
Shewing the Course of Capt Cowleys Voyage Round it." Captain William Hacke,
ed.,* A Collection of Original Voyages *(1699). Named after the Flemish cartographer Gerardus Mercator, who designed it in 1569, the projection is formed as if a
cylinder of paper were slid over the globe, touching it only at the equator, with area
and direction projected accordingly upon the paper. The projection enlarges the
sizes of European countries relative to those closer to the equator, such as African
or Caribbean nations. This distortion flattered the imperialist imagination of
European globalizers while it permitted navigators to plot their bearings with
straight lines. The many-headed hydra thrived against such a mapping.*

Notes

Introduction

1. Stephen B. Baxter, "William III as Hercules: The Political Implications of Court Culture," in Lois G. Schwoerer ed., *The Revolution of 1688–1689: Changing Perspectives* (Cambridge: Cambridge University Press, 1992).

2. Frank H. Sommer, "Emblem and Device: The Origin of the Great Seal of the U.S.," *Art Quarterly* 24 (1961): 57–76, esp. 65–67. Also Gaillard Hunt, *The History of the Seal of the United States* (Washington D. C., 1909), 9.

3. Mauricius quoted in Richard Price, ed., *To Slay the Hydra: Dutch Colonial Perspectives on the Saramaka Wars* (Ann Arbor, Mich.: Karoma, 1983), 15.

4. Andrew Ure, *The Philosophy of Manufactures: Or, an Exposition of the Scientific, Moral; and Commercial Economy of the Factory System of Great Britain* (London, 1835), 367.

5. Cotton Mather, *Magnalia Christi Americana* (London, 1702), book 7.

Chapter One

1. William Strachey, *A True Reportory of the Wreck and Redemption of Sir Thomas Gates, Knight, upon and from the Islands of the Bermudas* (London, 1625), and Silvester Jourdain, *A Discovery of the Bermudas, Otherwise Called the Isle of Devils* (London, 1610), both republished in Louis B. Wright, ed., *A Voyage to Virginia in 1609* (Charlottesville, Va.: University of Virginia Press, 1964), 4–14, 105–7; *A True Declaration of the Estate of the Colonie in Virginia* (London, 1610), republished in Peter Force, comp., *Tracts and Other Papers Relating Principally to the Origin, Settlement, and Progress of the Colonies in North America, from the Discovery of the Country to the Year 1776* (1836; reprint, Gloucester, Mass.: Peter Smith, 1963), 3:14, 20.

2. Jourdain, *Discovery of the Bermudas*, 106.

3. Samuel Purchas, *Hakluytus Posthumus, or Purchas His Pilgrimes, Contayning a History of the World in Sea Voyages and Lande Travells by Englishmen and Others* (Glasgow: MacLehose and Sons, 1906), 16:111–12. The cahow (or cohow or cohoo), which flourished on Bermuda in the early seventeenth century, is now almost extinct.

4. Jourdain, *A Discovery of the Bermudas*, 109; Strachey, *A True Reportory*, 40; John Smith, *The Generall Historie of Virginia, New England, and the Summer Isles* (1624), in Edward Arber, ed., *Travels and Works of Captain John Smith, President of Virginia, and Admiral of New England, 1580–1631* (New York: Burt Franklin, 1910), 2:633, 637.

5. Quoted in Alexander Brown, ed., *Genesis of the United States* (Boston: Houghton Mifflin, 1890), 1:86–87.

6. Robert Rich, *Newes From Virginia, The Lost Flocke Triumphant* (London, 1610), republished in Wesley F. Craven, ed., *A Good Speed to Virginia (1609) and Newes From Virginia (1610)* (New York: Scholars Facsimiles and Reprints, 1937); *True Declaration*, 14, 20.

7. [Richard Johnson], *Nova Britannia: Offering Most Excellent fruites by Planting in Virginia* (London, 1609), republished in Force, *Tracts and Other Papers*, 1:8; "The Relation of Lord De-La-Ware, 1611," in Lyon Gardiner Tyler, ed., *Narratives of Early Virginia, 1606–1625* (New York: Charles Scribner's Sons, 1907), 213.

8. Strachey, *A True Reportory*, 41; George Percy, "A Trewe Relacyon of the Procedings and Ocurrentes of Momente wch have hapned in Virginia (1612)," *Tyler's Quarterly Historical and Genealogical Magazine* 3 (1921–22): 260–82 (quotation on 269); Emanuel van Meteren in John Parker, *Van Meteren's Virginia, 1607–1612* (Minneapolis: University of Minnesota Press, 1961), 67; Edmund S. Morgan, *American Slavery, American Freedom: The Ordeal of Colonial Virginia* (New York: W. W. Norton, 1975), 73; J. Frederick Fausz, "An 'Abundance of Blood Shed on Both Sides': England's First Indian War, 1609–1614," *Virginia Magazine of History and Biography* 98 (1990): 55–56.

9. On the *Mayflower*, Hopkins insisted that the magistrate's powers were limited and that the passengers, once ashore, were entitled to follow "their owne libertie." In this instance his protest led not to a sentence of death but to the formation of the Mayflower Compact, the Pilgrims' constitutional framework of civil self-government. See Captain Thomas Jones, "The Journal of the Ship Mayflower," in Azel Ames, ed., *The "Mayflower" and Her Log* (Boston: Houghton Mifflin, 1907), 254–58; Charles Edward Banks, *The English Ancestry and Homes of the Pilgrim Fathers* (Baltimore: Genealogical Publishing Company, 1968), 61–64.

10. Evidence about the intrigues comes from Strachey, *True Reportory*, and J. Smith, *General Historie*, 638, 640, where it is noted that conflict developed among the three who decided to remain on the island.

11. Investors in England continued to complain of "the revels and perpetuall Christmas kept [by settlers] in their Sommer Islands." See Edmund Howe, *Annals of John Stowe* (London, 1614), 942 (quotation); *True Declaration*, 21; Strachey, *True Reportory*, 87; Henry Wilkinson, *The Adventurers of Bermuda: A History of the Island from its Discovery until the Dissolution of the Somers Island Company in 1684* (London: Oxford University Press, 1933), 87.

12. Victor Kiernan, *Shakespeare: Poet and Citizen* (London: Verso, 1993); Robert Ralston Cawley, "Shakespeare's Use of the Voyagers in *The Tempest,*" *Publications of the Modern Language Association* 41 (1926): 688–726. Many scholars agree that Shakespeare read Strachey's account in manuscript soon after it was written in 1610. Its publication was delayed until 1625 because the leaders of the Virginia Company feared that the tales of resistance would discourage further investment.

13. Wesley Frank Craven, "An Introduction to the History of Bermuda," *William and Mary Quarterly*, 2d ser., 17 (1937): 182.

14. Wesley Frank Craven, *Dissolution of the Virginia Company: The Failure of a Colonial Experiment* (Gloucester, Mass.: Peter Smith, 1932; reprint, 1964), 24.

15. [Johnson], *Nova Britannia*, 10; Raphe Hamor, *A True Discourse of the Present Estate of Virginia and the successe of the affaires there till the 18 of Iune 1614* (London, 1615), 19; Brown, *Genesis*, 1:252; Rich, *Newes from Virginia;* [Richard Johnson], *New Life of Virginea: Declaring the Former Successe and Present State of that Plantation, Being the Second part of Nova Britannia* (London, 1612), republished in Force, comp., *Tracts and Other Papers*, 1:10.

16. Karl Marx, *Capital*, ed. Dona Torr, vol. 1, chap. 26, "The Secret of Primitive Accumulation." J. R. Wordie has estimated that 2 percent of England's land was enclosed in the sixteenth century; 24 percent in the seventeenth century; 13 percent in the eighteenth century; and 11.6 percent in the nineteenth century. See his "The Chronology of English Enclosure, 1500–1914," *Economic History Review*, 2d ser., 36 (1983): 483–505. See also Roger B. Manning, *Village Revolts: Social Protest and Popular Disturbances in England, 1509–1640* (Oxford: Oxford University Press, 1988), 92; E. K. Chambers, *William Shakespeare: A Study of Facts and Problems* (London: Sidgwick and Jackson, 1925), 2:144–52.

17. William Harrison, in his *The Description of England* (1587; reprint, ed. Georges Edelen, Ithaca, N.Y.: Cornell University Press, 1968), reports (page 193) that some seventy-two thousand rogues were hanged during the reign of Henry VIII.

18. A. V. Judges, ed., *The Elizabethan Underworld: A Collection of Tudor and Early Stuart Tracts and Ballads* (New York: E. P. Dutton, 1930); Gamini Salgado, *The Elizabethan Underworld* (London: J. M. Dent, 1977).

19. A. L. Beier, *Masterless Men: The Vagrancy Problem in England, 1560–1640* (London: Methuen, 1986), 4; Manning, *Village Revolts*, 208.

20. Karl Marx and Frederick Engels, "The German Ideology" (1845–46), in Marx and Engels, *Collected Works* (New York: International Publishers, 1976), 5:69.

21. Christopher Hill, "The Many-Headed Monster," in *Change and Continuity in Seventeenth-Century England* (Cambridge, Mass.: Harvard University Press, 1974), 189; Bacon, "Of Seditions and Troubles," in *The Essayes or Counsels, Civill and Morall*, ed. Michael Kiernan (Cambridge, Mass.: Harvard University Press, 1985), 45; Beier, *Masterless Men*, 161–64; A. Roger Ekirch, *Bound for America: The Transportation of British Convicts to the Colonies, 1718–1775* (Oxford: Clarendon Press, 1987), 8.

22. Robert Gray, *A Good Speed to Virginia* (London, 1609), republished in Craven, ed., *A Good Speed to Virginia and Newes From Virginia*, 7.

23. In composing Gonzalo's speech, Shakespeare drew heavily on Michel de Montaigne's essay "Of Canibals," which was written in 1579 and translated into English in 1603. The word *cannibal*, many believe, is a corruption of "Carib," the name of

the Indians who fiercely resisted European encroachment in the Americas and who were rewarded for their efforts with a lasting image of flesh-eating monstrosity. Montaigne, however, turned the image on its head, praising the courage, simplicity, and virtue of those routinely called "savage" by many Europeans. See *The Essays of Michel de Montaigne*, ed. Jacob Zeitlin (New York: Alfred A. Knopf, 1934), 1:178–90.

24. Ronald Hutton, *The Rise and Fall of Merry England: The Ritual Year, 1400–1700* (Oxford: Oxford University Press, 1996); A. Feuillerat and G. Feuillerat, eds., *Documents Relating to the Revels at Court in the Time of King Edward VI and Queen Mary* (Louvain: A. Uystpruyst, 1914), 89. See also Sandra Billington, *Mock Kings in Medieval Society and Renaissance Drama* (Oxford: Clarendon Press, 1991) and Hal Rammel, *Nowhere in America: The Big Rock Candy Mountain and Other Comic Utopias* (Urbana and Chicago: University of Illinois Press, 1990). For a satire of plebeian traditions of the world turned upside down by a contemporary of Shakespeare, see [Joseph Hall], *Mundus Alter et Idem* (1605), reprinted as *Another World and Yet the Same*, trans. John Millar Wands (New Haven: Yale University Press, 1981).

25. Gray, *A Good Speed to Virginia*, 19; William Strachey, *The Historie of Travell into Virginia Britania* (London, 1612), reprint ed. Louis B. Wright and Virginia Freund (London: Hakluyt Society, 1953), 92; "The Voyage of Sir Henry Colt" (1631), in V. T. Harlow, ed., *Colonising Expeditions to the West Indies and Guiana, 1623–1667*, 2d ser., no. 56 (London: Hakluyt Society, 1925), 93. We are indebted here to William Brandon, *New Worlds for Old: Reports from the New World and Their Effect on the Development of Social Thought in Europe, 1500–1800* (Athens, Ohio: Ohio University Press, 1986), chap. 1.

26. Montaigne, "Of Canibals," in *Essays*, 1:181. Montaigne drew upon Andre Thevet, *Singularitez de la France Anarctique* (1558), and especially on Jean de Lery, *Histoire d'un Voyage Fait en la Terre du Bresil* (1578).

27. Cawley, "Shakespeare's Use of the Voyagers," 703–5; Kipling quoted in Charles Mills Gayley, *Shakespeare and the Founders of Liberty in America* (New York: Macmillan, 1917), 74.

28. Strachey, *Historie of Travell*, 24, 26; Hamor, *A True Discourse*, 16, 23–24; Sumner Chilton Powell, *Puritan Village: The Formation of a New England Town* (New York: Doubleday, 1963).

29. J. Smith, *General Historie*, 638–39; Parker, *Van Meteren's Virginia*, 67.

30. Alden T. Vaughan and Virginia Mason Vaughan, *Shakespeare's Caliban: A Cultural History* (Cambridge: Cambridge University Press, 1991). See also Ronald Takaki, "The Tempest in the Wilderness: The Racialization of Savagery," *Journal of American History* 79 (1992): 892–912, and the exchange involving Vaughan, J. R. Pole, and Takaki, letters to the editor, *Journal of American History* 80 (1993): 764–72.

31. Chambers, *William Shakespeare*, 2:334–35.

32. Peter Fryer, *Staying Power: The History of Black People in Britain* (London: Pluto,

1984), 6–7; C. H. Herford, Percy Simpson, and Evelyn Simpson, eds., *Ben Jonson* (Oxford: Clarendon Press, 1941), 7:173; Walter Raleigh, *The Discovery of the Large, Rich and Beautiful Empire of Guiana* (1596), in Gerald Hammond, ed., *Sir Walter Raleigh: Selected Writings* (London: Fyfield Books, 1984), 98; K. G. Davies, *The Royal African Company* (New York: Atheneum, 1970), 1, 9; R. Porter, "The Crispe Family and the African Trade in the Seventeenth Century," *Journal of African History* 9 (1968): 57–58; Ira Berlin, *Many Thousands Gone: The First Two Centuries of Slavery in North America* (Cambridge, Mass.: Harvard University Press, 1998), chap. 1.

33. Kenneth R. Andrews, *The Spanish Caribbean: Trade and Plunder, 1530–1630* (New Haven: Yale University Press, 1978), 141.

34. *True Declaration,* 9; "Instruccons orders and constitucons . . . issued to Sir Thomas Gates Knight Governor of Virginia" (1609), in Susan Myra Kingsbury, ed., *The Records of the Virginia Company of London* (Washington, D.C.: Government Printing Office, 1933), 3:16.

35. W. G. Perrin, ed., *Boteler's Dialogues* (London: Navy Records Society, 1929), 16; Manning, *Village Revolts,* 199, 207–10. John Cordy Jeaffreson, *Middlesex County Records* (London, 1887), 2:xvii; Michael R. Watts, *The Dissenters: From the Reformation to the French Revolution* (Oxford: Clarendon Press, 1978); John Nichols, ed., *The Progresses, Processions, and Magnificent Festivities of King James the First* (London, 1828), 1:69.

36. Michael Roberts, "The Military Revolution," in *Essays in Swedish History* (London: Weidenfeld and Nicolson, 1967), 195–225; Geoffrey Parker, *The Military Revolution: Military Innovation and the Rise of the West, 1500–1800* (Cambridge: Cambridge University Press, 1988), 18–22.

37. Wilkinson, *Adventurers of Bermuda,* 65, 114; John Pory, Secretary of Virginia, to Sir Dudley Carlton, in Lyon Gardiner Tyler, ed., *Narratives of Early Virginia, 1606–1625* (New York: Charles Scribner's Sons, 1907), 283 (second quotation); Darrett B. Rutman, "The Historian and the Marshal: A Note on the Background of Sir Thomas Dale," *Virginia Magazine of History and Biography* 68 (1960): 284–94, and "The Virginia Company and Its Military Regime," in *The Old Dominion: Essays for Thomas Perkins Abernathy* (Charlottesville, Va.: University of Virginia Press, 1964), 1–20. See also Stephen Saunders Webb, *The Governors-General: The English Army and the Definition of the Empire, 1569–1681* (Chapel Hill, N.C.: University of North Carolina Press, 1979), 5–6, 67, 78, 437.

38. *True Declaration,* 15; Percy, "A Trewe Relacyon," 67; John Smith, *A Map of Virginia* (1612), in Philip L. Barbour, ed., *The Jamestown Voyages under the First Charter, 1606–1609* (Cambridge: Cambridge University Press, 1969), 3:333; Henry Spelman, "Relation of Virginea" (c. 1613), in Arber, ed., *Travels and Works,* 1:ciii; Fausz, "Abundance of Blood Shed," 55–56; Nicholas Canny, "The Permissive Frontier: The Problem of Social Control in English Settlements in Ireland and Virginia, 1550–1650," in K. R. Andrews, N. P. Canny, and P. E. H. Hair, eds., *The Westward Enterprise: English Ac-*

tivities in Ireland, the Atlantic, and America, 1480–1650 (Detroit: Wayne State University Press, 1979), 32 (Smith quoted). See also Canny's *The Elizabethan Conquest of Ireland: A Pattern Established, 1565–1576* (New York: Harper and Row, 1976).

39. William Strachey, comp., *For the Colony in Virginea Britania: Lawes Divine, Morall and Martiall, etc.,* ed. David Flaherty (Charlottesville, Va.: University of Virginia Press, 1969); Craven, *Dissolution of the Virginia Company,* 32; Wilkinson, *Adventurers of Bermuda,* 65; J. Smith, *Generall Historie,* 654, 666 (quotation); Morgan, *American Slavery, American Freedom,* 79–81; Rutman, "The Historian and the Marshal," 15; Stephen Greenblatt, "Martial Law in the Land of Cockaigne," in *Shakespearean Negotiations: The Circulation of Social Energy in Renaissance England* (Berkeley, Calif.: University of California Press, 1988), 129–63.

40. Smith, *A Map of Virginia,* 2:370; Percy, "A Trewe Relacyone," 266; Helen C. Rountree, *The Powhatan Indians of Virginia: Their Traditional Culture* (Norman, Okla.: University of Oklahoma Press, 1989), and *Pocahantas's People: The Powhatan Indians of Virginia through Four Centuries* (Norman, Okla.: University of Oklahoma Press, 1990). See also Kirkpatrick Sale, *The Conquest of Paradise: Christopher Columbus and the Columbian Legacy* (New York: Alfred A. Knopf, 1990), 271, 301; James Axtell, "The White Indians of Colonial America," *William and Mary Quarterly,* 3d ser., 32 (1975): 55–88. Rountree (*The Powhatan Indians of Virginia,* 87) calls Powhatan society an "incipient class system," but the evidence for this is unpersuasive. What minimal social distinctions there were did not grow out of differentiation of economic function or property holding, but rather were based on hunting ability or capacity for leadership.

41. On Markham (or Marcum), see [Captain Gabriel Archer?], *A relatyon . . . written . . . by a gent. of ye Colony* (1607), in Barbour, ed., *Jamestown Voyages,* 1:82; J. Frederick Fausz, "Middlemen in Peace and War: Virginia's Earliest Indian Interpreters, 1608–1632," *Virginia Magazine of History and Biography* 95 (1987): 42.

42. Percy, "A Trewe Relacyon," 280.

43. J. Smith, *General Historie,* 646–48; Craven, "Introduction to the History of Bermuda," 177.

Chapter Two

1. Joyce Appleby, *Economic Thought and Ideology in Seventeenth-Century England* (Princeton, N.J.: Princeton University Press, 1978), 132.

2. Stephen B. Baxter, "William III as Hercules: The Political Implications of Court Culture," in Lois G. Schwoerer, ed., *The Revolution of 1688–1689: Changing Perspectives* (Cambridge: Cambridge University Press, 1992), 95–106.

3. Francis Bacon, *Of the Wisdom of the Ancients* (1609).

4. Katharine Park and Lorraine J. Daston, "Unnatural Conception: The Study of

Monsters in Sixteenth- and Seventeenth-Century France and England," *Past & Present* 92 (1981).

5. Against Charles Tilly, whose view of European proletarianization emphasizes "natural" increases in fertility, ignores enclosure, and occludes terror, we return to the interpretation of Marx, who says that expropriation is "written in the annals of mankind in letters of blood and fire." Indeed, the branding of the recalcitrant (with letters made from the admixture of blood and fire) was part of the terror. Where Tilly ignores slavery, Marx writes, "It is a notorious fact that conquest, enslavement, robbery, murder, in short, force, played the greatest part." Charles Tilly, *As Sociology Meets History* (New York: Academic Press, 1981), chap. 7, and "Demographic Origins of the European Proletariat," in David Levine, ed., *Proletarianization and Family History* (New York: Academic Press, 1984).

6. *On the Spirit of Patriotism* (1736).

7. *Northern Star* (1838), quoted in Gareth Stedman-Jones, *Languages of Class: Studies in English Working-Class History, 1832–1982* (Cambridge: Cambridge University Press, 1983), 104.

8. C. Osborne Ward, *The Ancient Lowly: A History of the Ancient Working People from the Earliest Known Period to the Adoption of Christianity by Constantine* (Chicago, 1888), 1:39.

9. George Jackson, *Soledad Brother: The Prison Letters* (New York: Bantam, 1970), 123. H. N. Brailsford, *The Levellers and the English Revolution* (Palo Alto, Calif.: Stanford University Press, 1961); also Norah Carlin, "Liberty and Fraternities in the English Revolution: The Politics of London Artisans' Protests, 1635–1659," *International Review of Social History* 39 (1994): 252; George Unwin, *Industrial Organization in the Sixteenth and Seventeenth Centuries* (Oxford: Clarendon Press, 1904), 207–10; Swift, *On the Wretched Condition of Ireland* (1729); James Connolly, *Erin's Hope . . . The End & The Means* (Dublin, 1909); Cyril Brigg's *Crusader*, April 1921; Nelson Mandela's closing address to the African National Congress, July 1991.

10. Robert Albion, *Forests and Seapower: The Timber Problem of the Royal Navy, 1652–1862* (Cambridge, Mass.: Harvard University Press, 1926), 127.

11. [Richard Johnson], *Nova Britannia: Offering Most Excellent fruites by Planting in Virginia* (London, 1609), republished in Peter Force, comp., *Tracts and Other Papers Relating Principally to the Origin, Settlement, and Progress of the Colonies in North America, From the Discovery of the Country to the Year 1776* (1836; reprint, Gloucester, Mass.: Peter Smith, 1963), 1:14; David Freeman Hawke, *Everyday Life in Early America* (New York: Harper and Row, 1988), 15; Charles F. Carroll, *The Timber Economy of Puritan New England* (Providence, R. I.: Brown University Press, 1973), 54; Patricia Seed, *Ceremonies of Possession in Europe's Conquest of the New World, 1492–1640* (Cambridge: Cambridge University Press, 1995), 19–23.

12. *Polyolbion* (1613). Michael Williams, *The Draining of the Somerset Levels* (Cam-

bridge: Cambridge University Press, 1970); Joan Thirsk, ed., *The Agrarian History of England and Wales*, vol. 5, *1640–1750: Agrarian Change* (Cambridge: Cambridge University Press, 1985), 323.

13. Jeremy Purseglove, *Taming the Flood: A History and Natural History of Rivers and Wetlands* (Oxford: Oxford University Press, 1988); Oliver Rackham, *The History of the Countryside* (London: J. M. Dent, 1986), 390; Keith Lindley, *Fenland Riots and the English Revolution* (London: Heineman, 1982), 34, 38, 72, 77.

14. Rackham, *History of the Countryside*; see also Raymond Williams, *The Country and the City* (New York: Oxford University Press, 1975), 32, 48.

15. John Merrington, "Town and Country in the Transition to Capitalism," *New Left Review*, no. 93 (September–October 1975).

16. Adam Ferguson, *An Essay on the History of Civil Society* (Edinburgh, 1767).

17. *New Life of Virginea: Declaring the Former Successe and Present State of that Plantation* (London, 1612), republished in Force, comp., *Tracts and Other Papers*, 1:14; A. W. Lawrence, *Trade Castles and Forts of West Africa* (Palo Alto, Calif.: Stanford University Press, 1964), 293.

18. J. M. Postma, *The Dutch in the Atlantic Slave Trade, 1600–1815* (Cambridge: Cambridge University Press, 1990), 158.

19. "The Woman's Brawl," in *Samuel Pepys' Penny Merriments*, ed. Roger Thompson (New York: Columbia University Press, 1976), 247–52.

20. Bridget Hill, *Women, Work, and Sexual Politics in Eighteenth-Century England* (Oxford: Blackwell, 1989), 103ff.

21. Anna Davin, *Growing Up Poor: Home, School, and Street in London, 1870–1914* (London: Rivers Oram Press, 1996), 186–89.

22. *Man: A Paper for Ennobling the Species*, no. 25 (18 June 1755).

23. E. P. Thompson, *Customs in Common* (London: Merlin Press, 1991), and R. H. Tawney, *The Agrarian Problem in the Sixteenth Century* (London: Longman, 1912).

24. William Fennor, *The Counter's Commonwealth; Or, A Voyage made to an Infernal Island* (London, 1617); Historical Manuscript Commission, *Rutland MSS*, 1:334; J. A. Sharpe, *Crime in Early Modern England, 1550–1750* (London: Longman, 1984), 150; Pieter Spierenburg, *The Prison Experience: Disciplinary Institutions and Their Inmates in Early Modern Europe* (New Brunswick, N.J.: Rutgers University Press, 1991).

25. *Taylor's Travels of Hamburgh in Germanie* (1616) and *The Praise and Vertue of a Jayle and Jaylers with the most excellent mysterie and necessary use of all sorts of Hanging*, in *All the Works of John Taylor the Water Poet 1630* (facsimile edition, London, 1977).

26. J. S. Cockburn, *A History of English Assizes, 1558–1714* (Cambridge: Cambridge University Press, 1972), 98; King James the First, *Daemonologie in Forme of a Dialogue, Diuided into three Bookes* (1597), ed. G. B. Harrison (London: John Lane, 1924); Sil-

via Federici, "The Great Witch Hunt," *The Maine Scholar* 1 (1988): 31–52; Frederic A. Youngs, Jr., *The Proclamations of the Tudor Queens* (Cambridge: Cambridge University Press, 1976), 76; Edmund Spenser, *A View of the Present State of Ireland* (1596), ed. W. L. Renwick (Oxford: Clarendon Press, 1970), 63.

27. *The Black Dog of Newgate* was first published in 1596; it was published in another edition in 1638 as *The Discovery of a London Monster.*

28. A. V. Judges, ed., *The Elizabethan Underworld: A Collection of Tudor and Early Stuart Tracts and Ballads* (New York: E. P. Dutton, 1930), 506–7.

29. Spenser, *View of the Present State of Ireland.*

30. Michael Taussig, *Shamanism, Colonialism, and the Wild Man: A Study in Terror and Healing* (Chicago: University of Chicago Press, 1987).

31. Sir George Peckham, "A true Report of the late discoveries, and possession taken in the right of the Crowne of England of the Newfound Lands, By that valiant and worthy Gentleman, Sir Humfrey Gilbert Knight," in Richard Hakluyt, ed., *The Principal Navigations, Voyages, Traffiques & Discoveries of the English Nation* (1589; reprint, New York: AMS Press, Inc., 1965), 3:102–3, 112; A. L. Beier, *Masterless Men: The Vagrancy Problem in England, 1560–1640* (London: Methuen, 1985), 150.

32. Cockburn, *English Assizes,* 126; M. Oppenheim, ed., *The Naval Tracts of Sir William Monson* (London: Navy Records Society, 1923), 4:109.

33. James Horn, "Servant Emigration to the Chesapeake in the Seventeenth Century," in Thad W. Tate and David L. Ammerman, eds., *The Chesapeake in the Seventeenth Century* (New York: W. W. Norton, 1979), 72; Richard S. Dunn, "Servants and Slaves: The Recruitment and Employment of Labor in Colonial America," in J. R. Pole and Jack P. Greene, *Colonial British America: Essays in Early Modern History* (Baltimore: Johns Hopkins University Press, 1984); Abbot Emerson Smith, *Colonists in Bondage: White Servitude and Convict Labor in America, 1607–1776* (New York: W. W. Norton, 1947), 8–12, 13, 16; Eric Williams, *Capitalism and Slavery* (New York: Capricorn Books, 1966), 19.

34. Scott Christianson, *With Liberty for Some: 500 Years of Imprisonment in America* (Boston: Northeastern University Press, 1998), 16, 18.

35. Jill Sheppard, *The "Redlegs" of Barbados: Their Origins and History* (Millwood, N.Y.: KTO Press, 1977), 12; Carl and Roberta Bridenbaugh, *No Peace beyond the Line: The English in the Caribbean, 1627–1690* (New York: Oxford University Press), 27; *A Publication of Guiana Plantation* (London, 1632), quoted in Smith, *Colonists in Bondage,* 285–86; Rafael Semmes, *Crime and Punishment in Early Maryland* (Baltimore: Johns Hopkins University Press, 1938), 81; John Donne, "A Sermon Preached to the Honourable Company of the Virginian Plantation," in *The Sermons of John Donne,* ed. George R. Potter and Evelyn M. Simpson (Berkeley, Calif.: University of California Press, 1959), 4:272.

36. A series of riots against spirits and kidnappers in the 1640s and 1650s led to legislation

designed to regulate the servant trade and hence also to the first set of records, kept in Bristol beginning in 1654, upon which statistical analysis of the trade has been based.

37. Robert C. Johnson, "The Transportation of Vagrant Children from London to Virginia, 1618–1622," in Howard S. Reinmuth, ed., *Early Stuart Studies: Essays in Honor of David Harris Willson* (Minneapolis: University of Minnesota Press, 1970), 137–51; Walter Hart Blumenthal, *Brides from Bridewell: Female Felons Sent to Colonial America* (Rutland, Vt.: Charles E. Tuttle Co., 1962), 65, 105, 107; Smith, *Colonists in Bondage,* 69–70.

38. James Revel, *The Poor Unhappy Transported Felon's Sorrowful Account of his Fourteen Years Transportation at Virginia in America* (London, n.d.), edited by John Melville Jennings and republished in the *Virginia Magazine of History and Biography* 56 (1948): 180–94 (Jennings shows that Revel arrived in Virginia between 1656 and 1671); "The Trapanned Maiden," *Virginia Magazine of History and Biography* 4 (1896–97): 218–21.

39. [Johnson], *Nova Britannia,* republished in Force, comp., *Tracts and Other Papers,* 1:27–28, 19.

40. E. D. Pendry, *Elizabethan Prisons and Prison Scenes* (Salzburg: Institut für Englische Sprache und Literatur, 1974), 1:2, 15.

41. [Samuel Rid], *Martin Markall, beadle of Bridewell, His Defense and Answers to the Bellman of London* (London, 1610).

42. *The American Anthropologist* 90 (1988): 406.

43. Jane Ohlmeyer, "The Wars of Religion, 1603–1660," in Thomas Bartlett and Keith Jeffery, eds., *A Military History of Ireland* (Cambridge: Cambridge University Press, 1996), 168.

44. Francis Bacon, *The New Atlantis* (London, 1629).

45. P. Dan, *Histoire de la Barbarie et de ses Corsaires* (Paris, 1637), quoted in Stephen Clissold, *The Barbary Slaves* (Totowa, N.J.: Rowman and Littlefield, 1977), and Peter Lamborn Wilson, *Pirate Utopias: Moorish Corsairs and European Renegadoes* (New York: Autonomedia, 1995).

46. Thomas Harman, *A Caveat for Common Cursitors Vulgarly Called Vagabonds* (1567).

47. Page Dubois, "Subjected Bodies, Science, and the State: Francis Bacon, Torturer," in Mike Ryan and Avery Gordon, eds., *Body Politics: Disease, Desire, and the Family* (Boulder, Colo.: Westview Press, 1994), 184.

48. *Appius and Virginia* (1625–27?).

49. Brian Manning, *The English People and the English Revolution, 1640–1649* (London: Heineman, 1976), 292.

50. Anne Chambers, "The Pirate Queen of Ireland: Grace O Malley," in Jo Stanley, ed., *Bold in Her Britches: Women Pirates across the Ages* (London: HarperCollins, 1995), 104.

51. Thomas Edwards, *Gangraena, or, A Catalogue and Discovery of Many of the Errors, Heresies, Blasphemies, and pernicious practices of the Sectaries of this time* (1646–47).

52. Thomas Nashe, *The Unfortunate Traveller; Or, the Life of Jacke Wilton* (1594).

53. Edwards, *Gangraena*, 121.

54. *The Kingdomes Faithfull and Impartiall Scout*, 6–13 April 1649, in Edwards, *Gangraena*, 268.

55. *The True Informer*, 21–28 February 1646, in Edwards, *Gangraena*, 262.

56. Cyril Outerbridge Packwood, *Chained on the Rock: Slavery in Bermuda* (New York: Eliseo Torres & Sons, 1975), 85.

57. Manning, *The English People and the English Revolution*, 92. See Hobbes, *Behemoth: The History of the Causes of the Civil Wars in England*, quoted in Christopher Hibbert, *Charles I* (New York: Harper and Row, 1968), 149–50.

58. Hibbert, *Charles I*, 149–50.

Chapter Three

1. Christopher Hill, *The World Turned Upside Down: Radical Ideas during the English Revolution* (London: Penguin, 1972), and H. N. Brailsford, *The Levellers in the English Revolution* (Palo Alto, Calif.: Stanford University Press, 1961), 11.

2. Robert Brenner, *Merchants and Revolution: Commercial Change, Political Conflict, and London's Overseas Traders, 1550–1653* (Princeton, N.J.: Princeton University Press, 1993); Phyllis Mack, *Visionary Women: Ecstatic Prophecy in Seventeenth-Century England* (Berkeley, Calif.: University of California Press, 1992); and David Sacks, *The Widening Gate: Bristol and the Atlantic Economy, 1450–1700* (Berkeley, Calif.: University of California Press, 1991).

3. Nigel Smith, *Perfection Proclaimed: Language and Literature in English Radical Religion, 1640–1690* (New York: Oxford University Press, 1989), and Peter Fryer, *Staying Power: The History of Black People in Britain* (London: Pluto, 1984), have noted her remarkable presence.

4. Christopher Hill, *The English Bible and the Seventeenth-Century Revolution* (London: Viking, 1993), 200. See also C. R. Cragg, *Puritanism in the Period of the Great Persecution of 1660–1688* (Cambridge: Cambridge University Press, 1957).

5. The Broadmead Records were published by E. B. Underhill in 1847. A second edition, printed in 1865 by Nathaniel Haycroft, preserved much of the orthography, emphatic typography, capital letters, and paragraph divisions of the original. This formed the basis of a third edition, published in 1974, edited and with a long, scholarly introduction by Roger Hayden. Our analysis is based on a scrutiny of the manuscript text at the Broadmead Church in Bristol.

6. Roger Hayden, introduction to *The Records of a Church of Christ in Bristol, 1640–1687* (Bristol: Bristol Record Society, 1974).

7. Bridget Hill, *Women, Work, and Sexual Politics in Eighteenth-Century England* (Oxford: Blackwell, 1989), 133.

8. Alice Clark, *Working Life of Women in the Seventeenth Century* (London: Routledge, 1919), and Susan Dwyer Amussen, *An Ordered Society: Gender and Class in Early Modern England* (Oxford: Blackwell, 1988), 158. See also Elliot V. Brodsky, "Single Women in the London Marriage Market: Age, Status and Mobility, 1598–1619," in R. B. Outhwaite, ed., *Marriage and Society: Studies in the Social History of Marriage* (New York: St. Martin's, 1981), and P. J. P. Goldberg, *Women, Work, and Life Cycle in a Medieval Economy: Women in York and Yorkshire, c. 1300–1520* (New York: Oxford University Press, 1992).

9. Paul Bayne, *An Entire Commentary upon the Whole Epistle of the Apostle Paul to the Ephesians* (1643).

10. Nell Painter, *Sojourner Truth: A Life, a Symbol* (New York: W. W. Norton, 1996), 71.

11. A. S. P. Woodhouse, ed., *Puritanism and Liberty* (Chicago: University of Chicago Press, 1951), 103.

12. Patricia Crawford, *Women and Religion in England, 1500–1720* (London: Routledge, 1993), 123.

13. David Harris Sacks, "Bristol's 'Wars of Religion,'" in R. C. Richardson, ed., *Town and Country in the English Revolution* (Manchester: Manchester University Press, 1992), 103.

14. Hayden, introduction to *Records of a Church of Christ in Bristol,* 27:85.

15. Claire Cross, "'He-Goats Before the Flocks': A Note on the Part Played by Women in the Founding of Some Civil War Churches," in G. J. Cuming and Derek Baker, eds., *Popular Belief and Practice* (Cambridge: Ecclesiastical History Society/Cambridge University Press, 1972).

16. G. F. Nuttall, *Visible Saints; The Congregational Way, 1640–1660* (Oxford: Blackwell, 1957), 35.

17. Ian Gentles, *The New Model Army in England, Ireland, Scotland, 1645–1653* (Oxford: Blackwell, 1992), 103.

18. J. F. McGregor, "The Baptists: Fount of All Heresy," in J. F. McGregor and B. Reay, eds., *Radical Religion in the English Revolution* (New York: Oxford University Press, 1984), 44.

19. Underhill, the nineteenth-century editor, changed this to "libertinism," surely a different thing from "Libertisme," yet itself not without its advocates in the 1640s: Abiezer Coppe in *A Fiery Flying Roll,* 1:1–5, taught that God's service was "perfect freedom and pure libertinism."

20. Laurence Clarkson, *Generall Charge* (1647).

21. Edwards, *Gangraena* 3:27, 163.

22. G. F. Nuttall, *The Welsh Saints, 1640–1660* (Cardiff: University of Wales Press, 1957), 34; 1–37.

23. C. Hill, *The World Turned Upside Down*, 40.

24. Karen Kupperman, *Providence Island, 1630–1641: The other Puritan Colony* (New York: Cambridge University Press, 1993), 179. A useful overview is Elaine Forman Crane, *Ebb Tide in New England: Women, Seaports, and Social Change, 1630–1800* (Boston: Northeastern University Press, 1998).

25. *The New Law of Righteousness* (1649), 216; *The Law of Freedom* (1652), 524.

26. Lodovick Muggleton, *Joyful News from Heaven* (1658; reprinted 1854), 45.

27. N. Smith, *Perfection Proclaimed*, 2.

28. *Human Nature* (1640); *Works*, 4:40–41.

29. Woodhouse, ed., *Puritanism and Liberty*, 390–6.

30. *Eikon Basilike*, chap. 9.

31. Underhill quoted in Alfred Cave, *The Pequot War* (Amherst, Mass.: University of Massachusetts Press, 1996), 152.

32. And, "whereas the Scriptures say, That the Creator of all things is no Respecter of persons, yet this Kingly Power doth nothing else but respect persons, preferring the rich and the proud . . . ," *The Law of Freedom* (1652), 508, 530.

33. Hugh Barbour and Arthur O. Roberts, *Early Quaker Writings, 1650–1700* (Grand Rapids, Mich.: Eerdmans, 1973), 165. See also *The Quaker's Catechism* (1655).

34. John F. Mackeson, *Bristol Transported* (Bristol: Redcliffe, 1987).

35. Mack, *Visionary Women*.

36. *The Exceeding Riches of Grace Advanced* (1651 and 1658), 122–25. Barbara Ritter Dailey, "The Visitation of Sarah Wright: Holy Carnival and the Revolution of the Saints in Civil War London," *Church History* 55, no. 4 (December 1986): 449–50.

37. William Haller, *The Rise of Puritanism* (New York: Columbia University Press, 1938), 79.

38. John Saltmarsh, *Smoke in the Temple* (1600s), quoted in Woodhouse, *Puritanism and Liberty*, 179.

39. Woodhouse, ed., *Puritanism and Liberty*, 184.

40. Emery Battis, *Saints and Sectaries: Anne Hutchinson and the Antinomian Controversy in Massachusetts Bay Colony* (Chapel Hill, N.C.: University of North Carolina Press, 1962), 69.

41. Cave, *The Pequot War*, 139.

42. Carol Karlsen, *The Devil in the Shape of a Woman: Witchcraft in Colonial New England* (New York: Vintage, 1987).

43. John Winthrop, *A Short Story of the Rise, Reign, and Ruine of the Antinomians, Familists, and Libertines* (London, 1644), reprinted in David D. Hall, *The Antinomian Controversy, 1636–1638: A Documentary History*, 2d ed. (Durham, N.C.: Duke University Press, 1990), 139.

44. Ibid., 218; Edward Johnson, *Johnson's Wonder-Working Providence, 1628–1651,* ed. J. Franklin Jameson (London, 1654; reprint, New York: Charles Scribner's Sons, 1910), 124–125.

45. Silvia Federici, "The Great Witch Hunt," *The Maine Scholar* 1 (1988): 32.

46. Ibid.

47. Mack, *Visionary Women,* 123.

48. Ibid., 104; Woodhouse, ed., *Puritanism and Liberty,* 367.

49. See also Leo Damrosch, *The Sorrows of the Quaker Jesus: James Nayler and the Puritan Crackdown on the Free Spirit* (Cambridge, Mass.: Harvard University Press, 1996), 2.

50. *A Publicke Discovery of the Open Blindness of Babel's Builders* (1656).

51. *A Few Words Occassioned* (1654).

52. James Nayler, *Saul's Errand to Damascus* (London, 1653), *A Discovery of the First Wisdom* (London, 1653), *An Answer to the Book called the Perfect Pharisee* (London, 1653), 22.

53. James Nayler, *The Lamb's Warre* (1657).

54. H. N. Brailsford, *A Quaker from Cromwell's Army* (London, 1926).

55. C. Hill, *The English Bible,* 165–66; Cragg, *Puritanism in the Period of the Great Persecution.*

56. Nathaniel Ingelo, *The Perfection, Authority, and Credibility of the Holy Scripture* (1659), and *A Discourse Concerning Repentance* (1677).

57. Christopher Hill, *The Experience of Defeat: Milton and Some Contemporaries* (New York: Viking, 1984), 164.

58. Richard Ligon, *A True & Exact History of the Island of Barbadoes* (London, 1657).

59. Hilary Beckles, *A History of Barbados: From Amerindian Settlement to Nation-State* (Cambridge: Cambridge University Press, 1990), 43.

60. We see it also in Henry Jessie, who in the 1658 edition of *The Exceeding Riches of Grace Advanced* introduces Dinah as "a Moor not born in England," an ethnic marker added eleven years after the first edition of 1647.

61. Christopher Hill, *A Tinker and a Poor Man: John Bunyan and His Church, 1628–1688* (New York: Alfred A. Knopf, 1988).

62. James H. Cone, *For My People: Black Theology and the Black Church* (Maryknoll, N.Y.: Orbis, 1984), 71, commenting on Fanon.

63. Marcus Garvey, *Vanity Fair; Or the Tragedy of White Man's Justice* (1926), in Robert A. Hill and Barbara Bair, eds., *Marcus Garvey: Life and Lessons* (Berkeley, Calif.: University of California Press, 1987), 115–39.

64. Lodovick Muggleton, *The Acts of the Witnesses of The Spirit* (1699; reprinted 1764), 73–74.

65. Painter, *Sojourner Truth,* 30.

66. Andrew Hopton, ed., *Tyranipocrit Discovered with his wiles, wherewith he vanquisheth* (1649; reprint, London: Aporia Press, 1991), 29.

67. For the term "Atlantic Mountains," See Peter Linebaugh, "All the Atlantic Mountains Shook," *Labour/Le Travailleur*, no. 10 (1982): 87–121, whose title quotes William Blake's song beginning book 2 of *Jerusalem* (1804).

68. *Three Guineas* (New York: Harcourt Brace, 1938), 103.

Chapter Four

1. Daniel Lysons, *The Environs of London* (1791).

2. *A Vindication of the Army* (1647); *Short Memorials of Thomas Lord Fairfax* (1699), 104–6.

3. Dan M. Wolfe, *The Purple Testament: Life Stories of Disabled Veterans* (Garden City, N.Y.: Doubleday, 1946).

4. A. S. P. Woodhouse, ed., *Puritanism and Liberty: being the Army debates (1647–9) from the Clarke manuscripts with supplementary documents*, 1st ed. (London: Dent, 1938); and see the prefaces by Ivan Roots to the 1974 edition and to the Everyman edition of 1986.

5. After the death of Frederick Engels, Edouard Bernstein published *Socialism and Democracy in the Great English Revolution* (1895); English translation by H. J. Stenning, *Cromwell & Communism: Socialism and Democracy in the Great English Revolution* (London, 1930).

6. See Thompson's "Edgell Rickword," in *Persons & Politics* (London: Merlin, 1994).

7. "Celticus" [Aneurin Bevan], *Why Not Trust the Tories?* (London: Gollancz, 1945); Raphael Samuel, "British Marxist Historians, 1880–1980, Part One," *New Left Review* 120 (1980): 27–28.

8. Ras Makonnen, *Pan-Africanism from Within*, ed. Kenneth King (Oxford: Oxford University Press, 1973), 170.

9. Ivan Roots, ed., *Puritanism and Liberty: Being the Army Debates (1647–9)*, 3d ed. (London: Dent, 1986).

10. Scott MacRobert, *Putney and Roehampton: A Brief History* (Putney: The Putney Society, 1992). For the enclosure of Richmond Park, see Clarendon's *History of the Rebellion and Civil Wars;* Lysons, *Environs of London*, 314; Christopher Hill, *Puritanism and Revolution* (London: Secker and Warburg, 1958), 267ff.

11. Ian Gentles, *The New Model Army in England, Ireland and Scotland, 1645–1653* (Oxford: Blackwell, 1992), 35; Dan M. Wolfe, *Leveller Manifestoes of the Puritan Revolution* (New York: Nelson and Sons, 1944).

12. William Bullock, *Virginia Impartially Examined* (1649), 47.

13. Vincent Harlow, *A History of Barbados, 1625–1685* (Oxford: Clarendon Press, 1926), 300.

14. *A Remonstrance of Many Thousand Citizens* (1646).

15. E. C. Pielou, *Fresh Water* (Chicago: University of Chicago Press, 1998), 109.

16. *Taylor on Thame Isis* (1632); *A Dialogical Brief Discourse between Rainborough and Charon* (1648).

17. Vittorio Dini, *Masaniello: L'eroe e il mito* (Rome, 1995), trans. Steven Colatrella; Rosario Villari, *The Revolt of Naples*, trans. James Newell (Cambridge, Mass.: Polity Press, 1993).

18. Wolfgang Goethe, *Italian Journey* (1786–88).

19. Francis Midon, *The History of the Rise and Fall of Masaniello, the Fisherman of Naples* (1729), 95.

20. Francis Haskell, *Patrons and Painters: A Study in the Relations between Italian Art and Society in the Age of the Baroque* (New Haven, Conn.: Yale University Press, 1980), 199.

21. Midon, *Masaniello*, 199.

22. Gigliola Pagano de Divitiis, *English Merchants in Seventeenth-Century Italy*, trans. Stephen Parkin (Cambridge: Cambridge University Press, 1997); H. G. Koenigsberger, *Estates and Revolutions: Essays in Early Modern European History* (Ithaca, N.Y.: Cornell University Press, 1971).

23. James Howell, *The Exacte historie of the late Revolutions in Naples, and of their Monstrous Successes* (1650).

24. N. A. M. Rodger, *The Safeguard of the Sea: A Naval History of Britain 660–1649* (London: HarperCollins, 1998), 401.

25. John Colerus, *The Life of Benedict de Spinosa* (London, 1706).

26. James Tyrrell, *Biblioteca Politica* (1694), 3d dialogue; Locke, *First Treatise of Government* (1690), para. 79.

27. Christopher Hill, "The English Revolution and the Brotherhood of Man," in *Puritanism and Revolution: Studies in Interpretation of the English Revolution of the Seventeenth Century* (New York: Schocken Books, 1958), 123–152.

28. C. H. Firth, ed., *The Clarke Papers* (London: Camden Society, 1894), 2:153–63.

29. *Pseudodoxia Epidemica* (1646); *Works*, ed. Geoffrey Keynes, vol. 2.

30. Samuel Chidley, *A Cry against a Crying Sin: Or, a just Complaint to the Magistrates, against them who have broken the Statute Laws of God, by Killing of men merely for Theft* (London, 1652), republished in William Oldys and Thomas Park, eds., *Harleian Miscellany* (London, 1811), 8:485.

31. *An Appeale to All Englishmen*, March 1649, and *A Letter to the Lord Fairfax*, June 1649; Lewis H. Berens, *The Digger Movement in the Days of the Commonwealth* (London: Merlin, 1961); Andrew Hopton, ed., *Digger Tracts, 1649–1650* (London: Aporia Press, 1989).

32. George H. Sabine, ed., *The Works of Gerrard Winstanley* (New York: Russell and

Russell, 1965), 492. Richard Overton led the soldiers in objecting to hanging for theft in his *An Appeal from the Commons to the Free People* (1647).

33. *A New-Yeers Gift for the Parliament and Armie* (1 January 1650), in Sabine, ed., *Works*, 388; *A Mite Cast into the Common Treasury* (1649), ed. and with an introduction by Andrew Hopton (London: Aporia Press, 1989).

34. Chidley, *A Cry against a Crying Sin*, 481; Anon., *More Light Shining in Buckinghamshire* (1649); Robert Zaller, "The Debate on Capital Punishment during the English Revolution," *American Journal of Legal History* 31, no. 2 (1987): 126–44.

35. Hawke, *The Right of Dominion, and Property of Liberty* (1656), 77–78.

36. James Connolly, *Labour in Irish History* (Dublin, 1910), and Christopher Hill, "Seventeenth-Century English Radicals and Ireland," in his *A Nation of Change and Novelty: Radical Politics, Religion and Literature in Seventeenth-Century England* (London: Routledge, 1990), 133–51.

37. Chris Durston, "'Let Ireland be quiet': Opposition in England to the Cromwellian Conquest of Ireland," *History Workshop Journal* 21 (1986): 105–12; Norah Carlin, "The Levellers and the Conquest of Ireland in 1649," *Historical Journal* 22 (1987).

38. J. G. Simms, "Cromwell at Drogheda, 1649," in his *War and Politics in Ireland, 1649–1730*, ed. D. W. Hayton and Gerard O'Brien, (London: Hambledon Press, 1986), 1–10; T. W. Moody et al., eds., *A New History of Ireland* (Oxford: Clarendon Press, 1976), vol. 3, *Early Modern Ireland, 1534–1691*, 339–41.

39. Richard Bagwell, *Ireland under the Stuarts and during the Interregnum* (London: Longman, 1909–16), 2:194. C. H. Firth, *Cromwell's Army: A History of the English Soldier during the Civil Wars, the Commonwealth, and the Protectorate* (London: Methuen, 1901), 337.

40. Bagwell, *Ireland under the Stuarts*, 2:329, 330; S. R. Gardiner, "The Transplantation to Connaught," *English Historical Review* 14 (1899): 703; John Davis, *A Discovery of the True Causes why Ireland was never entirely Subdued* (1612), 169.

41. John P. Prendergast, *Cromwellian Settlement of Ireland*, 3d ed. (Dublin: Mellifont Press, 1922), 427.

42. Firth, ed., *Clarke Papers*, 2:208.

43. F. H. A. Aalen et al., *Atlas of the Irish Rural Landscape* (Toronto: University of Toronto Press, 1997), 60, 74, 80.

44. Joseph J. Williams, *Whence the "Black Irish" of Jamaica?* (New York: Dial Press, 1932), 36.

45. Theodore Allen, *The Invention of the White Race* (New York: Verso, 1994), 1:258.

46. Eogan Ruadh O' Sullivan quoted in James Clarence Mangan, *The Poets and Poetry of Munster* (Dublin, 1885), 181.

47. Robert Boyle, *The Excellency and Grounds of the Corpuscular or Mechanical Philosophy* (1674), in Mari Boas Hall, ed., *Robert Boyle on Natural Philosophy: An Essay with*

Selections from His Writings (Bloomington, Ind.: Indiana University Press, 1965), 195.

48. Richard Ligon, *A True & Exact History of the Island of Barbados* (London, 1657), 45–6.

49. George Downing to John Winthrop, Jr., 26 August 1645, in Elizabeth Donnan, *Documents Illustrative of the History of the Slave Trade to America*, vol. 1, *1441–1700* (Washington, D.C.: Carnegie Institution, 1930, 1969); George Gardyner, *A Description of the New World* (1651); Ligon, *A True & Exact History*, 86.

50. Alexander Gunkel and Jerome S. Handler, "A German Indentured Servant in Barbados in 1652: The Account of Heinrich von Uchteritz," *Journal of the Barbados Museum and Historical Society* 33 (1970): 92; George Fox, *To the Ministers, Teachers, and Priests (So called, and so Stileing your Selves) in Barbados* (London, 1672), 5; Gary A. Puckrein, *Little England: Plantation Society and Anglo-Barbadian Politics, 1627–1700* (New York: New York University Press, 1984), 98, 106.

51. *Great Newes from Barbados, or, a True and Faithful Account of the Grand Conspiracy of the Negroes against the English* (London, 1676), 6–7.

52. David Watts, *Man's Influence on the Vegetation of Barbados, 1627–1800* (Hull: University of Hull, 1966); Edward Kamau Brathwaite, *Mother Poem* (Oxford: Oxford University Press, 1977); Hilary McD. Beckles, *White Servitude and Black Slavery in Barbados, 1627–1715* (Knoxville, Tenn.: University of Tennessee Press, 1989), 5, 64, 77, 78.

53. See "Extracts of the Minute Book of the Council of Barbados (1654–9)," in the Reverend Aubrey Gwynn, ed., "Documents Relating to the Irish in the West Indies," *Analecta Hibernica* 4 (1932): 236–37; Father Andrew White, "A Briefe Relation of the Voyage unto Maryland," in Clayton Colman Hall, ed., *Narratives of Early Maryland, 1633–1684* (New York: Charles Scribner's Sons, 1910), 34.

54. "Extracts of the Minute Book," in Gwynn, ed., "Documents Relating to the Irish," 234; Beckles, *White Servitude*, 111.

55. *The Negro's and Indians Advocate* (1680).

56. Puckrein, *Little England*, 113; Beckles, *White Servitude*, 168–76.

57. K. G. Davies, *The Royal African Company* (New York: Atheneum, 1970), 1; John C. Appleby, "A Guinea Venture, c. 1657: A Note on the Early English Slave Trade," *The Mariner's Mirror* 79, no. 1 (February 1993): 84–88; George Frederick Zook, *The Company of Royal Adventurers Trading into Africa* (1919; reprint, New York: Negro University Press, 1969), 6; J. M. Gray, *A History of the Gambia* (1940; reprint, New York: Barnes and Noble, 1966), 31; Davies, *Royal African Company*, chap. 1; David Eltis, "The British Transatlantic Slave Trade before 1714: Annual Estimates of Volume and Direction," in Robert L. Paquette and Stanley Engerman, eds., *The Lesser Antilles in the Age of European Expansion* (Gainesville, Fla.: University Press of Florida, 1996), 182–205.

58. Léopold Senghor, *On African Socialism,* trans. Mercer Cook (New York: Praeger, 1967).

59. Richard Jobson, *The Golden Trade; Or, A Discovery of the River Gambra* (1623), 124.

60. Charlotte A. Quinn, *Mandingo Kingdoms of the Senegambia: Traditionalism, Islam, and European Expansion* (Evanston, Ill.: Northwestern University Press, 1972), 7–8; Abdallah Laroui, *The History of the Maghrib: An Interpretative Essay* (Princeton, N.J.: Princeton University Press, 1977); Jamil M. Abun-Nasr, *A History of the Maghrib* (Cambridge: Cambridge University Press, 1971).

61. J. W. Blake, "The Farm of the Guinea Trade," in H. A. Cronne, T. W. Moody, and D. B. Quinn, eds., *Essays in British and Irish History in Honour of James Eadie Todd* (London: Frederick Muller, 1949), 86–106.

62. Donald R. Wright, *The World and a Very Small Place in Africa* (Armonk, N.Y.: M. E. Sharpe, 1997), 121–22; Ligon, *A True & Exact History,* 57; The Guinea Company to James Pope, 17 September 1651, in Donnan, *Documents Illustrative,* 1:128; Robert Farris Thompson, *Flash of the Spirit: African and Afro-American Art and Philosophy* (New York: Vintage, 1984), chap. 4.

63. Eliot Warburton, *Memoirs of Prince Rupert, and the Cavaliers,* vol. 3 (London, 1849), 358.

64. Donald R. Wright, *Oral Traditions from the Gambia,* vol. 1, *Mandinka "Griots,"* Ohio University Africa ser. no. 37 (1979): 104, 144.

65. Bernard Capp, *Cromwell's Navy: The Fleet and the English Revolution 1648–1660* (Oxford: Clarendon Press, 1989), 236.

66. Patrick Morrah, *Prince Rupert of the Rhine* (London: Constable, 1976), 269.

67. Richard Ollard, *Man of War: Sir Robert Holmes and the Restoration Navy* (London: Hodder and Stoughton, 1969), 89.

68. Ibid., 67–68; Donnan, *Documents Illustrative,* 177–80; Wright, *The World and a Very Small Place in Africa.*

69. *The Pleasant History of the Life of Black Tom* (1686); Roger Thompson, ed., *Samuel Pepys' Penny Merriments* (New York: Columbia University Press, 1976), 212.

70. John Towill Rutt, ed., *Diary of Thomas Burton, Esq., Member in the Parliaments of Oliver and Richard Cromwell, from 1656 to 1659* (New York: Johnson Reprint Corporation, 1974), 255.

71. Ibid., 256.

72. Ibid., 257.

73. Ibid., 259, 273, 308.

74. Ibid., 260, 262, 265, 268.

75. Ibid., 264, 270, 271, 304.

76. Christopher Hill, *The Experience of Defeat: Milton and Some Contemporaries* (New York: Viking, 1984), 285–87.

77. Richard L. Greaves, *Deliver Us from Evil: The Radical Underground in Britain, 1660–1663* (New York: Oxford University Press, 1986), 31, 38, 40, 53; Philip F. Gura, *A Glimpse of Sion's Glory: Puritan Radicalism in New England, 1620–1660* (Middletown, Conn.: Wesleyan University Press, 1984), 143.

78. Hilary McD. Beckles, "English Parliamentary Debate on 'White Slavery' in Barbados, 1659," *Journal of the Barbados Museum and Historical Society* 36 (1982): 344–52.

79. Greaves, *Deliver Us from Evil,* 33, 40, 58, 92 (quotation), 166, 229; Abbot Emerson Smith, *Colonists in Bondage: White Servitude and Convict Labor in America, 1607–1776* (New York: W. W. Norton, 1947), 170; Gura, *A Glimpse of Sion's Glory,* 4, 39, 78, 86.

80. "The Servants Plot of 1663," *Virginia Magazine of History and Biography* 15 (1908): 38–43.

81. Philip Ludwell to George Chalmers, 17 July 1671, Chalmers Collection, vol. I, f. 49; *Virginia Magazine of History and Biography* 19 (1911): 355–56; William Waller Hening, ed., *The Statutes at Large, being a Collection of all the Laws of Virginia* (1819–23; reprint, Charlottesville, Va.: University of Virginia Press, 1969), 2:509–11; 2:195; 3:398–400.

82. Joseph Douglas Deal III, *Race and Class in Colonial Virginia: Indians, Englishmen, and Africans on the Eastern Shore during the Seventeenth Century* (New York: Garland Press, 1993), chap. 3.

83. Warren M. Billings, "A Quaker in Seventeenth-Century Virginia: Four Remonstrances by George Wilson," *William and Mary Quarterly,* 3d ser., 33 (1976): 127–40.

84. "An Account of Our Late Troubles in Virginia, Written in 1676, by Mrs. An. Cotton, of Q. Creeke," in Peter Force, ed., *Tracts and Other Papers Relating Principally to the Origin, Settlement, and Progress of the Colonies in North America, from the Discovery of the Country to the Year 1776* (1836; reprint, Gloucester, Mass.: Peter Smith, 1963).

85. *Strange News from Virginia; Being a Full and True Account of the Life and Death of Nathanael Bacon, Esquire* (London, 1677).

86. "A True Narrative of the Late Rebellion in Virginia, by the Royal Commissioners," in Charles M. Andrews, ed., *Narratives of the Insurrections, 1675–1690* (New York: Charles Scribner's Sons, 1915), 140.

87. Aphra Behn, *The Widow Ranter* (1690).

88. "Defense of Col. Edward Hill," *Virginia Magazine of History and Biography* 3 (1895–96): 239; *Archives of Maryland* (Baltimore: Maryland Historical Society, 1885), 15:137; 5:153–54; 281–82; Notley to Baltimore, Chalmers Collection, Papers Relating to Virginia, vol. 1, f. 50; William Berkeley to Colonel Mason, 4 November 1676, *William and Mary Quarterly* 3 (1894–95): 163; in Andrews, ed., *Narratives of the Insurrections,* 31.

89. Riva Berleant-Schiller, "Free Labor and the Economy in Seventeenth-Century

Montserrat," *William and Mary Quarterly*, 3d ser., 46 (1989): 550; Richard S. Dunn, *Sugar and Slaves: The Rise of the Planter Class in the English West Indies 1624–1713* (Chapel Hill, N.C.: University of North Carolina Press, 1972), 244.

90. Planters in Antigua (1677), St. Kitts (1679), Barbados (1682, 1688, 1696), Montserrat (1693), South Carolina (1698), Nevis (1701), and Jamaica (1672, 1701, 1703) sought to privilege the servant, who was becoming a protector rather than a producer of property. David W. Galenson, *White Servitude in Colonial America: An Economic Analysis* (Cambridge: Cambridge University Press, 1986), 154; K. G. Davies, *The North Atlantic World in the Seventeenth Century* (Minneapolis: University of Minnesota Press, 1974), 98.

91. Hening, *Laws of Virginia*, 2:481–82, 492–93; 3:447–62. See also Kathleen M. Brown, *Good Wives, Nasty Wenches, and Anxious Patriarchs: Gender, Race and Power in Colonial Virginia* (Chapel Hill, N.C.: University of North Carolina Press, 1996), part 2.

92. Hugo Prospero Leaming, *Hidden Americans: Maroons of Virginia and the Carolinas* (New York: Garland, 1995), xv, 35, 48, 51, 68–71, 109, 116, 125; Hugh F. Rankin, *Upheaval in Albemarle: The Story of Culpeper's Rebellion* (Raleigh, N.C.: The Carolina Charter Tercentenary Commission, 1962), 10, 35, 40–41, 55; "Representation to the Lords Proprietors of Carolina Concerning the Rebellion in that Country," in William L. Saunders, ed., *The Colonial Records of North Carolina* (Raleigh, N.C.: P. M. Hale, 1886), 1:259, 261; Sir Peter Colleton, "The Case [of] Thomas Miller," in Andrews, ed., *Narratives of the Insurrections*, 152–56; Virginia General Assembly to Sir Joseph Williamson, 2 April 1677, *Virginia Magazine of History and Biography* 14 (1906–7), 286.

93. *True Levellers Standard Advanced* (1649) and *A Watch Word to the City of London* (1649).

94. Christopher Hill, introduction to *Winstanley: The Law of Freedom and Other Writings* (London: Penguin, 1973), 35.

95. R. J. Dalton, "Winstanley: The Experience of Fraud, 1641," *The Historical Journal* 34, no. 4 (1991): 973.

96. Ibid., 983.

97. *A Declaration from the Poor oppressed People of England* (June 1649).

98. *Truth Lifting Up Its Head* (October 1648).

99. Ibid.

100. The pause in economic development or democratic practice in England has long been noticed—e.g., by Gooch, Brailsford, Thompson, Orwell, Hobsbawm, and Anderson.

101. *Truth Lifting Up Its Head* (October 1648), s. 101, and *The New Law of Righteousness* (1649), s. 169.

Chapter Five

1. Richard Brathwaite, *Whimzies* (London, 1631), quoted in Christopher Lloyd, *The British Seaman, 1200–1860: A Social Survey* (Rutherford, N.J.: Fairleigh Dickinson University Press, 1970), 74.

2. Bernard Capp, *Cromwell's Navy: The Fleet and the English Revolution, 1648–1660* (Oxford: Clarendon Press, 1989), 42, 58, 66, 72, 396; L. A. Wilcox, *Mr. Pepys' Navy* (New York: A. S. Barnes and Co., 1966), 77.

3. Capp, *Cromwell's Navy*, 76; Lawrence A. Harper, *The English Navigation Laws* (New York: Columbia University Press, 1939), 38, 48–49, 53, 57, 60, 341; Ralph Davis, *The Rise of the English Shipping Industry in the Seventeenth and Eighteenth Centuries* (London: Macmillan, 1962), 17–20.

4. Capp, *Cromwell's Navy*, 219; J. D. Davies, *Gentlemen and Tarpaulins: The Officers and Men of the Restoration Navy* (Oxford: Clarendon Press, 1991), 95–96, 227; Maxwell P. Schoenfeld, "The Restoration Seaman and His Wages," *American Neptune* 25 (1965): 285.

5. Sir William Petty, *A Treatise of Taxes* (London, 1662), chap. 10, 12.

6. Sir William Petty, *Political Anatomy of Ireland* (London, 1691), 1:102.

7. Sir William Petty, *Political Arithmetick* (London, 1690), republished in C. H. Hull, ed., *The Economic Writings of Sir William Petty* (London, 1899), 1:259–60.

8. J. H. Parry, *Trade and Dominion: The European Overseas Empires in the Eighteenth Century* (New York: Praeger, 1971), 19, 13; P. K. Kemp and Christopher Lloyd, *Brethren of the Coast: Buccaneers of the South Seas* (New York: St. Martin's, 1960), 128; C. H. Haring, *The Buccaneers in the West Indies in the Seventeenth Century* (1910; reprint, Hamden, Conn.: Archon Books, 1966), 233.

9. *Gloria Britannia: Or, the Boast of the British Seas* (London, 1689), quoted in J. D. Davies, *Gentlemen and Tarpaulins*, 1.

10. Ernest Fayle, *A Short History of the World's Shipping Industry* (London: George Allen & Unwin, 1933), 207; Harper, *The English Navigation Laws*, 61, 161; Ian K. Steele, *The Politics of Colonial Policy: The Board of Trade in Colonial Administration 1696–1720* (Oxford: Clarendon Press, 1968), 44, 54; James A. Rawley, *The Transatlantic Slave Trade: A History* (New York: W. W. Norton, 1981), 163; Barry Supple, *Royal Exchange Assurance: A History of British Insurance, 1720–1970* (Cambridge: Cambridge University Press, 1970), 3.

11. As we have argued in Peter Linebaugh, "All the Atlantic Mountains Shook" and reply to Robert Sweeny, in *Labour/Le Travail* 10 (1982): 87–121 and 14 (1984): 173–81; and Marcus Rediker, *Between the Devil and the Deep Blue Sea: Merchant Seamen, Pirates, and the Anglo-American Maritime World, 1700–1750* (Cambridge: Cambridge University Press, 1987).

12. Conrad Gill, *Merchants and Mariners of the Eighteenth Century* (London: Edward

Arnold, 1961), 91; Edward Ward, *The London Spy* (1697; reprint, London: Cassell, 1927); Barnaby Slush, *The Navy Royal: Or a Sea-Cook Turn'd Projector* (London, 1709); C. L. R. James, "The Atlantic Slave Trade," in his *The Future in the Present* (London: Allison and Busby, 1977).

13. The pamphlet literature included George St.-Lo, *England's Safety* (London, 1693); *England's Interest, Or, a Discipline for Seamen* (London, 1694); Robert Crosfield, *Truth Brought to Light* (London, 1694); *Encouragement for Seamen and Manning* (London, 1695); William Hodges, *Dialogue concerning the Art of Ticket-Buying* (London, 1695); *Great Britain's Groans* (London, 1695); *Misery to Misery* (London, 1695); *Humble Proposals for the Relief, Encouragement, Security, and Happiness of the Seamen of England* (London, 1695); John Perry, *Regulation for Seamen* (London, 1695); *Discourse upon Raising Men* (London, 1696); Thomas Mozin and Nicholas Jennings, *Proposal for the Incouragement of Seamen* (London, 1697); and *Ruin to Ruin* (London, 1699).

14. J. R. Jones, *The Anglo-Dutch Wars of the Seventeenth Century* (London: Longman, 1996); J. D. Davies, *Gentlemen and Tarpaulins*, 15; John Ehrman, *The Navy in the War of William III, 1689–1697: Its State and Direction* (Cambridge: Cambridge University Press, 1953).

15. Harper, *English Navigation Laws*, 55; E. H. W. Meyerstein, ed., *Adventures by Sea of Edward Coxere: A Relation of the Several Adventures by Sea with the Dangers, Difficulties, and Hardships I Met for Several Years* (New York and London: Oxford University Press, 1946), 37; Petty, *Political Arithmetick*, 281; Ehrman, *Navy in the War of William III*, 115.

16. Michael Cohn and Michael K. H. Platzer, *Black Men of the Sea* (New York: Dodd, Mead, 1978).

17. "Richard Simons Voyage to the Straits of Magellan & S. Seas in the Year 1689," Sloane MSS. 86, British Library, f.57; William Matthews, "Sailors' Pronunciation in the Second Half of the Seventeenth Century," *Anglia: Zeitshrift für Englische Philologie* 59 (1935): 193–251.

18. Robert McCrum, et al., *The Story of English* (New York: Viking, 1986), chap. 6; B. Traven, *The Death Ship: The Story of an American Sailor* (New York: Collier, 1962), 237.

19. J. L. Dillard, *All-American English* (New York: Random House, 1975), develops the thesis of maritime languages. See also Nicholas Faraclas, "Rivers Pidgin English: Tone, Stress, or Pitch-Accent Language?" *Studies in the Linguistic Sciences* 14, no. 2 (fall 1984): 75; Ian F. Hancock, "A Provisional Comparison of the English-based Atlantic Creoles," *African Language Review* 8 (1969).

20. Nicholas Faraclas, "Rumors of the Demise of Descartes Are Premature," *Journal of Pidgin and Creole Languages* 3 (1988): 119–35. Robert C. Ritchie, *Captain Kidd and the War against the Pirates* (Cambridge, Mass.: Harvard University Press, 1986), 86;

Mechal Sobel, *Trabelin' On: The Slave Journey to an Afro-Baptist Faith* (Westport, Conn.: Greenwood Press, 1979), 30.

21. Arthur L. Hayward, ed., *Lives of the Most Remarkable Criminals . . .* (London, 1735), 37.

22. Ritchie, *Captain Kidd*, 147–51.

23. Jones, *The Anglo-Dutch Wars;* Capp, *Cromwell's Navy*, 259, 264, 287–88; *To his Highness Lord Protector* (London, 1654).

24. Richard Overton, *A Remonstrance of Many Thousand Citizens* (London, 1646); Don M. Wolfe, ed., *Leveller Manifestoes of the Puritan Revolution* (New York: T. Nelson and Sons, 1944), 80, 95, 227, 287, 347, and 405.

25. Kemp and Lloyd, *Brethren of the Coast;* Carl Bridenbaugh and Roberta Bridenbaugh, *No Peace beyond the Line: The English in the Caribbean, 1624–1690* (New York: Oxford University Press, 1972); Haring, *Buccaneers in the West Indies*, 71, 73; J. S. Bromley, "Outlaws at Sea, 1660–1720: Liberty, Equality, and Fraternity among the Caribbean Freebooters," in *History from Below: Studies in Popular Protest and Popular Ideology in Honour of George Rudé*, ed. Frederick Krantz (Montreal: Concordia University, 1985), 3.

26. See A. L. Morton, *The English Utopia* (London: Lawrence & Wishart, 1952), chap. 1; F. Graus, "Social Utopias in the Middle Ages," *Past and Present* 38 (1967): 3–19; William McFee, *The Law of the Sea* (Philadelphia: Lippincott, 1951), 50, 54, 59, 72.

27. Kemp and Lloyd, *Brethren of the Coast*, 3; Bridenbaugh and Bridenbaugh, *No Peace Beyond the Line*, 62, 176; Richard Price, ed., *Maroon Societies: Rebel Slave Communities in the Americas*, 2d ed. (Baltimore: Johns Hopkins University Press, 1979). Pirates continued to lead what they called the "marooning life" into the 1720s. See Examination of Thomas Jones, Feb., 1724, High Court of Admiralty Papers (HCA) 1/55, fo. 52, Public Record Office, London.

28. Christopher Hill, "Radical Pirates?" in *The Origins of Anglo-American Radicalism*, ed. Margaret Jacob and James Jacob (London: George Allen & Unwin, 1984), 20; William Dampier, *A New Voyage around the World* (London, 1697), 219–20; Kemp and Lloyd, *Brethren of the Coast*, 17; Bromley, "Outlaws at Sea," 6, 8, 9.

29. "Simsons Voyage," Sloane MSS 86, 43; Bromley, "Outlaws at Sea," 17; Marcus Rediker, "The Common Seaman in the Histories of Capitalism and the Working Class," *International Journal of Maritime History* 1 (1989): 352–53.

30. James Boswell, *The Life of Samuel Johnson . . .* (London, 1791), 86; Jesse Lemisch, "Jack Tar in the Streets: Merchant Seamen in the Politics of Revolutionary America," *William and Mary Quarterly*, 3d ser., 25 (1968): 379, 375–76, 406; Richard B. Morris, *Government and Labor in Early America* (New York: Columbia University Press, 1946), 246–47, 257, 262–68; Captain Charles Johnson, *A General History of the Pyrates*, ed. Manuel Schonhorn (1724, 1728; reprint, Columbia, S. C.: University of South Carolina Press, 1972), 244, 359 (hereafter cited as C. Johnson, *History*); A. G.

Course, *The Merchant Navy: A Social History* (London: F. Muller, 1963), 61; Davis, *Rise of the English Shipping Industry,* 144, 154–55.

31. Gov. Lowther to Council of Trade, in W. Noel Sainsbury et al., eds., *Calendar of State Papers, Colonial Series, America and the West Indies* (London, 1860–), 39:350; *Piracy Destroy'd* (London, 1700), 3–4, 12; R. D. Merriman, ed., *Queen Anne's Navy: Documents concerning the Administration of the Navy of Queen Anne, 1702–1714* (London: Navy Records Society, 1961), 170–72, 174, 221–22, 250; C. Lloyd, *The British Seaman,* 124–49; Peter Kemp, *The British Sailor: A Social History of the Lower Deck* (London: Dent, 1970), chaps. 4, 5.

32. Course, *Merchant Navy,* 84; C. Lloyd, *The British Seaman,* 57. Edward Cooke, *A Voyage to the South Sea* (London, 1712), v–vi, 14–16; Woodes Rogers, *A Cruising Voyage Round the World,* ed. G. E. Manwaring (1712; reprint, New York: Longmans, Green and Co., 1928), xiv, xxv; George Shelvocke, *A Voyage Round the World* (London, 1726), 34–36, 38, 46, 157, 214, 217; William Betagh, *A Voyage Round the World* (London, 1728), 4.

33. Rediker, *Between the Devil and the Deep Blue Sea,* chap. 6.

34. C. Johnson, *History,* 213, 423; Examination of John Brown (1717) in John Franklin Jameson, ed., *Privateering and Piracy in the Colonial Period: Illustrative Documents* (New York: Macmillan, 1923), 294; William Snelgrave, *A New Account of Some Parts of Guinea and the Slave Trade* (1734; reprint, London: Frank Cass, 1971), 199; Hayward, ed., *Lives of the Most Remarkable Criminals,* 37; C. Johnson, *History,* 42, 296, 337.

35. See *An Account of the Conduct and Proceedings of the Late John Gow, alias Smith, Captain of the Late Pirates* . . . (1725; reprint, Edinburgh: Gordon Wright Publishing, 1978), introduction.

36. C. Johnson, *History,* 338, 582; "Proceedings of the Court held on the Coast of Africa," HCA 1/99, fo. 101; *Boston Gazette,* 24–31 October 1720, 21–28 March 1726; Snelgrave, *New Account,* 225, 241; *Boston News-Letter,* 14–21 November 1720; Testimony of Thomas Checkley (1717), in Jameson, ed., *Privateering and Piracy,* 304; *The Trials of Eight Persons Indited for Piracy* (Boston, 1718), 11.

37. *An Account of . . . the Late John Gow,* 3; C. Johnson *History,* 244, 224. Bartholomew Roberts's crew was taken in 1722 because many of the men were drunk when the time came for an engagement. See C. Johnson, *History,* 243, and John Atkins, *A Voyage to Guinea, Brazil, & the West Indies* . . . (1735; reprint, London: Frank Cass, 1970), 192.

38. C. Johnson, *History,* 129, 135, 167, 205, 209, 211, 212, 222, 280, 308, 312, 343, 353, 620; *American Weekly Mercury,* 17 March 1720; Snelgrave, *New Account,* 233–38.

39. Walter Hamilton to Council of Trade and Plantations, 6 January 1718, Colonial Office Papers (CO) 152/12, fo. 211, Public Record Office, London; *Boston Gazette,* 6–13 July 1725; James Vernon to Council of Trade and Plantations, 21 December 1697, *Calendar of State Papers, Colonial Series* 16 (1697–98), 70; *Tryals of Thirty-Six Persons*

for Piracy (Boston, 1723), 3; Clive Senior, *A Nation of Pirates: English Piracy in Its Heyday* (New York: Crane, Russak & Co., 1976), 22; Kenneth Kinkor, "From the Seas! Black Men under the Black Flag," *American Prospects* 10 (1995): 27–29.

40. *American Weekly Mercury*, 17 March 1720; C. Johnson, *History*, 82; Information of Joseph Smith and Information of John Webley (1721), HCA 1/18, fo. 35; Information of William Voisy (1721) HCA 1/55, fo. 12. Native Americans also manned pirate ships, though in much smaller numbers. See *The Trials of Five Persons for Piracy, Felony, and Robbery* (Boston, 1726).

41. Testimony of Richard Hawkins, *Political State of Great Britain* 28 (1724): 153; *Boston News-Letter*, 17–24 June 1717; *The Tryals of Major Stede Bonnet and Other Pirates* (London, 1719), 46; C. Johnson, *History*, 173, 427, 595. See also *Boston News-Letter*, 29 April–6 May 1717.

42. *Boston News-Letter*, 4–11 April 1723.

43. John Gay, *Polly, An Opera* (London, 1729).

44. R. Reynall Bellamy, ed., *Ramblin' Jack: The Journal of Captain John Cremer* (London: Jonathan Cape, 1936), 144; Hugh F. Rankin, *The Golden Age of Piracy* (New York: Holt, Rinehart and Winston, 1969), 82. See Virginia Council to the Board of Trade, 11 August 1715, CO 5/1317.

45. C. Johnson, *History*, 273.

46. H. Ross, "Some Notes on the Pirates and Slavers around Sierra Leone and the West Coast of Africa, 1680–1723," *Sierra Leone Studies* 11 (1928): 16–53; C. Johnson, *History*, 131; L. G. Carr Laughton, "Shantying and Shanties," *Mariner's Mirror* 9 (1923): 48–50; Trial of John McPherson and others, Proceedings of the Court of Admiralty, Philadelphia, 1731, HCA 1/99, fo. 3; Information of Henry Hull (1729) HCA 1/56, fo. 29–30.

47. Marcus Rediker, "Liberty beneath the Jolly Roger: The Lives of Anne Bonny and Mary Read, Pirates," in Margaret Creighton and Lisa Norling, eds., *Iron Men, Wooden Women: Gender and Atlantic Seafaring, 1700–1920* (Baltimore: Johns Hopkins University Press, 1995). Dianne Dugaw, *Warrior Women and Popular Balladry, 1650–1850* (Cambridge: Cambridge University Press, 1989), and Jo Stanley, *Bold in Her Breeches: Women Pirates across the Ages* (London: HarperCollins, 1995).

48. Cotton Mather, *Instructions to the Living, From the Condition of the Dead: a Brief Relation of Remarkables in the Shipwreck of above One Hundred Pirates . . .* (Boston, 1717), 4; Meeting of 1 April 1717, in H. C. Maxwell Lyte, ed., *Journal of the Commissioners for Trade and Plantations . . .* (London: H. M. S.O., 1924), 3:359; C. Johnson, *History*, 7; *American Weekly Mercury*, 24 November 1720; *New England Courant*, 19–26 March 1722.

49. C. Johnson, *History*, 115–6; "Proceedings," HCA 1/99, fo. 158; Snelgrave, *New Account*, 203.

50. C. Johnson, *History*, 244; Bromley, "Outlaws at Sea," 11, 12; Atkins, *Voyage*, 191.

51. *Parker v. Boucher* (1719), HCA 24/132; *Wise v. Beekman* (1716), HCA 24/131. For

other instances of conflicts that ended up in court, see *Coleman v. Seamen* (1718) and *Desbrough v. Christian* (1720), HCA 24/132; *Povey v. Bigelow* (1722), HCA 24/134; *Wistridge v. Chapman* (1722), HCA 24/135. All, Public Record Office, London.

52. Information of Alexander Thompson (1723), HCA 1/55, fo. 23; see also Petition of John Massey and George Lowther (1721), CO 28/17, fo. 199.

53. "Proceedings," HCA 1/99, fo. 4–6; see also Atkins, *Voyage*, 91, 186–87.

54. Philip D. Curtin, *The Atlantic Slave Trade: A Census* (Madison, Wisc.: University of Wisconsin Press, 1969), 150. "The Memoriall of the Merchants of London Trading to Africa" (1720), Admiralty Papers (ADM) 1/3810, Public Record Office, London; *American Weekly Mercury*, 30 March–6 April 1721.

55. *Boston Gazette*, 13–20 June 1720; "Anonymous Paper relating to the Sugar and To-bacco Trade" (1724), CO 388/24, fo. 186–87.

56. Atkins, *Voyage*, 98; Rawley, *The Transatlantic Slave Trade*, 155; *Boston Gazette*, 27 August–3 September 1722; *New England Courant*, 3–10 September 1722.

57. "Proceedings," HCA 1/99, fo. 98; Stanley Richards, *Black Bart* (Llandybie, Wales: C. Davies, 1966), 107.

58. Rawley, *The Transatlantic Slave Trade*, 162.

59. Ibid., 164, 165; Curtin, *Atlantic Slave Trade*, 150.

60. Douglas North and Gary B. Walton emphasize the destruction of piracy as a major source of productivity advance in eighteenth-century shipping. See their "Sources of Productivity Change in Colonial American Shipping," *Economic History Review* 67 (1968): 67–78.

61. C. Johnson, *History*, 43; Leo Francis Stock, *Proceedings and Debates of the British Parliaments respecting North America* (Washington, D.C.: Carnegie Institute, 1930), 3:364, 433, 453, 454; Ritchie, *Captain Kidd*, 235–37. Walpole's direct involvement can be seen in Treasury Warrant to Capt. Knott, T52/32 (10 August 1722), P. R. O., and in *American Weekly Mercury*, 1–8 July 1725. Anne Pérotin-Dumon, "The Pirate and the Emperor: Power and the Law on the Seas, 1450–1850," in James D. Tracy, ed., *The Political Economy of Merchant Empires* (Cambridge: Cambridge University Press, 1991), 196–227, and Janice E. Thomson, *Mercenaries, Pirates, and Sovereigns: State-Building and Extraterritorial Violence in Early Modern Europe* (Princeton, N.J.: Princeton University Press, 1994).

62. W. E. May, "The Mutiny of the *Chesterfield*," *Mariners' Mirror* 47 (1961): 178–87; Aimé Césaire, "Nursery Rhyme," in *The Collected Poetry of Aimé Césaire*, trans. Clayton Eshleman and Annette Smith (Berkeley, Calif.: University of California Press, 1983), 265.

Chapter Six

1. Daniel Horsmanden, *A Journal of the Proceedings in the Detection of the Conspiracy formed by Some White People, in Conjunction with Negro and other Slaves, for Burning*

the City of New-York in America, and Murdering the Inhabitants (New York, 1744), edited and republished by Thomas J. Davis in *The New York Slave Conspiracy* (Boston: Beacon Press, 1971), 15, 443, 16, 452, 448–49. (All subsequent references are to this edition, hereafter cited as Horsmanden, *Journal.*)

2. Horsmanden, *Journal*, 15, 16, 155, 409, 446–47, 448; *Boston Gazette*, 15–22 June 1741; Lieutenant Governor George Clarke to Lords of Trade, 24 August 1741, in E. B. O'Callaghan, ed., *Documents Relative to the Colonial History of the State of New York* (Albany: Weed, Parsons & Co., 1855), 4:201–3.

3. Horsmanden, *Journal*, 29. See also T. J. Davis, *A Rumor of Revolt: The "Great Negro Plot" in Colonial New York* (New York: The Free Press, 1985), 78.

4. Horsmanden, *Journal*, 112, 160, 159, 42, 198, 418, 313, 246, 458, 436.

5. Ibid., 441, 432, 6, 10, 11, 12.

6. Anonymous letter to Cadwallader Colden, 23 July (?) 1741, in Letters and Papers of Cadwallader Colden, 1715–1748, *Collections of the New-York Historical Society* (1937), 8:270–72; Winthrop Jordan, *White over Black: American Attitudes toward the Negro, 1550–1812* (Chapel Hill, N.C.: University of North Carolina Press, 1968), 116, 121, 118, 119; Edgar J. McManus, *A History of Negro Slavery in New York* (Syracuse, N.Y.: Syracuse University Press, 1966), 13–139.

7. William Smith, Jr., *The History of the Province of New York* (1757; reprint, ed. Michael Kammen, Cambridge, Mass.: Belknap Press of Harvard University Press, 1972), 1:24–59; Ferenc M. Szasz, "The New York Slave Revolt of 1741: A Re-examination," *New York History* 48 (1967): 215–30; Leopold S. Launitz-Schurer, Jr., "Slave Resistance in Colonial New York: An Interpretation of Daniel Horsmanden's New York Conspiracy," *Phylon* 41 (1980): 137–52.

8. T. J. Davis, *Rumor of Revolt*, xii, xiii, 44, 226, 250, 258, 260, 277.

9. Gary B. Nash, *The Urban Crucible: Social Change, Political Consciousness, and the Origins of the American Revolution* (Cambridge, Mass.: Harvard University Press, 1979), chap. 5; Jacob Price, "Economic Function of American Port Towns in the Eighteenth Century," *Perspectives in American History* 8 (1974): 173; Horsmanden, *Journal*, 217, 34, 204, 211, 211, 288, 258.

10. Horsmanden, *Journal*, 58, 59. George William Edwards, *New York as an Eighteenth-Century Municipality* (New York: Columbia University Press, 1917), 2:109. See also Lawrence Leder, " 'Dam'me Don't Stir a Man': The Trial of New York Mutineers in 1700," *New-York Historical Society Quarterly* 42 (1958): 261–83.

11. Horsmanden, *Journal*, 322; 68, 93, 190, 194; 119, 271, 296, 302, 102; 33, 120, 413.

12. Samuel McKee, *Labor in Colonial New York, 1664–1776* (New York: Columbia University Press, 1935), 65, 66; *New York Gazette*, 3–10 July 1738; Lieutenant Governor Clarke to Lords of Trade, 2 June 1738, in O'Callaghan, ed., *Documents*, 115.

13. Horsmanden, *Journal*, 77–78; 459; 277, 282.

14. *The Colonial Laws of New York, from the Year 1664 to the Revolution* (Albany: James B.

Lyon, 1894), 2:679; Horsmanden, *Journal*, 229; 41, 44; 418. On weapons, see *Colonial Laws*, 2:687; 218; 174; 72, 132; 263, 231, 417, 418, 253, 417; 263; 417; 301; 217; 318–19; 257; 152, 169; 453.

15. *New York Gazette*, 31 January–7 February 1738; Horsmanden, *Journal*, 66, 448, 323, 13.

16. Horsmanden, *Journal*, 419; 82; 81; 148, 174; 210; 81; 191, 196; 461; 59; 210; 143; 191; 81; 173, 268; 255.

17. Ibid., 239. By calling each of these key organizers a "headman," Hughson and others appealed to the dominant meaning of the term in the middle of the eighteenth century: a headman was a leader of an ethnic group; see *Oxford English Dictionary*, s.v. "headman."

18. Horsmanden, *Journal*, 245, 193. Papa, or Pawpaw, slaves had played a major part in the slave revolt of 1712. See Kenneth Scott, "The Slave Insurrection in New York in 1712," *New-York Historical Society Quarterly* 45 (1961): 43–74. For an account of the early development of the African American community of New York, see Joyce D. Goodfriend, *Before the Melting Pot: Society and Culture in Colonial New York City, 1664–1730* (Princeton, N.J.: Princeton University Press, 1992), 111–32.

19. Horsmanden, *Journal*, 118, 120, 460, 461; Monica Schuler, "Akan Slave Rebellions in the British Caribbean," *Savacou* 1 (1970): 15, 16, 23; and idem, "Ethnic Slave Rebellions in the Caribbean and the Guianas," *Journal of Social History* 3 (1970): 374–85; Ray A. Kea, *Settlements, Trade, and Polities in the Seventeenth-Century Gold Coast* (Baltimore: Johns Hopkins University Press, 1982), 92–93, 131, 149; Kwame Yeboa Daaku, *Trade and Politics on the Gold Coast: A Study of the African Reaction to European Trade* (Oxford: Clarendon Press, 1970), and J. K. Fynn, *Asante and Its Neighbours, 1700–1807* (London: Longman, 1971); John Thornton, "African Dimensions of the Stono Rebellion," *American Historical Review* 96 (1991): 1101–13.

20. Horsmanden, *Journal*, 437, 284, 297; Z. Maurice Jackson, "Some Combination of Villains: The Unexplored Organizational Sources of the New York Conspiracy of 1741," unpublished paper, Georgetown University, 1993; Orlando Patterson, "The Maroon War," in Richard Price, ed., *Maroon Societies: Rebel Slave Communities in the Americas* (Baltimore: Johns Hopkins University Press, 1979), 262; *A Genuine Narrative of the Intended Conspiracy of the Negroes at Antigua* (Dublin, 1737), 7; David Barry Gaspar, *Bondmen and Rebels: A Study of Master-Slave Relations in Antigua, with Implications for Colonial British America* (Baltimore: Johns Hopkins University Press, 1985); Fynn, *Asante*, 58–60. For a contemporary's comments on thunder and lightning and some of their cultural meanings on the Gold Coast, see P. E. H. Hair, Adam Jones, and Robin Law, eds., *Barbot on Guinea: The Writings of Jean Barbot on West Africa, 1678–1712* (London: The Hakluyt Society, 1992), 2:398, 458, 579, 581, 589, 674.

21. Horsmanden, *Journal*, 59; Governor Hunter to the Lords of Trade, 23 June 1712, in O'Callaghan, *Documents*, 5:341–42. See McManus, *History of Negro Slavery*, 122–26;

Scott, "The Slave Insurrection," 62–67, 57 (quotation); David Humphreys, *An Historical Account of the Incorporated Society for the Propagation of the Gospel in Foreign Parts* (London, 1730), 240–42.

22. Horsmanden, *Journal,* 106, 547, 549, 200, 204; Scott, "The Slave Insurrection," 52, 54–56; *New York Weekly Journal,* 7 March 1737.

23. Horsmanden, *Journal,* 106, 59, 182, 80, 81, 111, 118, 120, 163, 172, 228.

24. Ibid., 277, 279, 281, 282, 285, 292, 293, 305, 341, 346–47, 460; Susan E. Klepp and Billy G. Smith, eds., *The Infortunate: The Voyages and Adventures of William Moraley, an Indentured Servant* (1743; reprint, University Park, Pa.: Penn State University Press, 1992), 94–96.

25. Audrey Lockhart, *Some Aspects of Emigration from Ireland to the North American Colonies between 1660 and 1775* (New York: Arno Press, 1976), 17, 22, 23; David Noel Doyle, *Ireland, Irishmen, and Revolutionary America, 1760–1820* (Dublin and Cork: Mercier Press, 1981), 62, 64; Kerby A. Miller, *Emigrants and Exiles: Ireland and the Irish Exodus to North America* (New York: Oxford University Press, 1985), 142; *New England Courant,* 4–11 January 1725 (quotation).

26. Lockhart, *Some Aspects of Emigration,* 98, 102, 152.

27. Kenneth Coleman and Milton Ready, eds., *The Colonial Records of the State of Georgia* (Athens, Ga.: University of Georgia Press, 1982), 20:365, 366; Edwards, *New York as an Eighteenth-Century Municipality,* 113; Lockhart, *Some Aspects of Emigration,* 90.

28. Miller, *Emigrants and Exiles,* 147; the Reverend Aubrey Gwynn, ed., "Documents Relating to the Irish in the West Indies," *Analecta Hibernica* 4 (1932): 281–82; Lockhart, *Some Aspects of Emigration,* 130.

29. Horsmanden, *Journal,* 28, 93, 182, 319.

30. Ibid., 167, 117, 179, 81.

31. Ibid., 179, 81, 147; see also 199, 197, 181.

32. Ibid., 180, 151, 28; see also 173, 181, 182. On the earlier use of fireballs in the Caribbean, see, for example, Alexander O. Exquemelin, *The Buccaneers of America* (1678; reprint, ed. Robert C. Ritchie, Annapolis, Md.: Naval Institute Press, 1993), 178, 180.

33. Horsmanden, *Journal,* 350–51, 370; for references to the popish plot, see 341, 350, 387, 413, 420, 431–32. Oglethorpe's letter is also excerpted in O'Callaghan, *Documents,* 6:198–99.

34. The historical literature on the Great Awakening is vast. See Nash, *The Urban Crucible,* 206, 211, 216, 219; Charles Hartshorn Maxson, *The Great Awakening in the Middle Colonies* (Chicago: University of Chicago Press, 1920); Frank Lambert, *"Pedlar in Divinity": George Whitefield and the Transatlantic Revivals* (Princeton, N.J.: Princeton University Press, 1994). The slave James Albert Ukawsaw Gronniosaw wrote some years later, "I knew Mr. Whitefield very well.—I had heard him preach in New York." See his *A Narrative of the Most Remarkable Particulars in the Life of*

James Albert Ukawsaw Gronniosaw, An African prince, Written by Himself (Newport, R.I., 1774).

35. J. Richard Olivas, "Great Awakenings: Time, Space, and the Varieties of Religious Revivalism in Massachusetts and Northern New England, 1740–1748" (Ph.D. diss., University of California, Los Angeles, 1997); Nash, *The Urban Crucible*, 208, 210, 482; Charles Chauncey, *Seasonable Thoughts on the State of Religion* (Boston, 1742), iii–xxx; Carl Bridenbaugh, ed., *Gentleman's Progress: The Itinerarium of Dr. Alexander Hamilton, 1744* (Chapel Hill, N.C.: University of North Carolina Press, 1948), 33.

36. Horsmanden, *Journal*, 105, 158, 203, 267, 300, 386. The religious instruction of slaves had long been a controversial issue in New York, as slaveowners feared the meetings and messages of Quakers, Baptists, and even the Church of England's conservative Society for the Propagation of the Gospel in Foreign Parts. The society's catechist Elias Neau, a former sailor and galley slave, had been blamed for the slave revolt of 1712. See McManus, *History of Negro Slavery*, 70, 73, 75; Humphreys, *An Historical Account*, 235–43; Nash, *The Urban Crucible*, 211.

37. George Whitefield, "Letter to the Inhabitants of Maryland, Virginia, North and South Carolina," in *Three Letters from the Reverend G. Whitefield* (Philadelphia, 1740). See also Kenneth P. Minkema, "Jonathan Edwards on Slavery and the Slave Trade," *William and Mary Quarterly*, 3d ser., 54 (1997): 823–34.

38. *South Carolina Gazette*, 10–17 and 17–24 April 1742, as quoted in Alan Gallay, "The Great Sellout: George Whitefield on Slavery," in Winfred B. Moore and Joseph F. Tripp, eds., *Looking South: Chapters in the Story of an American Region* (New York: Greenwood Press, 1989), 24; Alexander Garden, *Regeneration, and the testimony of the Spirit* (Charleston, 1740); *George Whitefield's Journals* (Guildford: Banner of Truth Trust, 1960), 442; William Smith, *A Natural History of Nevis and the rest of the English Charibee Islands . . .* (Cambridge, 1745), 230.

39. Horsmanden, *Journal*, 360; Daniel Horsmanden to George Clarke, 20 May 1746, in Minutes of the Council in Assembly, Parish Transcripts, New-York Historical Society, ff. 24–25. William D. Piersen has aptly written, "It sometimes seemed to conservatives that the worst fears of [The Reverend H. A.] Brockwell and [the Reverend Charles] Chauncey had come true, and the old antinomian heresy had returned in a black light whereby slaves in a state of grace thought themselves above the law of their masters." See his *Black Yankees: The Development of an Afro-American Subculture in Eighteenth-Century New England* (Amherst, Mass.: University of Massachusetts Press, 1988), 71.

40. Originally published in the *Weekly Miscellany*, 27 June 1741, and republished in the *New Weekly Miscellany*, 15 August 1741, and in *Scots Magazine*, August 1741, 367–368. Whitefield himself worried that his preaching had incited insurrection, and in his anonymously published *Letter to the Negroes Lately Converted to Christ in America* (London, 1743), he told slaves that it was better to die than to disobey one's master.

In subsequent years he would become a slaveowner and campaign for the legalization of slavery in Georgia, thereby making peace with the Devil. See Gallay, "The Great Sellout," in Moore and Tripp, eds., *Looking South*, 24–27, and Stephen J. Stein, "George Whitefield and Slavery: Some New Evidence," *Church History* 42 (1973): 243–56.

41. Writing on the historiography of slavery, Peter H. Wood observed, "There have been no successful longitudinal studies analyzing periods of intensive slave resistance throughout the Atlantic community, such as the late 1730s or the early 1790s." See his " 'I Did the Best I Could for My Day': The Study of Early Black History during the Second Reconstruction, 1960 to 1976," *William and Mary Quarterly*, 3d ser., 35 (1978): 185–225. Two fine studies on the subject have since been written: David Barry Gaspar, "A Dangerous Spirit of Liberty: Slave Rebellion in the West Indies during the 1730s," *Cimarrons* 1 (1981): 79–91, and Julius Sherrard Scott III, "The Common Wind: Currents of Afro-American Communication in the Era of the Haitian Revolution" (Ph.D. diss., Duke University, 1986).

42. Herbert Aptheker, *American Negro Slave Revolts* (New York: International Publishers, 1943, 1974), 80, 191, 191–92, 189; *American Weekly Mercury*, 26 February–5 March 1734; Peter H. Wood, *Black Majority: Negroes in Colonial South Carolina from 1670 through the Stono Rebellion* (New York: W. W. Norton, 1974), 308–26; "A Ranger's Report of Travels with General Oglethorpe, 1739–1742," in Newton Mereness, ed., *Travels in the American Colonies* (New York: Macmillan, 1916), 223.

43. Charles Leslie, *A New and Exact Account of Jamaica* (Edinburgh, 1739), 80; Mavis Campbell, *The Maroons of Jamaica, 1655–1796: A History of Resistance, Collaboration, and Betrayal* (South Hadley, Mass: Bergin and Garvey, 1988), 76, 6, 59–61.

44. Michael Craton, *Testing the Chains: Slave Resistance in the British West Indies* (Ithaca, N.Y.: Cornell University Press, 1983), cites the Journals of the House of Assembly, Jamaica, 3:98, 100. See also Campbell, *Maroons of Jamaica*, 54, 61, 78, 101, 143–44.

45. Craton, *Testing the Chains*, 90; Campbell, *Maroons of Jamaica*, 151.

46. Richard Price, ed., *To Slay the Hydra: Dutch Colonial Perspectives on the Saramaka Wars* (Ann Arbor, Mich.: Karoma, 1983), 15; Cornelius Ch. Goslinga, *The Dutch in the Caribbean and the Guianas, 1680–1791* (Assen/Maastricht, Netherlands: Van Gorcum, 1985), 541, 554, 676.

47. Coleman and Ready, eds., *Colonial Records of the State of Georgia*, vol. 20, quotations at 365, 271, 366, 241, 246, 272, 284, 285, 270–71, 246; James Oglethorpe to George Clarke, 22 April 1743, Parish Transcripts, f. 20; Miller, *Emigrants and Exiles*, 146–47. For other instances of Irish resistance, see *A Genuine Narrative of the Intended Conspiracy of the Negroes at Antigua*, 15; *Boston News-Letter*, 24 May 1739; Aptheker, *American Negro Slave Revolts*, 187; Doyle, *Ireland, Irishmen, and Revolutionary America*, 49; *Boston Evening-Post*, 7 January 1745; Philip D. Morgan and George D. Terry, "Slavery in Microcosm: A Conspiracy Scare in Colonial South Carolina," *Southern Studies* 21 (1982): 121–45. On Priber, see Verner W. Crane, "A Lost Utopia of the First

American Frontier," *Sewanee Review* 27 (1919): 48–60, and two articles by Knox Mellon, Jr.: "Christian Priber and the Jesuit Myth," *South Carolina Historical Magazine* 61 (1960): 75–81, and "Christian Priber's Cherokee 'Kingdom of Paradise,' " *Georgia Historical Quarterly* 57 (1973): 310–31.

48. Gwin, Bastian, and Jonneau belonged to the baker John Vaarck; Tom, to the baker Divertie Bradt; Pablo, to the brewer Frederick Becker; and Primus, to the distiller James Debrosses. It was observed in court that a "baker's servants, from the nature of their business . . . have always a command of fire." See Horsmanden, *Journal*, 390. On arson in colonial New England, see Lawrence W. Towner, "A Good Master Well Served: A Social History of Servitude in Massachusetts, 1620–1750" (Ph.D. diss., Northwestern University, 1955), 279.

49. Gaspar, "A Dangerous Spirit of Liberty," 87; *American Weekly Mercury*, 26 February–5 March 1734; Coleman and Ready, *Colonial Records of Georgia*, 20:241, 246, 258, 270; *American Weekly Mercury*, 19–26 May and 23–30 June 1737; *New England Weekly Journal*, 10 October 1738.

50. *South Carolina Gazette*, 11–18 August 1739; *Boston News-Letter*, 20 November 1740; *American Weekly Mercury*, 22–29 January 1741; *London Evening Post*, 10 January 1741; *Boston Gazette*, 29 June–6 July 1741; *Boston News-Letter*, 7–14 May 1741; *American Weekly Mercury*, 10–17 September 1741; *Boston News-Letter*, 1 October 1741; Morgan and Terry, "Slavery in Microcosm," 122.

51. *South Carolina Gazette*, 1–7 January 1741, as quoted in Gallay, "The Great Sellout," in Moore and Tripp, eds., *Looking South*, 23 (it was finally concluded that the fire in Charleston was not set by slaves); J. H. Easterby, R. Nicholas Oldsberg, and Terry W. Lipscomb, eds., *The Colonial Laws of South Carolina: The Journal of the Commons House of Assembly* (Columbia, S. C., 1951–   ), 3:461–62, quoted in Gallay, "The Great Sellout," 24.

52. Horsmanden, *Journal*, 387. On the design against the city on the anniversary of the burning of Fort George, see the Minutes of the Council in Assembly, 18 March 1742, Parish Transcripts, folder 162, f. 171.

53. Bridenbaugh, *Gentleman's Progress*, 41, 44, 46 (quotation), 48, 221.

54. William I. Davisson and Lawrence J. Bradley, "New York Maritime Trade: Ship Voyage Patterns, 1715–1765," *New-York Historical Society Quarterly* 35 (1971): 309–17; Colden quoted in Michael Kammen, *Colonial New York: A History* (New York: Charles Scribner's Sons, 1975), 169. See also Goslinga, *The Dutch in the Caribbean*, 220.

55. James G. Lydon, "New York and the Slave Trade, 1700 to 1774," *William and Mary Quarterly*, 3d ser., 35 (1978): 375–94; Ira Berlin, "Time, Space, and the Evolution of Afro-American Society on British Mainland North America," *American Historical Review* 85 (1980): 49, 50; McManus, *History of Negro Slavery*, 27.

56. Gaspar, *Bondmen and Rebels*, 35–37.

57. Lydon, "New York and the Slave Trade," 35; McManus, *History of Negro Slavery,* 35; Governor Rip Van Dam to the Lords of Trade, 2 November 1731, in O'Callaghan, *Documents,* 5:927–28; Governor William Cosby to House of Assembly, April 1734, Parish Transcripts, ff. 30–31. See also two articles by Darold D. Wax, "Negro Resistance to the Early American Slave Trade," *Journal of Negro History* 61 (1966): 13–14, and "Preferences for Slaves in Colonial America," *Journal of Negro History* 58 (1973): 374–89. Some of the complaining was hypocritical, as New York's merchants carried slaves of "marked unruliness" to the "southern colonies to be sold." See McKee, *Labor in Colonial New York,* 123.

58. McManus, *History of Negro Slavery,* 35; Lydon, "New York and the Slave Trade," 385; James A. Rawley, *The Transatlantic Slave Trade: A History* (New York: W. W. Norton, 1981), 334.

59. Horsmanden, *Journal,* 9–10, 107; *Pennsylvania Gazette,* 26 February 1745.

60. Horsmanden, *Journal,* 212; Ray A. Kea, " 'When I die, I shall return to my own land': An 'Amina' Slave Rebellion in the Danish West Indies, 1733–1734," in John Hunwick and Nancy Lawler, eds., *The Cloth of Many Colored Silks: Papers on History and Society Ghanaian and Islamic in Honor or Ivor Wilks* (Evanston, Ill.: Northwestern University Press, 1996), 159–93.

61. Horsmanden, *Journal,* 267.

62. Ibid., 259, 319, 70, 249, 118, 54, 419, 59–60, 283; Clarke to Lords of Trade, 20 June 1741, in O'Callaghan, *Documents,* 6:197.

63. *New York Weekly Journal,* 23 June 1741; Horsmanden, *Journal,* 271, 269, 266, 224, 210–11, 290; 61, 98, 166, 282, 297, 440.

64. Jane Landers, "Gracia Real de Santa Teresa de Mose: A Free Black Town in Spanish Colonial Florida," *American Historical Review* 95 (1990): 9–30; idem, "Spanish Sanctuary: Fugitives in Florida, 1687–1790," *Florida Historical Quarterly* 62 (1984): 296–313; John J. TePaske, "The Fugitive Slave: Intercolonial Rivalry and Spanish Slave Policy, 1687–1764," in Samuel Proctor, ed., *Eighteenth-Century Florida and Its Borderlands* (Gainesville, Fla.: The University Presses of Florida, 1975), 1–12.

65. Güemes to Montiano, 2 June 1742, and (for more evidence of the plan of Spanish authorities to use North American slaves) Montiano to José de Campillo, 12 March 1742, both in *Collections of the Georgia Historical Society* 7 (1913): 33–34, 26 (these are translations of original documents located in the General Archives of the Indies in Seville). See also Larry E. Ivers, *British Drums on the Southern Frontier: The Military Colonization of Georgia, 1733–1749* (Chapel Hill, N.C.: University of North Carolina Press, 1974), 151, 242.

66. On early May timing for the rising, see *Boston News-Letter,* 7–14 May 1741, and *American Weekly Mercury,* 7 May 1741; Horsmanden, *Journal,* 111. On Quack's grudge, see T. J. Davis, *A Rumor of Revolt,* 90, 148; on Spanish privateers, see *Daily Gazette,* 7 July 1741, and Carl E. Swanson, *Predators and Prizes: American Priva-*

teering and Imperial Warfare, 1739–1748 (Columbia, S. C.: University of South Carolina Press, 1991), 144, 148. The New York Assembly acknowledged the privateering threat by voting a special allowance of four hundred pounds to defend the city.

67. Horsmanden, *Journal,* 82, 411.

68. Ibid., 389, 411–12. The authorities also regulated the city's wells, where drawers of water had exchanged plans and news of the insurrection.

69. Lydon, "New York and the Slave Trade," 378, 388. For a similar response by South Carolina's slave traders and owners, see Darold D. Wax, " 'The Great Risque We Run': The Aftermath of Slave Rebellion at Stono, South Carolina, 1739–1745," *Journal of Negro History* 67 (1982): 136–47.

70. "Petition of Sundry Coopers of New York touching Negroes in the Trade," 1743, Parish Transcripts, folder 156, f. 1; Horsmanden, *Journal,* 19, 16; 309; 49; 311. It is important to remember that "white" as a cultural definition was relatively new, having made its first official appearance in the North American continent (in Virginia) only in 1680. The dichotomy of white and black began slowly to replace the older dichotomies of cultural difference such as English/African, Christian/pagan or heathen, and civilized/savage. See Jordan, *White over Black,* 95.

71. Horsmanden, *Journal,* 346; 284; 81; 101; 282; 54; 311, 309.

72. Ibid., 12, 82, 137, 383, 419, 431. The long-term successes of teaching "whiteness" in New York can be seen in the publication history of the legal documents surrounding the trials. The first edition of Horsmanden's collection was, as noted above, entitled *A Journal of the Proceedings in the Detection of the Conspiracy formed by Some White People, in Conjunction with Negro and other Slaves, for Burning the City of New-York in America, and Murdering the Inhabitants.* Originally published in New York in 1744 and republished in London in 1747, the volume, through its title, made "Some White People" central actors in the conspiracy and refused, moreover, to make "negro" and "slave" perfect equivalents, for there were "other" slaves (Indians, to be precise) also involved in the plot. The next edition, which appeared in 1810, was called *The New-York Conspiracy, or a History of the Negro Plot, with the Journal of the Proceedings against the Conspirators at New-York in the Years 1741–2.* Later in the nineteenth century, the event came to be known as simply the Great Negro Plot, the very name of which thus erased the participation of the conspirators of European (or Native American) descent.

73. Horsmanden, *Journal,* 273, 11, 276.

Chapter Seven

1. Henry Laurens to J. B., Esq., 26 Oct. 1765, Laurens to John Lewis Gervais, 29 January 1766, and Laurens to James Grant, 31 January 1766, all in George C. Rogers, Jr., David R. Chesnutt, and Peggy J. Clark, eds., *The Papers of Henry Laurens* (Columbia, S. C.: University of South Carolina Press, 1968–   ), 5:38–40, 53–54, 60; Bull

quoted in Pauline Maier, "The Charleston Mob and the Evolution of Popular Politics in Revolutionary South Carolina, 1765–1784," *Perspectives in American History* 4 (1970): 176.

2. Jesse Lemisch, "Jack Tar in the Streets: Merchant Seamen in the Politics of Revolutionary America," *William and Mary Quarterly* (hereafter *WMQ*), 3d ser., 25 (1968): 371–407; Marcus Rediker, *Between the Devil and the Deep Blue Sea: Merchant Seamen, Pirates, and the Anglo-American Maritime World, 1700–1750* (Cambridge: Cambridge University Press, 1987), chap. 5.

3. Dora Mae Clark, "The Impressment of Seamen in the American Colonies," *Essays in Colonial History Presented to Charles McLean Andrews by His Students* (New Haven, Conn.: Yale University Press, 1931), 217; Richard Pares, "The Manning of the Navy in the West Indies, 1702–1763," *Royal Historical Society Transactions* 20 (1937): 48–49; Daniel Baugh, *British Naval Administration in the Age of Walpole* (Princeton, N.J.: Princeton University Press, 1965), 162.

4. Peter Warren to the Duke of Newcastle, 18 June 1745, in Julian Gwyn, ed., *The Royal Navy and North America: The Warren Papers, 1736–1752* (London: Navy Records Society, 1973), 126.

5. Charles Knowles to ?, 15 October 1744, Admiralty Papers (hereafter ADM) 1/2007, f. 135, Public Record Office, London; "The Memorial of Captain Charles Knowles" (1743), ADM 1/2006; Peter Warren to Thomas Corbett, 2 June 1746, in Gwyn, ed., *The Warren Papers*, 262.

6. Thomas Hutchinson, *The History of the Colony and Province of Massachusetts Bay*, ed. Lawrence Shaw Mayo (Cambridge, Mass.: Harvard University Press, 1936, 1970), 2:330–31; William Shirley to Lords of Trade, 1 December 1747, Shirley to Duke of Newcastle, 31 December 1747, Shirley to Josiah Willard, 19 November 1747, all in Charles Henry Lincoln, ed., *Correspondence of William Shirley, Governor of Massachusetts and Military Commander of America, 1731–1760* (New York: Macmillan, 1912), 1:415, 416, 417, 418, 421, 422; John Lax and William Pencak, "The Knowles Riot and the Crisis of the 1740s in Massachusetts," *Perspectives in American History* 19 (1976): 182, 186 (Knowles quoted, our emphasis), 205, 214; Douglass Adair and John A. Schutz, eds., *Peter Oliver's Origin and Progress of the American Rebellion: A Tory View* (Palo Alto, Calif.: Stanford University Press, 1961), 41, 39; William Roughead, ed., *Trial of Captain Porteous* (Toronto: Canada Law Book Co., 1909), 103.

7. Lax and Pencak, "The Knowles Riot," 199; John C. Miller, *Sam Adams: Pioneer in Propaganda* (Palo Alto, Calif.: Stanford University Press, 1936), 15–16.

8. *Independent Advertiser*, 4 January 1748; Shirley to Lords of Trade, 1 December 1747, in *Correspondence of William Shirley*, 1:412; Resolution of the Boston Town Meeting, 20 November 1747, and Resolution of the Massachusetts House of Representatives, 19 November 1747, both in the *Boston Weekly Post-Boy*, 21 December 1747; Hutchinson, *History of Massachusetts Bay*, 2:332; William Douglass, *A Summary, Historical and Political, of the First Planting, Progressive Improvements, and Present State of the British Settlements in North America* (Boston, 1749), 254–55; *Independent Advertiser*,

28 August 1749; Amicus Patriae, *An Address to the Inhabitants of the Province of Massachusetts-Bay in New-England; More Especially, To the Inhabitants of New England; Occasioned by the late Illegal and Unwarrantable Attack upon their Liberties* (Boston, 1747), 4.

9. *Independent Advertiser,* 8 February 1748; 6 March 1749; 18 April 1748; 25 January 1748; 14 March 1748; 11 January 1748.

10. Jonathan Mayhew, *A Discourse Concerning Unlimited Submission* (Boston, 1750), reprinted in Bernard Bailyn, ed., *Pamphlets of the American Revolution: 1750–1776,* vol. 1, *1750–1765* (Cambridge, Mass.: Belknap Press of Harvard University Press, 1965), 213–247; Charles W. Akers, *Called unto Liberty: A Life of Jonathan Mayhew, 1720–1766* (Cambridge, Mass.: Harvard University Press, 1964), 53, 67, 84.

11. Lord Colvill to Philip Stephens, 9 September 1764 and 30 November 1764, ADM 1/482, ff. 386, 417–419; Neil R. Stout, "Manning the Royal Navy in North America, 1763–1775," *American Neptune* 23 (1963): 175.

12. Rear Admiral Colvill to Mr. Stephens, 26 July 1764, in John Russell Bartlett, ed., *Records of the Colony of Rhode Island and Providence Plantations in New England* (Providence: Knowles, Anthony & Co., 1861), 6:428–29; Thomas Hill, "Remarks on board His Maj[esty]'s Schooner St. John in Newport Harbour Rhode Island," ADM 1/482, f. 372; Thomas Langhorne to Lord Colvill, 11 August 1764, ADM 1/482, f. 377. See also *Newport Mercury,* 23 July 1764; Colvill to Stephens, 12 January 1765, ADM 1/482, f. 432.

13. Governor Samuel Ward to Captain Charles Antrobus, 12 July 1765, in Bartlett, ed., *Records of the Colony of Rhode Island,* 6:447; Lords of Admiralty to Mr. Secretary Conway, 20 March 1766, in Joseph Redington, ed., *Calendar of Home Office Papers of the Reign of George III, 1766–1768* (London, 1879), 2:26; Hutchinson, *History of Massachusetts Bay,* 3:138; Donna J. Spindel, "Law and Disorder: The North Carolina Stamp Act Crisis," *North Carolina Historical Review* 57 (1980): 10–11; *Pennsylvania Journal,* 26 December 1765; Adair and Schutz, eds., *Peter Oliver's Origin,* 69; Lemisch, "Jack Tar in the Streets," 392; David S. Lovejoy, *Rhode Island Politics and the American Revolution, 1760–1776* (Providence: Brown University Press, 1958), 157; Paul A. Gilje, *The Road to Mobocracy: Popular Disorder in New York City, 1763–1834* (Chapel Hill, N.C.: University of North Carolina Press, 1987), 63.

14. *Oxford English Dictionary,* s.v. "strike"; C. R. Dobson, *Masters and Journeymen: A Prehistory of Industrial Relations, 1717–1800* (London: Croom Helm, 1980), 154–70; Oliver M. Dickerson, *The Navigation Acts and the American Revolution* (Philadelphia: University of Pennsylvania Press, 1951), 218–19.

15. J. Cunningham, *An Essay on Trade and Commerce* (London, 1770), 52, 58. On Wilkes, see Pauline Maier, *From Resistance to Revolution: Colonial Radicals and the Development of American Opposition to Britain, 1765–1776* (New York: Vintage Books, 1972), 162–69; George Rudé, *Wilkes and Liberty: A Social Study of 1763–1774* (Oxford: Clarendon Press, 1962).

16. Nauticus, *The Rights of the Sailors Vindicated, In Answer to a Letter of Junius, on the*

5th of October, wherein he asserts The Necessity and Legality of pressing men into the Service of the Navy (London, 1772); William Ander Smith, "Anglo-Colonial Society and the Mob, 1740–1775" (Ph.D. diss., Claremont Graduate School and University Center, 1965), 108; Nicholas Rogers, "Liberty Road: Opposition to Impressment in Britain during the War of American Independence," in Colin Howell and Richard Twomey, eds., *Jack Tar in History: Essays in the History of Maritime Life and Labour* (Fredericton, New Brunswick: Acadiensis Press, 1991), 53–75.

17. Prince Hoare, *Memoirs of Granville Sharp* (1820); Edward Lascelles, *Granville Sharp and the Freedom of Slaves in England* (London: Oxford University Press, 1928); John Fielding, *Penal Laws* (London, 1768).

18. R. Barrie Rose, "A Liverpool Sailors' Strike in the Eighteenth Century," *Transactions of the Lancashire and Cheshire Antiquarian Society* 68 (1958): 85, 89, 85–92; "Extract of a Letter from Liverpool, Sept. 1, 1775," *The Morning Chronicle and London Advertiser*, 5 September 1775, republished in Richard Brooke, *Liverpool as it was during the Last Quarter of the Eighteenth century, 1775 to 1800* (Liverpool, 1853), 332.

19. *A Letter To the Right Honourable The Earl of T---e: or, the Case of J--- W---s, Esquire* (London, 1768), 22, 39; Maier, *From Resistance to Revolution*, 161; Adair and Schutz, eds., *Peter Oliver's Origin*, 56; *The Trial at Large of James Hill . . . , Commonly known by the Name of John the Painter . . . ,* 2d edition (London, 1777).

20. Edward Long, *The History of Jamaica, or General Survey of the Antient and Modern State of that Island; Reflections on its Situation, Settlements, Inhabitants, Climate, Products, Commerce, Laws, and Government* (London, 1774), 2:462; Mervyn Alleyne, *Roots of Jamaican Culture* (London: Pluto, 1988), chap. 4.

21. Douglas Hall, ed., *In Miserable Slavery: Thomas Thistlewood in Jamaica, 1750–1786* (London: Macmillan, 1989), 106; Michael Craton, *Testing the Chains: Resistance to Slavery in the British West Indies* (Ithaca, N.Y.: Cornell University Press, 1982), 125–39.

22. Long, *History of Jamaica*, 2:460; Hall, ed., *In Miserable Slavery*, 98. Sailors in the Royal Navy, it should be noted, did apparently assist in putting down the rebellion in a couple of areas. See Craton, *Testing the Chains*, 136, 132–33.

23. J. Philmore, *Two Dialogues on the Man-Trade* (London, 1760), 9, 7, 8, 10, 14; David Brion Davis, *The Problem of Slavery in the Age of Revolution, 1770–1823* (Ithaca, N.Y.: Cornell University Press, 1975), and idem, "New Sidelights on Early Antislavery Radicalism," *WMQ*, 3d ser., 28 (1971): 585–94.

24. Philmore, *Two Dialogues*, 45, 51, 54; Anthony Benezet, *A Short Account of that Part of Africa Inhabited by the Negroes . . .* (Philadelphia, 1762); idem, *Some Historical Account of Guinea* (Philadelphia, 1771); D. Davis, *Problem of Slavery*, 332.

25. James Otis, *The Rights of the British Colonies Asserted and Proved* (Boston, 1764), republished in Bailyn, ed., *Pamphlets of the American Revolution*, 1:419–82; *Boston News-Letter*, 19 June, 10 July, 18 September, and 30 October 1760, 2 February 1761.

26. Charles Francis Adams, ed., *The Works of John Adams* (Boston: Little, Brown, 1856), 10:247, 272, 314–16; Adair and Schutz, eds., *Peter Oliver's Origin*, 35.

27. Craton, *Testing the Chains*, 138, 139, 140; O. Nigel Bolland, *The Formation of a Colonial Society: Belize, from Conquest to Crown Colony* (Baltimore: Johns Hopkins University Press, 1977), 73.

28. See Peter Wood, " 'Taking Care of Business' in Revolutionary South Carolina: Republicanism and the Slave Society," in Jeffrey J. Crow and Larry E. Tise, eds., *The Southern Experience in the American Revolution* (Chapel Hill, N.C.: University of North Carolina Press, 1978), 276, and idem, " 'The Dream Deferred': Black Freedom Struggles on the Eve of White Independence," in Gary Y. Okihiro, ed., *In Resistance: Studies in African, Caribbean, and Afro-American History* (Amherst, Mass.: University of Massachusetts Press, 1986), 170, 172–73, 174–75; Jeffrey J. Crow, "Slave Rebelliousness and Social Conflict in North Carolina, 1775 to 1802," *WMQ*, 3d ser., 37 (1980): 85–86; Herbert Aptheker, *American Negro Slave Revolts* (New York: International Publishers, 1943, 1974), 87, 200–202; Benjamin Quarles, *The Negro in the American Revolution* (Chapel Hill, N.C.: University of North Carolina Press, 1961), 14.

29. Sylvia R. Frey, *Water from the Rock: Black Resistance in a Revolutionary Age* (Princeton, N.J.: Princeton University Press, 1991), 38, 61–62, 202.

30. Gary B. Nash, *Forging Freedom: The Formation of Philadelphia's Black Community, 1720–1840* (Cambridge, Mass.: Harvard University Press, 1988), 72; Quarles, *Negro in the American Revolution*, 84; Lemisch, "Jack Tar in the Streets," 375; Shane White, " 'We Dwell in Safety and Pursue Our Honest Callings': Free Blacks in New York City, 1783–1810," *Journal of American History* 75 (1988): 453–54; Ira Dye, "Early American Merchant Seafarers," *Proceedings of the American Philosophical Society* 120 (1976): 358; Philip D. Morgan, "Black Life in Eighteenth-Century Charleston," *Perspectives in American History*, new ser., 1 (1984): 200; Wood, " 'Taking Care of Business,' " in Crow and Tise, eds., *The Southern Experience*, 276; Crow, "Slave Rebelliousness," 85; Henry Laurens to John Laurens, 18 June and 23 June 1775, in *Papers of Laurens*, 10:184, 191.

31. F. Nwabueze Okoye, "Chattel Slavery as the Nightmare of the American Revolutionaries," *WMQ*, 3d ser., 37 (1980): 12; Anthony Benezet to Granville Sharp, 29 March 1773, in Roger Bruns, ed., *Am I Not a Man and a Brother: The Antislavery Crusade of Revolutionary America, 1688–1788* (New York: Chelsea House Publishers, 1977), 263.

32. John M. Bumsted and Charles E. Clark, "New England's Tom Paine: John Allen and the Spirit of Liberty," *WMQ*, 3d ser., 21 (1964): 570; Bruns, ed., *Am I Not a Man and a Brother*, 257–62; Thomas Paine, "African Slavery in America" (1775), in Philip S. Foner, *The Collected Writings of Thomas Paine* (New York: The Citadel Press, 1945), 17, 19. Wood, "The Dream Deferred," 168, 181.

33. Sharon Salinger, *"To Serve Well and Faithfully": Indentured Servitude in Pennsylvania,*

1682–1800 (Cambridge: Cambridge University Press, 1986), 101–2; Morgan, "Black Life," 206–7, 219.

34. Arthur Meier Schlesinger, "Political Mobs and the American Revolution, 1765–1776," *Proceedings of the American Philosophical Society* 99 (1955): 244–50; Lemisch, "Jack Tar in the Streets"; Pauline Maier, "Popular Uprisings and Civil Authority in Eighteenth-Century America," *WMQ*, 3d ser., 27 (1970): 3–35; Dirk Hoerder, *Crowd Action in Revolutionary Massachusetts, 1765–1780* (New York: Academic Press, 1977).

35. Hutchinson, *History of Massachusetts Bay*, 2:332; Carl Bridenbaugh, *Cities in Revolt: Urban Life in America, 1743–1776* (New York: Capricorn Books, 1955), 309; Jeremiah Morgan to Francis Fauquier, 11 September 1767, ADM 1/2116; Miller, *Sam Adams*, 142; Lemisch, "Jack Tar in the Streets," 386, 391; Colden to General Gage, 8 July 1765, in Colden Letterbooks, Letters and Papers of Cadwallader Colden, 1760–1765, *Collections of the New-York Historical Society* (1877), 23; Elaine Forman Crane, *A Dependent People: Newport, Rhode Island in the Revolutionary Era* (New York: Fordham University Press, 1985), 113.

36. Oliver Morton Dickerson, ed., *Boston Under Military Rule, 1768–1769, as revealed in A Journal of the Times* (Boston: Chapman and Grimes, Mount Vernon Press, 1936), entry for 4 May 1769, 94, 95, 110; John Allen, *Oration on the Beauties of Liberty* (1773), in Bruns, ed., *Am I Not a Man*, 258, 259 (emphasis in original).

37. Gary B. Nash, *The Urban Crucible: Social Change, Political Consciousness, and the Origins of the American Revolution* (Cambridge, Mass.: Harvard University Press, 1979), 366; Schlesinger, "Political Mobs," 244; Edmund S. Morgan and Helen M. Morgan, *The Stamp Act Crisis: Prologue to Revolution* (Chapel Hill, N.C.: University of North Carolina Press, 1953), 162, 208, 231–39; Adair and Schutz, eds., *Peter Oliver's Origin*, 51.

38. Hutchinson quoted in Anthony Pagden, *Spanish Imperialism and the Political Imagination: Studies in European and Spanish-American Social and Political Theory, 1513–1830* (New Haven, Conn.: Yale University Press, 1990), 66; Lovejoy, *Rhode Island Politics*, 105; Redington, ed., *Calendar of Home Office Papers*, 1:610; Morgan and Morgan, *Stamp Act Crisis*, 196; Lloyd I. Rudolph, "The Eighteenth-Century Mob in America and Europe," *American Quarterly* 11 (1959): 452; Spindel, "Law and Disorder," 8; *Pennsylvania Journal*, 21 November and 26 December 1765; Alfred F. Young, "English Plebeian Culture and Eighteenth-Century American Radicalism," in Margaret Jacob and James Jacob, eds., *The Origins of Anglo-American Radicalism* (London: George Allen and Unwin, 1984), 193–94; Gage quoted in Schlesinger, "Political Mobs," 246.

39. Lemisch, "Jack Tar in the Streets," 398; Lovejoy, *Rhode Island Politics*, 156, 159, 164.

40. Lee R. Boyer, "Lobster Backs, Liberty Boys, and Laborers in the Streets: New York's Golden Hill and Nassau Street Riots," *New-York Historical Society Quarterly* 57 (1973): 289–308; Hiller B. Zobel, *The Boston Massacre* (New York: W. W. Norton, 1970); L. Kinvin Wroth and Hiller B. Zobel, eds., *Legal Papers of John Adams* (Cam-

bridge, Mass.: Belknap Press of Harvard University Press, 1965), 3:266; Hoerder, *Crowd Action*, chap. 13.

41. Timothy quoted in Maier, "Charleston Mob," 181; Edward Countryman, *A People in Revolution: The American Revolution and Political Society in New York, 1760–1790* (Baltimore: John Hopkins University Press, 1981), 37, 45; Gage to Conway, 4 November 1765, in Clarence Edwin Carter, ed., *The Correspondence of General Thomas Gage, with the Secretaries of State, 1763–1775* (New Haven, Conn.: Yale University Press, 1931), 1:71; Barrington quoted in Tony Hayter, *The Army and the Crowd in Mid-Georgian London* (Totowa, N.J.: Rowman and Littlefield, 1978), 130; Charles G. Steffen, *The Mechanics of Baltimore: Workers and Politics in the Age of Revolution, 1763–1812* (Urbana, Ill.: University of Illinois Press, 1984), 73.

42. Albert G. Greene, *Recollections of the "Jersey" Prison-Ship from the Original Manuscripts of Captain Thomas Dring* (Morrisania, N.Y., 1865).

43. Jesse Lemisch, "Listening to the 'Inarticulate': William Widger's Dream and the Loyalties of American Revolutionary Seamen in British Prisons," *Journal of Social History* 3 (1969–70): 1–29; Larry G. Bowman, *Captive Americans: Prisoners during the American Revolution* (Athens, Ohio: Ohio University Press, 1976), 40–67; John K. Alexander, "Forton Prison during the American Revolution: A Case Study of the British Prisoner of War Policy and the American Prisoner Response to That Policy," *Essex Institute Historical Collections* 102 (1967): 369.

44. Clarence S. Brigham, *Paul Revere's Engravings* (Worcester, Mass.: American Antiquarian Society, 1954), 41–57; Quarles, *Negro in the American Revolution*, 125.

45. Steffen, *The Mechanics of Baltimore*, 73; Gouverneur Morris to Mr. Penn, 20 May 1774, in Peter Force, ed., *American Archives*, 4th ser., 1 (Washington, D.C., 1837): 343; Maier, "Charleston Mob," 185; Leonard W. Labaree, ed., *The Papers of Benjamin Franklin* (New Haven, Conn.: Yale University Press, 1961), 3:106; Adair and Schutz, eds., *Peter Oliver's Origin*, xv, 35, 51–55, 88, 107; Joseph Chalmers, *Plain Truth* (Philadelphia, 1776), 71.

46. Richard B. Morris, *Government and Labor in Early America* (New York: Harper and Row, 1946), 189; Lovejoy, *Rhode Island Politics*, 159; Leonard quoted in Esmond S. Wright, *Fabric of Freedom, 1763–1800*, rev. ed. (New York: Hill and Wang, 1978), 77–78.

47. Rush quoted in Eric Foner, *Tom Paine and Revolutionary America* (New York: Oxford University Press, 1976), 138; David S. Lovejoy, *Religious Enthusiasm in the New World: Heresy to Revolution* (Cambridge. Mass.: Harvard University Press, 1985), 223–24; D. Davis, *Problem of Slavery*, 333.

48. Don M. Wolfe, *Leveller Manifestoes of the Puritan Revolution* (New York: Thomas Nelson and Sons, 1944), 227, 300, 125, 287, 320, 405. See also Robin Blackburn, *The Overthrow of Colonial Slavery, 1776–1848* (London: Verso, 1988), chap. 1. Recent examinations of the Declaration of Independence have been disappointingly narrow,

ignoring the motley crew, the Levellers, and huge bodies of relevant literature from seventeenth-century England. See Pauline Maier, *American Scripture: Making the Declaration of Independence* (New York: Alfred A. Knopf, 1997), 51ff; Garry Wills, *Inventing America: Jefferson's Declaration of Independence* (Garden City, N.Y.: Doubleday, 1978).

49. Maier, *From Resistance to Revolution*, 76, 97–100; Gilje, *Road to Mobocracy*, 48; Wroth and Zobel, eds., *Legal Papers of John Adams*, 3:269; C. Adams, ed., *Works of John Adams*, 2:322.

50. Carl Becker, *The Declaration of Independence: A Study in the History of Political Ideas* (New York: Harcourt Brace, 1922), 214.

51. Alyce Barry, "Thomas Paine, Privateersman," *Pennsylvania Magazine of History and Biography* 101 (1977): 459–61.

52. Maier, "Charleston Mob," 181, 186, 188, and idem, "Popular Uprising and Civil Authority," 33–35; Hoerder, *Crowd Action*, 378–88; Gordon S. Wood, *The Creation of the American Republic, 1776–1787* (Chapel Hill, N.C.: University of North Carolina Press 1969), 319–28.

53. Charles Patrick Neimeyer, *America Goes to War: A Social History of the Continental Army* (New York: New York University Press, 1996), chap. 4; Quarles, *Negro in the American Revolution*, 15–18; Frey, *Water from the Rock*, 77–80.

54. James Madison, "Republican Distribution of Citizens," *National Gazette*, 3 March 1792, republished in *The Papers of James Madison*, ed. William T. Hutchinson and William M. E. Rachal (Chicago: University of Chicago Press, 1962–85), 14:244–46; David Humphreys, Joel Barlow, John Trumbull, and Dr. Lemuel Hopkins, *The Anarchiad: A New England Poem (1786–1787)*, ed. Luther G. Riggs (Gainesville, Fla.: Scholars' Facsimiles & Reprints, 1967), 29, 56, 38, 69, 14, 15, 34.

55. Madison's Notes and Abraham Yates's Notes, 26 June 1787, in Max Farrand, ed., *The Records of the Federal Convention of 1787* (New Haven, Con.: Yale University Press, 1937), 1:423, 431.

56. Staughton Lynd, "The Abolitionist Critique of the United States Constitution," in his *Class Conflict, Slavery, and the United States Constitution* (Indianapolis: Bobbs-Merrill, 1967), 153–54.

57. James D. Essig, *The Bonds of Wickedness: American Evangelicals against Slavery, 1770–1808* (Philadelphia: Temple University Press, 1982), 132.

58. Barbara Jeanne Fields, "Slavery, Race, and Ideology in the United States of America," *New Left Review* 181 (1990): 101; Frey, *Water from the Rock*, 234–36. Adams quoted in Schlesinger, "Political Mobs," 250.

59. Sidney Kaplan and Emma Nogrady Kaplan, *The Black Presence in the Era of the American Revolution*, rev. ed. (Amherst, Mass.: University of Massachusetts Press, 1989), 68–69; Forrest McDonald, "The Relation of the French Peasant Veterans of the American Revolution to the Fall of Feudalism in France, 1789–1792," *Agricul-*

tural History 25 (1951): 151–61; Horst Dippel, *Germany and the American Revolution, 1770–1800: A Sociohistorical Investigation of Late Eighteenth-Century Political Thinking,* trans. Bernard A. Uhlendorf (Chapel Hill, N.C.: University of North Carolina Press, 1977), 228, 236.

60. Arthur N. Gilbert, "The Nature of Mutiny in the British Navy in the Eighteenth Century," in Daniel Masterson, ed., *Naval History: The Sixth Symposium of the U.S. Naval Academy* (Wilmington, Del.: Scholarly Resources, Inc., 1987), 111–21; Richard B. Sheridan, "The Jamaican Slave Insurrection Scare of 1776 and the American Revolution," *Journal of Negro History* 61 (1976): 290–308; Julius Sherrard Scott III, "The Common Wind: Currents of Afro-American Communication in the Era of the Haitian Revolution," (Ph.D. diss., Duke University, 1986), 19, 204, 52.

61. Lord Balcarres to Commander-in-Chief, 31 July 1800, CO 137/104, quoted in Scott, "The Common Wind," 33.

62. Hoare, *Memoirs of Granville Sharp;* Lascelles, *Granville Sharp and the Freedom of Slaves in England.*

63. Thomas Clarkson, *The History of the Rise, Progress, and Accomplishment of the Abolition of the African Slave-Trade by the British Parliament* (London, 1808), 2:297.

64. Diogenes Laertius, 6:63, and Oliver Goldsmith, *Citizen of the World* (London, 1762); David Hancock, *Citizens of the World: London Merchants and the Integration of the British Atlantic Community, 1735–1785* (Cambridge: Cambridge University Press, 1995); Alfred F. Young, "*Common Sense* and *The Rights of Man* in America: The Celebration and Damnation of Thomas Paine," in K. Gavroglu, ed., *Science, Mind, and Art* (Amsterdam: Kluwer Academic Publishers, 1995), 411–39.

Chapter Eight

1. *Morning Post,* 22 February 1803. See the analysis of Despard's speech by David Worrall in his *Radical Culture: Discourse, Resistance and Surveillance, 1790–1820* (Detroit: Wayne State University Press, 1992), 58.

2. P. C. 1/3553; *The Trial of Edward Marcus Despard, Esquire,* 94, 126; T. B. Howell, *A Complete Collection of State Trials* (1820); Examination of John Emblin, TS 11/121/332.

3. Chaplain's Letters and Notes, Despard Family MSS., London.

4. PRO, P. C. 1/3564, 14 February 1803.

5. PRO, HO 42/70, 20 February 1803; *Political Register,* 26 February 1803; A. Aspinall, ed., *The Later Correspondence of George III* (Cambridge: Cambridge University Press, 1968), 4:80.

6. Despard Family MSS., [Elizabeth Despard], *Recollections on the Despard Family* (c. 1850), 22.

7. Bodleian Library, Burdett Papers. Ms. English History, c. 296, fols. 9–11; M. W. Pat-

terson, *Sir Francis Burdett and His Times 1770–1844*, (1931), 1:68; PRO, P. C. 1/3553, Examination by Richard Ford; Valentine Lord Cloncurry, *Personal Recollections* (Dublin, 1847), 45. *Authentic Memoirs of the Life of Col. E. M. Despard* (London, 1803), 22; *The Annual Register*, 1803, 142–43.

8. Joseph Farington, *Farington Diary*, ed. James Geig (London: Hutchinson, 1923), 2:83; *Authentic Memoirs*, 22.

9. *Labour in Irish History* (1910), chap. 9.

10. Rolf Loeber, "Preliminaries to the Massachusetts Bay Colony: The Irish Ventures of Emanuel Downing and John Winthrop, Sr.," in T. Barnard, D. ó Cróinin, and K. Simms, eds., *A Miracle of Learning: Studies in Manuscripts and Irish Learning: Essays in Honor of William O'Sullivan* (Brookfield, Vt.: Ashgate, 1998).

11. James Bannantine, *Memoires of Edward Marcus Despard* (London, 1799). Communication of Archdeacon H. H. J. Gray, St. Peter's Rectory, Mountrath. PRO of Northern Ireland (Belfast), T. 1075/34. Genealogical notes.

12. John Feehan, *Laois: An Environmental History* (Bailykilcavan, 1983), 289–91.

13. Angus Calder, *Revolutionary Empire: The Rise of the English-Speaking Empires from the Fifteenth Century to the 1780s* (New York: Dutton, 1981), 672–75.

14. Maurine Wall, "The Whiteboys," in Desmond T. Williams, ed., *Secret Societies in Ireland* (Dublin: Gill and Macmillan, 1973), 16; James S. Donnelly, Jr., "The Whiteboy Movement, 1761–5," *Irish Historical Studies* 21 (1978–9): 28.

15. Charles Coote, *Statistical Survey of Queen's County* (1801).

16. John Feehan, *The Landscape of Slieve Bloom: A Study of Its Natural and Human Heritage* (Dublin: Blackwater, 1979), 116.

17. Despard Family MSS., Jane Despard, *Memoranda connected with the Despard Family recollections* (1838).

18. [Elizabeth Despard], *Recollections on the Despard Family*.

19. Thomas Bartlett and Keith Jeffery, eds., *A Military History of Ireland* (Cambridge: Cambridge University Press, 1996), 257.

20. Benjamin Moseley, *A Treatise on Tropical Diseases; on Military Operations; and on the Climate of the West Indies*, 2d ed. (London, 1789), 184. Kenneth F. Kiple, *The Caribbean Slave: A Biological History* (Cambridge: Cambridge University Press, 1984), 5.

21. R. R. Madden, *A Twelvemonth's Residence in the West Indies during the Transition from Slavery to Apprenticeship* (London, 1835), 2:117; Barbara Bush, *Slave Women in Caribbean Society, 1650–1838* (Kingston, Jamaica: Heinemann, 1990).

22. Douglas Hall, ed., *In Miserable Slavery: Thomas Thistlewood in Jamaica, 1750–1786* (London: Macmillan, 1989).

23. Anonymous, "Observations on the Fortifying of Jamaica, 1783," Add. Ms. 12,431, fo. 8, British Library.

24. Major General Archibald Campbell, "A Memoir Relative to the Island of Jamaica" (1782), King's 214, British Library.

25. [Elizabeth Despard,] *Recollections on the Despard Family,* 22.

26. Douglas W. Marshall, "The British Engineers in America, 1755–1783," *Journal of the Society of Army Historical Research* 51 (1973): 155.

27. Edward K. Brathwaite, *The Development of Creole Society in Jamaica, 1770–1820* (Oxford: Oxford University Press, 1971), 126–129; J. G. Links, ed., *The Stones of Florence* (New York: Hill & Wang, 1960), 244–45.

28. Henry Rule, *Fortification* (London, 1851), 145; Peter Way, *Common Labour: Workers and the Digging of North American Canals, 1780–1860* (Cambridge: Cambridge University Press, 1993), 47.

29. Kevin Whelan, *Fellowship of Freedom: The United Irishmen and 1798* (Cork: Cork University Press, 1998), 6.

30. J. K. Budleigh, *Trench Excavation and Support* (London: Telford, 1989), 62.

31. Thomas More Molyneux, *Conjunct Operations* (1759).

32. *Collections of the New-York Historical Society* (1884), entries for 23 April, 27 May, 21 June.

33. *Narrative of Sir Alexander Leith, Lieut. Col. 88th Regiment,* 49, Germain MSS., William L. Clements Library, University of Michigan.

34. Edward Davis to Kemple, 28 September, Kemple MSS., vol. 1, William L. Clements Library, University of Michigan.

35. Peter Hulme points out that *barbeque* and *canoe* are both etymologically Caribbean words. See his *Colonial Encounters: Europe and the Native Caribbean, 1492–1797* (London: Routledge, 1986), 210–11.

36. Olaudah Equiano, *The Interesting Narrative of the Life of Olaudah Equiano* (1789), chap. 11.

37. Bell, *Tangweera: Life and Adventures among Gentle Savages* (1899; reprint Austin, Tex.: University of Texas Press, 1989); George Pinkard, *Notes on the West Indians* (1816); see also Eduard Conzemius, *Ethnographical Survey of the Miskito and Sumu Indians of Honduras and Nicaragua* (Washington, D.C.: Government Printing Office, 1932).

38. Thomas Dancer, *A Brief History of the Late Expedition Against Fort San Juan So Far as it Relates to the Diseases of the Troops* (Kingston, 1781), 12.

39. *Collections of the New-York Historical Society* (1884), entry for 21 March.

40. See Governor Dalling's defense of his role in his *Narrative of the Late Expedition to St. Juan's Harbour and Lake Nicaragua,* 13; Germain MSS., vol. 21.

41. Moseley, *Treatise on Tropical Diseases.*

42. Silvia R. Frey, *Water from the Rock: Black Resistance in a Revolutionary Age* (Princeton, N.J.: Princeton University Press, 1991), chap. 4.

43. John Marrant, *A Narrative of the Lord's Wonderful Dealing with John Marrant, a Black* (1785); Graham Hodges, ed., *The Black Loyalist Directory: African Americans in Exile after the American Revolution* (New York: Garland, 1996).

44. C. O. 700/13.

45. Grant D. Jones, *Maya Resistance to Spanish Rule: Time and History on a Colonial Frontier* (Albuquerque: University of New Mexico Press, 1989), 21, 274; George Henderson, *An Account of the British Settlement of Honduras* (London, 1811), 70; Wallace R. Johnson, *A History of Christianity in Belize, 1776–1838* (Lanham, Md.: University Press of America, 1985), 12.

46. William Dampier, "Mr. Dampier's Voyages to the Bay of Campeachy," in his *A Collection of Voyages,* 4th ed. (London, 1729), 89; Anonymous, "A Voyage to Guinea, Antego, Bay of Campeachy, Cuba, Barbadoes, &c., 1714–1723," Add. Ms. 39,946, British Library; Malachy Postlethwayt, *Universal Dictionary of Trade and Commerce* (London, 1755?).

47. Robert A. Naylor, *Penny Ante Imperialism: The Mosquito Shore and the Bay of Honduras, 1600–1914, A Case Study in British Informal Imperialism* (Rutherford, N.J.: Associated University Presses, 1989), 41; F. O. Winzerling, *The Beginning of British Honduras, 1506–1765* (New York: North River Press, 1946), 81; Edwin J. Layton, *Thomas Chippendale: A Review of His Life and Origin* (London: J. Murray, 1928).

48. "Convention of London," 14 July 1786, in Sir John Alder Burdon, *Archives of British Honduras* (London: Sifton, Piraed and Co., 1931), 1:154–57.

49. Quoted in Narda Dobson, *A History of Belize* (London: Longman, 1973), 67; see also José A. Calderón Quijano, "Un Incidente Militar en los establecimientos ingleses in Río Tinto (Honduras) en 1782," *Annuario de Estudios Americanos* 2 (1945): 761–84; Robert White, *The Case of the Agent to the Settlers on the Coast of Yucatan; and the late Settlers on the Mosquito Shore* (London, 1793), 10.

50. Henderson, *An Account,* 134; CO 123/5, 24 August 1787; Burdon, *Archives of British Honduras,* 1:161; Despard to ?, 11 January 1788, CO 123/6.

51. Despard to Lord Sydney, 23 February 1787, CO 123/4, fo. 49; Despard to Lord Sydney, 24 August 1787, CO 137/50; Burdon, ed., *Archives of British Honduras,* 1:159, 161.

52. Despard to Sydney, 24 August 1787, CO 123/5; Edward Marcus Despard, "A Narrative of the Publick Transactions in the Bay of Honduras from 1784 to 1790," 8 March 1791, CO 123/10.

53. Quoted in O. Nigel Bolland, *The Formation of a Colonial Society: Belize from Conquest to Crown Colony* (Baltimore: Johns Hopkins University Press, 1977), 38. Burdon, ed., *Archives of British Honduras,* 1:159; Despard to Lord Sydney, 24 August 1787, CO 137/50.

54. Despard, "Appendix to the Narrative of Publick Transactions in the Bay of Honduras 1784–1790," CO 123/11. Perhaps she was the Catherine Ernest included among a list of the "poor people of colour" from the Mosquito Shore. Her name does not recur on the list of new settlers who received the lots in Belize Town distributed by Des-

pard several months later, a fact consistent with the hypothesis that Catherine had meanwhile become his wife. See Robert White, *The Case of the Agent to the Settlers on the Coast of Yucatan.*

55. Mary Thale, ed., *Selections from the Papers of the LCS 1792–1799* (Cambridge: Cambridge University Press, 1983), 8, 18.

56. *A Narrative of the Proceedings of the Black People during the late awful calamity in Philadelphia in the year 1793* (1794).

57. *The Proceedings at the Old Bailey*, February 1790, 15 September 1802, April 1803, Dec. 1802, 27 October 1802, 4 July 1802, 15 September 1802.

58. Herbert Aptheker, ed., *A Documentary History of the Negro People in the United States* (New York: Citadel Press, 1951); and idem, *American Negro Slave Revolts* (New York: International Publishers, 1943, 1974).

59. Worrall, *Radical Culture;* Iain McCalman, *Radical Underworld: Prophets, Revolutionaries, and Pornographers in London, 1795–1840* (New York: Cambridge University Press, 1993); and Roger Wells, *Wretched Faces: Famine in Wartime England, 1793–1803* (New York: St. Martin's, 1988); Malcolm Chase, *"The People's Farm": English Radical Agrarianism, 1775–1840* (Oxford: Clarendon Press, 1988).

60. Carolyn Fick, *The Making of Haiti: The Saint Domingue Revolution from Below* (Knoxville: University of Tennessee Press, 1990); 217–24; Iowerth Prothero, *Artisans and Politics in Early Nineteenth-Century London: John Gast and His Times* (Baton Rouge, La.: Louisiana State University, 1979).

61. *A Treatise on the Commerce and Police of the River Thames* (1800), 210.

62. *Pig's Meat*, iii, 56, 212–13, and W. H. Reid, *The Rise and Dissolution of the Infidel Societies in the Metropolis* (1800), 14, 93. See also Olivia Smith, *The Politics of Language, 1791–1819* (Oxford: Clarendon Press, 1984).

63. P. C. 1/3514 f. 100.

64. R. R. Madden, *The Life and Times of Robert Emmet* (New York, 1896), 13. Thomas Spence, *The Restorer of Society to its Natural State* (1801). PRO, P. C. 1/3117, pt. 1, fol. 87; T. S. 11/121/332. f. 37.

65. *Paddy's Resource Being a Select Collection of Original and Modern Patriotic Songs, Toasts and Sentiments Compiled for the use of the People of Ireland* (Belfast, 1795).

66. Jim Smyth, *The Men of No Property: Irish Radicals and Popular Politics in the Late Eighteenth Century* (New York: St. Martin's, 1992), 151.

67. Kevin Whelan, *The Tree of Liberty: Radicalism, Catholicism and the Construction of Irish Identity, 1760–1830* (Cork: University of Cork Press, 1996).

68. Thomas Russell, *Address to the People of Ireland* (1796).

69. Viscount Stewart Castlereagh, *Memoirs and Correspondence*, ed. Charles Vane II (London, 1850), 417.

70. *Detection of a Conspiracy Formed by the United Irishmen* (Philadelphia, 1798), 28ff.

71. Roger Wells, *Insurrection: The British Experience* (Gloucester: Alan Sutton, 1983), 134.

72. Despard's brother considered his part in the mob to be "extremely foolish; had he possessed common prudence he might now be in comfortable circumstances." Despard Family MSS., Letter to Andrew Despard from J. Despard, 28 May 1796.

73. Examination of Arthur Graham, TS 11/221/332, f. 46. Iain McCalman, "Newgate in Revolution: Radical Enthusiasm and Romantic Counterculture," *Eighteenth-Century Life* 22, no. 1 (1998).

74. Joyce M. Bellamy and John Saville, eds., *Dictionary of Labour Biography* (Clifton, N.J.: A. M. Kelley, 1972).

75. Ralph Manoque, "The Plight of James Ridgway, London Bookseller and Publisher, and the Newgate Radicals, 1792–1797," *Wordsworth Circle* 27 (1996).

76. Doug Hay, "The Laws of God and the Laws of Man: Lord George Gordon and the Death Penalty," in John Rule and Robert Malcolmson, eds., *Protest and Survival: Essays for E. P. Thompson* (London: Merlin, 1993), 60–111.

77. PRO, P. C. 1/3553, Examination by Richard Ford.

78. PRO. KB 1/31, pt. 1.

79. David Levi, *Dissertations on the Prophecies of the Old Testament*, 3 vols. (1793–1800).

80. A. L. Morton, *The Everlasting Gospel: A Study in the Sources of William Blake* (London: Lawrence and Wishart, 1958), 36. E. P. Thompson, *Witness against the Beast: William Blake and the Moral Law* (New York: The New Press, 1994).

81. Quobna Ottobah Cugoano, *Thoughts and Sentiments on the Evil of Slavery*, ed. Vincent Carretta (London: Penguin, 1999), 93, 110, 111.

82. Michael Duffy, *Soldiers, Sugar, and Seapower: The British Expeditions to the West Indies and the War against Revolutionary France* (London: Oxford University Press, 1987), 387.

83. O. Smith, *Politics of Language*, 71.

84. Will Chip, *Village Politics, addressed to all the mechanics, journeymen and day labourers in Great Britain, by Will Chip, a country carpenter* (1793).

85. Joan Dayan, *Haiti, History, and the Gods* (Berkeley, Calif.: University of California Press, 1995).

86. John Hunter, *Observations on the Disease of the Army in Jamaica* (1788), and Charles White, *An Account of the Regular Gradation in Man . . .* (1799).

87. David V. Erdman, *Commerce des Lumières: John Oswald and the British in Paris, 1790–1793* (Columbia, Mo.: University of Missouri Press, 1986).

88. Donna T. Andrew, *London Debating Societies, 1776–1799* (London: London Record Society, 1994), 281.

89. Alan Wharam, *The Treason Trials 1794* (London: Leicester University Press, 1992), 110.

Chapter Nine

1. Inventory Book, 1B/11/3, vol. 135, National Archives, Spanish Town, Jamaica.

2. Robert Wedderburn, *The Horrors of Slavery* (London, 1824), republished in Iain McCalman, ed., *"The Horrors of Slavery" and Other Writings by Robert Wedderburn* (Edinburgh: Edinburgh University Press, 1991). Wedderburn chooses italic, bold, and upper-case characters from the typographer's case, breaking with the English conventions of printed expression, because he feels that his own character, or type, requires that English conventions of printing and writing, in addition to those of political thinking, be modified to make room for a voice such as his own. The printing parallels Wedderburn's unconventional interruption described in Cruikshank's print *The City of London Tavern* (1817). See page 325.

3. Robert Hamilton, *The Duties of a Regimental Surgeon Considered*, 2 vols. (1794).

4. Joan Dayan, *Haiti, History, and the Gods* (Berkeley, Calif: University of California Press, 1995).

5. The *Political Register*, July 1809; see also The *Examiner*, September 1810. The punishment was meant to terrorize and to silence. Anna Clark examined the Old Bailey *Proceedings* and concluded that after 1795 the court began to suppress the testimony of women against violence, rape, and beatings. Deborah Valenze shows that this was the period of the devaluation of women's labor: the violence against them and the silencing of their complaints were means of making their wages subsubsistence, their work supersubmissive, and themselves an ideal subject for the horrors of the factory. Anna Clark, *Women's Silence, Men's Violence: Sexual Assault in England, 1770–1845* (London: Pandora, 1987), 17; Deborah Valenze, *The First Industrial Woman* (New York: Oxford University Press, 1995), 89.

6. Wedderburn, *Horrors of Slavery*.

7. Iain McCalman, "Anti-Slavery and Ultra-Radicalism in Early Nineteenth-Century England: The Case of Robert Wedderburn," *Slavery and Abolition* 7 (1986): 101–3.

8. See his *Truth Self-Supported; or A Refutation of Certain Doctrinal Errors Generally Adopted in the Christian Church* (c. 1802), republished in McCalman, ed., *"The Horrors of Slavery" and Other Writings*.

9. *The Axe Laid to the Root*, no. 4 (1817).

10. Ian McCalman, *Radical Underworld: Prophets, Revolutionaries, and Pornographers in London, 1795–1840* (Cambridge: Cambridge University Press, 1988); Henry Lewis Gates, Jr., *The Signifying Monkey: A Theory of African American Literary Criticism* (New York: Oxford University Press, 1988).

11. James Cone, *A Black Theology of Liberation*, 2d ed. (Maryknoll, N.Y.: Orbis, 1986), 31.

12. *Political Register*, October 1809; Malcolm Chase, "From Millennium to Anniversary: The Concept of Jubilee in Late Eighteenth- and Nineteenth-Century En-

gland," *Past and Present* 129 (1990): 132–47. In 1795 Coleridge had lectured with deep scholarship on jubilee and open sympathetic fraternity to the poor.

13. Peter Linebaugh, "Jubilating; Or, How the Atlantic Working Class Used the Biblical Jubilee against Capitalism, with Some Success," *Radical History Review* 50 (1991): 143–80; James Harrington, *Oceana* (London, 1656), and idem, *The Art of Lawgiving* (London, 1659); John Bunyan, *The Advocateship of Jesus Christ* (London, 1688).

14. P. M. Ashraf, *The Life and Times of Thomas Spence* (Newcastle upon Tyne: Frank Graham, 1983), 101. See also Thomas R. Knox, "Thomas Spence: The Trumpet of Jubilee," *Past and Present* 76 (1977); Malcolm Chase, *"The People's Farm": English Radical Agrarianism, 1775–1840* (Oxford: Clarendon Press, 1988); Alan Dean Gilbert II, "Landlords and Lacklanders: The Radical Politics and Popular Political Economy of Thomas Spence and Robert Wedderburn" (Ph.D. diss., SUNY Buffalo, 1997).

15. See "The Marine Republic (1794)," in *Pig's Meat,* 2d ed., 2:68–72 (emphasis in original); A. L. Morton, *The English Utopia* (London: Lawrence and Wishart, 1952), 164, 165 (quotation).

16. Joel W. Martin, *Sacred Revolt: The Muskogees' Struggle for a New World* (Boston: Beacon Press, 1991). In his last published writing, *The Giant Killer* (1814), Spence wrote about slavery. See Ashraf, *Life and Times.*

17. John Wesley, *Thoughts Upon Slavery* (London, 1774), 55–56.

18. John Rylands Library (Deansgate, Manchester), Methodist Archives Center, Thomas Coke Papers, PLP/28/4/10.

19. *Commentary,* 481–83.

20. Nathan O. Hatch, *The Democratization of American Christianity* (New Haven, Conn.: Yale University Press, 1989), 102–13.

21. Sterling Stuckey, *Slave Culture: Nationalist Theory and the Foundations of Black America* (New York: Oxford University Press, 1987), chap. 1.

22. Douglas R. Egerton, *Gabriel's Rebellion: The Virginia Slave Conspiracies of 1800 and 1802* (Chapel Hill, N.C.: University of North Carolina Press, 1993).

23. Edward A. Pearson, eds., *Designs against Charleston: The Trial Record of the Denmark Vesey Slave Conspiracy of 1822* (Chapel Hill, N.C.: University of North Carolina Press, 1999); Douglas R. Egerton, *He Shall Go Out Free: The Lives of Denmark Vesey* (Madison, Wisc.: Madison House, 1999).

24. David Walker, *Appeal to the Coloured Citizens of the World, but in particular, and very expressly, to those of The United States of America* (1829; reprint ed. James Turner, Baltimore: Black Classic Press, 1993); Peter H. Hinks, *To Awaken My Afflicted Brethren: David Walker and the Problem of Antebellum Slave Resistance* (University Park, Pa.: Pennsylvania State University Press, 1997).

25. Henry Mayer, *All on Fire: William Lloyd Garrison and the Abolition of Slavery* (New York: St. Martin's Press, 1998), 188.

26. Vicki L. Eaklor, *American Antislavery Songs: A Collection and Analysis,* Documentary Reference Collections series (New York: Greenwood Press, 1988).

27. Elizabeth Campbell may have been related to the several Campbells among the Trelawny maroons, who after their defeat in the Second Maroon War were tricked into being deported to Nova Scotia. Other maroons lived outside their communities without giving up their maroon status. See Mavis C. Campbell, *Nova Scotia and the Fighting Maroons: A Documentary History,* no. 41 (January 1990) of *Studies in Third World Societies,* 196, 207, 211, 238. The *Jamaica Almanac* of 1818 lists an Elizabeth Campbell of Amity Hall in Trelawny as the owner of fifteen slaves. See the *Inventory Book,* volume 130, page 236 (20 August 1818), and *Index to Manumissions,* volume 1, number 47, National Library (Kingston). The Feurtado Manuscript notes the death of one Elizabeth Campbell, aged thirty-three, in 1825, and identifies her as a matron in the Public Hospital in Kingston; see National Archive (Spanish Town).

28. Alfred Hasbrouck, *Foreign Legionaries in the Liberation of Spanish South America* (New York: Columbia University Press, 1928); Mavis Campbell, *The Dynamics of Change in a Slave Society: A Sociopolitical History of the Free Coloureds of Jamaica, 1800–1865* (Rutherford, N.J.: Fairleigh Dickinson University Press, 1976), 71.

29. *Barbados Mercury and Bridgetown Gazette,* 7 September 1816, quoted in Hilary McD. Beckles, *Black Rebellion in Barbados: The Struggle against Slavery, 1627–1838* (Barbados: Antilles Publications, 1987), 95–113; Horace Campbell, *Rasta and Resistance from Marcus Garvey to Walter Rodney* (Trenton, N.J.: Africa World Press, 1987), 28; Seymour Drescher, *Capitalism and Antislavery: British Mobilization in Comparative Perspective* (New York: Oxford University Press, 1987), 107; Robin Blackburn, *The Overthrow of Colonial Slavery, 1776–1848* (London: Verso, 1988), 323–25.

30. *A Correct Report of the Trial of James Watson, Senior, for High Treason* (1817); *The Life and Opinions of Thomas Preston* (1817); *The Trial of James Watson* (1817), 1:72; Malcolm Chase, "Thomas Preston," in Joyce M. Bellamy, John Saville, and David Martin, eds., *Dictionary of Labour Biography,* vol. 8 (London: Mcmillan, 1987).

31. *Votes of the Honourable House of Assembly, 28 October–16 December 1817,* 127, National Library of Jamaica.

32. See *Copp's Return* in Andrew Hopton, ed., *Abiezer Coppe: Selected Writings* (London: Aporia, 1987), 72.

33. Mervyn C. Alleyne, *Roots of Jamaican Culture* (London: Pluto Press, 1988), 83–96; Erna Brodber, *Myal, A Novel* (London: New Beacon, 1988). See also Edward Long, *History of Jamaica* (London, 1774); Monica Schuler, *"Alas, Alas, Kongo": A Social History of Indentured African Immigration into Jamaica, 1841–1865* (Baltimore: Johns Hopkins University Press, 1980), 33–36; and John Thornton, *Africa and Africans in the Making of the Atlantic World, 1400–1680* (Cambridge: Cambridge University Press, 1992).

34. *A Brief Account of the Life, Experience, Travels and Gospel Labours of George White, An*

African Written by Himself and Revised by a Friend (New York, 1810); J. Ann Hone, *For the Cause of Truth: Radicalism in London, 1796–1821* (Oxford: Clarendon Press, 1982), 225; Thomas Paine, *The Age of Reason,* part 1, reprinted in *The Thomas Paine Reader,* ed. Michael Foot and Isaac Kramnick (London: Penguin, 1987), 413; Thomas Spence, *The Restorer of Society to its Natural State* (London, 1801), 16–18; HO 42/199 (29 November 1819), PRO.

35. Violet Smythe, "Liberators of the Oppressed: Baptist Mission in Jamaica 1814–1845" (B. A. thesis, University of the West Indies [Mona], 1983). See also Albert J. Raboteau, *Slave Religion: The "Invisible Institution" in the Antebellum South* (New York: Oxford University Press, 1978).

36. Mary Turner, *Slaves and Missionaries: The Disintegration of Jamaican Slave Society, 1787–1834* (Urbana, Ill.: University of Illinois Press, 1982), 88; *The Life, History, and Unparalleled Sufferings of John Jea, the African Preacher* (Portsea, 1817); Matthew Gregory Lewis, *Journal of a West India Proprietor* (London, 1834), 187.

37. Thomas Evans, *Christian Policy, the Salvation of the Empire* (London, 1816), 19; *The Axe Laid to the Root,* no. 4 (1817).

38. Lewis, *Journal,* 173–74. Donald G. Mathews, *Slavery and Methodism 1780–1845* (Princeton, N.J.: Princeton University Press, 1965); Wesley, *Thoughts Upon Slavery;* M. Turner, *Slaves and Missionaries;* Edward K. Brathwaite, *The Development of Creole Society in Jamaica, 1770–1820* (Oxford: Clarendon Press, 1971), 259.

39. Orlando Patterson, "Slavery and Slave Revolt: A Sociological Analysis of the First Maroon War, 1655–1740," *Social and Economic Studies,* 1970, and Mavis C. Campbell, *The Maroons of Jamaica, 1655–1796: A History of Resistance, Collaboration & Betrayal* (South Hadley, Mass.: Bergin and Garvey, 1988); *The Axe Laid to the Root,* no. 4 (1817).

40. *The Axe Laid to the Root,* no. 4 (1817).

41. Lewis, *Journal,* 39, 179; *The Axe Laid to the Root,* no. 6 (1817).

42. Campbell, *The Maroons.* See chapter 4 above.

43. M. W. Patterson, *Sir Francis Burdett and His Times,* 2 vols. (London: Macmillan, 1931).

44. Douglas Hall, ed., *In Miserable Slavery: Thomas Thistlewood in Jamaica, 1750–1786* (London: Macmillan, 1989), 26; M. Turner, *Slaves and Missionaries,* 47; Julius Scott, "Afro-American Sailors and the International Communication Network: The Case of Newport Bowers," in Colin Howell and Richard J. Twomey, eds., *Jack Tar in History: Essays in the History of Maritime Life and Labour* (New Brunswick: Acadiensis Press, 1991).

45. Ira Dye, "Physical and Social Profiles of Early American Seafarers, 1812–1815," in Howell and Twomey, eds., *Jack Tar in History.*

46. *The Axe Laid to the Root,* no. 6 (1817). See also Graham Hodges, ed., *Black Itinerants of the Gospel: The Narratives of John Jea and George White* (Madison, Wisc.: Madison

House, 1993); W. Jeffrey Bolster, *Black Jacks: African American Seamen in the Age of Sail* (Cambridge, Mass.: Harvard University Press, 1997), 33, 211.

47. Brathwaite, *Development of Creole Society,* 170 (quoting 1 Geo. III c. 22 [1760]); *The Axe Laid to the Root,* no. 1 (1817).

48. *The Axe Laid to the Root,* no. 4 (1817); Lewis, *Journal,* 405. For suggestions about the "Shariers," we thank Dr. Kenneth Ingram of the National Library of Jamaica and Professor Mavis Campbell.

49. Barry Higman, *Jamaica Surveyed: Plantation Maps and Plans of the Eighteenth and Nineteenth Centuries* (Kingston: Institute of Jamaica Publications, Ltd., 1988), 261–62; Sidney W. Mintz, "The Historical Sociology of Jamaican Villages," in Charles V. Carnegie, ed., *Afro-Caribbean Villages in Historical Perspective* (Kingston: African-Caribbean Institute of Jamaica, 1987).

50. Examination of William Plush (1819), *Rex V. Wedderburn* (TS 11/45/167, PRO, reprinted in McCalman, ed., *"Horrors of Slavery,"* 120); *The "Forlorn Hope," or A Call to the Supine* (n.d., 1800s).

51. A. J. Peacock, *Bread or Blood: A Study of the Agrarian Riots in East Anglia, in 1816* (London: Gollancz, 1965), 18.

52. *"Forlorn Hope,"* 15; *The Axe Laid to the Root,* no. 5 (1817).

53. HO 42/195, PRO, published in McCalman, ed., *"Horrors of Slavery,"* 111.

54. *The Axe Laid to the Root,* no. 4 (1817); E. P. Thompson, *The Making of the English Working Class* (London: Gollancz, 1963), 632.

55. *Old Bailey Proceedings,* 15 January 1817; *Political Register,* No. 21 (1817).

56. *The Axe Laid to the Root,* no. 6 (1817); *The Horrors of Slavery.*

57. National Library (Kingston), Nugent Papers, MS 72, Box 3 (1804–1806), fol. 279.

58. *The Axe Laid to the Root,* no. 2 (1817).

59. Ibid., ibid., no. 5 (1817).

60. *The Axe Laid to the Root,* no. 4 (1817).

61. Wedderburn, *Truth Self-Supported,* in McCalman, ed., *"Horrors of Slavery,"* 57, 100.

62. Ibid., 82; Hone, *For the Cause of Truth,* 307; Iowerth Prothero, "William Benbow and the Concept of the 'General Strike,'" *Past and Present* 63 (1974): 147; McCalman, ed., *"Horrors of Slavery,"* 81, 116.

63. James Kelly, *Voyage to Jamaica,* 2d ed. (Belfast, 1838), 29–30; Barry M. Higman, *Slave Population and Economy in Jamaica, 1807–1834* (Cambridge: Cambridge University Press, 1976), 147; Pierce Egan, *Life in London* (1821), 320–21.

64. Benjamin Waterhouse, *A Journal of a Young Man of Massachusetts* (Boston, 1816) reprinted in the *Magazine of History,* no. 18 (1911).

65. Michael Ventura, "Hear that Long Snake Moan," in *Shadow Dancing in the U.S.A.* (Los Angeles: Jeremy P. Tarcher, 1985), 103–162; W. T. Lhamon, Jr., *Raising Cain* (Cambridge, Mass.: Harvard University Press, 1998).

66. *Old Bailey Proceedings*, 15 January 1817, and McCalman's introduction to "*Horrors of Slavery*," 15; Stanley Palmer, *Police and Protest in England and Ireland, 1780–1850* (Cambridge: Cambridge University Press, 1988), 169; Iowerth Prothero, *Artisans and Politics in Early Nineteenth-Century London: John Gast and His Times* (Baton Rouge, La.: Louisiana State University, 1979), 90.

67. Wedderburn, *Truth Self-Supported*, in McCalman, ed., "*Horrors of Slavery*," 67, 82, 98; *The Axe Laid to the Root*, nos. 1 and 4 (1817); Robert Wedderburn, *High-Heel'd Shoes for Dwarfs in Holiness*, 3d ed. (London, 1820), 8; M. Turner, *Slaves and Missionaries*, 58.

68. Examination of William Plush, in McCalman, ed., "*Horrors of Slavery*," 120; Wedderburn, *The Address of the Rev. R. Wedderburn*, in ibid. 134.

69. Chapters 20–22. The theory stems from Charles DuPuis, *Origines de toutes les Cultes* (1795).

70. *King v. Wedderburn*, TS 11/45/167 in McCalman, ed., "*Horrors of Slavery*," 125.

71. *The Axe Laid to the Root*, no. 1 (1817); McCalman, "Anti-Slavery and Ultra-Radicalism," 112; Julius S. Scott, "A Perfect Air of Slavery: British Sailors and Abolition," unpublished manuscript, courtesy of the author. For a useful debate on workers and abolitionism, see James Walvin, "The Impact of Slavery on British Radical Politics, 1787–1838," in Vera Rubin and Arthur Tuden, eds., *Comparative Perspectives on Slavery in New World Plantation Societies* (New York: New York Academy of Sciences, 1977), 343–67; Patricia Hollis, "Anti-Slavery and British Working-Class Radicalism in the Years of Reform," in Christine Bolt and Seymour Drescher, eds., *Anti-Slavery, Religion, and Reform: Essays in Memory of Roger Anstey* (Folkstone: Archon Books, 1980), 297–311; Drescher, *Capitalism and Anti-Slavery*.

72. Walvin, "Impact of Slavery," 346; M. Turner, *Slaves and Missionaries*, 200.

Conclusion

1. Adam Smith, *The Wealth of Nations* (1776), book 5, chapter 1, part 3, article 2; and Karl Marx, *Capital*, trans. Ben Fowkes (London: Penguin, 1976), chap. 14, 476, 549.

2. Thomas Bartlett, ed., *Life of Wolfe Tone* (Dublin: Lilliput, 1998), 437.

3. Gwyn A. Williams, *Search for Beulah Land* (New York: Holmes and Meier, 1980), 71.

4. *Rights of Nature* (1796), in Gregory Claeys, ed., *Political Writings of the 1790s* (Brookfield, Vt.: Pickering and Chatto, 1995), 4:407.

5. *Thoughts and Sentiments on the Evil of Slavery* (1787, 1791), 36–37. In 1934 Samuel Beckett translated an article during the anglophone moment of *négritude:* "If the race of Negroes should happen to disappear tomorrow, no doubt, their absence would be deprecated by the white man; as transatlantic stokers, as hewers and carriers of water it would be a matter of some difficulty to replace them." See Nancy Cunard, *The Negro Anthology* (London: Nancy Cunard at Wishart, 1934), 580.

6. Brit. Lib., Add. MSS 33122 (Pelham Papers), "Minutes Relating to the Trial of Col. Despard."

7. Joan Dayan, "Haiti, History, and the Gods," in Gyan Prakash, ed., *After Colonialism: Imperial Histories and Postcolonial Developments* (Princeton, N.J.: Princeton University Press, 1995), 83ff.

8. Francis Midon, *The History of the Rise and Fall of Masaniello, the Fisherman of Naples* (1729), 204–5.

9. Lura Pedrini, *Serpent Imagery and Symbolism: A Study of the Major English Romantic Poets* (Utica, N.Y.: State Hospitals Press, 1962), 31.

10. *A Social History of England* (London: Penguin, 1983), 198; *Agrarian Justice* (1795).

11. See Mumia Abu-Jamal, *Live from Death Row* (Reading, Mass.: Addison Wesley, 1995).

12. The address is reprinted in E. P. Thompson, *The Making of the English Working Class* (London: Gollancz, 1963), 199–202. Iowerth Prothero, *Artisans and Politics in Early Nineteenth-Century London: John Gast and His Times,* (Baton Rouge, La.: Louisiana State University, 1979), 68, 182. Peter Gaskell described the factory proletariat as "but a Hercules in the cradle," in *The Manufacturing Population of England* (1833), 6.

13. William Jeremiah Moses, *Afrotopia: The Roots of African American Popular History* (Cambridge: Cambridge University Press, 1998).

14. *Reflections on the Revolution in France* (1790).

15. Olaudah Equiano, *The Interesting Narrative and other Writings,* ed. Vincent Carretta (New York: Penguin, 1995), 38.

16. T. C. Smout, *A History of the Scottish People, 1560–1830* (London: Collins, 1969), 302.

17. M. D. George, *London Life in the Eighteenth Century* (New York: Alfred A. Knopf, 1925).

18. Peter Fryer, *Staying Power: A History of Black People in England* (London: Pluto Press, 1984).

19. R. B. McDowell, *Ireland in the Age of Imperialism and Revolution* (New York: Oxford University Press, 1979), 348; Kevin Whelan, *The Tree of Liberty: Radicalism, Catholicism and the Construction of Irish Identity, 1760–1830* (Cork: University of Cork Press, 1996), 100.

20. Nini Rodgers, "Equiano in Belfast: A Study of the Anti-slavery Ethos in a Northern Town," *Slavery and Abolition* 18 (1997), 80.

21. Thomas Hardy, *Memoir of Thomas Hardy* (London, 1832), 8–9.

22. Albert Goodwin, *The Friends of Liberty: British Democratic Movements at the Time of the French Revolution* (Cambridge, Mass.: Harvard University Press, 1979).

23. *State Trials for High Treason,* part 2, *The Trial of John Horne Tooke* (1794), 53.

24. John Wilson, ed., *The Songs of Joseph Mather* (Sheffield, 1862), 63–66.

25. Roy Porter, *Doctor of Society: Thomas Beddoes and the Sick Trade in Late-Enlightenment England* (London and New York: Routledge, 1992).

26. As we read in the "Original Letter Book of the Corresponding Society." British Library Add. MS. 27,811, The Place Papers, fols. 4v–5r.

27. Roger Anstey, *The Atlantic Slave Trade and British Abolition, 1760–1810* (Atlantic Highlands, N.J.: Humanities Press, 1975), 276.

28. Lydia's letter is quoted in Clare Midgley, *Women against Slavery: The British Campaigns, 1780–1870* (London and New York: Routledge, 1992), 39. David Brion Davis, *The Problem of Slavery in the Age of Revolution, 1770–1823* (Ithaca, N.Y.: Cornell University Press, 1975), 429–39; Philip D. Curtin, *The Atlantic Slave Trade: A Census* (Madison, Wisc.: University of Wisconsin Press, 1969), 136, 140.

29. R. Coupland, *Wilberforce: A Narrative* (Oxford: Clarendon Press, 1923), 159.

30. David Erdman, *Blake: Prophet against Empire*, 3d ed. (Princeton, N.J.: Princeton University Press, 1977), 238. Seymour Drescher, *Capitalism and Antislavery* (New York: Oxford University Press, 1987), 84, 220, 229; J. R. Oldfield, *Popular Politics and British Anti-Slavery: The Mobilisation of Public Opinion against the Slave Trade, 1787–1807* (Manchester: Manchester University Press, 1995), 3.

31. Carl Ludwig Lokke, "London Merchant Interest in the St. Domingue Plantations of the Émigrés, 1793–1798," *American Historical Review* 43, no. 4 (1938): 799–800.

32. Adrian Randall, *Before the Luddites: Custom, Community, and Machinery in the English Woollen Industry, 1776–1809* (New York: Cambridge University Press, 1991), 265.

33. T. B. Howell, ed., *State Trials* 25:1099.

34. C. F. Volney, *The Ruins, Or, Meditation of the Revolutions of Empires: and The Law of Nature* (reprint, Baltimore: Black Classic Press, 1991), 66.

35. Mary Thale, ed., *Selections from the Papers of the LCS 1792–1799* (Cambridge: Cambridge University Press, 1983), entry for April 1798, 435.

36. A. Ruy, *A primeira revoluçao social brasileria 1798* (1942), quoted in R. R. Palmer, *The Age of the Democratic Revolution: A Political History of Europe and America, 1760–1809* (Princeton, N.J.: Princeton University Press, 1964), 2:512.

37. *The Patriot*, 21 May 1793; Gwyn A. Williams, "Morgan John Rhys and Volney's *Ruins of Empires*," *Bulletin of Celtic Studies* 20 (1962); Whelan, *Tree of Liberty*, 63, 78, 80.

38. Henry Redhead Yorke, *Letters from France in 1802* (London, 1802), 2:328; C. F. Volney, *The Ruins: Or, A Survey of the Revolutions of Empires* (London: J. Johnson, 1795), 146–48. Thomas Jefferson translated the first twenty chapters, which formed the basis of Joel Barlow's translation of 1801–2. Jefferson asked Volney to burn the manuscript of his translation. See Gilbert Chinard, *Volney et l'Amérique* (Baltimore: Johns Hopkins University Press, 1923), 110–11.

39. Volney, *The Ruins,* 39.

40. This is from the 1795 translation, page 29, rather than the 1802 translation.

41. Jean Gaulmier, *Un Grand Témoin de la Révolution et de l'Empire: Volney* (Paris: Hachette, 1959), 21.

42. James Morton Smith, *Freedom's Fetters: The Alien and Sedition Laws and American Civil Liberties* (Ithaca, N.Y.: Cornell University Press, 1956), 50–51, 160, Adams quoted at 162; James Morton Smith, ed., *The Republic of Letters: The Correspondence between Thomas Jefferson and James Madison, 1776–1826* (New York: Norton, 1995), vol. 2, entry for 3 May 1798.

43. Erdman, *Blake;* and John Gabriel Stedman, *Narrative of a Five Years Expedition against the Revolted Negroes of Surinam—Transcribed for the First Time from the Original 1790 Manuscript,* ed. Richard Price and Sally Price (Baltimore: Johns Hopkins University Press, 1988).

44. Stedman, 359.

45. E. P. Thompson, *Witness against the Beast: William Blake and the Moral Law* (New York: The New Press, 1993), 212.

46. William Wells Brown, *The Black Man, His Antecedents, His Genius, His Achievements* (1863), 32–33. Almost half of the fourth chapter consists of footnotes substantiating the proposition that civilization began in Africa. Otherwise, American editions expunged the priority that Volney gave to African civilization. "Who built the seven gates of Thebes?" Brecht asked in his poem "A Worker Reads History," on the aftermath of the invasion of Ethiopia in 1935. George W. Williams coined the expression "crimes against humanity" advancing Volney's dearest cause.

ᴄᴧcknowledgments

Oᴜʀ ᴄᴏʟʟᴀʙᴏʀᴀᴛɪᴏɴ ᴏʀɪɢɪɴᴀᴛᴇᴅ at a conference on "The World Turned Upside Down," held in 1981 with the assistance of the University of Pennsylvania and the Philadelphia Center for Early American Studies in honor of Christopher and Bridget Hill. We furthered the collaboration at subsequent conferences, in Miami, Baltimore, Claremont, Milan, Atlanta, New Orleans, Halifax (Nova Scotia), Boston, Moscow, Chicago, Amsterdam, London, Detroit, Pittsburgh, Toledo, Durham, and Los Angeles. We thank those who organized the meetings and those who commented on our work. We also thank Bryan Palmer and Gregory Kealey, who gave us an opportunity to publish some of our early findings, and the Midnight Notes Collective, which helped us to think. We thank those whose kindred projects have been so important to us: Julius Scott, Robin D. G. Kelley, Robin Blackburn, Michael West, Paul Gilroy, Susan Pennybacker, James Holstun, Dave Roediger. Thanks to Staughton and Alice Lynd and the Youngstown Workers' Solidarity Club. We thank the comrade remembrancers who passed on before we finished: John Merrington, George Rawick, Raphael Samuel, Edward Thompson, Jim Thorpe, Gwyn Williams. We thank especially our colleagues at Beacon Press: Edna Chiang, always helpful; Dorothy Straight, for gracious and meticulous copyediting; and our editor, Deb Chasman, who first contacted us about this project seven years ago, and since then has given it her catalytic intelligence, energy, humor, and wisdom. We are deeply grateful.

I, Peter Linebaugh, thank family—especially Grandmother Jean, Nick and Joanne, Andy and Linda, Lisa and Scott, Dave, Tom and Charlotte, and Kate—ever ready with the jolly boat. Thanks to Janet Withers and her hospitable moorings. Thanks to Denis and Edna for showing the chalk cliffs again. Thanks to Dan Coughlin and Dave Riker for labor at the capstan, "La Ciudad," and shanties of parting and welcome. Thanks to Silvia Federici, George Caffentzis, Nancy Sheehan, John Willshire,

Nancy Kelley, Monty Neill, and Massimo De Angelis for their heave-ho! Thanks to Bettina Berch for hospitality behind the cays of Belize. Thanks to Riley Ann, a seasoned shipmate from the Caribbean Sea to the Irish Sea, and to Michaela Brennan who hauled side by side in Spanish Town, Belize, the British Museum, Dublin, Kew Gardens, and Chancery Lane, where we dove together into archival waters. "History from the ground up" includes the bump of irreverence, and she found Despard's ancestral home through a laugh and a word with the shoemaker of Mountrath.

I thank the Fulbright Travel Fellowship for visits to Rio de Janeiro, São Paulo, and Bahia in 1982, where I saw the southern sky and the Hydra. Thanks to support at the University of Toledo from the College of Arts and Sciences and the History Department, particularly from Carol Menning, Al Cave, Roger Ray, and Ruth Herndon, as well as Abdul Alkalimat of Africana Studies and the Black Radical Congress. Thanks to my students Ty Reese, Jeff Howison, Jason Hribal, and Manuel Yang, who scrambled nimbly in the shrouds and manned the hand-pumps. Thanks to the History and Literature Department of Harvard College, especially Janice Thaddeus, Noel Ignatiev, Brenda Coughlin, Jonathan Taylor, and Philipe di Wamba. Great sailors! Closer to the harbor, at University of Massachusetts, special thanks to Richard Horsley and Charlie Shively for clear bells in foggy conditions. In Boston thanks to Carol Flynn and her quadrant and Edward Kamau Brathwaite and his conch. Thanks to Bill Jones, Bill W., and my friends at Grace. Thanks to helpers and critics Iain and Gillian Boal of the Retort Group in Berkeley, Philip Corrigan, Jim Holstun, Rip Lhamon, Jr., Jo Stanley, Lew Daly, Winston James, Alan Dean Gilbert III, Deborah Valenze, Steven Colatrella, Marty Glaberman, Ferruccio Gambino, Olivia Smith, and Dorothy Thompson. Thanks to John Roosa for work in the Burdett Papers at Oxford. Thanks to Peter King for help with the Assizes Records. Thanks to Yann Moulier Boutang for *De l'esclavage au salariat: Économie historique du salariat bridé* (Paris: Presses Universitaires de France, 1998). Thanks to Kevin Whelan for introducing the Green Atlantic, and to Luke Gibbons, Tommy Graham, and Daire Keogh, who welcomed me to the fellowship of '98 and the Bicentenary Conference in Belfast and Dublin. Thanks to Robert Scally of Irish House at New York University, Alf Lüdtke and Hans Medick of the Max Planck Institute in Göttingen, and Richard Price and Sally Price in Martinique.

Gracious thanks to Glyn Duggan for help in the muniments room of the Broadmead Baptist Church in Bristol; to the Venerable H. H. J. Gray, St. Peter's Mountrath, Co. Laois, Eire; to the Reverend D. Vidler, Priests House, Putney, London; and to J. Joseph Wisdom, the librarian of St. Paul's Cathedral, for their generosity with their records and knowledge. Thanks to Mr. and Mrs. M. H. Despard, Chelsea, London, for permission to use the Despard Family Papers. Thanks to the staffs at the Boston Public Library, Arlene Shy at the William L. Clements Library (University of Michigan), the Houghton Library (Harvard University), the Institute of Historical Research (London), the Wellcome Institute for the History of Medicine, Malcolm Thomas at the Friends Library (London), the Detroit Public Library, the National Archives of Brazil (Rio), the National Library of Ireland, the National Archives of Ireland, the National Library of Jamaica (Kingston) and the National Archives (Spanish Town), the Public Record Office of Northern Ireland (Belfast), the Rylands Library in Manchester, the Bodleian at Oxford, and the special collections of the university libraries of Toledo and Notre Dame.

I, Marcus Rediker, join Peter in thanking the people and institutions above, and I add to the list the many helpful folks at the Public Record Office of Great Britain, Chancery Lane and Kew Gardens, the British Library and Manuscript Collections, the Library of Congress, the New York Public Library, the New-York Historical Society, the Virginia State Library, the Carnegie Library of Pittsburgh, and the Hillman and Darlington Libraries at the University of Pittsburgh. Thanks, too, to the National Endowment for the Humanities, the John Simon Guggenheim Memorial Foundation, the Andrew P. Mellon Foundation, and the University of Pittsburgh (especially the Richard D. and Mary Jane Edwards Endowed Publication Fund) for grants that supported the project.

Thanks to the friends who have generously helped me over the years: Joseph Adjaye, Reid Andrews, Ira Berlin, Eric Cheyfitz, Jim Collins, Susan G. Davis, Seymour Drescher, David Goldfrank, Graham Hodges, Shan Holt, David Johnson, Paula Kane, Jesse Lemisch, John Markoff, Gary B. Nash, Robert Resch, Rob Ruck, Satan and Adam (Sterling Magee and Adam Gussow), Sharon Salinger, Dan Schiller, Hisham

Sharabi, Richard Sheldon, Dale Tomich, Judith Tucker, Daniel F. Vickers, Shane White, Alfred F. Young, and Michael Zuckerman. Thanks to Norman O. Brown, who after long discussion of the Atlantic proletariat remarked happily, "*Eppur si muove!*" Thanks to my gang, the members of the Working-Class History Seminar in Pittsburgh: Wendy Goldman, Maurine Greenwald, Michael Jiménez, Richard Oestreicher, Steven Sapolsky, Csaba Toth, and Joe White. Thanks to my students past and present Thomas Barrett, Thomas Buchanan, Alan Gallay, Gabriele Gottlieb, Douglas R. Egerton, Rick Halpern, Forrest Hylton, Maurice Jackson, Craig Marin, Margaret McAleer, Charles Neimeyer, Scott Smith, and Cornell Womack, whose own work has been an inspiration. Thanks to the motley Free Mumia crew, and in particular to Mu himself, who encouraged this project by letter, by intense discussion in the tiny visitor's cubicle at SCI-Greene prison (Waynesburg, Pennsylvania), and by his example of thinking freely, courageously, and joyously though incarcerated on death row.

And finally, special thanks to my wife, Wendy Goldman, who helped to make the book possible, not least by reading endless drafts and saying what she really thought, which was not always what I wanted to hear. Thanks, too, to Ezekiel and Eva, and to brother Shayne. My mother, Faye Ponder, did not live to see this book completed, but I nonetheless want to say to her, in memory, that the circle is unbroken.

Index

Page numbers for illustrations appear in italic

Abyssinia Baptist Church, 334
Act Concerning Aliens of 1798, 344
"Act Concerning Servants and Slaves, An"
  (1705), 138
"Act for the more effectual suppression of
  piracy," 149
Act for the Settlement of Ireland, 121
Act of Trade of 1696, 149
Act of Uniformity (1662), 73
"Act to Restrain the Wanderings of Servants
  and Negroes, An," 126
Adams, John, 2, 224, 232, 234, 237, 240, 344
Adams, Samuel, Jr., 216, 217, 218
"Address of a Journeyman Cotton Spinner,"
  333–334
Address to the People of Ireland (Russell), 278
Advertisement Touching an Holy War, An
  (Bacon), 37, 39, 61
Africa, 41, 82, 91, 111, 128, 170. *See also* West
  Africa
African Americans: diaspora of, 266–267;
  excluded from revolutionary settlement,
  267; fighting press-gang, 228; identity,
  origins of, 213; jubilee and, 268, 296, 297,
  300; religious beliefs of, 282; slavery and,
  213–214, 227, 239; as vector of revolution,
  242, 247. *See also* Africans
African Baptist Church, 334
African Institute, 302
African National Congress, 41
Africans: banishment legislation and, 57; diaspora of, 334; Hannibal's army and, 66; hewers of wood and drawers of water and, 41; as
  pirates, 165–167, 169–170; slavery and, 72,
  77, 99, 110, 124–125, 126, 132, 137. *See also*
  African Americans

Afro-Christianity, 226
Age of Reason, The (Paine), 307
Agreement of the Free People of England (May
  1649), 235
Agreement of the People, 78, 110, 157
Agricultural State of the Kingdom, The, 315
Aitken, James (Jack the Painter), 221
Akan religion, 221–222
Albion Mills, 250
al-Din, Nasir, 128
Algonquians, 33–34
Allen, John, 227, 229
Allen, Richard, 274
alternative ways of life, 20–24, 26
America, a Prophecy (Blake), 344, 345, 347
American Revolution, 211–247; Blake on, 347–
  348; counterrevolution and, 236–240; jubilee
  in, 292; mobs and, 227–236; sailors and, 214–
  221; slavery and, 221–227, 236; vectors of,
  241–247
American Sons of Liberty, 221
Anabaptists, 64–66, 87, 102, 159
anarchia, 235
"Anarchiad, The," 239
Anatomy of Melancholy, The (Burton), 332
Ancient Lowly, The, 41
Andover, Thomas, 138
Angello, Nathaniel, 81, 96
Annesley, Arthur, 133
Annis, John, 245
antinomian, 81, 138, 224, 227, 247, 322–
  323
antinomianism: Bunyan on, 99; controversy,
  90, 91; in Declaration of Independence, 235;
  defeat of, 138; peak of, 80; radical, 94, 190;
  slaves and, 192; Terrill on, 87; theological

sign of, 282; in Virginia, 135; Winstanley
and, 140
apartheid, 41
*Appeal to the Coloured Citizens of the World, but
in particular, and very expressly, to those of
The United States of America* (Walker), 299
Appleby, Joyce, 36
April Compromise, 274, 340
Areopagitica (Milton), 79–80
Argument on Behalf of the Catholics of Ireland
(Tone), 285, 337
Articles of War of 1652, 145, 146
Asbury, Francis, 299
Ascham, Anthony, 70
assassins, 63–64
Assiento, 171
Atkins, John, 169
Atlas of the West Indies (Jefferys), 261, *262*
Attucks, Crispus, 232, 240
*Axe Laid to the Root, or a Fatal Blow to Oppressors, Being an Address to The Planters and
Negroes of the Island of Jamaica, The* (Wedderburn), 301, 305, 306, 309, 313, 316, 318

backra, 53–54
Backhouse, Matthew, 128–129, 132, 140
Bacon, Francis, 6, 18, 19, 20, 33, 37–40, 102, 139.
   See also monstrosity, Bacon's theory of
Bacon, Nathaniel, 136, 137
Baker, Moses, 306, 307
Balcarres, Earl of (Alexander Lindsay), 242
Banana Bottom (McKay), 313
banishment legislation, 57
Bank of England, 148
Bannantine, James, 256
Baptists, 80, 87, 94, 97, 291, 297–298, 306, 307
Baptist War (1831), 326
Barbados, 44, 46, *98*, 123–127, 302
Barnaby Rudge (Dickens), 48
Barrington, Lord (William Wildman, Viscount Barrington), 232
Barrow, James, 165
Bartholomew Fair (Jonson), 36, 50, 115
Bastian, 182
Batts, Nathaniel, 138

Bayne, Paul, 76
Beake, Major John, 134
Beaumont, Francis, 36
Becker, Carl, 237
Beckles, Hilary McD., 126, 134
Beggars Act of 1597/1598, 56
Beggars' Christmas Riot (1582), 19
Beggar's Opera, The, 166
begging, 56
Behn, Aphra, 137
Beier, A. L., 18
Belize, 267–272
Bellamy, Sam, 169
Bell, Charles Napier, 265
Bellingham, John, 316
Benbow, William, 320
Benezet, Anthony, 227
Bennet, Colonel Benjamin, 168
Bentivoglio and Urania (Angello), 96
Bermuda, 9–10, 27, 32, 35
Bernstein, Edouard, 107
Bevan, Aneurin, 107, 108
Bible: Bacon on, 39; on blackness, 78; class in,
   306; Despard conspiracy and, 282; Ezekiel,
   quote from, 71; glory in, 83–84; Great Awakening and, 190; Hazzard compared to figures
   in, 79; hewers of wood and drawers of water
   and, 40–41, 42, 47–48; Joel, quote from, 71;
   jubilee and, 290–292, 296–298; no respecter
   of persons phrase in, 84; for proletariat, 351;
   used for oaths, 191
Biet, Father Antoine, 125
Bishop, George, 97
black dog myth, 53–56
Black Dog of Newgate (Hutton), 53
Black Dwarf, The (Wooler), 301, *303*, 306, 321–
   322, 333
"Black Irish," 126
blackness, 78, 86–87, 89–90, 114
Black River Negroes, 266
Blackymore Maide. *See* Francis (Blackymore
   Maide)
Blake, William, 5, 246, 250, 344–351; on American Revolution, 347–348; Orc, as symbol,
   346, 347; poetry of, 254, 282–283, 345–349,

351; and revolt of slaves, 351; tiger, as symbol, 348–349

Blasphemy Act, 96

Blow to the Root, A (Leland), 307

Bolingbroke (Henry St. John), 41

Bonny, Anne, 167

Boscawen, Edward, 134

Boston, 215, 221, 228, 229

Boston Massacre, 232, 233, *234*, 237, 240

Boston Tea Party, 221

bourn, 22–23

Bow Street Runners, 220

Boyle, Robert, 123

Braithwaite, Richard, 143

Brand, Joseph, 285

Brathwaite, E. K., 260

Briggs, Asa, 331–332

Bristol (England), 77, 78, 97

British and Foreign Bible Society, 309

"British Prison Ship, The," 233

Broadmead Baptist Church, 73, 94

Bromley, J. S., 159

Brothers, Richard, 286, 322

Brown, Tom, 96

Browne, Robert, 13, 31, 65

Browne, Thomas, 116–117

Bry, Theodore de, *11*

Bryan, Cornelius, 126

Bryan, Hugh, 198

buccaneers, 157, 158–159

Buccaneers of America, The, 143

Buchan, William, 339

Bull, William, 211

Bunyan, John, 88, 97–99, 100, 292, 300

Burdett, Sir Francis, 311

Burke, Edmund, 89, 284

Burnaby, William, 269

Burns, Robert, 335

Burrough, Edward, 135

Burton, Robert, 332

Bussa's Rebellion, 302, 305, 320

Byron, George Gordon (Lord), 305

Cadiz expedition (1596), 56

Calley, John, 48

Calvin, John, 68

Calvinism, 80

Campbell, Archibald, 261

Campbell, Elizabeth, 290, 301, 305–306, 309–310, 312–313

Campbell, Horace, 302

Canne, John, 87

Cape Coast Castle (West Africa), 46

capitalism: Act of Trade and, 149; anticapitalist traditions, 35; Atlantic, 145, 328; commoning economy and, 44; in England, 212, 328; exploitation of human labor with, 149; foundations for, 145; growth of, 138; hanging and, relationship between, 51–52; hewers of wood and drawers of water and, 42, 49; hydra as symbol of, 36; hydrarchy and, 145, 172; multi-ethnic class and, 6–7; origins of, 14, 15, 327; parturition, need for control over, 93; piracy and, 170; ports as essential to, 45–46; servants under, 76; ships and, 144, 150; slavery and, 28, 141; speculative, 72; workers as necessary for, 42

capital punishment: abolition of, 105; Bacon on, 39; Chidley on, 118–119; class discipline and, 30–31, 33, 316–317; in English America, 13; first in the United States of America, 286; hewers of wood and drawers of water and, 50; in Ireland, 121; King's (Charles) execution, 116; Lockyer's execution, 116; for Luddites, 305; New York Conspiracy of 1741 and, 177, 185, 186; opposition to, 101; piracy and, 149, 173; proletarian movements and, 316–317; revolutionary challenges to, 116; ships and, 145, 146; terror and, 50–52; witchcraft and, 52

Capp, Bernard, 130

Caribbean, 97, 326

Carlisle, Richard, 331

Carson, Rachel, 1

Cary, Mary, 88

Cashman, John, 321

Cast-Iron Parsons, or Hints to the Public and the Legislature, on Political Economy (Wedderburn), 317

Cerquozzi, Michelangelo, 113

Certain Queries Propounded to the Considera-tion of such as were Intended of the Service of Ireland, 120
Césaire, Aimé, 173
Chalmers, Joseph, 234
Chandler, Henry, 63
Charles I, King, 70, 71, 85, 109, 217
Charles II, King, 73
Chesapeake (Virginia), 137–138
Chidley, Samuel, 117, 118–119
Child, Sir Josiah, 58
children, 59, 111, 351
Chippendale, Thomas, 269
Christianity: Afro-, 226; Baptist version of, 306; Great Awakening and, 191, 192; growth of, 86; jubilee and, 293, 296–298; Philmore on, 223; Wedderburn on, 308, 324; Wight on, 89
Christian Policy, the Salvation of the Empire (Evans), 308
Christianson, Scott, 58
Christ in Triumph Coming to Judgment (1795), 279
citizen of the world, 246, 247
Citizen of the World (Goldsmith), 246
Clarendon, Earl of (Edward Hyde), 109
Clark, Adam, 47–48
Clark, Lieutenant Governor George, 182
Clark, Peter, 161–162
Clarkson, Laurence, 81
Clarkson, Thomas, 111, 242–243
class: in Bible, 306; Blackymore Maide and, 72, 103; common people as social, 140; Despard conspiracy and, 254; proletariat as unified cultural, 332; in relation to subsistence and the commons, 272; struggles, 145; superior-ity, 271; system in Jamaica, 307; Wedderburn on, 314; working, 333
class discipline, imposition of, 29–35; capital punishment in, 30–32, 33; Laws Divine, Moral, and Martial in, 33, 35; military disci-pline in, 32; Native Americans and, 33–35; by Virginia Company, 30
Cobbett, William, 279, 306, 344
Coke, Edward, 19, 51

Coke, Thomas, 297
Coleridge, Samuel Taylor, 290, 330
Collier, Thomas, 84
colonial rebellions, 193–195, 197–198
colonization, 14, 15–16, 20, 29, 35, 56, 60
Colt, Sir Henry, 24
Columbus, Christopher, 152
Colvill, Admiral Alexander, 218
Combe, William, 18
Combination Act (1799), 288
Commentary on the Holy Bible (Coke), 297
committee of correspondence, 235
commoners, 108–109, 276–277
commonism, 106, 128
commons, 140–142
Common Sense (Paine), 237–238
communism: advocate of, 101; Anabaptists and, 65, 66; in Bible, 190; City of Refuge society of, 197; of early Christians, 308; prim-itive (in Belize), 268; rebels at Hughson's tav-ern practicing, 176; Winstanley and, 140
Company of Adventurers of London Trading to Gynney and Bynney by James I, 28
Company of Royal Adventurers, 134
Condent, Edward, 165
Cone, James, 99, 291
Connecticut Wits, 239
Connolly, James, 41, 120
Constitution, U.S., 240
Conventicle Act (1664), 73
Convention of London, 269
cooperation, human, 26–29, 47
Coote, Charles, 257
Coppe, Abiezer, 119
Corbett, Michael, 229
Coriolanus (Shakespeare), 19
Corker, Jerry, 186
Cornish Rising (1497), 19
Coromantee, 184, 202
Corporation Act (1661), 73
Coster, Robert, 118
Council of State, 128
counterrevolution, 94, 100, 134, 236–240
Courier, 311
Coxere, Ned, 151

Coxon, William, 130
Craddock, Walter, 79, 81
Craven, Wesley Frank, 15
criminal code, 18–19
Critical Review, 152
Cromwell, Henry, 123
Cromwell, Oliver: Barbados and, 126; Dutch and, 127; in expedition to conquer Ireland, 120; hewers of wood and drawers of water and, 45, 70; in Ireland, 121; on Levellers, 119; on Lockyer, 116; maritime state and, 145; on Putney Debates, 105; revolution and, 71, 72; slavery and, 101
Cromwellian Republic, 94
Cry Against a Crying Sin, A (Chidley), 119
Cry of the Poor for Bread, The (1796), 279
Cugoano, Ottobah, 283, 329
Culpeper, John, 138–139
customs service, British, 228, 231
Cutlers Company, 338
Cylchgrawn Cymraeg, 329

Daemonologie (James I), 52
Dale, Sir Thomas, 32, 33, 34, 35
Dalling, John, 261–267
Dalton, R. J., 140
Dan, Father, 63
Dartmoor Prison, 321
Daughter of Adoption; A Tale of Modern Times, The, 259
Davidson, William "Black," 322
Davis, Howell, 163
Davis, Sir John, 121
Davis, T. J., 178
Dayan, Joan, 284
Deal, Douglas, 135
Dean, John, 243
Declaration of Independence, 235, 237, 240
Dekker, Thomas, 50, 63
democracy, 233, 234, 247
Despard, Catherine, 252–254, 272–275, 281
Despard conspiracy, ideas and ideals that motivated, 281–286; notion of equality, 281–282; race, 283–286; religious ideas, 282–283. See also Despard, Edward Marcus

Despard conspiracy, social forces behind, 275–281; Irish, 278–281; lost commoners of England, 276–277; sailors and dockworkers, 277–278; slavery, 275–276. See also Despard, Edward Marcus
Despard, Edward Marcus, 255; in Belize, 267–272; conspiracy of, 248–249; death of, 251, 316; in England, 272–275; as Irishman, 254–258; in Jamaica, 258–261; on land distribution, 270–272; in Nicaragua, 261–267; on religion, 251–252
Dessalines, 330
Dickens, Charles, 48
Diggers, 72, 85, 98, 101, 117, 118, 292
"Digger's Song, The," 120
Dinah ("the Moor"), 88, 89, 101
"Discourse Concerning Unlimited Submission and Non-Resistance to the Higher Powers, A" (Mayhew), 217
Discovery of The Main Grounds and Original Causes of all the Slavery in the World, but chiefly in England (1649), 101
Donne, John, 59
Downing, George, 96, 124
Down survey, 122, 147
Drayton, Michael, 10, 45
"Dream" (Heywood), 353
Dring, Thomas, 232
Dryden, John, 131, 168
Du Bois, W. E. B., 41, 128, 152
Dudingston, Lieutenant William, 231
Dunmore, Earl of (John Murray), 239
Dunmore's Proclamation (1774), 267
Dutch, 145, 146, 148, 150, 195, 197
Dutch soldiers and guide in a Suriname swamp, 5
Dyer, Mary, 90, 91

Easton, Peter, 63
Edwards, Thomas, 65, 66, 67–68, 69, 93, 282
Ehrman, John, 151, 151–152
Elizabethan Statue of Artificers (1814), 288
Elizabeth I, Queen, 57
Ellenborough, Earl of (Edward Law), 251, 281
Ellis, Thomas, 73
Elmina, 46, 47, 77–78

Emmanuel Appadocca (Phillip), 41

Emmet, Robert, 254

enclosure, 16, 17–18, 19, 21, 40, 44, 52, 118, 315, 332

End of Oppression; Or, A Quartern Loaf for Two-Pence; being a Dialogue between an Old Mechanic and a Young One, The (Spence), 294

Engels, Friedrich, 20

England: April Compromise of, 274, 340; Barbados as wealthiest colony of, 124; as capitalist power, 212; as center of European seafaring, 114; children shipped to Virginia from, 59; Christians in, 141; Church of, 29, 73; civil war in, 71; colonization for, 56; commoning in, 22–24, 26; criminalization of women in, 92; customs service in, 228, 231; Despards in, 272–275; displacing the Dutch as the hegemonic Atlantic power, 146; doctrine of white supremacy for, development of, 134; dominance in Africa following suppression of piracy, 172; economic changes in, 72; expropriation in, 17–20; fens in, draining of the, 44–45; ports in, 46; protecting plantation economy in, 148; shipping expansion for, 145, 146; ships and sailors as basis of wealth and power in, 147; slavery in, 28, 57, 82, 128, 149, 172, 273, 274; social and economic changes in, 16; Virginia as colony of, 8. *See also* English Revolution; Parliament; Royal Navy

England, Edward, 168

English Revolution, 40, 61, 71–73, 86, 102–103, 132, 138, 158–159, 318–319

English Soldiers' Standard, The, 120

Enslow Hill Rebellion (1596), 19, 37

Equiano, Olaudah, 220, 243, *244*, 245–246, 265, 285, 334–338, 340

Erbery, Dorcas, 94

Erskine, Thomas, 285–286

Essay on the Causes of the Variety of Complexion and Figure of the Human Species, An (Smith), 284

Ethiopianism, 334

Evans, Benjamin, 165

Evans, Thomas, 308

Everard, William, 117–118

Ewins, Thomas, 94

Exact History of the Late Revolutions in Naples; and of Their Monstrous Successes, An (Giraffi), 114

expropriation, 15–20; classification of dispossessed from, 19–20; colonization and, 56; in countries other than England, 28; in England, 17, 49; Evans on, 308; fens and, 44; as fuel for colonization, 20; hewers of wood and drawers of water and, 42, 43–45; as mobilizing disenfranchised, 276; resistance to, 18–19, 335; as source of capital, 16; terror and, 49; Wedderburn on, 313–314; workers from, new kinds of, 40

Exquemelin, Alexander, 143, 151, 158, 159

factories, 28, 46, 150, 242

Fairfax, Lord Thomas, 105, 118

fatigue, meanings of the word, 260

Federici, Silvia, 52

Felt-Makers' Riot (1591), 19

fens, 44–45

Ferguson, Adam, 46

Fernandez, Lucas, 28

Ferrers, George, 22

Fielding, John, 220

Fiery Flying Roll: A Word from the Lord to All the Great Ones, A (Coppe), 119

Fifth Monarchist workers, 134

"1st Security against Insurrections," 259

Fisk Jubilee Singers, 300

Fitzgerald, Edward, 285

Five Mile Act (1665), 73

Fly Boys, 183

Ford, Richard, 252

forests, 43–44, 125

Fort Wilson Riot, 238

Fox, George, 94–95, 125, 138

Foyle, Oxenbridge, 132, 133

France, 148, 212, 241, 274

Francis (Blackymore Maide): as Anabaptist, 78–79, 102; from Bristol (England), 77; on community, 82; ethnicity of, 78, 86; as hydra, 102; message of, 82; as prophet, 88; religious fellowship of, 78–80, 82; as servant, 76–77; on slavery, 82; social relations, within context of, 74, 76; spiritual power of, 101; survival of her ideas, 100; Terrill on, 73–74, 75

Franklin, Benjamin, 1

Free African Society of Philadelphia, 334

Frend, William, 338

Fryer, Peter, 77, 242

Fuller, Thomas, 45

Gage, Thomas, 231, 232

Gambia (River), 127–132

Gangraena: Catalogue and Discovery of many of the Errours, Heresies, Blasphemies and pernicious Practices of the Sectaries of this time (Edwards), 65, 282

Garden, Reverend Alexander, 192

Gardiner, Samuel, 121

Garrison, William Lloyd, 299–300

Garvey, Marcus, 41, 99, 100

Gast, John, 331

Gates, Sir Thomas, 9, 13–14, 16, 23, 29–30, 32, 33

Gateward's Case, 50

Gay, John, 143, 162, 166

gender, 72, 103

General History of the Pyrates, A, 167

genocide, 40, 61

Gentleman and Cabinet Maker's Director, The (Chippendale), 269

George, David, 226

George I, King, 170

George III, King, 290

Germain, Lord George, 266

German peasant revolt, 87

Gerrard, Joseph, 285

Gewen, Thomas, 134

Ghana, 28, 47

Giant Killer, Or, Anti-Landlord, The (Spence), 296, 307

Gilbert, Sir Humphrey, 56

Giraffi, Alexander, 114

Glas, John, 292–293

"Glimpse of Sion's Glory, A" (Hanserd), 84

globalization, 327, 328, 353

glory, 82–86, 100

Godwyn, Morgan, 126, 139

Golden Hill Riot, 231

Goldsmith, Oliver, 246

Gordon, Lord George, 280, 285, 294

Gordon Riots, 48, 283, 288

Goree Island, 46

Gorgon, 302, 331

Grantham, Thomas, 137

Gray, Robert, 20–21

Great Awakening, 190–193

Great Instauration, The (Bacon), 38

Green, Thomas, 18

Greene, Robert, 63

Grigg, Nanny, 302

grometta, 129

Grotius, Hugo, 17

Güemes, Juan Francisco de, 205

Guianese Arawaks, 124

Guinea Company, 128, 129

Guy, Hannah, 89

Gwin, John, 174, 176, 177, 183, 206

Gypsies, 57

habeas corpus, 220–221, 245

Haitian Revolution, 241, 242, 273, 274, 301, 319–320, 330, 334, 340–341

Hakluyt, Richard, 16, 20, 56

Hamilton, Alexander, 191, 198, 199

Hamilton, Elizabeth, 284

Hamlet (Shakespeare), 28

Handbook of Freedom (Rickword and Lindsay), 108

Hannibal's army, 66

Hardy, Lydia, 334, 335, 336, 337, 340

Hardy, Thomas, 334, 335, 336, 337, 338, 339, 340

Harman, Thomas, 63

Harrington, James, 93, 292

Harriss, John, 120

Hawkins, Jane, 90

Hawkyns, John, 28

Haymarket Massacre (1886), 331

Haynes, Samuel, 41

Hazzard, Dorothy, 73, 78–79, 80

Hercules, *30;* Bacon on, 37–39, 39–40; as executioner, 329; hewers of wood and drawers of water and, 60; Hobbes on, 69–70; in Raleigh's *History of the World*, 36–37; Shakespeare and, 28; significance of, 6; as symbol, 2–4, 234, 330–331

Hercules and Iolaus slaying the Lernean Hydra, Eritrian amphora, 3

heresies, 67, 68, 88, 93, 282

Hesilrige, Arthur, 134

hewers of wood and drawers of water, 40–70; children as, 59; genocide for, 61–65; mechanization on, influence of, 48–49; origins of, 40–42; self-organization of, 60–61, 65, 69; as slaves, 49, 69, 329; women as, role of, 47–48; as workers, 42, 329

hewers of wood and drawers of water, functions of, 43–49; for building ports, 45–47; for labors of expropriation, 43–45; for maintaining communities, 45–47

hewers of wood and drawers of water, role of terror for, 49–54, 56–60; banishment legislation, 57; black dog myth and, 53–56; capital punishment, 50–52; forced overseas labor, 57–58; prisons, 56–57, 58–59; servitude in, 57–60; witches, 52; women, 52

Heywood, Peter, 353

High-Heel'd Shoes for Dwarfs in Holiness (Wedderburn), 323

Higman, Barry, 313

Hill, Bridget, 48

Hill, Christopher, 72, 140, 158

Historie of Serpents (Topsell), *30*

History of Jamaica (Long), 284

History of the World (Raleigh), 36

Hobbes, Thomas, 69, 84, 109

Holdip, James, 125

Holland, 114

Hollister, Dennis, 94

Holmes, Robert, 131, 148

Holy War, The (Bunyan), 99

Hopkins, Stephan, 13, 29, 31, 65, 92

Horsmanden, Daniel, 183, 184, 192, 194, 199, 201, 231

Hortop, Job, 9

House of Burgesses, 135, 136

Howard, Martin, Jr., 229

Howell, James, 114, 247

Hughson, John, 174, 176, 177, 182–183, 184, 186, 189, 191, 203, 209

human solidarity, doctrine of, 86

"Humble Petition of the Seamen, belonging to the Ships of the Commonwealth of England," 156–157

Hume, David, 139

Hunt, Henry, 331

Hunter, Robert, 188

Hutchinson, Anne, 88, 90, 91

Hutchinson, Thomas, 215, 218, 229, 232

Hutton, Luke, 53

Hyacinth, 274

hydra, 3–6, *30*, 331, 353; Bacon on, 37, 40, 65; counterrevolutionary forces in terms of, 330; Francis (Blackymore Maide) and, 102; Hobbes's interpretation of, 69–70; mobs and, 228, 233; pirates and, 173; proletariat described in terms of, 329; in Raleigh's *History of the World*, 36

"Hydra Decapita" (Mather), 5–6, 92

hydrarchy, 144, 145, 147, 154, 167–173, 294

hydrarchy, sailors', 154, 156–162; buccaneers of, 157–159; comparing ship to jail in, 160; conditions of, 159–160; defeat of, 173; impressment in, 157, 160; piracy in, 160–161; resistance of sailors in, 156–157; stages of, 156

Hydra Rebellion, 302

imperialism, 145, 147, 152, 234, 319

Imperial Registry Bill of 1815, 302

impressment, 145, 157, 160, 214, 217, 219, 228–229, 235–236, 237

Independent Advertiser, 217, 218

industrial revolution, 250

"Insurrections of the Slaves in some of the West India Islands," 320

Interesting Narrative of Olaudah Equiano or Gustavus Vassa the African, The, 285, 336–337

Intolerable Acts, 228

Ireland, 120–123; Act for the Settlement of, 121; Baptists in, 97; capital punishment in, 121;

colonization, 20; "cutthroat expedition" to, 116; Despard conspiracy and, 254–258; English Revolution and, 71; expedition to conquer, 120; hewers of wood and drawers of water in, 328; Orange Order in, 283; ports in, 46; Quakers in, 97; slaves in, 123, 125, 126; war in, 147

Ireton, Henry, 106, 121

Irish: banishment legislation and, 57; Black, 126; Despard conspiracy and, 278–281; hewers of wood and drawers of water and, 41; history of betraying English, 187–188; Methodists, 297; New York Conspiracy of 1741 and, 186–188; pirate queen O'Malley, 64; prisoners, 94

Irish Rebellion of 1798, 250, 278

Jackson, George, 41

Jamaica: Baptist War in, 326; buccaneers in, 148; class-leader system in, 307; Despard conspiracy and, 258–261; jubilee in, 312; maroons of, 194–195, 309–311; plantations in, 272; slaves in, 201. *See also* Tacky's Revolt

Jamaica Discipline, 158, 159

James, C. L. R., 108, 254

James I, King, 44, 52

Jea, John, 311–312

Jefferson, Thomas, 214, 237, 299, 343–344

Jefferys, Thomas, 261

Jeremiah, Thomas, 226

Jessey, Henry, 89

Jessup, John, 168

Jobson, Richard, 128

Johnson, Edward, 91

Johnson, Francis, 138

Johnson, Joseph, 344

Johnson, Samuel, 160

Jones, Absalom, 274

Jones, Joshua, 270–271

Jonson, Ben, 28, 36, 49, 50, 114

Jourdain, Silvester, 9

Joyce, James, 112

jubilee, 290–300; African Americans carrying message of, 268; biblical tradition of, 290; Coke and, 297; elements of, 290; Evans on,

308; Garrison and, 299–300; in modern era, 292–294; opposition to slavery and, 296–300; as restoration of manufacturing rights, 339; Spence and, 292–296; Wedderburn's proletarian version of, 291. *See also* Wedderburn-Campbell correspondence

"Jubilee Hymn; Or, A Song to be sung at the Commencement of the Millennium, The" (Spence), 292–293

Justification of the Mad Crew, A (Ranters), 85

Kane, William, 185, 186

Karlsen, Carol, 90

Kelley, James, 321

Kerry, Margaret, 174, 177, 187, 204, 206

Kett's Rebellion (1549), 19

Kiffin, William, 97

King, Boston, 226

King Street Riot, 231–232

Kinte, Kunta, 130

Kipling, Rudyard, 24

Knight of the Burning Pestle, The (Beaumont), 36

Knolly, Hanserd, 84

Knowles, Charles, 215

Knowles Riot, 216

Labat, Père, 159

labor. *See* hewers of wood and drawers of water; sailors; slavery

labor code, 18

Lamb, Charles, 330

Lamb, Thomas, 232

lançados, 129

Land of Cockaygne, 158

land rovers, 63

languages, on ships, 152–154

Latchett, Sarah, 93

Laurens, Henry, 211

Lavenham Rising (1525), 19

Lawes, Nicholas, 164

Law of the Privateers, 158

Laws Divine, Moral, and Martial, 33, 35

lazzaroni, 63

Leaming, Hugo, 138

Legate, Bartholomew, 31
Leland, John, 307
Lemisch, Jesse, 228
Lenthall, Sir John, 134
Leonard, Daniel, 235
Leslie, Charles, 195
Letters from the Dead to the Living (Brown),
    96
Levant Company, 114
Levellers: Bunyan and, 98; Canne on, 87; on
    impressment, 157; on Ireland, 120–121; as law
    advocates, 105; opposition to impressment,
    235–236; origins of, 80; as political party, 105;
    as radical voice, 72; Rainborough as leader
    of, 105; resistance to expropriation, 19; on
    slavery, 111; survival of ideas of, 119–120
Lewis, "Monk," 312
libertism, 87
Liberty Riot, 228
Liele, George, 226, 307
Light Shining in Buckinghamshire, A (Diggers),
    101, 108
Ligon, Richard, 124
Lilburne, John, 97
Lincolnshire Rebellion (1536), 19
Lindsay, Jack, 108
Locke, John, 114, 139
Lockyer, Robert, 119
Lok, John, 28
London, 116–120, 132–135
London Corresponding Society, 274, 288, 329,
    337, 338, 339
London Spy, The (Ward), 152
Long Bridge Boys, 183
Long, Edward, 221, 222, 284
Lovejoy, David S., 235
Lovelace, Richard, 60
Lowther, George, 169
Loyal American Rangers, 269
Luddites, 303–304
Ludgate Prison Riot (1581), 19
Ludlow, Edmund, 121
lumpenproletariat, 63
Lydon, James G., 199, 201, 208
Lysons, Daniel, 104

MacIntosh, Ebenezer, 229
Mack, Phyllis, 88
MacNamara, John, 249
Madden, R. R., 259
Madison, James, 239, 240
Magnalia Christi Americana (Mather), 92
Making of the English Working Class, The
    (Thompson), 100
Makonnen, Ras Tefari, 108
Malthus, Thomas, 276
Mandela, Nelson, 41
Mansfield's army (1624), 56
marine insurance industry, 148
Marine Republic, The (Spence), 277, 294
maritime labor, 150, 151
maritime radicalism, 173
maritime state, 144, 145, 147, 148
Markall, Martin, 61
Markham, Robert, 34
maroons, 194–195, 309–311
Marriage of Heaven and Hell, The (Blake), 345
Marryat, Frederick, 312
martial laws, 33, 146
Marvell, Andrew, 136
Marxism, 107
Marx, Karl, 20, 332
Masaniello (Naples fisherman), 112, 113, 114, *115*,
    116
Masque of Blacknesse, The (Jonson), 28
Massachusetts's Riot Act of 1786, 238
Mather, Cotton, 5–6, 91–92
Mather, Joseph, 273
Mathews, Governor William, 193
Maurice of Orange, 32
Maurice, Prince, 127
Mauricius, J. J., 4
Mayhew, Jonathan, 217, 218
McKay, Claud, 313
McManus, Edgar J., 200
Mediterranean, 46
Medusa; Or, Penny Politician, 302, 331
Memoirs of a Modern Philosopher (Hamilton),
    284
merchant shipping industry, 150
Mercurius Militaris, 120

Merrington, John, 45–46
Methodists, 291, 296–298, 307, 309
middle passage, 17, 172
Midlands Revolt of 1607, 19, 335
military discipline, 32
Miller, Kerby A., 197
Milton, John, 79–80, 90, 245, 292, 336
mobs, 227–229, 231–236; in Boston, 229;
    description of, 228; hydra and, 228, 233;
    against impressment, 228–229; multiracial,
    228, 234, 235; prisons and, 232–233; resistance
    to Townshend Revenue Act, 231; riots and,
    231–232
Moffat, Thomas, 229
Molyneux, Thomas More, 263
Molyneux, Tom, 321
Monson, Sir William, 56
monstrosity, Bacon's theory of, 39, 40, 61, 62,
    63, 64, 65, 91, 137, 341
Montaigne, Michel de, 24
More, Thomas, 17, 24
Moreton, J. B., 258
Morgan, Lewis Henry, 268
Morris, Richard B., 234
Morton, Thomas, 62
Moseley, Benjamin, 258
Mosquito Indians, 158, 265–266, 267, 281
motley crew, 27–28, 151, 212–214, 235, 246, 331
Moutapass (formerly Robert Markham), 34
Mr. Midshipman Easy (Marryat), 312
Muggletonians, 96, 101, 135
Muggleton, Lodovick, 83
Munster, 64–65
Murray, James, 293
mutiny, 130, 156–157, 165, 173, 277
myalism, 306

Naples (Italy), 112–116
Narrative (Stedman), 349
Nashe, Thomas, 65
Nash, Gary B., 190
Nassau Street Riot, 231
Native Americans: alternative ways of life for,
    24, 26; colonists and, 33–35; communist soci-
    ety for, 197; cooperation and, 27; hewers of

wood and drawers of water and, 61, 62, 68; as
    slaves, 124; Spence on, 295–296; struggles on
    the frontier, 214
"Nauticus," 219–220
Navigation Act of 1651, 145, 151
Navigation Acts, 72, 145–146, 151
Nayler, James, 86, 94, 95, 96–97, 101, 292
Negro inferiority, doctrine of, 139
Negro Seaman Act (1822), 299
Netherlands, 32
New Account of Some Parts of Guinea and the
    Slave Trade, A, 171–172
New Atlantis (Bacon), 37, 62, 102
New Chains Discovered, 157
Newcomen, Thomas, 48
New Engagement, or, Manifesto, 157
New English Canaan, or New Canaan (Mor-
    ton), 62
New Model Army, 71, 80, 84, 104, 134
New Orleans at Congo Square (1817), 321
Newport, Christopher, 9
New River Company, 49
New World as paradise, The (Bry), 11
New York at Catherine Market (1821), 321
New York Conspiracy of 1741, 174–210; assis-
    tance from Britain's imperial enemies, 204–
    205; colonial rebellions and, 193–195, 197–
    198; conditions for insurrection, 203; conse-
    quences of, 207–210; controversy of, 177;
    debates about, 178; executions resulting
    from, 177; factors contributing to, 179; fail-
    ure of insurrection, 205–206; fear of, 176–
    177; Great Awakening and, 190–193; Hors-
    manden, Daniel, 177; Hughson's house and,
    182; Irish and, 186–188; journal about, 177;
    multiracial waterfront problem, 206–207;
    "negro oath" and, 185; religious dimension
    of, 190–192; slavery and, 179, 182, 184–185;
    Spanish America and, 188–190; story of
    Gwin and Kerry, 174–176; trade patterns in,
    198–203; waterfront and, 179–184; West
    Africa and, 184–186
Nicaragua, 261–267
Nicaraguan expedition of 1780, 272
Noell, Martin, 133

no respecter of faces, phrase, 103
no respecter of persons, phrase, 82, 84, 85–86, 96, 100, 102, 103, 116, 118, 190
North Carolina, colony of, 139
Nova Britannia, 60
Nugent, Sir George, 317

Oceana (Harrington), 93
"Ode to the Virginian Voyage" (Drayton), 10
"Of Empire" (Bacon), 37
"Of Plantations" (Bacon), 37
"Of Seditions and Troubles" (Bacon), 37
Of the Confusions and Revolutions in Government (Ascham), 70
Ogle, Captain Challoner, 170
Oglethorpe, James, 190
okofokum, 184
Oliver, Andrew, 229
Oliver, Peter, 229, 236
O'Malley, Grace, 64
O'Neill, Hugh, 123
Orange Order, in Ireland, 283
"Oration on the Beauties of Liberty, An" (Allen), 227
Orc, as symbol, 344, *345*, 346, 347
Oroonoko, 301
Oswald, John, 285
Othello (Shakespeare), 321
Otis, James, Jr., 223–224
Overton, Richard, 111
Owen, John, 65

Paddy's Resource, 278
Paine, Thomas, 214, 227, 237, 284–285, 307, 332, 339
Painter, Nell, 77, 101
Pan-African Congress, 108
pan-Africanism, 212, 299, 312, 334
Paradise Lost (Milton), 245, 336
Parliament, 71, 105, 119, 132–134, 149, 211, 250, 323
Parry, J. H., 148
parturition, 93
Patience, 13
patriarchy, 76, 103
Patterson, Orlando, 125

Peacham, Edmund, 63
Peasant's Revolt of 1381, 29, 318
Pembroke Prize, 215
Pepys, Samuel, 45, 48, 146
Pequot War, 91
Peter, Hugh, 89, 121
Peterloo Massacre of 1819, 320, 331
Petty, Sir William, 62, 122, 123, 139, 146–147, 151
Philanthropic Hercules, 331
Philip, Maxwell, 41
Philmore, J., 223, 319
pidgin English, 153, 154
Pig's Meat; Or, Lessons for the Swinish Multitude (Spence), 342
Pilgrimage of Grace (1536), 19
Pilgrim's Progress (Bunyan), 98, 99, 100
piracy, 160–161, 170, 172, 173. *See also* pirates
Piracy Destroy'd, 160
pirates, 162–167; in Africa, 170; Africans as, 165–167; Bacon on, 62–63; as class-conscious, 163; as damagers of world shipping, 172; as defenders of hydrarchy freedoms, 167–168; as egalitarian, 163; extermination of, 171–172; insistence on right to subsistence, 164; as issue for Parliament, 149; as justice-seeking, 163; limitation on captain's power for, 162–163; as motley, 164–165; sailor's hydrarchy and, 156, 160; social order of, 162; women, 167. *See also* piracy
Place, John, 173
Plaisterers' Insurrection (1586), 19
plantations: accession of Negroes in, 147; attacks on, 139; crisis in, 195; formation of, 46; labor for, 149; as new system, 138; proletariat of, 139; resistance of workers in, 135, 136, 137; vagrants shipped to, 124; workers as chattels on, 125
Political Anatomy of Ireland (Petty), 146
political economy, 146
Political Register (Cobbett), 306, 311
Polly: An Opera, 143, 162, 166
Poole, Elizabeth, 97, 116
Poor Law, 18
Poor Man's Catechism, The (1798), 279
Popham, Sir John, 19, 45, 53

Porteous, Captain John, 216
ports, 45–47
poverty, 108
Powhatan, 33–34
Prayer Book Rebellion (1549), 19
Prendry, E. D., 60–61
Press Act of 1659, 146
press-gangs, 151, 214, 215–216, 218, 219, 228, 229
Preston, Thomas, 302
Price, Richard, 89
Priestley, Joseph, 344
prisons, 50, 56–57, 58–59, 60–61, 101, 232–233, 252–253, 280–281
privateers, 158, 161
Privy Council, 59
proletariat, 330–333; Bible for, 351; Blackymore Maide and, 76, 101, 102, 103; description as many-headed hydra, 329; as hewers of wood and drawers of water, 328–329; idea of liberty, 219; origins of term, 93, 332; plantation, 137; resistance, 318; in revolutionary movement, 40, 69; sailors and, 132, 150; slaves and, 132; Wedderburn on, 301, 313, 321
Protestantism, 82
Puritans, 71, 87, 90, 94
Purnel, Robert, 94
Putney Debates of 1647, 97, 104, 105–106, 107–108, 108–109
putting-out system, 149

Quakers: banned from Virginia, 136; emigration to West Indies, 159; founder of, 94–95; jubilee and, 292; leaving England, 135; as "new age" entrepreneurs, 97; rewritten history of, 96; rise of, 80; Wedderburn on, 319
Quartering Acts, 228
Quarterly Review, 311
Queen Mab (Shelley), 307
Queen Sieve, 256–257
quietism, 94
Quin, Daniel, 243

race, 72, 97, 99, 101, 103, 271, 274, 283–286
racism, 97, 100, 101, 139, 352

Rainborough, Colonel Thomas, 80, 104, 105, 106, 109, 109–110, 111, 116
Rainborough, William, 111
Raleigh, Sir Walter, 31, 36–37
Rankin, Hugh, 166
ranterism, 94
Ranters, 85, 98, 99, 135, 137, 159
Rawley, James A., 172
Read, Mary, 167
Rebellion of Naples, The, 114, 114–115
rebellions, colonial, 193–195, 197–198
rebellions, Tudor, 18–19
Rebel's Doom, The, 29
Records of a Church of Christ in Broadmead, Bristol, 1640–1687, The (Terrill), 73, 82
Red String Conspiracy, 197
Reeves, John, 283–284
Reflections on the Revolution of France (Burke), 284
regicides, 135, 217
Reid, William Hamilton, 282
Reign of Felicity, The (Spence), 294–295
"Religious Musings" (Coleridge), 290–291
respecter of faces, phrase. See no respecter of faces, phrase
respecter of persons, phrase. See no respecter of persons, phrase
Restoration, 101, 135
Restorer of Society, The (Spence), 307
Revel, James, 59
Revenge of Whitehall (ship), 131
Revere, Paul, 217, 233
Revolt of Masaniello, The (Cerquozzi), 113
revolution. See American Revolution; English Revolution; Haitian Revolution
Rhys, Morgan John, 328–329
Rich, Colonel Nathaniel, 106
Rich, Robert, 10
Richard II (Shakespeare), 28
Rickword, Edgell, 108
Ridgway, James, 280
Rights of Infants; Or, the Imprescriptable Right of MOTHER'S to such a Share of the Elements as is Sufficient to Enable them to Suckle and Bring up their Young (Spence), 285, 323
Rights of Man, The (Paine), 284–285, 323, 339

Rights of Nature, The (Thelwall), 285
Rights of the British Colonies Asserted and Proved, The (1764), 224
Rights of the Sailors Vindicated, The (Nauticus), 219
Rights of Women, The (Wollstonecraft), 323
Rise and Dissolution of the Infidel Societies in this Metropolis, The (Hamilton), 282
rivers, 111–112. *See also* Gambia (River)
Rivers, Marcellus, 132, 133
Roberts, Bartholomew, 163, 164, 168, 169, *171*
Robin Hood Club of London, 220
Rodney, Walter, 128
Rogers, Woodes, 161
Roots, 130
Royal African Company, 131, 148, 170
Royal Navy, 145, 146, 148, 150, 160, 171, 288
Ruins; Or, Meditation on the Revolutions of Empires, The (Volney), 285, 341–342
Rumor of Revolt: The "Great Negro Plot" in Colonial New York, A (Davis), 178
Rupert, Prince, 79, 80, 127, 129, 130, 131
Rush, Benjamin, 235
Ruskin, John, 47, 260
Russell, Thomas, 278

sailors: Braithwaite on, 143–144; as crew, 153; Despard conspiracy and, 277–278; as essential to English expansion, 144; as individualists, 153; as labor, 147, 151; language of, 152–154; multiracial, 132; self-organization of, 144; as vector of revolution, 241; Wedderburn on, 321–322. *See also* hydrarchy, sailors'
sailors, in the American Revolution: abolitionist movement of, 220–221; attack on naval property, 218–219; press-gang resistance and, 216–217; resisting impressment, 214–216; revolts of, 219; strike of, 220–221; Tacky's Revolt and, 221–224
Saltmarsh, John, 89–90, 101
Saltonstall, Richard, 89
Savery, Thomas, 48
Scale of Creatures, The (Petty), 139
scientific racism, 139
Scotland, 46, 71
Scott, Julius, 241

Searle, Governor Daniel, 125
Sea-Venture, wreck of the, 8–35; alternative ways of life and, 20–24, 26; in Bermuda, 9–10, 12–13; class discipline and, 29–35; cooperation and, 26–29; expropriation and, 15–20; historical significance of, 14–15; Shakespeare on, 14; voyage to Virginia, 8–9, 11–12, 13–14
Second Charter of the Virginia Company (1609), 33
Second Part of Masaniello . . . The End of the Commotions, The, 114
"2nd Security against Foreign Invasion," 259
Secotan (Nathaniel Batts), 138
self-organization, 65, 69
"Sermons To Asses" (Murray), 293
servants, 124, 125–126, 127, 135–139, 197
servitude, 57–60
Seven Years' War, 212, 218, 268
Sexby, Edward, 78
Shakespeare, William, 29; on alternative ways of life, 21–22, 24, 26; on class discipline, 30–32; on cooperative resistance, 27; expropriation and, 18; Hercules myth and, 28; Midlands Revolt influence on, 19; on *Sea-Venture* wreck, 14
Sharpe, Sam, 326
Sharp, Granville, 220
Shaw, Alexander, 265
Shays' Rebellion, 238, 239
Sheffield Constitutional Society, 274
Sheffield (England), 273–274, 338
Shelley, Percy Bysshe, 100, 307
ships, 111–112, 128, 129, 130, 131, 149–154; as basis of English wealth and power, 147; *Bounty, H.M.S.,* 277; as communication between continents, 152; crew on, 153; *Dragon,* 28, 165, 170; as engines of capitalism, 144; English merchant, 129, 146; English seaman on, 150; as factory prototype, 150; felons on, 147; *Gaspee,* 231, 235; labor for, 151; languages on, 152–154; mortality on slave, 242–243; to Naples, sailors on, 114; New York Conspiracy of 1741 and, 199; press-gangs on, 151; prison, 232–233; as setting of resistance of revolutionaries, 144–145; slang terms for abducting persons on, 110; slave, 28, 165, 169, 170, 215,

222; use of violence and terror to man, 150–151; *Wager,* H.M.S., 215, 222. *See also* mutiny

Shirley, William, 215, 216

Shyllon, F. O., 242

Sierra Leone, 242, 247

Sieve, Queen, 242

Simmonds, Martha, 94

Simmonds, Richard, 322

slavery, 140–142; abolished in England, 274; abolitionist movement, 242–243, 340–341; African, 91, 110; in America, 118; Baptists on, 298; in Barbados, 124–125; black, 134; British Caribbean end to, 326; children and, 111; defined, 111; Despard conspiracy and, 275–276; Diggers and, 117; as foundation of Atlantic capitalism, 141; as Great Awakening issue, 191–192; Irish slaves, 123; Levellers on, 111; Methodists on, 297; "new covenant" and, association between, 88; new kind of, 40; New York Conspiracy of 1741 and, 185; opposition to, 97, 101, 101–102, 139, 236, 299–300; Parliamentary debate on, 132–135; Putney Debates and, 106, 108; racialized, 101; resistance to, 124; revolts against, 82, 221–224, 226–227, 239, 269; sailors and, 111, 220–221; ship mortality and, 242–243; soldiers at Putney opposition to, 105; Volney on, 342–343; Wedderburn on, 302–308, 324–326; white supremacy and, 240; Winstanley on, 118. *See also* servitude

slaves: African, 99; colonial rebellions and, 194, 198; communist society for, 197; division between servants and, 127; England as greatest transporter of, 149; hewers of wood and drawers of water and, 49, 69; in Jamaica, 201; in New York, 191, 199–203; oaths for, 191; as vector of revolution, 241–242; in Virginia, 135–139

slave trade: abolition of, 90; African, 72, 77, 126, 170; antinomianism and, 94; Christians and, 97; DuBois on, 152; in England, 28, 57; Francis (Blackymore Maide) and, 82; hydrarchy as danger to, 168–169; as important to imperial planning, 147; Naylor on, 96; piracy and, 165, 170–171; port of Goree Island, 46; protest against, 89; Rainborough on, 109–

110; at River Gambia, 128; U.S. Constitution and, 240; workers in, 131–132. *See also* servitude

Slush, Barnaby, 150

Smith, Adam, 327

Smith, Captain Abel, 215

Smith, John, 14, 33, 186

Smith, Samuel, 284

Smith, William, 192

Smith, William, Jr., 178

Smith, William, Sr., 191

Snelgrave, William, 171

social democracy, 107

Somerset, James, 220

Somers, Sir George, 9, 13

Songs of Experience (Blake), 345, 348–349

Songs of Innocence (Blake), 282

Sons of Liberty, 234, 235, 237

South Carolina Council of Safety, 233

Southey, Robert, 311

South Sea Company, 171

Southwark Butter Riot (1595), 19

Southwark Candle-Makers' Riot (1592), 19

Spa Fields Riots, 302–304, 305, 322

Spain, 204–205, 269

Spanish America, 188–190

Speed, John, 46

Spelman, Henry, 33

Spence, Thomas, 276, 277, 285, 288, 292–296, 295, 307, 323–324, 342

Spencian doctrine, 311

Spenser, Edmund, 50, 54

Spirits, 110

Spriggs, Francis, 165

Stamp Act, 211, 228, 229, 230, 231

Statute of Artificers, 18

St. Bendito, Antonio de, 189

steam engine, 48

Stedman, John Gabriel, 5, 344, 346, 347, 348, 349

Steere, Bartholomew, 37

Stephen, James Fitzjames, 51

St. Johns expedition, 261–267, 263, 267, 284

Stones of Venice, The (Ruskin), 47

Stono Rebellion, 198

Strachey, William, 8, 12, 24, 26, 27, 33

Strange News from Virginia, 136
Stranger, Hannah, 94
Strong, Jonathan, 220
Stuart, Charles, 97
sugar production, 125, 127, 133, 319
superlucration, 147
Swift, Jonathan, 41

Tacky's Revolt, 221–224, 319
Tahiti, 353
Tar, Jack, 218
Taylor, John, 48, 51–52
Tea Act, 228
Tempest, The (Shakespeare), 14, 16–17, 21–22, 24, 27, 28, 29, 30–31, 168
Terrill, Edward: on Canne (John), 87; on Francis (Blackymore Maide), 73–74, 77, 78, 82, 86; on Hazzard, 79; on no respecter of faces phrase, 86; on religion, 80–81; sugar industry involvement of, 97; on women's spiritual role within the community, 88
Test Act (1673), 73
Theatre of the Empire of Great Britain, The (Speed), 46
Thelwall, John, 259, 285, 329
Third Institute (Coke), 51
Thistlewood, Arthur, 322
Thistlewood, Thomas, 222, 311
Thompson, Edward, 100, 108, 285, 332
Thoughts and Sentiments on the Evil of Slavery (Cugoano), 283
Thoughts on Slavery (Wesley), 296–297
tilth, 22–23
Timothy, Peter, 232
Tom Paine Methodists, 338
Tone, Wolfe, 41, 285, 328, 337
"Topographical Description and Admeasurement of the Yland of Barbados in the West Indies with the M[aste]rs Names of the Severall Plantacons," 97
Topsell, Edward, *30*
Torch, The, 342
tories, 122–123
Townshend Revenue Act, 228, 231
"Trapann'd Maiden" (anonymous woman), 59–60

Trapnel, Anna, 92–93
Traven, B., 153
Treaty of Paris, 268
Trelawny, Edward, 193, 201
Trinculo's Trip to the Jubilee, 292
True Leveller's Standard Advanced (1649), 85
Truth Self-Supported (Wedderburn), 307, 319
Truth, Sojourner, 71
Tsenacommacah, 33
Tucker, Daniel, 32
Tudor rebellions, 18–19
Turkey, 86
Turner, Mary, 307, 323, 326
"Tush, they can shift," policy of, 126–127
Two Dialogues on the Man-Trade (Philmore), 223
"Tyger, The," (Blake), 348–349
Tyler, Wat, 318
Tyndale, William, 42
Tyranipocrit Discovered, 101–102, 118
Tyrrell, James, 115

underclass, 63
Underhill, Captain, 85
United Irishmen, 336, 337
Universal Patriot, 285
Ure, Andrew, 4
Ury, John, 192
U.S. Constitution, 240
Utopia (More), 17, 24

vagabond laws, 18–19
Vagrancy Act, 81
Vala, or the Four Zoas (Blake), 345–346, 351
Van Dam, Rip, 200
Vane, Sir Henry, 133
Vanity Fair (Bunyan), 300
Vanity Fair (Garvey), 100
Venner, Thomas, 134
Verney, Thomas, 58
Vesey, Denmark, 298–299
Vindication of the Rights of Women, The (Wollstonecraft), 285
Virginia, 135–139; children shipped to, 59; clearing land in, 43; colonization in, 20; confusion between Bermuda and, 10–11;

Jamestown, 47; military in, 35; resistance in, 32, 33; *Sea-Venture* voyage to, 8–9, 11–12, 13–14; servitude in, 58–59; substitution of African slaves for European servants in, 137

Virginia Company of London, 9, 13, 14, 15–16, 27, 33, 37, 59

Visions of the Daughters of Albion (Blake), 254, 345

Volney, Constantin François, 285, 341–344

von Uchteritz, Heinrich, 124

Wahunsonacock, 33–34
Walker, David, 299
Walpole, Robert, 170, 173
Ward, Edward (Ned), 150, 152
Ward, John, 63
Ward, John "Zion," 322
Ward, Osborne, 41
War of Spanish Succession in 1713, 171
Warren, Peter, 215, 236
Watkinson, Jonathan, 338, 339
Watson, James, 302
Webber, John, 231
Webster, John, 63–64
Wedderburn-Campbell correspondence, 301–313; on Christianity, 308; hymns and, 307–308; on jubilee, 312; on maroons, 309–311; on mechanization, 305; on Methodists, 309; on slavery, 302–308

Wedderburn, Robert, 287–326, *289;* as antinomian, 322–323; background of, 241; on Bussa's Rebellion, 320; on capital punishment, 316–317; on cast-iron idea, 317–318; as central actor in revolutionary traditions, 289–290; on Christianity, 324; disciplinary violence and, 287–288; on English Revolution, 318–319; on expropriation, 313–314; Haitian Revolution and, 319–320; on land and private property, 314–316; on proletariat, 318, 321; on sailors, 321–322; on slavery, 314–317, 324–326; Tacky's Revolt influence on, 319; as theorist of Atlantic proletariat, 313; universal war of, 314. *See also* jubilee

Wedgwood, Josiah, 273
Wesley, John, 296–297

West Africa, 28, 46, 127, 128, 134, 150, 166, 169, 184–186. *See also* Africa
Western Rising (1629–31), 64
West Indies, 46, 72, 123, 159, 199, 261, *262*
Weston, John, 126
Weston, William, 126
White, Charles, 284
White, George, 306–307
white identity, 102, 208–210
white supremacy, 99, 139, 240, 284
Whitefield, George, 190, 191, 192–193
Whitman, Walt, 330
Whitsuntide Riots (1584), 19
Widow Ranter, or a History of Bacon in Virginia, The, 137
Wight, Sarah, 88, 89, 90, 101
Wilberforce, William, 302, 324–325, 340
Wilkes, John, 219, 220
Wilkinson, Jemima, 285
Wilkinson, Moses, 226
Williams, Eric, 58
Willson, George, 163
Wilson, George, 136
Winstanley, Gerrard, 83, 85, 106, 118, 139, 140, 141, 292
Winthrop, John, 90
witchcraft, 90
witches, 52, 92, 93
Wolfe, Dan, 105
Wollstonecraft, Mary, 285, 323
"Woman of Ely" (prophet), 88
women: armed, 64; black, 101; capitalist patriarchy on, 103; criminalization of, 92; as hewers of wood and drawers of water, 47–48; as preachers, 68; as prophets, 88–93; reproduction crisis for, 92, 93; as target for extirpation, 64; as witches, 52, 92, 93
Wooden World Dissected, The (Ward), 152
Wooler, Thomas, 301, 306
Woolf, Virginia, 103
Wrightman, Edward, 31

Yorke, Henry Redhead, 341
Young, Arthur, 257, 315

Zong, 242